Immanent Distance

POETS ON POETRY

Marilyn Hacker and Kazim Ali, Series Editors
Donald Hall, Founding Editor

New titles

David Baker, *Show Me Your Environment*
Bruce Bond, *Immanent Distance*
Andrew Hudgins, *Diary of a Poem*
T. R. Hummer, *Available Surfaces*
Lawrence Joseph, *The Game Changed*
Marilyn Krysl, *Yes, There Will Be Singing*
David Mason, *Two Minds of a Western Poet*
Joyelle McSweeney, *The Necropastoral*
Natasha Sajé, *Windows and Doors*
Cole Swensen, *Noise That Stays Noise*
David Wojahn, *From the Valley of Making*

Recently published

Kazim Ali, *Orange Alert*
Martín Espada, *The Lover of a Subversive Is Also a Subversive*
Annie Finch, *The Body of Poetry*
Marilyn Hacker, *Unauthorized Voices*

Also available, collections by

Elizabeth Alexander, Meena Alexander, A. R. Ammons, John Ashbery, Robert Bly, Philip Booth, Marianne Boruch, Hayden Carruth, Amy Clampitt, Alfred Corn, Douglas Crase, Robert Creeley, Donald Davie, Thomas M. Disch, Ed Dorn, Tess Gallagher, Sandra M. Gilbert, Dana Gioia, Linda Gregerson, Allen Grossman, Thom Gunn, Rachel Hadas, John Haines, Donald Hall, Joy Harjo, Robert Hayden, Edward Hirsch, Daniel Hoffman, Jonathan Holden, John Hollander, Paul Hoover, Andrew Hudgins, Laura (Riding) Jackson, Josephine Jacobsen, Mark Jarman, Galway Kinnell, Kenneth Koch, John Koethe, Yusef Komunyakaa, Maxine Kumin, Martin Lammon (editor), Philip Larkin, David Lehman, Philip Levine, Larry Levis, John Logan, William Logan, William Matthews, William Meredith, Jane Miller, David Mura, Carol Muske, Alice Notley, Geoffrey O'Brien, Gregory Orr, Alicia Suskin Ostriker, Ron Padgett, Marge Piercy, Grace Schulman, Anne Sexton, Karl Shapiro, Reginald Shepherd, Charles Simic, William Stafford, Anne Stevenson, May Swenson, James Tate, Richard Tillinghast, C. K. Williams, Alan Williamson, Charles Wright, James Wright, John Yau, and Stephen Yenser

Bruce Bond

Immanent Distance

POETRY AND THE METAPHYSICS OF THE NEAR AT HAND

UNIVERSITY OF MICHIGAN

Ann Arbor

Published in the United States of America by
The University of Michigan Press
Manufactured in the United States of America
♾ Printed on acid-free paper

2018 2017 2016 2015 4 3 2 1

A CIP catalog record for this book is available from the British Library.
ISBN 978-0-472-07283-5 (hardcover : alk. paper)
ISBN 978-0-472-05283-7 (pbk. : alk. paper)
ISBN 978-0-472-12136-6 (e-book)

Acknowledgments

Chapters from this book first appeared in modified form in the following journals:

The Age of Technique: *Coldfront*

Empathy and the Poetic Imagination: *Coldfront*

The Wind in the Fire: *The Georgia Review*
Sentimentality and the Movement of the Mind

An Abundance of Lack: *Kenyon Review*
The Fullness of Desire in the Poetry of Robert Hass

Authenticity and the Myth of the Lyric Subject: *Kenyon Review*
The Summons of Olson's Legacy

Mercury's Passage: *Kenyon Review*
Poetry, Fracture, and the Talking Cure

Zeno's Arrow, Cupid's Bow: Structure, *Kenyon Review*
Process, and Poetry's Dream of the Unified Field

The Double Fall of Madame I: *The Ohio Review*

The Postmodern Split: Poetry, Theory, *Philosophy and Literature*
and the Metaphysics That Would Not Die

Metaphysics of the Image in Charles Wright's *The Southern Review*
"Homage to Paul Cezanne"

The Genius of the Medium: *32 Poems*
Identity and Alterity in Poetic Practice

The Limits of Metaphor: *Western Humanities Review*

Form's Future: *The Writer's Chronicle*
Negative Capability, Apprenticeship, and the Poetic Line

The author would like to thank the following people for their help during the completion of this manuscript: Gabriel Cervantes, J. Baird Callicot, Stephen Corey, B. H. Fairchild, David Holdeman, Steven Karl, David Lynn, Michael Mejia, Dahlia Porter, and Mark Wagenaar.

Contents

Introduction

The Glass Island

Crusoe
We say was
'Rescued'.
So we have chosen.
—George Oppen, "Of Being Numerous"

The self, like the other, has no home, or none in particular. Nor does it constitute a home. Although it carries the burden and authority of some inwardness, it has no exterior, no discernible core. Its inner space is more vast than its imagined contours. It has a body, but it cannot be its body, and too often it is not home there. It is wandering some abstracted place that is nowhere and everywhere. Although the self has no boundary, it has not rid itself of boundaries. It *has* a name, we say, which tells us it cannot *be* its name, nor vanish from the presumption of *having*, from the imaginary seat of possession. To say the contingent nature of the self makes of selfhood an illusion says nothing. The claim dissolves the terms of its assertion. One might as well say our experience is a dream, as if subjectivity could swallow up the world and remain a subject. None of this is new. "No man is an island," claimed John Donne. "He is a peninsula," replied Peter Bergman, the founder of the 1970s comedy group the Firesign Theater. Admit it, the joke says, the self is not exactly landlocked either. It has an island's sense of vulnerability, its sense of exile, its impeded access to the objects of desire. It cannot feel what another feels, cannot appropriate or embody another's integrity of thought and affect, and even if it did, it could not know it did. The self is part island, part droplet in the oceanic community of others. It is the child of both its volition and context, its relational experience, which is both like and unlike any other. In gazing out from the promontory of some great loss or disappointment, a person might feel what it is to be surrounded in the shush of no one in particular, to experience the unassailable singularity of one's fleeting experience, mine, yours, isolate and yet bound as is the present to the past. Poems give voice to this complex experience of self and the world to which it owes its emergence, transcendence, and renewal.

Especially in difficult times, when language cracks under the pressure of experience, we may feel drawn to what poems have to offer. We may find in them the privacy of our singularity, however much tragedy may bring us together, drawn by the silence we break like bread. As little as we know about just what the self is, poems remind us of two things: the self can never occupy the space of the other, nor can the self extricate otherness from its nature. Perhaps less obvious is that we cannot quite extricate some trace of selfhood from our experience of the other. Even the metaphysical construct of otherness as beyond experience is haunted by the ghost of our imagination. Desire lights the imagination by virtue of the self/other paradox, the sense of the inner other, the outer self, and our imagined exile from the very being we embody. "I is not an I," as Rimbaud says, but neither is it a you or an us. The I defies the power of words and so invites them in the form of poetry. We cannot embody those we know, any more than banish them from memory, from the fabric of thought with its untraceable origins, its ache of social debt, social want, social repulsion, the appropriated gestures of love that articulate the realm of the intimate. To complicate matters, the otherness inextricable from selfhood has both an inward and outward character, the summoning distances of consciousness and world that likewise cannot be extricated from one another.

When Paul Eluard reportedly stated, "There is another world, and it is this one," he gave voice to the fundamental tension that drives the poetic imagination, that must render the near at hand as seen through the lens of desire. Without a hunger for the deeper resources of being, there is no poetry, no poetic wonder, no eros as the bridge made of the distance to be bridged. Poetry has long thrived on the paradox of otherness as both immanent and distant, how, as the imagination journeys inward, it finds its emotional access to the world, its empathy, however flawed. It finds the deft intelligence of the waking dream that makes the world into something we can love. For this reason, it is often helpful for the apprentice poet to write about others as though they were oneself and to write about oneself as though one were another. The commerce between otherness and selfhood provides the friction that kindles the fire, that gives a poem its animating necessity, its urgency in terms of what is at stake, what calls subjectivity not merely to invest but to make manifest its imaginative riches in the world.

Thus, for the poetic imagination, the otherness of the psyche's depths occupies both an inward and outward space, embedded as it is in a sensorial realm that includes the numberless, material expressions of culture and the natural world. The poet must therefore go inward by going outward and go outward by going inward. For a philosopher such as Heidegger, to speak of the complex relational being of poetry with precision is to put the language under such pressure that it requires a new nomenclature. It is to engage in an activity close in spirit to that of poetry, full of metaphor and contradiction, to register a heightened phenomenological awareness and precision. Poetry, according to Heidegger, "speaks Dasein" or the relational manifestation of being. As the embodiment of our felt sense of being, embedded in the "thereness" of being, poetry refuses to extract the world from the self or the self from the world. It aspires not simply to objectify the world, but to participate in the affective plenitude of its emergence. We might add, therefore, that poetry does not simply "express" emotion; it creates it. It does not render the ready-made; it bodies forth that which is coming into being. It is not an escape from the real, but a restoration of the real conceived relationally, inclusive of our being-in-the-world.

Poetry's particular kind of precision, its deep attention to the act of attention, is predicated on desire, on longing for a being that is inaccessible to language. Thus, as will be explored through this book, poems make manifest the metaphysical yearning that drives all language, and in recognition of deeper resources of being outside their grasp, poems tend to inquire, crack, evoke, hush, and elude. Poetry, as true to its relational being, must preserve the elusive nature of its subject even as it commits itself to the power of revelation, in large part because its "subject" is always in part the imagination itself.

To say that all language relies upon and embodies a metaphysics requires a clarification of the concept of the metaphysical. The object of metaphysical speculation, accurately speaking, does not constitute a body of knowledge, although it is suggestive of the real. The long association of metaphysics with the positing of a metaphysical "ground" invokes the paradoxical, physical metaphor of empirical stability to characterize something beyond the empirical. The "ground" or intimation of reality in metaphysics must be in another sense "groundless," beyond representation and thus haunted, as faith must be, by doubt. The metaphysics implicit in poetry and discussed throughout this book characteristically owes more to the negative capability of faith than some style of certitude that would systemize that which is not only beyond the senses but, more largely, beyond experience as a clearly constituted whole. This is not to say metaphysics does not require or spring from experience. On the contrary, metaphysics implics a knowledge led to the limits of knowledge, so that the poem, as metaphysical, summons a more dynamic form of expressive precision than that implied by the positing of some static, ahistorical, metaphysical "ground." Poems are metaphysical insofar as their voices reach into dark recesses that, mercifully, will not relinquish their darkness, at least not all of it.

The metaphysical *intimation* of reality as expressive of something outside the limits of representation is absolutely critical to the quality of desire, necessity, and ethos in a poem and in language more largely. As will be explored later in this book, a resistance to metaphysics gives rise to a poetry enervated in its capacity for urgency and commitment, but it should be added that even anti-metaphysical poetic posturing will be haunted by metaphysical speculations, if only in an attempt to parody and dismantle them. To enact the dynamism of being-in-the-world, poems of urgency must appear to move toward a real that remains forever at a distance. Without the intuition of the real, poems go nowhere, or nowhere of significance. It is in the sensation of meaningful search, this sense of eros drawn toward some absent presence or groundless ground, that poems in turn would "move" us as engaged in a world that matters.

The self too might be said to be a "groundless ground," whether accorded the objective status of "the real" or not. The self remains the source of organizing tension within the developing psyche, and its very elusive nature as contingent upon and inhabited by alterity is what drives its stubbornly dynamic nature. What could be closer than the self? What could be more elusive and uncanny? In its felt presence as both structural and dynamic, it cannot be described with precision without calling upon poetic resources of paradox and metaphor. If the self is an island, it is an island made of glass. Hard to know just where the ocean ends, the land begins. Taken as a whole, the otherness upon which the self depends borrows the metaphorical nomenclature so often applied to the absolute—oceanic, uncontrollable, sublime, temperamental, at times even chaotic. As Wallace Stevens suggests in his poem "Sunday Morning," it is difficult to dispense some intuition of totality, some vague sense of a larger, more inclusive version of things, however failed our attempts to understand. It is our exile and inability to comprehend that makes possible the hunger so central to the imagination:

> We live in an old chaos of the sun,
> Or old dependency of day and night,
> Or island solitude, unsponsored, free,
> Of that wide water, inescapable.
> (l. 110–113)

The ocean here is of two natures. It divides us from the absolute—the mainland, the community, the real—but it likewise takes on the language of the absolute. Distance is central to its immediate felt presence and the feeling of awe of those on shore. Each in her singularity is "free," disconnected, and yet bound by that same feeling of disconnection to something beyond view. The ocean is thus a summons, as is all poetry, to pay attention to the near at hand and to see in the act of attention the ghost of the unknown. Thus poetry weds the act of witness inextricably to faith, just faith enough, to call us to look more closely at the world and, by grace of the imagination, to look again.

I.

The Hunger for Being

The Postmodern Split

Poetry, Theory, and the Metaphysics That Would Not Die

Postmodernism, in spite of its exaggerations and myopias, has left us with many gifts, including two strains of the critical tradition that struggle to reconcile with one another. Those strains grow from two undeniable truths: that the self can never occupy the space of the other, nor can the self extricate the other from its nature. Given the conflict between these truths, the postmodern resistance to metaphysics can never be quite as rigorous as it imagines, for the self, as inextricable from what it can never be, must be an object of faith, its origin and agency rooted in an eclipsed otherness beyond our capacity to witness or understand. A sense of this, acknowledged or not, haunts the contradictions of recent critical and literary culture, a postmodern approach that, in rejecting metaphysical models of meaning for more politically exigent and skeptical forms of rigor, has adopted a faith in the limits of our language as the limits of our world. In spite of this shift, metaphysical assumptions, embedded in that language, stubbornly persist. We are what we are not, which is to say we embody vast reaches of reverie, memory, and incommunicable nightmare, the mysteries of both free will and all that circumscribes it. In us and before us, an otherness persists, intuited by way of its effects, by the ghosts of missing presences among our most immediate objects of experience: our bodies, our psyches, our silences, and the words we speak.

Since to say the word "I" is to invoke both a self and an other, the word has a little of poetry's penchant for paradox in it. As a yoking of opposites, it is mythic. It does what the poetic imagination does constantly in our daily discourse: it creates a language for something we intuit as beyond our language. It goes where reason cannot. It speaks the unspeakable, clarifies our felt relation to it, our sense of ontological wonder, hunger, and awe. If we accept that poetry is by definition a metaphysical activity, speculative in ways that summon faith, then the phrase "postmodern poetry" seems like a bit of an oxymoron. Admittedly, the word "postmodern" blurs from abuse and overuse, though in poetry criticism it has come to describe poets who follow in the theoretical footsteps of Jacques Derrida, who, in rejecting naive notions of meaning as a stable essence buried in words, would in general resist affirmations of the real as something buried and so beyond appearance. This spirit of disciplined resistance is not new with Derrida and continental philosophy of the post-war years. Rather it is an intensification of Husserl's phenomenological method that prides itself on a rigorous adherence to immanent data, to being as appearance, as embodied in the near at hand. Husserl, in defiance of Kantian speculations about "the thing in itself" as something apart from the mind's categories of space and time, would "bracket off" from consideration all that lies beyond the realm of immediate experience. So too a postmodern sensibility would bracket off or discredit notions of the buried self as a center or ground, out of which grows consciousness as we know it.

A creative and critical culture devoted to skeptical rigor has engendered the poetic sensibility that Marjorie Perloff describes in defense of "language" poetry, a movement self-identified with a postmodernism that "no longer recognizes such 'depth models' as inside/outside, essence/appearance, latent/manifest, authenticity/ inauthenticity, signifier/signified, or depth/surface" (406). The political resonance of this defiance is in turn a demythologizing of the "self-made" man, defined apart from his social context, affirmed within a capitalist system that views individual freedom as exaggerated and success as consistent with character. Unfortunately postmodernist rhetoric, granted license as polemic, often falls victim to a reductio-ad-absurdum akin to the essentialist exaggerations that it would critique. To eliminate depth models, for instance, is to eliminate the conscious/unconscious duality, and so the metaphysical contributions of the psychoanalytic tradition must go and with them our intimations of hidden desires, histories, and fears. The postmodern rejection of depth models implies a rejection of our sense of the unseen mind in the felt mysteries of its emergence.

It is one thing to say that the self cannot be autonomous or an impervious monad, something other than fundamentally relational; it is another thing to say that it does not exist or that we have succeeded, by way of skeptical rigor, in dismantling the concept as meaningful. That is a bit like saying that because our behavior is to a large degree determined by our culture, we have no will at all. The experience of freedom is relevant here, since it lies at the core of our intuitive experience of selfhood. Naturally we can conclude that the self, as an object of metaphysics, does not exist, or that we have no way of knowing that it exists, though our language and behavior continue to assert precisely the opposite. The experience of self-agency as a felt phenomenon has become impossible to extricate from the process and production of meaning. Those who would "transcend the self" have already conceded that there is something to transcend. To transcend a self is to be led to the limits of language, to see a world beyond it, and so, from a postmodern point of view, to embrace an illusion. Poems risk just such an embrace constantly, but with the felt sense that fictions articulate what is genuine in our relation to something beyond our fictive structures.

"Even the death of the imagination," writes Wallace Stevens, "had to be imagined," and yet he continues, in the face of a contradictory aestheticism, to try to get outside the imagination that he so celebrates, obsessively hungering for the greater context. Stevens realizes that the imagination loves a problem. It loves a state of irresolution wherein desire for being continues to animate poetry as both homage and testament to that desire. True, Stevens is in the Romantic tradition, such that he sees the poet as a "metaphysician in the dark," looking to the unseen in the seen. Many poets conceive of their calling differently. But I would argue that even poets of a professed postmodernism cannot avoid what is endemic to metaphors that would subvert or dismantle the notion of "subjectivity." Even such poets sign their names to their works. The postmodern denial of depth models, including those that make meaningful the concept of self, has led to a host of epistemological problems, the most extreme of which being the conception of language as one vast self-referring system that constitutes the entirety of our experience. Given the instability of signs, it is the totalizing of experience as semiotic that leads to the greatest absurdities that bear little relation to the sense of the real and the authentic as they continue to inform our sense of what is at stake in and outside of language.

Even as the spell of unreality conjured by much postmodern hyperbole subsides, as it is increasingly obvious that the real as merely socially constructed ceases to fulfill the definition of the real, the anti-metaphysical strain of postmodern thought carries forward a phenomenological ideal of tough-mindedness, of paying close attention to the near at hand. But the near at hand, viewed as inextricable from the way we view it, tends to suggest something metaphysical, namely that what appears closest to us, one's own body for instance, eludes reliable representation or understanding. To talk this way is to call upon a metaphysical intuition of something outside of representation. In this sense, the immanent bears characteristics of the transcendent, and much of the speculative poetry since the Romantics increasingly registers the confusion, paradox, and wonder of the immanent as distant, the familiar, seen through the clarifying lens of the poem, as strange.

Ferdinand de Saussure's linguistic theory is extremely helpful in focusing the divergent trends of influence that have given rise to a postmodern and paradoxical view of language and its relation to subjectivity. Particularly his notion that all meaning in language appears by virtue of context and the relational production of difference suggests two fundamental principles: (1) All meaning has a private dimension since no two contexts are the same, and (2) all meaning is unstable since contexts shift and evolve. One can see in these simple insights the seeds of current critical thought. Language is both an individual and collective medium. It is where the private and the public find their most heated and meaningful tension. To reiterate, the self cannot occupy the space of the other, nor can it extricate otherness from its nature.

These two notions have given birth to a divide in critical culture, a postmodern split. Whereas a reader-response critic might emphasize the former, a more ideological critic might emphasize the latter, such that ideological associations in language need to be clear and stable enough to suggest political consequence and significance. When both interpretive play and collective connectivity appear to permeate the totality of consciousness, we see more sharply the postmodern split: all poems become political, and yet the political resonance and efficacy become diffuse thanks to language's fundamental instability and openness to interpretation. Taken together, the two points of emphasis can become useful if each perspective is not radicalized into absurdity but rather tempered by the other.

The postmodern split has led many to reconcile the divergent points of emphasis by politicizing semiotic closure itself and, via a close association of form and meaning, formal closure. We see such strategies in Frederic Jameson's *The Political Unconscious*, where a sense of narrative closure correlates to the forces of imperialist hegemony one finds in Conrad's *The Heart of Darkness*. Likewise an ironically limited reading of form appears in Ron Silliman's essay "The New Sentence," where syntactical models of coherence suggest hegemonic centering. Such arguments give support then to the attack on lyric form where formal closure provides a language for semiotic closure, and a tighter and more obviously structured musicality figures as both a metaphor for and embodiment of exclusionary control.

The irony of the sometimes strict association of formal closure with semiotic closure is that the interpretive play available to a poem's meaning becomes less available to form as metaphor, so that recursivity in lyric and narrative form narrows its connotations to that of hegemony, ego, essentialism, and control. Lyric practice thus rather strongly implies ideology, which it can do, but not without a residue of irony due to the exclusive interpretive practice that reads the lyric in that way. The sentence can likewise suggest hegemony, but it might also signify psychic integration, for that matter, where the parts of the mind are now talking to one another. It could model sanity as a genuinely healthy dynamic of psychic connectivity.

When one adds to Saussure's insights Wittgenstein's sense that the limits of our language are the limits of our world, then nothing in consciousness remains immune to the destabilizing contextual nature of semiotics. The self, as semiotically constructed, suffers the same fate and enjoys the same freedoms as all sign systems. As an added complication, the collectivity critical to self-construction is a product of both culture and the individual, for each self bears a slightly different collectivity, or rather a different mess of competing collectivities. Sameness cannot exist, only similitude. The insidious pursuit of sameness is a familiar postmodern theme, symptomatic of not only a naïveté but also a hegemonic intolerance of difference, the kind critiqued by Foucault in his account of Jeremy Bentham's Panopticon, the eighteenth century architectural structure wherein one can oversee and regulate all the inmates in an institution. What the postmodern split suggests is that each individual within an institution is something of a cultural construct and yet, in spite of institutional oversight, invisible to that culture. Each subjectivity is a monad, insofar as it cannot be dismantled, passed on, or fully understood by others, but no subjectivity is autonomous. The epistemology regarding the "self" gets caught up in a debate between, on the one hand, a desire to liberate the individual and, on the other, a need to call into question the very concept of the individual.

In literary studies, the strain on the word "self" finds its correlative in the strain on the word "text." Take for example Stanley Fish's famous monograph, *Is There a Text in This Class?* (1982), where the author examines the tenuous nature of the category "text" as something with an essentialized and objectified nature. He then points to the role of interpretive communities as sanctioning strategies whereby the sense of textual authority and identity are constructed. Fish's work provides a useful illustration of how the postmodern split would attempt to reconcile the divergent tendencies in contemporary thought that spring from the insight into meaning's contextual basis, and like much criticism of our time, Fish seeks to bring reader-response theory, with its more introverted individualism, into greater recognition of textual authority as a social construct. He represents an attempt to reconcile some of the more useful insights of reader-response theory with a more ideological and community-based criticism that will increasingly supersede it. He would recognize the sense of selfhood as embedded in collective otherness, but that otherness would remain as vague, as inextricably "other," as the concepts in reader-response theory that he would attack.

While the self cannot occupy the other nor extricate itself from otherness in part because the "self" is too blurry to constitute a bounded phenomenon, the same can be said for the concept of community. Nevertheless, Fish's theory must deploy the concepts of "individual" and "communal" to give any shape to his argument. What we see in Fish is evidence of how the culture wars of the Reagan era aroused in the academic world a greater hunger for political conviction at the expense of a more rigorously philosophical scrutiny of the contradictory discourse and slackened attentions that such conviction would engender. Ethics, or more precisely, politics, would increasingly trump aesthetics and epistemology in ways that would move the mainstream of literary studies away from expertise in the values most salient in poetry, a mode of writing conceived not simply as a formal discipline but as a mode of imaginative investigation where the dense, polysemous conflation of subjects and objects make political analysis problematic.

This is not to say that Fish is unconcerned with epistemology, but his epistemology is not terribly subtle in ways that become more obvious with the passage of time. Since the focus in Fish's monograph is on pedagogy and the politics of the classroom, Fish concerns himself especially with the role that power plays in rendering certain readings of texts "acceptable." In so doing, Fish exposes the epistemological shakiness of certain categories deployed by those less savvy to the contextual nature of meaning. His point of view thus carries forward something of the insights of previous reader-response criticism in moving toward a greater scrutiny of the untenable essentialism implicit in such categories as "text," but likewise his work has a decidedly political resonance that argues for less centralization of authority, particularly in matters of pedagogy and critical reception. Thus reader-response's emphasis on relative nature of the individual finds its correlative in the relative nature of interpretive community. On the other hand, Fish cannot make his argument without deploying the very categories that he chooses to dismantle, and a similar irony pervades the work of numerous theorists who would set aside the very metaphysics that they cannot escape.

A more inclusive phenomenology of reading would need to take into consideration the centrality of the urgent *sense* of the real, what Wallace Stevens calls the "pressure of the real." While the imagination cannot fully accommodate the real, according to Stevens, the imagination loses vitality without it:

> By pressure of reality, I mean the pressure of an external event or events on the consciousness to the exclusion of any power of contemplation. . . . We are confronting . . . a set of events, not only beyond our power to tranquillize them in the mind, beyond our power to reduce them and metamorphose them, but events that stir the emotions to violence that engage us in what is direct and immediate and real . . . a pressure real enough and prolonged enough to bring about the end of one era in the history of the imagination and, if so, then great enough to bring about the beginning of an era.
> (20, 22)

The pressure of the real might likewise be dubbed the pressure of necessity, and via this pressure ethics, as a mode of receptivity to otherness, forges its close relationship with epistemology. We might feel the pressure of the real most acutely when, for example, we read a newspaper in times of crisis, times that undermine the luxury of some radical relativism that rushes to defend the decentering of meaning as a form of liberation.

Tragedy asserts hierarchy. The sentence "The Holocaust happened" registers a sense of the real with a greater pressure of necessity than the sentence "Textual meaning is simply the product of interpretive communities." A horrifying look at the interpretive community that refuses to believe the first sentence might suggest as much. To be fair, Fish's concern is with *literary* texts, which by definition are open to interpretation, but his statements ring as more categorical as evidenced by the repeated lack of qualification to the word "text." If the argument is that our reading of *literary* texts (by definition interpretively open) is relativized by community, the statement is nearly circular and not much of a claim. He has simply added the social contingency of the self. Fish's rhetoric depends upon a grandeur of hyperbole characteristic of the performative theatricality of much French theory.

More importantly, Fish's famous attack on Wolfgang Iser demonstrates some of the recalcitrant metaphysical gesturing that cannot be extricated from our experience of language. This essay, though from 1981, has once again become the subject of greater scrutiny thanks in part to a recent essay by Michael Bérubé, who sees in Fish's attack a critical crossroads in terms of the weakening of reader-response theory in favor of a greater emphasis on the social construction of meaning ("There Is Nothing Inside the Text, or Why No One's Heard of Wolfgang Iser," 2004). The implication here is that Fish's critique was hugely influential in ways that beg a closer re-evaluation. The particular re-evaluation relevant to the question of the metaphysics might focus not so much on the difference between Fish and Iser as their similarity.

The notion that Fish deploys categories that he would dismantle is ironic, since this resembles the very strategy that he accuses Wolfgang Iser of deploying. First Fish must call into question Iser's essentialized notion of text:

> [Iser declares] "the text itself . . . offers 'schematized aspects' through which the actual subject matter of the work can be produced." . . . Iser is able to maintain this position because he regards the text as *a part of the world* (even though the process it sets in motion is not).

The phrase "the text itself" has a decidedly New Critical ring to it and hardly characterizes the main thrust of Iser's emphasis on the key interpretive agency of the reader. Fish exercises just such an agency as he later offers a reading of Fielding's *Tom Jones* contrary to Iser's and concludes:

> If gaps are not built into the text, but appear (or do not appear) as a consequence of particular interpretive strategies, then there is no distinction between what the text gives and what the reader supplies . . . I am *not* saying that it is impossible to give an account of *Tom Jones* which depends on a distinction between what is in the text and what the reader is moved, by gaps in the text, to supply; it is just that the distinction itself is an assumption which, when it informs an act of literary description, will *produce* the phenomena it purports to describe.

Once again, Fish's initial claim is barely a claim. Of course it is *possible* to give an account of *Tom Jones* in any number of ways. The larger claim is that the assumption of distinctions produces the phenomena of distinctions. If one does not recognize the critical metaphysics in language charged with necessity and the pressure of the real, then the problem Fish notes becomes the problem of *all* distinctions as products of interpretation. No distinction can be cleansed of the ghost of subjectivity engaged in the elusive process we intuit in the dialogically perceived nature of "relations." Distinctions are only perceived as "produced" by some interpretation relative to some alterity that is the thing that we would interpret. Fish does not explore a basis for distinctions among distinctions. This explains the rhetorical strategies of claims such as the sentence, "I am *not* saying that is impossible to give an account." This claim risks and says very little. Fish wishes to back off from a privileging of distinctions here, though he will focus on Iser's distinctions and, by virtue of selective dismantling, implicate Iser's hierarchy in what those distinctions would promote.

In the debate between reader-response criticism and community-based literary theory, it is not simply textual objectivity that comes under extreme pressure as untenable, but the related category, associated with Iser, of a text being "in the world." It is easy to attack the blurriness of some imagined objective status that lies outside the act of reading, but we could say the same thing about the agreed upon nature of readers and communities. Where are these if not "in the world" and thus accessible to Fish's categorical statements about them? Fish's very argument routinely employs both the category of "text" and "reader," as if he might displace the unreliable epistemological status of the former with the equally unreliable status of the latter. One might additionally ask the question, is there a reader in this class? Or: is there a community? Where exactly? Is not community a bit phantasmal, something no eye can see in its identifying boundaries? Are we not asked to exercise faith by intuiting a large structure such as a community from its inevitably dissimilar effects? Is not the identifiable dynamic of any community subject to individual interpretation, and are not individuals in turn deeply conflicted and provisional in their constructions?

Because cultural constructions are subject to the imaginations of individuals, a liberal discourse on collective identity finds itself deploying categories its sensitivities to individual difference would dismantle.

A criticism disciplined, like a poem, to the felt nature of experience requires a taste for nuance, for matters of degree, and a self-awareness about the limits of its approach. Differences of degree are messy and thus do not lend themselves readily to theory as a systematic practice nor to political polemics. As we see in the ironies of radical relativism, a "systemless system" is still a system, which a poem cannot credibly be. The irony is that, so long as critical theory pursues a tact that would radicalize its sense of language as characterizing the whole of consciousness, its pursuit of rigor will exacerbate its lack thereof—that is, it will prefer a seemingly tough-minded theoretical skepticism to the more elusive discipline of ontological description, a technique closer in spirit to that of poetry. Theory in denial of its metaphysics will miss the subtlety necessary to register the crucial summons to the faith that makes language possible. It will fail to fully complicate the epistemological status of "communal and individual agencies" as both problematic, contingent on unknown alterities, and yet oddly indispensible to our sense of purpose. It will turn away from the dark intuitive heart of both epistemology and its ethical bearing, away from the role that the pressure of necessity plays in the production of critical discourse and our sense of why it matters. Theory will fail to fully appreciate, as Heidegger did, that at the growing tip of thought, of new meaning, coming into being, is an encounter with and manifestation of a mindfulness, less theoretical or systematic than it is creatively ontological and therefore, in some measure, poetic.

Works Cited

Bérubé, Michael. "There is Nothing Inside the Text, or, Why No One's Heard of Wolfgang Iser." In *Postmodern Sophistry: Stanley Fish and the Critical Enterprise.* Gary A. Olson and Lynn Worsham, eds., 11–26. Albany, NY: State University of New York Press, 2004.

Fish, Stanley. *Is There A Text in This Class? The Authority of Interpretive Communities.* Cambridge: Harvard University Press, 1982.

Fish, Stanley. "Why No One's Afraid of Wolfgang Iser." *Diacritics: A Review of Contemporary Criticism* 11, 1 (1981): 2–13.

Jameson, Frederic. *The Political Unconscious: Narrative as a Socially Symbolic Act.* Cornell, NY: Cornell University Press, 1982.

Perloff, Marjorie. "Language Poetry and the Lryic Subject." *Critical Inquiry* 23 (1999): 405–434.

Silliman, Ronald. "The New Sentence." In *Claims for Poetry.* Donald Hall, ed. Ann Arbor: University of Michigan Press, 1983.

Stevens, Wallace. "The Noble Rider and the Sound of Words." In *The Necessary Angel.* New York: Random House, 1951.

Authenticity and the Myth of the Lyric Subject

The Summons of Olson's Legacy

Ever since 1950, when in his essay "Projective Verse" Charles Olson framed his summons to the ideals of a more spontaneous though no less formally conscious aesthetic, the notion of "the lyrical interference of the individual as ego" has appeared frequently in poetic theory to define by contrast a more inclusive and magnanimous poetics. The call for a poetry of greater candor and more inclusive attention, a more immediate participation in the unfolding of being, was not new. Rather it articulated a major strain of literary Romanticism, German and British in its roots, but taking on revolutionary poetic form in America, most visibly in the poetic practice of Whitman with his defiant, expansive, and politically contextualized shattering of the tight lyric vessel. Increasingly the term "spontaneous" has come to characterize not only compositional method at its most unguarded, but also the writing itself, as if that particular method left a relatively reliable transcription or embodiment of its process. The projective poem resonates not merely as code but also as an index, its words like footprints that, by virtue of causality, bear with them an intimacy with the temporal origins of the poem. What is at stake in the projective poem is its authenticity, which relies upon the language's precision as both mimetic of the real and, with regard to process, evidentiary.

While Olson made some effort to distance himself from the Romantic tradition, particularly in its obvious associations with individualism and the elevated epistemological and aesthetic status of subjectivity, his approach depends on a similar complication of what we understand to be subjectivity, the value of which relies heavily on its paradoxical nature as both personal and transpersonal. Both Olson and the Romantics gesture, either explicitly or implicitly, toward an elusive authenticity of language, a less artificial means of rendering consciousness, and such authenticity depends in turn upon a relative lack of self-consciousness, or posturing, and an increase in transpersonal awareness. This compensatory dynamic, so characteristic of poetic theory since the Romantics, relies upon the twin values of the individual and her larger context, in addition to the essential reciprocity and complication of the categories of self and other as the very dynamic that drives the visionary act.

Although the contemporary practice of free verse has lost its revolutionary identity, it maintains some of its cultural currency as democratic, inclusive, and unpretentious. Whereas "formality" implies, for some, a mask, free verse implies "nakedness," a term echoed in Stephen Berg and Robert Mezey's influential free verse anthology, *Naked Poetry,* first released in 1969. Although the metaphor of nakedness in poetry would be received with more skepticism now, certain critical biases implicit within the metaphor linger. In theoretical terms, few today would argue that a poem can indeed be naked, since, after all, it is the nature of language to mediate, but whatever their theoretical position, those who risk the aesthetic judgment of poetry may still catch themselves deploying categories such as "phony" and "artificial," as if to suggests a more naked poem is a more authentic one. The naked poem would be more intimate with being, such that our poetic means is just that, a means, a vehicle. The ego, in Olson's terms, is its obstacle. In contrast to the naked poem, the artifice of what Olson calls "closed verse," with its typically revisionary compositional demands, suggests for many an artifice of self, one that cannot keep pace with the great phenomenological river that is the fullness of consciousness and its imaginations.

What is defiantly non-Romantic about Olson's directive is the explicit complaint against the lyric as egocentric. Understanding the rationale for this attack is complicated by our many associations with the word "lyric," but if we accept the link Olson makes between the lyric and "closed verse," or recursive form, it makes sense that he would object to such form as not only "artificial" but also evidence of a hesitant, self-conscious compositional method incapable of authenticity. Since Olson's essay, the postmodern resistance to the lyric has likewise accepted his sense of the lyric as the province of the individual soul or the ego, but missing from this postmodern echo of Olson's critique is his metaphysics, that critical "stance toward the real" by which he justifies his approach. Moreover what the postmodern approach *does* appropriate from Olson is an imprecisely conceived association of lyric form with subjectivity, a bias born of an inadequately challenged conflation of lyric form with lyric content.

To demonstrate how the conflation of form and content breaks down, we enter into issues far more fundamental than those associated with projective versus postmodern aesthetics. We enter into the difficulty that lies at the heart of the problem of representation, how the more reliable models that articulate difference, such as that between form and content, likewise gesture toward continuity. The assault on the concept of authenticity reflects the error of seeing all experience as mediated by language rather than a more complex dynamic between binaries of differentiation and the monads of awareness.

Lyric and the Individual

Olson, in his attempt to construct a reliable model of the relationship between self and nature, in turn asserts a simultaneous continuity and difference that, however provocative, creates contradiction and confusion in his language. This confusion however is nonetheless preferable to the more crisply discriminatory and illusory sense of the self as purely autonomous, as mere ego. The self for Olson is authentically represented as a "creature of nature," which is to say, both continuous with nature and yet in some measure apart from and in relation to nature, which is for him an "object:"

> Objectism is the getting rid of the lyrical interference of the individual as ego, of the "subject" and his soul, that peculiar presumption by which western man has interposed himself between what he is as a creature of nature (with certain in-

> structions to carry out) and those other creations of nature which we may, with no derogation, call objects. (620)

This point of view may not be as different from Romanticism as Olson imagines, for he cannot shake the language of personal identity altogether. Nevertheless, projectivism, which implies for Olson "objectism," calls into question notions such as "soul," which would make a sacrament of nature while maintaining a personal identity in relation to it. Just why the lyric imposes its interference between us and nature is only implied, though it makes sense that he would object to the revised, refined, and frequently formal qualities of the lyric, which require a more hesitant compositional method, akin to the careful construction of a persona. The recursive dimension of the poem as "song" fits Olson's description of "closed" verse, something abandoned via the iconoclastic break that Pound attributed to Williams. To quote Olson once again,

> *The NON-Projective*
>
> (or what a French critic calls "closed" verse, that verse which print bred and which is pretty much what we have had, in English & American, and have still got, despite the work of Pound & Williams. (613)

The debt to Pound goes deeper than merely the break with the metrical tradition and the domination of the iamb. If by "lyric" we mean to suggest polysemous resonance, then Olson fits squarely into a lyric tradition as articulated by Pound via his love of speed, his "piths and gists," and his idea of poetic gesture as an instantaneous complex. The opening of Olson's essay sounds particularly Poundian in its leaps, which gather about the word "projective" a complex of words: "(projective (percussive (prospective vs. The NON-Projective" (613).

Given the inclusion here of the word "percussive," it is unlikely Olson meant to detract from musicality in general, another lyric virtue dear to Pound, but it could well be that the particular music of the lyric, the song with its repetitive pulse of strophes and measures, and the culture of correctness surrounding traditional, lyric form suggest something too far removed from all that is not art. A framing irony to my discussion of Olson is the fact that lyric, in its original connotation, embodies a primacy very close to that of a projective poem, which, like a song, takes the breath as its basic unit and so asserts an immediate physical presence, a sense of language as not just semiotic, but also corporeal, both inside and outside the play of signs. Music moves the listener with a speed that outraces semiotic interpretation, as if some arrow split the uncomprehending heart.

Olson's attack against closure in musical form as egoistic leads immediately to a criticism of poetic exhibitionism, as if to suggest a connection between closed form and narrow content. In criticizing Romantic tunnel-vision, Olson points to Wordsworth as an example of "the private-soul-at-any-public-wall" (613) but does not say that the individual self should not be a poet's subject. Rather he argues that the self must be objectified first and so appear as "out there," in the sense that objects are: neither inflated nor otherwise distorted by pride. He advocates a more objectivist aesthetic (which he labels "objectist") as an alternative to Wordsworth's "egotistical sublime." For the objectist, the subject-as-object is not the possession of the ego. What this suggests is that "self" in some of Olson's taxonomy is a larger phenomenon than the ego that is its representative:

> For a man is himself an object, whatever he may take to be his advantages, the more likely to recognize himself as such the greater his advantages, particularly at that moment that he achieves an humilitas sufficient to make him of use. (620)

This passage precedes some of the most paradoxical in Olson's manifesto, in which he echoes, with some irony, a view close to that of Wordsworth:

> It comes to this: the use of a man, by himself and thus by others, lies in how he conceives his relation to nature, that force to which he owes his somewhat small existence. If he sprawl, he shall find little to sing but himself, and shall sing, nature has such paradoxical ways, by way of artificial forms outside of himself. (620)

Here we find the dominant paradox of the lion's share of Romantic poetic theory. We see it in Blake, Shelley, Coleridge, Emerson, Whitman, and their contemporary offspring—all of whose ideals of individual liberation and authority depend heavily upon a complementary transpersonal awareness. Self-illumination is predicated upon self-transcendence, or, in Whitman's case, the radical expansion of sympathy and attention. Moreover, it is the sense of the transpersonal in "the common" or the near at hand that distributes authority to individuals. The door of the self leads to the world, the door of the world deeper inward.

The reciprocity of inward and outward movement not only defines the ideals articulated in Romantic poetic theory, it also describes the realm of what we might call, more generally, "the poetic." A richly complex dynamic between the self and other drives the verbal imagination to seek, even as it makes manifest, an ever elusive intimacy with alterity. For Olson and Wordsworth, this "other" bears the name "nature," which, however vague, suggests the otherness of *this* world (as opposed to the merely transcendent). It would be in keeping with Olson's phenomenological spirit to include language itself as a force of nature. We speak and so are spoken. As a collaboration with otherness, language, particularly that which requires adaptation to some demand, be it formal or epistemological, comes into being via an intimate and animating tension between subject and object.

Olson and the Postmodern

While it is generally acknowledged that manifestoes operate in hyperboles and broad, polemical strokes, an inherited confusion over the word "lyric" and its association with personal themes and subjectivity refuses to die a natural death. If there is such a thing as an avant-garde still in American poetics, it frequently positions itself against what is loosely called "the lyric," as the epitome of "the" tradition. Assumptions regarding the lyric's traditional subject matter and its closed form continue to converge to suggest that the lyric remains by some vague, causal necessity the province of the autonomous self or the writer who believes in such illusions. This politicized characterization of the lyric informs statements such as those by the writer Vanessa Place, who, at the Critical Voices Conference at the University of North Texas in 2011, claimed that she had no problem with those who chose to write in lyric forms, so long as they acknowledged their investment in an implied ideology of subjectivity. She on the other hand had abandoned an attachment to the notion of authorship and so simply "found" texts. Such gestures enter into the larger conversation of power relationships with an assumption that ideological identities attached to poetic form are intractable and should be obvious, therefore shared. Beyond that, the association of lyric form with "ego" or "autonomous self" honors no distinction or tension between the referential and non-referential dimensions of form, but rather conflates lyric form and lyric content with self-assured facility. Given the fixed assumptions that would pin themselves to the lyric as if they were its essentials, the identification of lyric with a breed of essentialism and ideology of self-interest appears ironic. Who, we might ask, does the closed reading of recursive form empower?

As Dadaism approaches its century mark, it still feels, to some, a little new. Indeed in subtle ways context makes it so, for in an age of postmodernism and its aftermath, the new Dadaists not only encourage authors to take themselves less seriously, but also to examine the viability (as opposed to mere value) of authorial selfhood altogether to see if it does not crumble as hegemonic illusion. For many the association of "the lyric" with "bourgeois complacency" or "reification of the self" owes much of its contemporary resonance less to Olson than to a postmodern poetic practice, such as L=A=N=G=U=A=G=E poetry, or more specifically the critical conversations that would make it credible. Marjorie Perloff's essay "Language Poetry and the Lyric Subject: Ron Silliman's Albany, Susan Howe's Buffalo" provides an illuminating example, wherein we encounter a distillation of values associated with postmodernism, including Barthes' sense of "the death of the subject" and his view of the unsustainable fabrication of the "bourgeois monad or ego or individual." Crucial to our understanding of what Perloff calls "postmodern" is its larger resistance to a metaphysics of reading that supposes a text has an interior and an exterior. As mentioned in the first chapter of this book,

"Postmodernism," according to Perloff, "no longer recognizes such 'depth models' as inside/outside, essence/appearance, latent/manifest, authenticity/ inauthenticity, signifier/signified, or depth/surface" (406). We might add to her list of suspect distinctions the dichotomy of form and content, their traditionally baffling relations now rendered simple by the impulse simply to "no longer recognize" the taxonomy as meaningful.

Doubtless the title of Perloff's essay resonates with Olson's, and yet there remain dramatic differences between their points of view, the most critical difference being the value that Olson invests in the concept of the real. Little is at stake in his advocacy of projective verse without what he calls "a stance toward reality." Nowhere does he claim that reality is fully accommodated by projective attempts, but the irresolution that fuels his process does nothing to undermine its significance and, in turn, the importance of its relative success or failure. To say the authority of a "stance toward reality" is relative is not to say it is arbitrary. A writer requires strict attention to authenticate a poem, and the breath as Olson's fundamental poetic unit facilitates such mindfulness with regard to the spontaneous nature of being. His claims for the breath suggest that he wishes to invoke a phenomenon of relative immediacy and primacy, much like the body itself, or, better yet, the dynamic process wherein the body and spirit comingle and surge.

Clearly the directionality of Olson's textual "stance *toward* reality" gestures beyond itself, to something other than a text, so he lacks the postmodern view, as framed by Perloff, that does not recognize the distinction between the signifier and the signified. If we follow the logic of postmodern nullification, the world would not simply be mediated through language but would be a creation of language. The presupposition about the wholly linguistic character of experience is key because if all experience is made possible and limited by language, then awareness becomes conflated with the endless play of differentiation. Such a point of view has yet to account for the experience of real presence associated with forms of corporeal immediacy, such as music. Nor does it make, as a Buddhist might, any distinction between awareness and cognition. Such a distinction does not require Buddhist meditation to reveal itself. We live in both worlds with some consistency, the worlds of seeing and thinking, though they are elusively embedded in each other, with cognition as a simultaneous facilitator of and obstacle to awareness. Thought is "intentional" in philosophical terms in the sense that there is always a distance between the thinker and the contents of thought. We think *about* things. The experience of music however is made possible via a greater intimacy with Being, a sense of overcoming or preceding the intentionality of cognition. We need not think *about* music to experience it. We need only be mindful in its presence.

Olson and Heidegger: Continuity and Difference in Models of the Real

Heidegger's somewhat poetic discourse proves useful in elucidating the projective project and its debt to mindfulness and the goal of authenticity. In granting art the power of authentication, he explores the notion of truthful representation via models akin to Olson's, metaphors that would assert in one gesture the senses of both continuity and differentiation that characterize our experience of the real. The concept of "intimacy," as understood by Heidegger, is especially helpful in characterizing the problematic nature of Olson's "stance" toward the real. As Heidegger argues in *Poetry, Language, Thought,* the purpose of the poetic is to overcome the "concealedness" implicit in separately articulated "things" or in propositions and thereby live in greater intimacy with being (54–56). It is true that, in keeping with his postmodern legacy, presence announces itself as absence for Heidegger. As Heidegger states, "Because presence conceals itself at the same time, it is itself already absence" (93). Nevertheless it is equally true that the aesthetic realm for Heidegger overcomes the concealedness of being. His example of Van Gogh's painting of shoes suggests things "attain their unconcealedness" by virtue of the aesthetic intensification of their being. In his words, "Beauty is one way that truth occurs as unconcealedness." Part of Heidegger's resistance to logic owes its complexity to two competing strains of thought: the sense of presence as absence, concealed, and yet capable of attaining unconcealedness. Because of the limitations of logic in its opposition to contraction, Heidegger seeks a means we might better call "poetic" with its mythic strategies for containing opposites in a single gesture. Being is not simply "revealed," for instance, it is "unconcealed" (from the German "unverborgen," based on the Greek word "aletheia" for "truth," which most literally means "not-concealed:" a-letheia). As opposed to the German word "Wahrheit" for "truth," "aletheia" or "unverborgenheit" still preserves the oppositional sense of concealment within it.

Little wonder poetry, with its ability to behold in simultaneous tension and reconciliation what the logic of non-contradiction cannot, occupies a special status for Heidegger. The poet, for him, is someone who summons the origin of thought and in turn empowers man to "dwell" on "earth," to live, via the creative activity of building and measuring, in greater intimacy with the given, material circumstance of his condition. By way of dwelling, a poet lives in a way "appropriate" to earth. "Poetry," he states, "is authentic or inauthentic according to the degree of this appropriation" (228). The concepts of "appropriation" and "intimacy," as alternatives to "union," provide ways of suggesting both a bond and a difference, such that poetry does not eliminate difference but rather would bring the elements of difference into closer relation and thereby speak in the space between them, between, as he later states, "world" (a monad) and "thing" (one among many) (202). Heidegger's intuitions on poetry and its primacy in engendering thought express a profound longing that drives and animates consciousness: the desire for the reconciliation of "the many" and "the one." With some frequency, his language works with some finesse and novelty to express as mutually inextricable both the articulations of difference and the unity of Being. "We can only say 'the same,'" he states, "if we think of difference" (218).

Heidegger's sense of a poet's calling closely resembles Olson's, which is, above all, to pay close attention and so forge an ever more intimate relation to being. As Heidegger states,

> The more poetic an author is—the freer (that is, the more open and ready for the unforeseen) his saying—the greater is the purity with which he submits what he says to an ever more

painstaking listening, and the further what he says is from the mere proposition statement that is dealt with solely in regard to its correctness or incorrectness. (216)

The impulse to be "correct" can ruin a poet. It stems from what Heidegger calls in *Being and Time* "the they-self, which we distinguish from the *authentic* Self" (167). As opposed to the will to conform, a poet's *listening*, so critical to both Heidegger and Olson, makes way for the authentic poem as evidenced by its "originality," not only in the sense of independence from the norm, but also in the sense of dwelling close to one's origins, of participating in the birth of thought, bringing new being into being. Out of this intimacy, the relationships between polarities—world and thing, self and nature, Being and beings, subject and object—suggest and undermine the binaries that make their meaning possible. With meaning, comes the summons to mean.

The Role of Beauty in Authenticity

One sharp contrast between Heidegger and Olson concerns Heidegger's reverential invocation of the concept of beauty, which occasions the true. While the word "beauty" might conjure traditional concepts of aesthetic form, with virtues such as balance, harmony, and closure, Olson prefers to focus on talk of poetic form, traditionally conceived as an aesthetic issue but defended here in epistemological and ethical terms. The page as a field becomes legitimized as a facilitator of veracity and humility rather than anything he frames as beauty. The omission likewise suggests that the discrediting of the lyric does not wish to engage the issue of the lyric's beauty or lack thereof, but rather its problematic epistemological and ethical status.

In omitting the concept of beauty, Olson likewise does not venture into discussion of the uneasy relationship between the beautiful and the true. The intimacy that Heidegger registers between beauty and truth has more to do with beauty's immanence than its possibility as a mediator of reality. It "unconceals" or "occasions" truth rather than conveys it. Thus the issue of possible euphemism does appear problematic. It may be hard to see where the example of music, including a poem's music, occasions truth. Music, of which the lyric is one example, exerts a nearness due to its intensity of presence and affect. Thus it may indeed feel primary, close to the fountainhead of the real. Nevertheless as the least referential art form, it seems to be the one least invested in truth, the most "about" its own form, its beauty. If music can be said to "be true," it is as an embodiment of the real rather than a sign of it. It is evidentiary as a participation in the real in the way projective verse aspires, in part, to be.

This point is key to understanding how poetic form, as an element of music, likewise resists our attempts to reduce it to true or false meanings. It does not quite enter into the epistemological or ethical conversation that Olson has struck up with regard to lyric form. On the other hand, it asserts some of the quality of immanence that we might rightly associate with Olson's approach. While we may differentiate pitches and sonorities within the phenomenological field of music, what we refer to as "the music" of that field asserts itself strongly *as* a field. So music, like Being itself, constitutes a monad, one character of which is the experience of difference. For this reason music occupies a special status for those, like Schopenhauer, who see music less as mimetic of anything than as an embodiment of the will. However referential music becomes by way of personal or cultural memory, aural mimesis, and synesthesia, it continues to assert its non-referential character as well, such that the postmodern view of sign systems as mediating all experience appears to be indicative less of how we actually are, in our vast complexity, than of how a certain language-centric personality perceives herself to be.

The Problem of Form and Content in Modeling Authenticity

In a larger sense, the notion that all our experience is mediated through language cannot account for the complexity of our experience of form and content. The postmodern, as defined by Perloff, might well refuse to recognize the depth model of form/content where form constitutes its difference as interior to form. However, a refusal to recognize such a model is no solution to the perennial conundrum of how content, given the pervasiveness and breadth of our experience, must be encountered as both different from and yet radically continent upon form. Creeley's claim, quoted by Olson, strives to be more nuanced in the simultaneous negotiation of continuity and difference. "FORM," he states, "IS NEVER MORE THAN AN EXTENSION OF CONTENT" (614). While a marriage of meaning and medium informs poetic theory since Aristotle, with Coleridge and Whitman raising the stakes, Creeley's language would make this marriage stronger still. The elusive word in his statement remains "extension," which, in metaphorical fashion, invokes the language of ontology, in which foundational reality is extensive with its articulations. Moreover binaries may be co-extensive. Such language is itself poetic, since it would assert two contradictory elements (the two as two and the two as one), relying upon the ghost of an image to bring dissonance into harmony, to spatialize that which extends. In so doing, the directionality of "extension" in Creeley's figure both calls into question and reasserts a strongly intuitive metaphysics, a sense of content as origin (something we can never confirm), form as that which makes it manifest.

The problem with lyric form remains, in Olson's terms, "interference," which might well suggest an "unnatural" opacity relative to the phenomenological field. Thus buried in Olson's assumptions lies a primitivism that seeks, instead of revisionary refinement, the veracity of the rough, raw, and, most importantly, original. The fact that primacy becomes impossible to achieve via the mediation of language is neither asserted nor denied by Olson, but the recognition of such failure need not make the pursuit of origins any less urgent. In fact Olson's fervor recalls a Calvinist, proselytizing discourse, in which he advocates a leap of faith into the page's open field. Some of Olson's manic energy may well register a recognition that this is a leap without arrival, thus requiring the insistence of a Jeremiad, part-screed, part-call for a new level of commitment to the as yet unseen. What remains unexplored in Olson's writings is the negative capability, and likewise faith, associated with lyric process as well.

While the lyric suggests self-consciousness and control, the question remains, whose control? Is not the form asserting its otherness, even as the writing subject asserts her subjectivity? Is not the writer of lyrics giving some power away? Moreover, what keeps a lack of self-consciousness from degenerating into self-indulgence? Is attention truly enough to sustain a poem without some principle of selection to spare the reader various genuine and spontaneous banalities? Lyric form as both opportunity and obstacle might indeed ease the grip of the ego. It might ask a writer to "let go" in the way that the patient must let go. The problem with lyric form appears to be less "the ego" than exclusion, hesitancy, and closure. While all form requires both repetition and variety to be form, the accent for Olson is on keeping pace with consciousness and thus moving ever toward the next needful thing. Degree matters. Nevertheless, what Olson's attack on closed form does not take into consideration is the fact that musical recursivity, less as compositional method than performance practice, has traditionally been a vehicle to break down the ego, as evidenced by the trans-cultural, trans-historical phenomenon of spiritual incantation.

If what we object to is the cleverness required to achieve form as a conspicuous display of the ego, it appears that the objection is more appropriately targeted at "decadence," as defined by Yvor Winters. Decadence might be one way of describing failed form, recursive or not, wherein the attention to the vehicle upstages all other concerns. The breed of poetic fracture that opens the field of signification so widely that it approaches meaninglessness might likewise be decadent. A total lack of conceptual commitment leaves us with mere form, what the language-poet Charles Bernstein praises in his book *A Poetics* as "the poetry of non-absorption," defended in Marxist terms as restoring us to the material basis of language. Such a conceptually enervated language finds its unlikely kin in that of some tiresome sestina that turtles along all too slowly at the level of insight and evocation, so we are left with the rather glaring "look-at-me" effect of the chorusing end-words. In either case, form upstages meaning, whereas lyric resonance, understood as a simultaneity of meaningful possibility, renders an abundance.

It is understandable that many fine poets have lost faith in formal writing in part because, according to their own process, formalism represented some patriarchy that was there to test them. To attempt a villanelle was to set out to prove something. Such is the dynamic that Donald Revell describes in his highly figurative and lyric essay entitled "The Moving Sidewalk," wherein he describes himself in his early attraction to form as "disguising envy as admiration" (179). Clearly he has the gift to write formally. The formal lyrics of his first two books, poems such as "Belfast" and "A Setting," remarkable not only for their music but also the abundance of resonance in their fierce figurations, testify both to his facility and to the capacity for formal writing to be meaningfully adventurous, wild within its measures. As an essay calling into question the motives that characteristically lead to formalism, "The Moving Sidewalk" likewise includes many moving admissions:

> When I first read the poems of Auden and Bogan, I understood their eloquence to be the gestures of a perfect complacency, their forms to be the ceremonies of unafflicted invention. I envied their facility too much to recognize (or to emulate) the courage of their minds or the deep colors of their humility. (179)

To write in forms was, for Revell, "to write the outside," to move away from "legitimacy" into "an outsider's empowerment" (177). For him formal writing represented power and escape. No doubt it does for many. Whether it does or should for all is another matter. The fact that traditional form is derivative may signify less if we see all acts of legitimacy and originality as conversations between the given and the made. We are made of the dead, as is language, and so take them to new neighborhoods

We might also view "the deep colors of [Bogan's and Auden's] humility" as indicative of the same sensibility that engenders and honors form. Formal writing foregrounds for a writer the collaborative dimension that describes all acts of language. We collaborate first and foremost with a medium, which is constructed, destabilized, made meaningful in part by the elusive process of its history. Beyond this, aesthetic affection is not quite the same as admiration, let alone envy. What Revell envied when young was *the poet* not the poem. The formal poem, as poet's surrogate, naturally aroused a focus on authorial persona. Any musical performer will tell you that there is a critical difference on stage between thinking about personae, yours or someone else's, and being in the music. Lyric form *is* music. While most music is measured, that need not suggest the superiority of metered poetry, for some metered poetry, as Pound pointed out, sounds unmusical by virtue of its regularity. Music in measures wears one of the many faces of beauty. We can hang any number of other faces on it, and still the music goes on, beneath our conversations, asserting both its immanence and its independence.

The assumption that lyric form leads causally and by necessity to lyric content, or vice versa, is true only insofar as a subcategory of the subject matter is the form. It would be narrow to suggest that this subject matter is "the" subject matter. The blurriness of conflating the senses of "lyric" as both a form and a content has led to decades of blurry thinking on the subject, and moreover a somewhat insistent reductio-ad-absurdum when it comes to the consideration of the lyric impulse. Revision, as an imaginative deepening, need not eclipse or preclude the spontaneous unfolding of being. One can in fact revise toward wildness. One can, in the spirit of Blake's and Eliot's re-association of the sensibility, imagine and be critical at the same time. The reductio-ad-absurdum that sees the lyric as an expression of untenable selfhood is hardly worthy of a theory-savvy culture, which you would imagine might see all language, and certainly imaginative language, as dependent upon an ever-expanding and temporal context, an ocean of contingencies that are, inextricably, both private and public in nature. Clearly no one can write from a position of "pure self," and the assumption that one can simply does not appear in defenses of the lyric impulse.

Mindfulness as the Argument For and Against the Lyric

The confusion that lyric form implies lyric selfhood stems not only from examples of past practice, but also from a sense that lyric form encourages hesitation, whereas a projectivist's speed as the means of outracing self-consciousness takes as its goal an unburdening of pretense. Olson's declaration that "one perception must must must MOVE, INSTANTER, ON ANOTHER!" looks forward to a beat aesthetic of fast, energetic, spontaneous candor as a form of resistance to a stilted mainstream of 1950's America, and as such it paves the way for Chogyam Trungpa's later assertion so often quoted by Ginsberg, "First thought, best thought." "Best" of course implies a hierarchy of values (as does Ginsberg's variorum edition of "Howl"), but the pursuit of such values is intriguingly problematic and paradoxical in ways reminiscent of a Buddhist path. To judge a thing that is not yet seen is to never see it, but the climate of value judgments that compromises vision also summons us to the discipline of seeing. The goal of meditation, like the goal of projective practice, is to achieve a certain transparency and readiness of vision, a mindful luminosity.

"Inclusiveness" is one of those terms, much like "subjectivity," that declares itself as conspicuously "under erasure," since it so obviously fails to characterize the effect or practice of a poem, or any other discourse, let alone any community or sensibility. That said, the formal demand of a lyric does provide more compositional resistance, and so the weight of judgment feels heavier, the force of exclusion more severe. While hesitation remains greatest for those out of practice or without that particular gift, one can improve and so internalize the summons of a more recursive music, while facilitating the lithe and vibrant movement of rhetoric, inflection, argument, and imaginative fire. In recent times, much of what we call "formal poetry" has, by virtue of the neo-formalist and neo-narrative movements, narrowed some of its cultural associations and become identified for many with values coded as conservative, such as story, accessibility, and realism, though there is no reason this need be the case, and in fact has not always been. Coincidence is not causality. Nor is practice principle.

Ironically, recent formal movements, as articulated by Dana Gioia and Robert MacDowell, imagine their approach as more inclusive, less self-involved, than a poetics that deploys strategies to destabilize meaning and thus create interpretive challenge, opportunity, or exasperation, depending on your point of view. Aesthetic populism, such as the one articulated by Gioia in *Can Poetry Matter*, often presumes that one should, let alone could, write a poetry that lots of people like, as if a poem's value were determined democratically with the goal that poetry might shed the elitist reputation and practices that make it a pleasure of the few. The question remains whether this, or *any* aesthetic polemic for that matter, is not another form of self-aggrandizement and exclusion.

Projective verse advocates an inclusiveness, not in terms of its position relative to the general taste, but in terms of its power to model and embody the process of being. The projective poem's process concerns itself less with failing the tastes of a majority than with failing the demands of a medium, in which the tension and intimacy between the individual and the cultural make meaning possible. Not that projective speed suggests that "anything goes." On the contrary, it requires, for Olson, alert care, however difficult it might be for a reader to discern faithful allegiance to the compositional moment in any given projective poem. While projective leaps and gestures may appear to the baffled less careful than carefree, a writer's over-concern with accessibility relative to an imaginary reader might well constitute a mode of interference, the inauthentic activity of a "they-self" that takes a poet outside the authority of spontaneous process, to seek what Revell calls "an outsider's empowerment."

In a 2009 interview with the Society for Critical Exchange, Perloff, in addition to defending the essentials of sound structure in poetry, reveals some of the curious logic with which the category of authenticity comes under scrutiny and constitutes for many a form of nostalgia empowered by a certain establishment. In addressing the implied assumptions that make for a friendly reception to Elizabeth Alexander's poem for Obama's inauguration, she states,

> It's really completely out of step, because now that you have everything digitized, everything is already mediated, this kind of flatness doesn't go with that at all, so you theoretically could "do talk" about Elizabeth Alexander's poem and show that, in a way, it's living in a world that doesn't exist. If I wanted to have this authentic statement about how people feel and how people are doing, there are no authentic statements like that today. I mean everything is always mediated, always recycled, always used. You can move it around on the screen.

> All photographs are treated photographs that we see. So what does it mean to try to have this authentic voice? ("Marjorie Perloff 3," *Youtube.*)

In the above comments, Perloff reverses the logic of her previous arguments, where she suggests that, in a contemporary image-inundated culture, poetry would be wise to resist, to contribute something new—that is, poetry should move from less dependence on the image and more on the discursive gesture. The above case concerning authenticity, on the other hand, maintains that cultural practice, where signs are more inauthentic than ever, diminishes the attempt to be authentic as "out of step." The spirit of rebellion vanishes. The negative valence of the phrase "out of step" suggests that perhaps the usefulness of the concept "authenticity" and certainly the poetic practice that values it are and should be relativized by cultural practice and intellectual fashion.

Resistance to implicit messages of popular culture might feel especially ill fated given how deeply entrenched the context is that shares her skepticism regarding the viability of the authentic as a possibility or virtue. However, while the concept of authenticity has become, for some, too blurry to be useful, it is difficult to imagine a credible epistemology without it, as either implicit or explicit, by way of some investigation of the reliability of representations that make knowledge possible. The gospel of seeing the limits of our language as the limits of our world has led to the error that all we know of the world comes to us via semiotic play. Given interpretive play, both endemic and cultivated within language, such a gospel, once inflected by a faith in the infinite nature (as opposed to possibility) of that play, leads to the untenable position of radical relativism. In such a "systemless" system, we find no gradations of truth. Rather we discover an ironically either/or position with regard to truth, either absolute or none at all. Radical relativism is hardly unstable. It is the mirror image of a rage for stability. It requires a good deal more negative capability to live in a world, and likewise understand it, where there are degrees of truth-value, where the real is a pressure that exerts itself in partial eclipse or partial distortion. When Perloff suggests that postmodernism "does not recognize" depth models that differentiate the authentic from the inauthentic and so give significance to the terms, she invokes stark diametrical oppositions that, as they leave us, take with them the gradations that would come closer than the extremities of conceptual binaries to describing the real. Nuance and degree are not accommodated via binary differentiation, or not yet, nor is a complexity of affect. Binaries do not describe or explain the phenomenon of the continuum, which may inform the impulse toward language without being adequately represented by it. The language-centric point of view makes the error of viewing the real as the creation of (or subject to the laws of) language rather than, in part, the other way around.

Wallace Stevens understood the importance of nuance in matters of truth when he came up with the phrase "the pressure of the real." His work is saturated with allusions to "the real" in spite (and in light) of the fact that the imagination cannot fully accommodate it. Still, as he argues in "Noble Rider and the Sound of Words," the imagination loses vitality as it loses touch with that pressure. Open a relatively reliable newspaper in a time of war, and there it is: "the pressure of the real." It is no coincidence that a postmodern indulgence in a sense of unreality took off in America during decades of relative peace, just after Vietnam had exhausted a generation and the culture glided toward disco and Derrida. The holocaust happened. To demonstrate the inauthenticity of that statement, by virtue of its mediation as language, is self-evidently frivolous. To suggest the ethical superiority of ambiguity in this context is offensive. True, that statement is not poetry but rather mere reportage. Nevertheless it might well inform an essential element within a poem, the real toad in our imaginary garden.

The Ego of Polemic and the Reclamation of the Lyric

More clear than Olson's rationale for condemning the lyric is something less specific to the realm of aesthetics: "the interference" that compromises our "stance toward reality" derives from modes of inauthenticity due to the ego's tendency to distort the real in defense of its own interest. While the "authentic" person is presumed to be sincere, "authenticity" is a larger category than "sincerity," in that it may refer to artifacts and need not imply personhood. The "authentic" artifact may be authentic due to a causal relation to the real rather than merely a constructed, semiotic one. In addition sincerity, unlike authenticity, points specifically to a reliable speaker, as if that author were the speaker. A dramatic monologue for instance might be authentic, but not "sincere." In the hands of a bad poet, sincerity could easily engender the kind of declarative and dominating literalism and interpretive closure that make a poem dull. In terms of poetry's essential interpenetration of self and other, such "poems" are not "poems." Nevertheless the impoverishment of sincerity altogether in a body of work might contribute to a radical irony in which all that is said is half-meant, and interpretive point of view goes slack or vanishes, taking with it the risk of commitment, the possibility of vision. The poem becomes a drone of evasions, each one emblematic of the same conceptual meta-gesture, the same spirit of evasion. For this reason theory about radical fracture and de-centering tends to be more dynamic, less conceptually diffuse and static, than practice. An avant-garde writer's love affair with philosophy may well attempt to compensate for the impoverished philosophical movement in the work itself.

The ego is a resourceful creature. It makes use of any aesthetic, any ideology, out there. Its opposite, or rather its partner in the ongoing conversation of consciousness, is not an idea, not a form, not an aesthetic, certainly not a spiritual or ethical philosophy, but a process of generosity and attention. To borrow Olson's metaphor, we enter a field of highly complex and shifting relationships when we write. We bring a sense of the individual to the world, the world to the individual. The stubborn and problematic dualism of self and world finds its correlative in the dualisms of content and form, mind and body. To say one is coextensive of the other is to assert both their inextricable relatedness and the recalcitrant difference that characterizes one way we experience them. In terms of offering a phenomenological model of who we are, let alone what a poem is or should be, monism appears as insufficient as dualism. Both models break down under pressure.

Nothing is more fundamental to the problem of epistemology than the impossible logical reconciliations of "the two" and "the one," dualism and monism, articulation and continuity. The "light" of being appears to be both a particle and a wave. Nothing is more fundamental to poetry than the notion that the imagination goes where logic cannot. What is the sound of one hand clapping? It is all sound, certainly music, all phenomena that assert themselves both within and outside the play of differentiation, which is only one dimension, the semiotic dimension, of language. The image of the singular, clapping hand, like Creeley's image of content extending into form, speaks to our longing to see the one in the two, the two in the one, to hold them together in imaginative space. As Maximus says, in Olson's poem "Maximus, to himself," we "learn the simplest things/ last. Which made for difficulties. . . . we grow up many/ And the single/ is not easily/ known." One reading of this passage suggests the individual fails to know herself; another reading suggests the individual fails to see herself as coextensive with the field of Being. Either way, the individual fails to be authentic.

While the projective poem would bring us into closer proximity with Being and the nature of our relation to it, we might say the same of music, including a lyric's breed of it, with its primacy, its form, its heartbreak, its grace, all that is far too embedded in our nervous system to be dismissed as mere escape. Escape from what remains a critical question. Many live their lives "fleeing the moment," which is to say, the vicissitudes of the near at hand, what the speaker's breath and the lyric's music summon us to encounter. Musical form, by nature recursive, brings to the play of differentiation the experience of something nearer still. In turn it makes problematic the argument that all our experience is mediated by language, or *is* a language, an infinite regress of mediations. Within a cultural competition for attention that engenders an oppositional stalemate if not dialectic, each side laying claim to an anticipation of what is to come, to see the future lyric as illegitimate, to discourage it as a genre defined by scale, intensity, and recursive musicality, is to impoverish our experience of the word. The lyric is no more exhausted in the poetic conversation than tonality is in the musical one, and what the examples of Palestrina and Bach teach us is that meaningfully innovative genius may appear antiquated to one's own time. Certainly the ambition to be ahead of one's time leads daily to a certain interference of the ego. Poetry resonates in so far as it dwells deeply *in* one's own time, including its historicity, its momentum, its complexity, wild with a diversity of legitimate paths to the attentive, the aesthetic, the ethical gesture. Generous focus, relatively undistracted by an ego's sense of correctness, is what both the projective poem and the lyric would authenticate, as does music in general—an attention, a physicality, a formal pressure that must move, must die, to live, carried forward, breath by breath.

Works Cited

Bernstein, Charles. *A Poetics.* Cambridge, MA: Harvard University Press, 1992.

Gioia, Dana. *Can Poetry Matter?* Saint Paul, MN: Graywolf, 1992.

Heidegger, Martin. *Being and Time.* John Macquarrie and Edward Robinson, trans. New York: Harper and Row, 1962.

Heidegger, Martin. *Poetry, Language, Thought.* Albert Hofstadter, trans. NY: Harper Collins, 1971.

Olson, Charles. "Maximus, to Himself." In *Postmodern American Poetry.* Paul Hoover, ed. 14–15. NY: Norton, 1994.

Olson, Charles. "Projective Verse." In *Postmodern American Poetry.* Paul Hoover, ed., 613–621. New York: Norton, 1994:

Perloff, Marjorie. "Language Poetry and the Lyric Subject." *Albany, Critical Inquiry* 23 (1999): 405–434.

Perloff, Marjorie. "Marjorie Perloff 3." *Youtube.* 2009. Interview with the Society for Critical Exchange. January 30, 2009. <http://www.youtube.com/watch?v=d37kHq1TQrk>

Revell, Donald. "The Moving Sidewalk." *Invisible Green.* Richmond, California: Omnidawn, 2005.

Stevens, Wallace. "The Noble Rider and the Sound of Words." *The Necessary Angel.* NY: Vintage Books, 1965.

Metaphysics of the Image in Charles Wright's "Homage to Paul Cézanne"

All my poems seem to be an ongoing argument with myself about the unlikelihood of salvation.
—Charles Wright

In search of the absolute, Charles Wright finds himself in a world of things, "the world of ten thousand things," as the title of his recent poetry collection would have it. In spite of their longing for transcendence, Charles Wright's poems remain forcefully visual, as if the image were both bridge and barrier to the unseen, the most immediate objects assuming a metaphysical inscrutability and allure. To quote Wright's notebook, "If you look at it long enough, you won't recognize it" (H, 30). Little wonder that Cézanne, with his ongoing struggle both to penetrate and submit to the world of appearances, would suggest a model for Wright's own conflicted sensibility. At the age of 67, Cézanne saw his art as ever unsatisfactory, the forms of nature still hopelessly out of reach. "Will I ever arrive at the goal, so intensely sought and so long pursued?" he asked. "I am still learning from nature, and it seems to me I am making slow progress" (Merleau-Ponty 9). His late paintings in particular, those watercolors of increasing gaps and disintegrations born paradoxically out of an impulse toward precision, inform Wright's deeply haunting "Homage to Paul Cézanne," in which all things take on a quality of depth and disquiet.

Both Cézanne and Wright, in their desire for direct access to natural forms, profess an elusive primitivism. "Primary force alone," writes Cézanne, "*id est* temperament, can bring a person to the end he must attain." The word "must" here leaves open the question of attainability, as does Wright's claim, "All great art tends toward the condition of the primitive" (H, 26). Just what constitutes "the primitive" remains vague, most often defined by what it is not, those mediating traces of culture, which, even if they could disappear, would take with them our very language, let alone any so-called primitive art. Unlike the transcendent, the primitive is by definition a starting point rather than a point beyond. It comes first, either temporally or in the figurative sense as ground and condition—the way that sensation serves as a condition of consciousness. Unlike the transcendent, the primitive connotes an anchoring in concrete existence. But Wright's phrase, "tends toward the condition of the primitive," places primary conditions at an ever energizing, prospective distance. Since the primitive can never be clearly defined, we can never be too certain about the character of our aesthetic progress towards it. Even the efficacy of our spontaneity, like prayer, remains open to question.

Throughout Wright's "Homage to Paul Cézanne," the dead, as emissaries of the unseen, emerge incarnate in an archetypal, "primitive" world, unnervingly tangible, if only to make us increasingly aware of their unbridgeable distance. They inhabit our most intimate objects—shirts, shoes, our very beds—cling like dirt to our hands, coming as close as possible without quite dissolving their identity and ours:

> At night, in the fish-light of the moon, the dead wear our
>   white shirts
> To stay warm, and litter the fields.
> We pick them up in the mornings, dewy pieces of paper and
>   scraps of cloth.
> Like us, they refract themselves. Like us,
> They keep on saying the same thing, trying to get it right.
> Like us, the water unsettles their names.
> Sometimes they lie like leaves in their little arks, and curl up
>   at the edges.
> Sometimes they come inside, wearing our shoes, and walk
> From mirror to mirror.
> Or lie in our beds with the gloves off

And touch our bodies. Or talk
In a corner. Or wait like envelopes on a desk.
(*TWOTTT,* 3, 1–11)

Wright's quiet directness, his declarative informality, as familiar as it is familiarizing, turns the poem itself into an intimate and inhabitable object for the dead. In spite of the implied auditor, the poem has the sparse, musing quality of interior speech. All the unmistakable strategies of heightening metaphysical tension—an elemental restlessness, the near ecstatic dissolution of identity, the transformative immersion into water—work by way of contrast with the ordinary thing and word: "shirts," "paper," "scraps of cloth."

These ordinary things, extraordinary in their suggestiveness, oneiric in their metamorphoses, quick to reflect an otherworldly light, provide Wright's landscape with white space, both literal and figurative, concrete and cryptic, and so resemble the patches of bare canvas so intriguing to Wright in Cézanne's later work:

> I like layers of paint on the canvas. I also know after I'm tired of lots of layers on the canvas, I'm going to want just one layer of paint and some of the canvas showing through . . . I've been trying to write poems . . . the way a painter might paint a picture . . . using stanzas in the way a painter will build up blocks of color, each disparate and often discrete, to make an overall representation that, taken in its pieces and slashes and dabs seems to have no coherence, but seen in its totality, when it's finished, turns out to be a very recognizable landscape, or whatever. Cézanne is someone who does this, in his later work, to an almost magical perfection.
> (H, 66, 85)

What we see in the occasional white space is the implication of a larger story, *the* larger story as Wright would have it. The understated canvas stands like a Platonic shadow this side of its source and subject, or like a sacrament, the body of what we cannot see. In Wright's thinking, blank spaces serve not merely as barriers to a fuller knowledge but also as windows of access into the invisible:

> ". . . he regarded the colors as numinous essences, beyond which he 'knew' nothing, and the 'diamond zones of God' remained white . . ." (Cézanne). Change "colors" to "words" and "white" to "blank" and you have something I believe . . .
> (H, 37)

As "the diamond zones of God," empty spaces encourage our interpretive approach, charge their subject with desire, and so invite all the pleasures of doubt and speculation. In so doing, they vitalize their subject, or, more precisely, they "keep it alive," maintaining the dimension of possibility by respecting a distance. "Art tends toward the certainty of making connections," Wright states; "The artist's job is to keep it apart, thus giving it tension and keeping it alive, letting the synapse spark" (H, 22).

The quality of vitality and remoteness in Cézanne's work stems not only from his blank spaces, but also from a prioritizing of color over outline to imply shape and movement. The foregrounding of chromatic relationships accounts for a simultaneous myopic distortion and sensuous intimacy. Blues recede; yellows come forward; complementary colors vibrate—all by way of how colors touch. Wright's literal near-sightedness provides him with a similar sense of distance and heightened color sensitivity:

> Their leaves lie in limes and tans
> Flocking the grass, vaguely pre-Cubist to me,
> And blurred, without my glasses, arranged
> In an almost-pattern of colors across the yard,
> The same colors Cézanne once used in the same way
> . . . .
> Still the colors and pure arrangements
> Oozing out of the earth, dropping out of the sky
> in memory of him each year.
> ("A Journal of English Days," *TWOTTT,* 127)

As if in a Platonic model of being, Wright's myopia makes the world of appearance seem incomplete, a teasing intimation of the real. But such distance becomes an end in itself, transmuted from failure into wonder. Light takes on a luxurious, animate quality, "oozing out of the earth," persuading in terms of mere sensation. "Often 'light' becomes literary in poems," Wright states. "I like to think I think of light as light. When you are nearsighted as I am . . . light is where it's at, as they used to say" (H, 146).

To give words a similar concrete insistence, to layer them in "discrete blocks of color" as Wright claims he does, he needs a unit of color, some correlative to the brush stroke itself. According to Wright, these units are aural, created at the level of word, line, and stanza in harmonized patterns of balance and contrast. Although there is a lot of cacophonous and spondaic grit in Wright's music that argues for the word as discrete unit, the poem "Homage" is most conspicuous and convincing in asserting the line as its brush stroke, something big enough to contain in itself an imagistic as well as a musical force:

> They reach up from the ice plant.
> They shuttle their messengers through the oat grass.
> Their answers rise like rust on the stalks and the spidery
> leaves.
>
> We rub them off our hands.
> (13–16)

Wright's lines characteristically favor a monosyllabic percussiveness and emphatic finish, contributing to a heightened physicality. As each line here cadences on a crisp image, the overall pattern moves around the color wheel from greens to yellows to the rising oranges, from recessed cool shades outward toward the intimacies of our hands. Like the colors they wear, the dead "reach up" line by line, intent on perceptual resurrection.

The appeal of the transcendent in Wright's work lies largely in its power to disturb, to raise questions, invigorate an otherwise too certain world. Any imaginary reclaiming of the dead by way of sacramental union thus remains ephemeral. Unappeasable as the grief they inspire, they appear neither wholly dead nor alive but in a state of perpetual rising into our lives:

> Each year the dead grow less dead, and nudge
> Close to the surface of all things.

They start to remember the silence that brought them there.
They start to recount the gain in their soiled hands.
(17–20)

The dead, like us, "refract themselves," fragmenting into a picture of uncertainty and longing. They too are haunted by mere intimations and a prospective memory always just starting out toward the horizon of the past. They too approach "the surface of things" with anxiety and wonder, imagining the other side.

Through the dead's eyes, we are the transcendent. The project of the poem—or of all Wright's poems for that matter—is to see ourselves this way as well, made expansive and unfamiliar in the world mirror:

High in the night sky the mirror is hauled up and
unsheeted.
In it we twist like stars.
(112–113)

Wright's poetry typically blurs and merges irreconcilable points of view, or plays them off one another like complementary colors. It testifies to his negative capability: how poem after poem, the dead see as the living, the living as the dead, the skeptic sees as the metaphysician, and so on—all in an effort to enlarge our range of feeling, to contain and be vitalized by contradiction.

Given his skepticism, Wright's nostalgia for an older metaphysics often expresses itself through acts of ventriloquism, by speaking through the sensibility of the dead, including such visionaries as Dante, Plato, and Cézanne. "Whose unction can intercede for the dead?" Wright's speaker asks in the final section of his "Homage." "Whose tongue is toothless enough to speak their piece?" (123–124). Clearly no one's, in spite of the fact that Wright has attempted just that and, if only momentarily, enjoyed the illusion of having succeeded:

And thus we become what we've longed for,
past tense and otherwise,
A BB, a disc of light,

song without words.
And refer to ourselves
In the third person, seeing that other arm
Still raised from the bed, fingers like licks and flames in the
boned air.

Only to hear it's not time.
(88–94)

The desire to pay homage to the dead, to speak their at best fragmentary piece, implies a longing not only to enlarge the self but also to redeem time, to become, by way of a multiplication of egos, "past tense and otherwise."

Though Wright's poem is deeply persuasive in creating a model of the object and character of Cézanne's obsessions, it likewise calls into question the final success of any such effort. Wright's instruments for redeeming time are the images of a riddling world in flux. In resisting the explicitly narrative conventions of the homage, Wright's "Homage to Paul Cézanne" focuses instead on what inspires and frustrates the narrative impulse. "*Remember me*," the dead chant, "*speak my name*." And yet the only proper name here appears in the poem's title. The absence of identifiable people in the body of the poem not only encourages objects to bear the full burden of aesthetic affect, but also accentuates a simultaneous privacy and archetypal breadth, the sense of an introspective look into collective being, full of blank spaces, partial stories.

Though historical narrative appeals to the dead as a means of resurrection, Wright's poem turns on the irony that to bear up the dead is to bear up an absence. As the dead "take in" the meanings of favorite words, language appears as one more puzzling and intimate object:

They point to their favorite words
Growing around them, revealed as themselves for the first
time:
They stand close to the meanings and take them in.
(24–27)

To say the dead are "revealed *as themselves*" is to imply the revelation of both their presence and their nature, which is to say their absence. Like the dead, language becomes something half-there, its meanings withdrawn into an otherworld of deferral and loss. The force of desire that drives words drives the ocean as it "explains itself, backing and filling/ What spaces it can't avoid" (1.37–38). While, as Helen Vendler argues, the conservation of matter in Wright's work may offer its small consolations for a failure of faith, it is likewise the mirror of such failings, consigned to redundancy—the waves, like the dead, "saying the same thing, trying to get it right." In a world where language never gets to the bottom of anything, what we know of eternity is an eternal desire to know.

The mystique of the inexplicable allows for Wright's characteristic transmutation of despondency into wonder. In light of his frequent praise for inaccessibility and near-completeness in art, an aesthetic failure to fill the spaces of nature appears not merely inevitable but also desirable, encouraging the assertions of a reconstructive imagination. But this desire is met in Wright and Cézanne by a contrary one, intent on an unlikely mimesis. Both artists see themselves as simultaneously resisting and aspiring toward something larger than the individual imagination. "All great art is Neoplatonic," Wright claims, "you're always trying to make something that's the best replica of what it really is" (H, 35). For Cézanne, the mere fact that nature so often figures as the commanding starting point in his discussions of the aesthetic process complicates any notion of his work as freely subordinating natural form to individual expression:

> One cannot be too scrupulous, too sincere, too submissive to nature, but one is more or less master of one's model, and above all one's means. Penetrate that which is before you, and persevere to express it as logically as possible.
> (Bernard 43)

Though there is a Platonic ring to Cézanne's metaphor of penetrating "that which is before" us, his emphasis on perceptual exactitude works against any metaphysical devaluation of appearances. It is as though the world of appearance itself, as ever elusive and humbling, took on a metaphysical dimension of depth.

In Wright's tribute, the omnipresent dead provide this dimension, charging natural forms with not only all the pathos attendant on human loss, but also the power of our need to participate more fully in being. In response to the question of who can intercede for the dead, Wright's speaker states:

> What we are given in dreams we write as blue paint,
> Or messages to the clouds.
> At evening we wait for the rain to fall and the sky to clear.
> Our words are words for the clay, uttered in undertones,
> Our gestures salve for the wind.
> (125–129)

Cézanne's parallel urge toward participation is key, for it sheds a possible light on the paradox of his later work, that paradox being, as Wright describes it, Cézanne's simultaneous disintegration of and attachment to natural form:

> The move toward a disintegration of the object in some of the most memorable works of a painter so passionately attached to objects is the attraction and riddle of Cézanne's last phase.
> (H, 21)

One perspective on the riddle is to see the disintegration of the object, those refractions and gaps that beg our interpretive approach, as Cézanne's very expression for his attachment to it—or more precisely, for his ongoing desire to access it fully. As Merleau-Ponty claims,

> [Cézanne] did not want to separate the stable things which we see and the shifting way in which they appear; he wanted to depict matter as it takes on form, the birth of order through spontaneous organization.
> ("Cézanne's Doubt," 13)

According to Merleau-Ponty, Cézanne's objects are charged by the artist's longing to become involved ever more actively and intimately in the "primary force" of their existent being, their spontaneous coming into form.

Given his phenomenological orientation, Merleau-Ponty does not qualify the birth of order as the birth of perceptual order, since he will not go on to make claims as to a distinguishing form of order preceding perception. In a phenomenological model, attempting as it does to "bracket" phenomena off from transcendent conditions, the otherness of imagined objects stems from their intentional status—that is, the fact that they appear as the contents of consciousness without being identical to consciousness itself. When we say we are conscious *of* something, the barrier and bridge of the "of," which is to say intentionality of consciousness, implies a distancing. According to Merleau-Ponty, sensation, as an absolute, an irreducible, primary condition of thought, precedes and resists the intentionality of consciousness. Cézanne's professed desire to realize sensation as art thus becomes for Merleau-Ponty a project of getting out of the way, of letting be, releasing meaning from objects rather than distancing them with the stylizations of imposed affect:

> The meaning Cézanne gave to objects and faces in his painting presented itself to him in the world as it appeared to him. Cézanne simply released this meaning.
> (CD, 21)

Through Merleau-Ponty's lens, Cézanne's representational liberties attempt not to abstract the physical but to resist abstraction, to wear thin the membrane between consciousness and its intentional object and so allow things to relinquish their delicate ontological light.

But Merleau-Ponty's statement is complicated by his mixed-metaphors of meaning as both "presented to" and "given by" the artist. The immediacy of sensation appears not merely "realized," as Cézanne had hoped, but consciously endowed. Wright's "Homage" is far more explicit in asserting the role of artists as masters of their means:

> The dead are a cadmium blue.
> We spread them with palette knives in broad blocks and
> planes.

We layer them stroke by stroke
In steps and ascending mass, in verticals raised from the
earth.

We choose and layer them in,
Blue and a blue and a breath.
(49–53)

Here the artist's powers of creative volition rival God's, raising the dead, supplying breath. Aesthetic form likewise rivals natural form, each giving shape to the ubiquitous dead. The mutual penetration of artist and nature blurs any clear distinction between the aesthetic and the natural. "Aren't nature and art different?" Emile Bernard once asked, to which Cézanne replied, "I want to make them the same" (Merleau-Ponty, 13). Of course art and nature, however similar, cannot be the same, anymore than the speaker in "Homage" can intercede unequivocally for the dead. Even to see the natural as seamlessly continuous with human nature is to tame the inscrutable power and demand of nature's otherness. In short, Cézanne's and Wright's sensibilities thrive on the prospect of ever-deferred unions.

The fact that natural form emerges as a new horizon of inaccessibility and command, as unrealizable and animating in consciousness as any divine ideal, testifies to the tenacity of metaphysical desire, its yearning to break the silence of things, to slip through the ontological white space. Even Merleau-Ponty's metaphor of meaning as "released from" objects invokes a stubbornly metaphysical model of secret and conditioning interiors. The notion of such interiors eroticizes being, encourages our intimacy, leads us on. Any aesthetic that professes a revolutionary commitment to mere immanence or surface, as sufficient to itself, free from the shadow of the ideal, faces a problem—that is, sufficiency breeds complacency. To adapt a claim from Merleau-Ponty, Cézanne and Wright are reluctant to separate stable things from our desiring perspectives through which they appear. The dead in Wright's "Homage" charge the visible world with not merely absence but lack, an impelling sense of inadequacy, of eros and grief. Much of the distinguishing power and immensity of Cézanne's and Wright's art lies in the way lack is transmuted into sacramental abundance, the way all things gesture toward a conditioning otherness—be it God or nature or being itself—which must be concealed to be revealed, inseparable as we know it from the way we long to know it, an otherness realized *as other* in the bold refractions of a loving eye.

Works Cited

Bernard, Emile. "Paul Cezanne." In *Cezanne in Perspective.* Judith Wechsler, ed. Englewood Cliffs, NJ: Prentice Hall, 1975.

Johnson, Galen A., and Smith, Michael, B., eds. *Ontology and Alterity in Merleau-Ponty.* Evanston, IL: Northwestern University Press, 1990.

Merleau-Ponty, Maurice. "Cezanne's Doubt." In *Sense and Non-Sense.* Evanston, IL: Northwestern University Press, 1964.

Rewald, John. *Cezanne.* New York: Abrams, 1986.

Vendler, Helen. *The Music of What Happens.* Cambridge, MA: Harvard University Press, 1988.

Vendler, Helen. *Part of Nature, Part of Us.* Cambridge, MA: Harvard University Press, 1980.

Wright, Charles. *Halflife.* Ann Arbor: University of Michigan Press, 1988.

Wright, Charles. *The World of Ten Thousand Things: Poems 1980–1990.* New York: Farrar Straus Giroux, 1990.

II.

The Becoming of Form

Zeno's Arrow, Cupid's Bow

Structure, Process, and Poetry's Dream of the Unified Field

It's easy to be mysterious about mystery. The difficult thing, the beautiful thing, is to be clear about mystery.
—B.H. Fairchild

Reason loves a paradox, especially those rendered with succinct opposition, rhetorically tight yet unresolved, the kind of puzzle that, like Keats's urn, would "tease us out of thought" (l. 44). Contrary to its reputation, reason loves the pleasures of contradiction and multiplicity or, beyond that, the sense of something unspoken, a suggestive silence, full of interpretive possibility, a sense of release from the drone of literalism, of logical consistency and utilitarian compulsion. Poems tend to love a little tension in their reason, to animate logos with a future tense, a feeling that there is something left over from the work of understanding, some conflict that does not resolve into the intellectual harmony of equations. That said, the paradox would be devoid of its animating tension if it were not for the hidden longing in logos for singularity, for the monotheism of the middle term, the resolution, the convergence of parallel rails in the distance. We seem hardwired to contemplate some common dominator or metaphysical ground—be it ethical, historical, or epistemological—that gives clarity to our experience, that gives it a sense of direction, a sense of the promised land.

Take the list of pre-Socratic philosophers who longed to find the basic building block of the material world. Is it air? Is it water? Or as Pythagoras curiously asked, is it number? We are still searching with our electron microscopes and particle accelerators, not to mention the hieroglyphic arcana of theoretical physics. We have survived this long as a species because of our innate longing to find unifying principles by which to predict patterns within the vicissitudes of nature, but what we discover along the way is the joy of discovery, the joy of longing, the joy of the old stabilities breaking down, filling us with wonder. Wonder, too, has a function. It invests the world with value not simply for what the world is but for what it might be. Ortega y Gasset has argued that in order to find meaning, we first must need to find it (13–27), and the pleasures of paradox give voice to that need, the hunger to know, to solve, and at the same time relish a certain release from the certainty of knowing. While there is a certain "logic" to the oppositional symmetry of the paradox, a certain conceptual strength via parallelism that holds contraries together, that yoking of opposites requires resistance, the kind we find in the sublimity of tensive metaphor. Conceptual boundaries are both crossed and reasserted. Within the logical parallelism of the paradox, we celebrate rebellion. We are led to the limits of reason where the abyss makes us small once again, susceptible to suggestion, dreaming awake, a little vulnerable in our rebellious nature, our imaginative hunger—in short, we are like children.

The innate human desire both to assert and to reconcile difference is the driving force of speculation itself, of logos as it proliferates a language that would forge ever new distinctions and in so doing make possible new connections. If we accept the notion that consciousness inherently desires greater scope and complexity, that this is the natural fulfillment of the power implicit in its semiotic play, its loves affair with being, then the mind to self-actualize longs for a progressive sense of that love affair. It longs to forge a new language within our language. Logos in turn longs to be infused with eros, that connective tendency in mind that desires a deeper relation to being, that gives to logos its amorous drive, its empathic expansiveness, its poetry. For eros to survive, we must reinvent the terms of eros. We must risk being a little confused. To think anew, to discover what eros longs to discover, we must broaden our tolerance for mystery and so take logos to a place where it glimpses its limitations. This precisely is what poetry does. It uses language to gesture beyond language, beyond the powers of semiotic logic implicit in the language arts. As Wallace Stevens says in his poem "Man Carrying Thing," "A poem must resist the intelligence / Almost successfully" (l. 1–2).

Poetry, largely conceived as a dimension of all language formation, wants to get close to the world, and thus it seeks to wed its medium not simply to the objects of perception but to our experience of those objects. It longs to render the world as restored to its relational emergence in experience, where self and other blur, invested in one another, untenable as conceptually discrete. It seeks to find the other in the self, the self in the other, to conceive its truth as neither exclusively inward nor outward, but always both. The famous adage attributed to Paul Éluard, frequently quoted and yet from an unknown source, articulates poetic truth in this way: "Il y a un autre monde mais il est dans celui-ci" ("There is another world, but it is in this one").

The paradox of immanence as transcendent brings a poem into its distinctive power as articulating the growing tip of awareness, of consciousness as participating in a natural process as it raises its architectures and constantly demolishes or renovates them. Poetry as a force of nature expresses nature, and the ground of nature, if it can be said to have one, appears both spontaneous in its proliferation of anomaly and orderly in its suggestion of pattern. Poems, like nature itself, appear to us as having a mixed nature, one suggestive of both order and chaos, change and continuity, creative will and material causation. As such, the poem bears traits of both a structure and a process, and thus refuses to resolve (and thus dissolve) its architectural and temporal powers into some unified field of absolute harmony. Poems are conflicted, like us.

Space as Time, Time as Space

Zeno's paradox is not strictly speaking a paradox but a confusion. Indeed it does have the ring of a paradox, one that importantly expresses the fundamental temptations of mind to seek a conflation of the categories of process and structure that are the driving forces of consciousness and, so far as we can tell, its perceived objects. What is commonly referenced as Zeno's paradox is actually one of several, though they all depend upon the same confusion between structure and process. They all articulate the universal desire to reconcile categories of understanding that cannot be reconciled—that is, conceptions of space and those of time. His most famous paradox claims that if an arrow is shot at a target, it must travel first half the distance to the target, then half of the remaining distance, the half that, and so on to infinity, which thus implies it will never hit its target. Of course the arrow does hit the target, hence the paradox. The logical conflict may well inspire a bit of wonder, as if the real world had been transformed into dream by force of reason. More accurately speaking, however, Zeno is not a figure of reason. His notion comes closer to poetry than it does to rational argument, for what he has seen in the phenomenon of spatial distance as it succumbs to measure is a metaphor for process, not process itself.

This metaphor verges toward transparency because it is so very common, implicit in the spatial ways that we tend to conceive of time, the ways we lend to the temporal the perceived stillness and orderliness of certain spaces. We spatialize time more than we temporalize space, in part because space clarifies, time blurs. In making time a space, we move imaginatively toward some sensation of mastery over time, over our anxieties about time and the pressure of non-being. For one thing, with spatial models, we have the power to move within the space according to the desires of engagement. We can walk so far, then walk back, and we have not violated the essentials distinctive to space, what makes space recognizable as such to immediate experience. When, historically, poems found repose in the pages of books, they were free to take on qualities of complexity that offered up their structures to the act of rereading. The spatial being of poems granted both reader and writer new freedoms of interpretive action, of how long we dwell with a text, how the temporal encounter with a poem as text might be restructured or resequenced.

Time, however, challenges the intellect with its slippery insistence. We may hear a striking passage of music and reflect upon it, but meanwhile the music goes on, leaving our ideas about music behind. To go back musically is to violate its sequential order in favor of a new one. We might see a scaled-down rendition of a painting in a book and, in doing so, still access some essentials relevant to the whole. The eye then is free to make its own movements, however cued by the composition. Music cannot, however, be sped up, shrunk in time, without obviously violating its essentials. Nor can it be excerpted to render a credible and affective experience of the whole. The temporal medium of music asserts itself in a way that requests greater surrender than a spatial medium in order to regard the aesthetic structure. Music leads, and if we are to regard it, we follow. Our footsteps are those of the music itself. It thus embodies the undeniable power that time has over us, and yet it makes of our master a companion. In music, the great tide of loss and arrival takes the shape of something we can love, something that, like us, lives and dies, that possesses a heart that beats, phrases that breathe, memories that come and go. It asserts within the context of loss and expectation the fleeting dominion of the present. Little wonder then that music ritualizes grief and celebration so often. Its scope impresses us as both immediate and transcendent, inward and immense. To embrace music is to embrace being itself, but especially that aspect of being that most affects the heartbeat: being-in-time.

Because of the greater sense of mastery and manipulation granted the interpretive mind in spatial models, the eye dominates as the sense most linked to logos. Moreover, the word *idea* comes from the Greek word *idein*, meaning "to see." Although recursivity, and thus order, belong both to time and space, to preserve a sense of temporal recursivity in music or the cycles of nature, those with the power to do so turn to space. They fashion models that are not temporal, but metaphors for the temporal. The very notion of a model tends to be spatial. To model time, we pour it into the visual media of treble clefs and calendars and so open time to a mode of investigation that would mitigate time's mastery. In the most dominant realms of metaphor, therefore, the relation between space and time mirrors the relation between rationality and irrationality or faith. Flux and the relentlessness of novelty and loss challenge our ability to measure, to reason, to conceptualize. Thus the moving target of the world comes to represent to the imagination a force of wonder and resistance.

We can further investigate the different emotional and conceptual valences of space and time through a phenomenology of the senses that align themselves roughly, metaphorically, with the categories of mind. Music, as the aesthetic medium most about time, is likewise invisible. Poetry, insofar as it is spoken and thus a form of music, also possesses a nature that is invisible. Music often represents a reality beyond or beneath the visual surface of things, which is why it can align itself with the mystical. The angels do not have paintbrushes. They have harps. Shepherds have flutes. Orpheus with his lyre possesses the animating power of nature itself. If music does not raise the dead, it nevertheless can raise our spirits, in part because it is a spirit, moving invisibly through us. Thus music offers a language for that which is beyond language, and so, as with Stevens's "blue guitar," it so often represents the imagination in general, its powers of faith, the aesthetic element of mystery as we find it in all the arts.

Seeing, of course, can do this as well, but less readily so. As a result, it is far more common to weep in response to music than in response to painting. To *see* what people are saying is to understand them, to grasp their idea. But hearing as a metaphor suggests something more intimate and empathic. Light travels farther than sound, so generally hearing implies closer proximity. *Hearing* what someone is saying is akin to *hearing someone.* The speaker is metonymy for what she is saying. Hearing represents therefore a more soulful or personal connection. When we read a science text, we may well see what an author is saying. Reason has traditionally borne the properties of light. If we are deeply moved by a poem, on the other hand, we hear what the poet says. If we are more moved still, we hear the poet.

In his book *Of Grammatology*, Derrida's challenge to the phonocentrism that privileges speech over inscription is precisely a challenge to see language increasingly in terms of the eye and not the ear. The ear attaches language to the personal realm of the speaker. Phonocentrism in turn reifies the illusion of autonomous identity, of author as origin. Derrida's argument greatly popularized the challenge to naïve versions of authorial autonomy implicit in our metaphors, but one is left to wonder, however, if in losing a sense of a writer having a voice, we lose something critical to the reading imagination, not to mention the epistemology of the creative act. It is not simply the case that we as readers are empowered by the experience of dismantling the author's authority as origin. We are also more alone. The extremes of anti-essentialism do not liberate us; there is no us. Derrida has bracketed off the messy phenomenon of individual creative will, what some might call a soul, such that the problem of personhood is too reductively handled, too easily caricatured and absorbed into a complementary naïveté. His bias in this sense resembles ironically that of a material determinism where the causal origin of process must always be material. We simply have no way of knowing this, and it does not account for our experience of consciousness as inherently creative, as bringing new being into being. The recognition of selfhood as relational and dynamic does not negate or explain originary volition within the psyche. The dream of unified fields of finitude and infinity, law and freedom, matter and spirit all elude us. On the other hand, the imagined warmth of a human voice in writing has the power to keep us company, to invite us inward. With a voice, a poem has a slightly hidden space, like us, and we connect more emotionally to the partially inaccessible depth than we do to the superficial. Eros needs a metaphysics. By way of its imperfect speculations by which we negotiate personal relations, we now perceive a boundary to be crossed, and our imaginative longing provides the connective principle.

The synesthetic resources of our language likewise bear testament to the mind's fundamental tendency to transgress, to cross boundaries, to both reify and subvert identities and thereby expand them. We may indeed see what we hear. At a more abstract level, we may, like Zeno, see stillness in movement. But if there is a paradox in Zeno's puzzle, it is the paradox of desire that takes pleasure in asserting two contrary states at once: connection and difference. Our love of paradox makes manifest the poetical and dual nature of consciousness, how the want that drives and potentially expands consciousness is itself paradoxical. We desire both unity and difference, both desire and the cessation of desire. Since the conceptual play of the mind longs both to unify and to differentiate being, its hunger for clarity remains unresolved. Our experience of intimacy with being breeds a language predicated on distance, on being as an object.

The Hunger for Wordlessness

In his essay "A Midwestern Poetics," the poet B. H. Fairchild explores the paradoxical nature of poetry's intimacy with being, the fact that poetry appears possible through a conflation of subject and object and yet likewise driven by a desire for this state and thus predicated on difference. He claims at one point that poetry reenacts the ontological magic that one first experiences at the dawn of a language. The ontological spirit throughout his essay owes much to Heidegger, since poetry can now be seen as a bodying forth of being and thus enacting the originary process whereby language comes into being:

> On the origins of language: It began, perhaps, as an ontological breakthrough of almost supernatural proportions. Suddenly, a sound made with the mouth makes the distant, removed, and unseeable present. That is, *it is a kind of poetry without the craft* [original emphasis]. It is not "referential" (at least in the modern sense). It embodies the thing. The thing is seemingly present in the very articulation of its name. The art of poetry attempts to recreate this first, stunning, magical effect, this primal ontological leap. (141)

Key to the above passage is its contradiction. Poetry "embodies" the thing as named, and yet the thing is only "seemingly present" in the articulation of its name. In Stevensian fashion, all that is is as is.

The contradiction here owes its mystique and power to the presumption that poetry embodies a unity that it nevertheless desires and therefore lacks. Fairchild, with reference to Jan Zwicky, explores this desire in terms reminiscent of Lacanian nostalgia, a longing for some prelinguistic unity of self and other:

> What we have lost is not so much silence as the unity, the wholeness, of the world before the great wall arose and the world was divided into subjective and objective, self and other.
>
> "Lyric art is the fullest expression of the hunger for wordlessness."
>
> Yes, and I would describe the "hunger" as a hunger for that world *where language is no longer required* [original emphasis]. (127)

Such a hunger might well have a bit of trepidation in it, for arriving at the desired ideal implies draining the energy of necessity from language itself. This energy of necessity gives poetry its vitality, its existential authenticity, its essentializing concentration. If lyric art were to embody the object of its desires, it would cease to be poetry. Thus, knowingly or not, poetry harbors a death wish. Fortunately for us, it also desires life, which is predicated on hunger. Life's principles of growth and survival are expansive, as hunger is, as consciousness must be.

If we are to believe, as Heidegger does, that poetry does not so much speak *about* its subject matter as *speak its subject*, then it longs to be not simply *about* being, but to embody it, and yet it is important here to note that the phrase "subject matter" with regard to poetry is elusive and misleading. Fairchild says early in his essay:

> It is not the purpose and certainly not the magic of poetry to speak about the thing (information), but rather to speak the thing, to perform the impossible task of making the absent present—palpably, tangibly present. (123)

Critical to the above passage is the word "impossible." Certainly we are not regressing to a medieval sense of spells and charms that flatter us with an axial, causal relation between word and thing. On the contrary, the subject matter of poems is not strictly speaking mere "things." What makes a poem a poem is the way its so-called subject matter resists dissociation from its form, its body, just as the world for the phenomenologist cannot be cleanly separated from our experienced relation to it. We can imagine the world as separate from our relation to it, but only at the cost of then having nothing to say about it. Thus a poet's subject is always some relation to a subject. Heidegger's name for this relational being is "Dasein." It comes as no surprise, therefore, that B. H. Fairchild's essay would reference Heidegger in relation to poetry's exceptional status among modes of discourse and their ways of conceiving and rendering what they reference:

> Reading Heidegger: poetry as the only way to speak *dasein, being-in-the-world* [original emphasis], since it cannot be spoken *about* without distorting it. (123)

What poetry *speaks*, according to Heidegger, is "Dasein," or being for which being is an issue. Dasein is self-reflexive being. As tempting as it is to refer to Dasein in English as "consciousness," more accurately it is consciousness being understood as embedded in a sense of being ("Sein") as "there" ("da"). Thus B. H. Fairchild translates Dasein into the Heidiggerian nomenclature: "Being-in-the-World." To borrow a phrase from Heidegger's *Poetry, Language, Thought,* poetry, as the bodying forth of Dasein, "worlds the world," which is no doubt paradoxical since world as worlded appears to preexist its existence.

In its paradoxical agency, poetry, for Heidegger, occupies an ancestral space in the cosmology of thought, its origin and means of expansion. It figures as the primary force that speaks Dasein into being and with it the mindful, relational experience of being. As B. H. Fairchild states once again:

> My definition of poetry: "The thinking mind bodied forth." (Note from Caputo's *The Mystical Element in Heidegger's Thought*: "Heidegger has repeatedly said that thinking and poetry dwell in the closest proximity. . . .") Again, H. in *The Basic Problems of Phenomenology*: Poetic language is "the elementary emergence into words, the becoming-uncovered of existence as Being-in-the-world." (124)

It is equally important to note that Heidegger does not exactly proffer the notion of a resolved and poetical unification of word and world. Such a notion would be absurd, since language would cease to operate as language without the poetic word's animating proximity and responsiveness to the unspeakable. Heidegger's nomenclature is more subtle and difficult. Dasein, after all, suggests "there-being," similarly connotative of the separation implied in the word "existence" as "being outside." Dasein is being that regards the there-ness of being. Poetry, in "speaking Dasein," both longs for and participates in the originary blossoming of thought.

While essential to the poetic is the element of amorous longing that seeks to close the gap between word and world, a certain "there-ness" to the world remains. Poetry seeks to unify the being of a particular language with the larger context of our ontological relations, and yet we can never regard the totality of those relations. We intuit them through the stubborn sense that there is always more to a particular act of language, to its affect and resonance, more to articulation than what we can articulate. Poetry makes this intuition conspicuous. It makes palpable the sense of the unspoken in language. For this reason, we might say that it speaks silence. And in turn, it "resists the intelligence almost successfully," even as it arouses and depends upon that same intelligence. In resisting adequate interpretation, poetry proliferates levels of interpretation. The poetic word therefore takes on the elusiveness of Zeno's arrow, its nature beyond measure, and we who speak it see our own elusive nature there speeding out of view.

Zeno the Poet

In Jorie Graham's richly suggestive and realized poem "Dawn Day One," she falsely associates Zeno's failed analogy with the failure of reason. However, this confusion expresses the bias of consciousness, to apply the terms of time to those of space. By association then, Zeno's spatialization of time represents reason's attempt to stabilize being via measures that break down under the pressures of the real, just as the language for selfhood breaks down under the pressures of temporality and contingency that make the experience of selfhood possible and desirable. Zeno thus articulates a force of illusion in Graham's musings on the origin of consciousness and selfhood as born of plurality and otherness:

> We come about first, into waking, as an us, I
> think. Sometime between the first and second instant
> there is still the current that carries one in
> and deposits one in singleness. The body's weight is
> a beaching. Back behind, or underneath: infinity
> or something which has no consequence. Then
> consequence, which
> feels like walls and the uprighting of self one has to do
> in them, then the step one has to take once roused, and how
> it

> puts one back on the walking-path one stepped off of
> last night. Zeno reasoned we would
> never get there. Reason in fact never gets there. (l. 4–14)

If Zeno is the rationalist here, he is a failed one. Zeno, in fact, falls into the fallacy of reasoning by false analogy. The two contrary truths that constitute his "paradox" are not in fact contrary. They do not provoke reason. They suspend disbelief.

Zeno's impulse, therefore, is that of a poet, perhaps unwittingly, for what he brings into focus is a poet's longing for the unified field that logos can never embody or prove. He demonstrates that an unbridgeable gap remains between measure and movement or, more largely, a spatial, numerical model of the world and the world itself as a process. To conceive the world as mere space is to fail its being-in-time. Zeno's particular deployment of reason collapses into wonder. His so-called paradox figures as mythic in the sense that it teases the imagination with oppositions that only the imagination can bring into conjunction, into some poetry of alignment. If not reconciled, mythic contraries are nonetheless linked by story or paradigm that articulates their animating friction. Zeno's so-called paradox gives voice to something fundamental about our condition: we want to impose constructs of imaginary stillness in a world that shakes them off. The mind, indebted to and destined for non-being, pressured therefore by anxiety and desire, seeks both the stillness of the principle and the life-force of the process. It seeks the knowable patterns of the past and the liberating novelty of the future.

Although Zeno figures as a representative of reason that "never gets there," in Graham's poem the poetic imagination never gets there either, if by "there" we mean the presumed target of the speaker's meditation—that is, the nature and origin of selfhood as contingent upon otherness and yet not identical with it. What the speaker enacts as she contemplates her own subjectivity, its presumed source, the myth of some center akin to a metaphysical ground, does not quite qualify as a rational ordering of experience. At best she engages the most poetic of all fields of philosophy: ontology, which is largely descriptive and intuitive, as is phenomenology.

Since what ontology describes lies outside the powers of description, an ontology such as Heidegger's uses negation to gesture toward such concepts as "truth" (characterized via the Greek word *aletheia* to mean "unconcealedness"). Thus presence appears conceptually wedded to its opposite in the spirit of theology's Via Negativa, blazing a path to the absolute by way of clarifying what it is not. Graham's poem similarly demystifies the failed, reductive models of selfhood in an effort to make vulnerable the mind to the infinity behind or below language. Mind, for the speaker, is not to be confused with model, let alone measure. So, too, the speaker's mind, like Zeno's mythical arrow, is in a state of perpetual approach. This is because her target keeps receding in thought as the object of thought. In touching her eyelid, longing to see the seer, she imagines a self that lies outside (or inside) the intentional nature of consciousness. She wants to arrive at what Husserl called "the transcendental ego," the unseen part of the mind this side of the objects of thought.

In short, she seeks a unified field. What she finds instead is a body, an orienting locus to reify the self, albeit provisionally, imaginatively, imperfectly. The body offers itself as a "beaching"—the surrogate to some more convincing metaphysical ground for the self. The poem thus gestures toward a process akin to Lacan's mirror stage, where the vague region of seeming continuity with the world yields to an experience of the body as an integrated whole and thus a model for the emergence of self-consciousness and sign systems in general. Critical to the authority of the poem is the speaker's prevailing stance of rigor and doubt, such that if there is what Lacan calls an imaginary stage (that stage of union with the [m]other that precedes the mirror stage), there is little one can say about it, or little that is clear. At best she can muse, "We come about first, into waking, as an us, I / think." The tentative qualification here registers the difficulty with the imaginary stage, how talk of it presumes constructions we must imaginatively negate. Prelinguistic experience calls here once again upon ontology and the poetry of negation.

The problem of representing prelinguistic experience mirrors the problem more largely of metaphysics and more specifically as the psychoanalytic school as a branch of metaphysics, inferring depth structures via our experience of the surface—that is, the immediate data of experience. Graham's speaker participates in a breed of postmodern resistance to metaphysical presupposition, while simultaneously embodying the fundamental metaphysical want that drives all language. Hers is the dilemma of so many caught in a postmodern, ant-imetaphysical zeitgeist that suggests discipline to immediacy but is also strongly counterintuitive. We could say the stubborn, intuitive metaphysics with its instrumental dailiness exists, in part because the death of metaphysical assumptions is so unsettling, but also because language produces a sense of its own inadequacy, its own desire to accommodate a greater sense of being outside of language, a sense of the extra-linguistic real that must be there for desire to have an object, a target.

As Graham's poem moves toward its elusive target, its meditation on selfhood cues a desire to close the intentional gap between seer and seen: if the body's weight is "a beaching," what is "beached"? Is it an "I?" We presume so. But the nature of this "I" is so problematic that both the word and the concept threaten to paralyze and simplify some dynamic complexity. The problematic nature of selfhood appears fundamental to poetry's imaginative impulse, as that which animates the tension and bond between self and other as instrumental in both the structure and process of consciousness. The body as a "beaching" offers us another language for the self and comes with its own contingencies and dynamism that call into question its autonomy. The body, therefore, is likewise an "us," a multiplicity, as are the embodied moments that come to define the poetic. Poems think with the body and therein lies much of their polysemous power. The poetic image, as defined by Pound, differs from description because its embodiment "presents an intellectual and emotional complex." Images think. In so far as they are complex, they resist translation. Like bodies, they cannot be replaced. Poems deploy the more corporeal elements of their medium, such as music and image, and so wed their polysemous resonance inextricably to a singular form. Irreducibility, therefore, is not to be confused with autonomy, however much both figure as key to the construction and experience of identity.

In Graham's terms, the body as a "beaching" makes possible not only the formation of the child's self, but also the poem's structure. The body figures as critical in structuring how a child, in all her poetical nature, thinks. The power of thought, however, comes under pressure at this point in Graham's speculations. Her syntax collapses the rhetoric of predication into the less committed and more impressionistic kinetics of fragments. Statement yields to something more tentative, fraught with epistemological difficulty. Corporeal coalescence evokes its contrary complement in the sublime. Finitude evokes infinitude. And in a fashion consistent with a post-psychoanalytic sense of the sublime, the world without limit takes on an inward cast: "Back behind, or underneath: infinity / or something which has no consequence." The limitless as behind or underneath suggests a source—either in the historical past or in the spontaneous depths of mindfulness. The unseen seer takes on aspects of the sublime as the interior other, infinite in the sense of without form, or none we can confirm. Form derives from the absence of form, or at least this is what the creative force of Dasein keeps suggesting via the novelty and proliferation of forms of thought—or more precisely this visionary expansion of Dasein in dialogue with its recombinant nature. The experience of will in the process of thought suggests the "ground" (or underworld) of the finite is infinite (or formless) and so inadequately modeled in material determinism.

As the speaker puts her hands to her eyes, she longs to touch the transcendental ego, to better understand its nature as beyond the false dichotomy of selfhood and otherness. She seeks a unified field:

> I put my hands over both my eyes and lie
> still. I think. The paradox says that you can never leave
> the room in which you are right now. First walk
> half the distance to the door, then half again, and so on.
>   These eyes,
> under my hands, I looked at in the mirror yesterday.
> Everything of course was silver, my skin, my gaze,
> and then the eyes, held in their lids. (l. 52–59)

If the desire to reconcile self and other via language is failed, it is not reason's failure alone. Thought, poetic or otherwise, is driven by the simultaneous assertion and dismantling of the self–other distinction. It also produces a residual sensation that gestures toward some origin outside of thought, outside of language, of form. The creative activity of thought creates not so much metaphysical knowledge as it does a sense of speculative wonder. Though these new structures derive from old ones, there is no denying that new being asserts its singularity, particularly so in the case of poems. So, too, the thought of poems cannot be simplified into moments of logos (as differentiation) and those of eros (as connectivity). As the fundamental consequence of semiotic play, the experience of connectivity will always be tainted with its opposite, as will the experience of difference. Both eros and logos participate in the structural tension of thought. Poetic thought intensifies this tension.

This implausibility of self-autonomy as an absolute reminds us of the tensions implicit in the very construction of a subjectivity. Graham's poem invokes Zeno to mirror the self that attempts to leave the room, as one might use reason to get outside the limitations of subjectivity. As that rational process mirrors in turn the poetical, the urge to get inside the subject, to see the seer, the person in the mirror becomes a stranger:

> One takes smaller and smaller steps
> according to Zeno to try to leave the room. If you return
> now
> to the glass, you can look at your eyes. After a short
> time, very short if you hold fast, don't blink, just stare,
> you will be looking at an other. (l. 65–69)

Poetry, as the mode of discourse that most illuminates and intensifies the powers and failures of language, requires both concealment and revelation. Poetry gestures toward the unspeakable as the imaginary fruition of what it has to say.

In turn, poetry gestures toward its reader. It invites the reader to give the poem a present tense, to enter the silence at the heart of the poem. The dramatic turn to the reader toward the poem's closure coincides then with its turn toward the present moment of the reading act. This, too, is a beginning. This, too, is affirmed as a source, *the* source, of being. New being comes into being even as it makes possible our experience of the past:

> Here. You are at the beginning of something. At the exact
> beginning. OK. This is awakening
> number two in here, in this poem. Then there are
> these: me: you: you there. I'm actually staring up at
> you, you know, right here, right from the pool of this page.
> Don't worry where else I am, I am here. Don't
> worry if I'm still alive, you are. (l. 84–90)

There are no rhetorical contingencies here. The speaker becomes quite authoritative and unequivocal in asserting the generative power of the present. What heightens the tension as we move forward is the force of that rhetoric coupled with the increasing implausibility of its claims. Thus Graham's speaker asserts, "I'm actually staring up at / you, you know, right here, right from the pool of this page." The passage relies upon the authority of what came before, where the failure of the terms "I" and "you" have already been laid bare. Clearly the body is not sufficient in locating or defining the relational nature of selfhood. If the "I" is not on the page, where is she? Why not here? And behind these questions lies the more self-reflective and unsettling question: why anywhere at all?

The force of the poem's final assertions is critical. It reaffirms the emotional energy by which structure finds its necessary place in a poem's journey. Zeno's poetic paradigm likewise loses all interest if the mind simply dismisses its instrumental fascination with measure and the modeling of a world in flux. The closure thus resembles that of Keats's "Ode on a Grecian Urn" in which the final emphatic simplification, in the voice of the urn, contains an element of the absurd as expressive of the overwhelming sensation of faith:

> "Beauty is truth, truth beauty,"—that is all
> Ye know on earth, and all ye need to know. (l. 49–50)

In a manner that would tease us out of thought, opposites would both reconcile and assert themselves at the same time. If we find the closure in either Keats's or Graham's poem convincing, it is because the terms of both poems begin to crack under the pressure of experience that finds expression in defiance of reason.

The concepts "you" and "I" can no more be conflated than the concepts "truth" and "beauty." As embedded as parts are in one another, they do not dissolve into a unified field without likewise dissolving into nonsense.

As if "beauty is truth" were not absurd enough, Keats, albeit as voicing his urn, intensifies the hyperbole with the notion that all knowledge can be reduced to this equation. Beauty as truth thus constitutes the unified field so desired through the anxious exploration of mortality and its relation to art in the poem. The final statement seeks to conflate not only truth and beauty, but the larger binaries of the poem, including art and life, eternity and mortality, structure and process, stasis and kinesis:

> Bold Lover, never, never canst thou kiss,
> Though winning near the goal—yet, do not grieve;
> She cannot fade, though thou hast not thy bliss,
> For ever wilt thou love, and she be fair! (l. 19–20)

In another of Zeno's paradoxes, he asks, if a process is made of instants and any one instant is a still place, how do we get from stillness to stillness? Obviously the world is not made of still places, nor is the imagination. The lovers on Keats's urn who hold still in anticipation are eternal precisely because they appear to be outside of time. Outside of process, they inspire the eternal: our sense of love as the imaginative desire for consummated love.

Beauty as metonymical for desire, both aesthetic and epistemological, reveals its hidden power that shapes our sense of what we choose to believe. Both in the argument of "Ode on a Grecian Urn" and also Keats's famous letter to Benjamin Bailey on the authenticity of the imagination (November 22, 1817), Keats offers far more support for beauty as truth than truth as beauty. The letter's opening after all is meant to comfort Bailey, who has presumably been hurt by a letter from their mutual friend, Benjamin Robert Haydon. The power of beauty is, for Keats, the power of consolation:

> O I wish I was as certain of the end of all your troubles as that of your momentary start about the authenticity of the Imagination. I am certain of nothing but of the holiness of the

> Heart's affections and the truth of Imagination—What the imagination seizes as Beauty must be truth—whether it existed before or not—for I have the same idea of all our passions as of love. . . . I am more zealous in this affair because I have never yet been able to perceive how anything can be known for truth by consecutive reasoning—and yet it must be. Can it be that even the greatest philosopher ever arrived at his goal without putting aside numerous objections? However it may be, O for a life of sensation rather than of thoughts! (36–37)

Beauty thus has the potential to overwhelm all other considerations. One could call the aesthetic trumping of reason "faith." Certainly faith seeks the truth, as Keats says he does, albeit truth as beauty or authenticated by the imagination. This kind of truth appears to be that of Dasein, relational, inclusive of the subjectivity, its responsiveness to beauty. On the other hand, what does Keats have faith in? Is it anything other than the vehicle of faith? What is actually believed here other than the fact that beauty has the power to overwhelm the needs of reason? Is truth reconceived, or simply laid aside?

A philosophical pragmatist such as William James might claim that we find things true simply because we first find it useful to believe they are true. What then is the use of pragmatism? Is it not unsettling? Why see all truth as a pragmatist does, as a production of need and our success in satisfying it? To make use of philosophical pragmatism, we must broaden the concept of "usefulness" beyond its more common valence to include among its goals the many varieties of emotional and conceptual satisfaction. Pragmatism might be useful psychologically, but so, too, are the forms of falsehood that we know to be false. Both Graham's and Keats's closures prove useful in that they voice the defeat of reason, but they in turn voice the anxiety that longs to defeat it. "Don't worry," says her speaker, who in speaking to the reader speaks to herself and thus belies her own anxiety, which finds appeasement in unsustainable terms that make one anxious. In the deployment of partial falsehoods, both poets have a lot in common with Zeno. They apply to being a conceptual medium that can never be as supple as being itself. Unlike Zeno, of course, they make no pretense of rationality, and so reason gives way to myth, to the imaginative negotiation of the irrational, to aesthetic form as that which makes the infinite something we can bear.

Form as Emptiness, Emptiness as Form

Graham's poem derives much authority from its intellectual energy and the lovely, broken-down engine of the intellect at the poem's closure. It conceptually honors being, which cannot *be* a concept. Being is Zeno's arrow as it moves, or rather it is the *movement* of the arrow. It defies formal definition, at the same time that process requires form to articulate its movement. The resulting difficulty with regard to the representation of being provides one path into a greater appreciation of the strange claims of "The Heart of Prajnaparamita Sutra," one of the most prominent texts of Mahayana Buddhism. The text, most commonly called "The Heart Sutra," appears as well as "The Heart of Perfect Understanding":

> Listen Shariputra,
> form is emptiness, and emptiness is form.
> Form is not other than emptiness, emptiness is not other
>   than form.
> The same is true with feelings, perceptions, mental
>   formations, and
>   consciousness.
> Listen, Shariputra, all dharmas are marked with emptiness.
> They are neither produced nor destroyed,
> neither defiled nor immaculate,
> neither increasing nor decreasing.
> Therefore, in emptiness there is neither form, nor feelings,
>   nor
>   perceptions,
> nor mental formations, nor consciousness.
> No eye, or ear, or nose, or tongue, or body, or mind. (1)

Like most English versions of this text, the above translation by Thich Nhat Hahn uses the word "emptiness" for the Buddhist term "sunyata" (or "shunyata"), which might also be translated as "no thing." In context the word suggests that there is no thing—including human existence—that has ultimate substantiality. Therefore no thing is either permanent or independent of everything else. All things are thus interconnected and in a state of continual flux, such that it becomes difficult to refer to them as "things." The notion of form as emptiness has a slightly different resonance than the notion of emptiness as form. Granted, the text says that they do not differ, and yet the two terms obviously do different work in leading consciousness out of the false conceptual dualities. The text asks us to let go of the illusory structures of cognition and look to their absence in an undifferentiating mindfulness wherein the self–other binary ceases to operate.

One enormous contribution of Buddhism to ontology is its experiential affirmation of mind as something that may include the play of differentiation without being defined by it. While the "emptiness" illuminated by moments of mindful awareness calls into question traditional categories of knowledge, epistemology likewise appears untenable without some larger sense of being as more than merely a product of language and cognition. Whether we embrace it or not, the notion of being itself as undifferentiated, as a unified field, creates an epistemological catch-22. Without this sense of being, semiotics appears groundless and thus unreal. With this sense of being, semiotics appears rigid and thus unreal. For a language to be true, it must admit its falseness.

As opposed to the claim "form is emptiness," the slightly more difficult notion "emptiness is form" could suggest another paradox: the reality of illusion. This might equally be called the reality of appearance. In other words, the lack of substantiality in Being nevertheless finds expression in that which appears to have substantiality. The mind, which includes cognition, has a nature. Moreover, it expresses nature. The experienced contemplation of being, however exiled from its object, is a manifestation of being. To look at a tree with its explosive spontaneity of forms that defy even fractal mathematics is nevertheless to see a certain tension between structural principle and spontaneous diversity, and that duality appears as both a creation of nature and our experience of it. The fact that the mind contributes its creative energy via conceptualization does little to tear us from the experience of natural principle as something both abstract and embedded in the multiplicities we see.

Herein lies the most persuasive residual appeal of Platonic idealism, which in its privileging of transcendence over immanence is quite alien in spirit to both Buddhism and postmodern anti-essentialism. The world appears in its recursivity of pattern amidst change to have a structure that is revealed not simply by observation of the particular, but by the particular in temporal context. We see in the specimen the shadow of the species. Platonism therefore is contingent upon historicity as key to revealing the metaphysics of underlying principles, patterns that prove not only useful to science, but also to the poetics of wonder. At the same time it is the ahistorical, eternal nature of the Platonic "idea" that makes it true. An individual triangle can be destroyed, but the mathematic principle embodied in that triangle cannot. Platonic truth is revealed through temporality, but it is not in itself temporal. Truth, to be truth, cannot die.

While the particular in all its integrity defies representation via the powers of categorization, so, too, the experience of emergent principles, however elusive and open to debate, questions the experience of the particular alone as sufficient to reveal nature's complexity of design. Though recursivity as the signature of principle occurs both in space and time, space figures as more suggestive of stability, time as more suggestive of instability. One might be tempted to apply metaphors of space to time in an effort to gain imaginative mastery, largely because space has a calming and clarifying effect on our experience of time. But this kind of clarity also harbors the dissonance of illusion.

In contrast, time as the dominant category of mind has the effect that we see in "The Heart Sutra." Mindfulness with its ability to move with the ongoing present sees through the less supple constructs of mind: boundaries, definitions, formal identities altogether. The calming effect of Buddha-mind is the dismantling of identity boundaries that produce attachment and anxiety. The "hunger for wordlessness" gives way to undifferentiating awareness. A poetry born of no hunger no longer longs to know. It knows. This, it would seem, would not make for a very energetic poetics. The poetry of "The Heart

Sutra," however, lies in the verbal and provocative tension of statements such as "emptiness is form." The language strains under the pressure of what it longs to convey. Like so many sacred texts, it deploys definition by negation, the fullness of being realized as empty, as "no thing." Like so many poems, it offers the pleasure of paradox to tease us out of thought, to open the interpretive mind to the authority of experience, to what interpretation can never fathom.

Infinity in a Grain of Sand

Einstein's space–time continuum is not to be confused with the unified field of felt experience. It is marvelous in part because it is so strongly counterintuitive. Moreover, it does not claim that the mental categories of space and time can be conflated in daily life. Nevertheless, Einstein's theories have some of the appeal of Zeno's paradox in provoking a search for harmony within the contrary forces that define us. Einstein's theory is both a rational and imaginative triumph because it sees beyond intuited contraries. Likewise, quantum physics moves to resolve another fundamental opposition that defines Newtonian physics: the separation between the perceiver and the perceived. That said, relativity and quantum physics as descriptions of extremities of scale (large and small) do not model a world of felt experience in its fullness. It is a fallacy to assume epistemological models remain equally successful as they change scale and thus their relation to subjectivity. Extreme models can, however, provide analogies and thus function poetically.

In the Newtonian scientific model, quantity trumps quality, largely because the truth it pursues would reify the objectivity of objects as expressed in verifiable, repeatable terms. For the scientific method to operate smoothly, the world beneath the microscope must appear divorced from our felt relation to it. The realm of the poetic, however, has a bit of the new physics in it, since the presence of relational experience changes our calculations. We see the seer in the seen, the stranger in the mirror. If poetry embodies a breed of truth specific to the poetic, it does so by expanding meaning as the felt embodiment of being, not only through its semiotic relation to the familiar, but also through the spontaneous creation of what is strange.

Poems participate in the unfolding and creative manifestation of being, of new forms of meaning wedded to their particular forms, the way music is wedded to it. Like music, poems are not so much *expressions* of feeling as they are *creators* of feeling. The singular feelings they embody did not precede their embodiment and await expression. Poems are inherently musical as resistant to translation and paradoxical in nature, both organized and unruly, immediate and evasive. Their structures put themselves under pressure via meaningful multiplicity key to structural singularity. It is not necessarily the case that a poetics of formal closure lends itself semiotic closure. On the contrary, the friction between aesthetics and semiotics can invigorate a poem. Poetic structure asserts the integrity of its given outlines, its feeling of necessity, beauty, and meaningful precision, and yet makes of that precision something dynamic, both in terms of the poem's movement and the reader's interpretive play. One might be reminded of the aesthetics of William Blake, who criticized the art of various contemporaries for their blurriness and advocated an art of clearer demarcation. Such an aesthetic, however, did little to diminish his enthusiasm for the experience of "infinity," a notion that he reiterates with an exuberance bordering on obsession. As he states in his annotations to "The Works of Sir Joshua Reynolds":

> Without Minute Neatness of Execution. The. Sublime cannot Exist! Grandeur of Ideas is founded on Precision of Ideas. (636)

Precision in art implies formal precision and suggests that form is being precise about something, that its neatness of execution is precisely adapted to serve or gesture toward being beyond the form.

Poems have bodies. Bodies have minds. The mind's forces of logos and eros find mutual expression in imaginations that, in Blake's system, work to bring the body, intellect, and heart into some semblance of the unity, a paradise regained. That at least is the longing enacted by the imagination, that it might bring the parts of the human subject (and its world) into greater conversation. Thus Blake holds up as ideal the archetype of the unified field. In systems as diverse as Blake's and Hegel's, consciousness drives toward greater and greater synthesis of its complexities, culminating in some final assimilation and realization of divine potential. The unified totality of being correlates in both systems to a monotheistic divine. Totality cannot be an object of experience. It, as imagined, is a way of coping with experience, of positioning oneself relative to unity. It posits an absolute by which the anxieties associated with temporality can be appeased by the cessation of conflict, and yet this very absolute, in its felt relation, also animates the desire for greater and greater vision.

Where Hegel's system posits assimilation by rational synthesis, Blake's posits penetration to the "infinite." Neither system, however, dismisses the instrumental essential of formal delineation. For Blake, the infinite expresses itself in the formal and the local, the grain of sand, for instance, or the sharply outlined figure of Adam in an illuminated book. Finitude bodies forth the experience of infinitude. Likewise in poems, voice bodies forth the voiceless. Once again, B. H. Fairchild proves useful:

> Poetry, as the only form of language able to "body forth" existence as "Being-in-the-world," has traditionally done so chiefly in the two modes of lyric, the "dwelling-in" existence (the verticality of moment) and narrative, the on-goingness of existence (the horizontal dimension of being-in-time). Speaking of lyric's vertical motion, its seeming arrest of or being out of time, Ed Hirsch says, "Perhaps the asocial nature of the deepest feeling, the 'too muchness' of human emotion is what creates the space for the lyric, which is a way of beating time . . . of verging on the infinite." (140)

The infinite here might best be understood in Sanskrit as "sunyata," as "no thing" once again or "emptiness." It certainly does not suggest the everlasting or permanent. The experienced sense of the infinite can suggest what Paul Tillich called "the eternal now," a sense of stepping outside the paradigm of horizontal time. Thus we can feel in poems some release from our ongoing enslavement to time.

Vertical time in poetry is traditionally thought of as lyric time, as opposed to narrative time. Lyric verticality thus enlivens the paradigmatic quality of language, as exemplified in metonymies, Freudian slips, and puns, conflationary superimpositions of meaning by way of displacement. The lyricism of the vertical in a poem intensifies where the resonance is strongest, where more than one thing happens at one time; and without lyric depth, even in a narrative poem, we may feel trapped in a dull literalism, a monological style where the reader's imagination becomes passive. The poetic image, as lyric, triggers a depth charge, an exploratory sense of plenitude in the instant, a feeling that meaning overflows the container of its language. We might as a result feel more summoned to the text as opposed to being dominated by it, less impoverished by the relentless horizontal pull that dominates the daily experience of time.

Doubtless poetry requires both horizontal and vertical time, but the move from utilitarian language to poetic language (in Valéry's terms, from walking to dancing) requires a move toward the vertical and thus toward greater resistance to translation, greater singularity. A poem, however radically conceived, earns the label "poem" because it has carved out an identity for itself, a conversation among the parts, a coalescence of character. And yes, this character's vitality depends equally upon the tensive, the discontinuous, the absurd, the contradictory, the enigmatic, the paradoxical. As empowering or reassuring as unity might promise to be, it does not negate the pleasure of paradox, of contrariness, of being "teased out of thought" without abandoning the medium of thought altogether. The body that carries us to the sublime abyss is nonetheless there, its heart perhaps beating a little fast.

Poetic movements often fall into Dionysian or Apollonian categories that strike extreme postures in order to compensate and self-promote, but the fact remains that poetry becomes untenable without both rationality and irrationality and their approximate correlatives in structure as stable and process as not. Just as structure and process can never be neatly dissociated from one another, so, too, can they never dissolve their identities into an undifferentiated, unified field. A poetics with a process orientation, such as Olson's projective verse, makes its case by way of reconceiving notions about ideal form, but this form can never be the equivalent of process. The projective poem attempts to keep pace with the process of consciousness as enacting in the process of composition itself. Closed form, for Olson, represents artifice; open form represents a more genuine stance toward the real. But form does not capture or constellate compositional process; it cannot, though some forms may stage their reenactments a bit more ardently. Form is the trace of process at best. It is the model of the arrow's flight, the thing left behind, as the glory of flight suffers the fate we all must suffer.

And what could be more fortunate. Without the failure of structure to accommodate the reality of process, we as readers are not called upon to long for what is missing. Beauty belongs not to form alone. It belongs to energy, to the perceiver's longing that inhabits form. Desire then is critical to the experience of the aesthetic. It is both the product and producer of imaginative vision. Where there is no loss, there is no music. Where there is no failure, there is no poetry. Zeno's failure is our own. He is a poet of the absurd who unveils a fundamental absurdity in the way desire seeks out fully realized, undifferentiated unities where none exist, not for us—we who live forward, but know in reverse; we who are arrows in Cupid's bow; we the fallen; we who look to poems less for the absolute perhaps than for the way the absolute transforms us, our world, our being-in-the-world; we who look to poems less for the wordlessness of heaven than for a little company.

Works Cited

Blake, William. *The Poetry and Prose of William Blake.* David V. Erdman, ed. New York: Doubleday, 1970.

Derrida, Jacques. *Of Grammatology.* Baltimore: Johns Hopkins University Press, 1974.

Fairchild, B. H. "A Midwestern Poetics." *New Letters* 78, 1 (Fall, 2011): 121–145.

Graham, Jorie. "Dawn Day One." In *Overlord 3–5.* New York: Harper Collins, 2005.

Hahn, Thich Nhat. *The Heart of Perfect Understanding.* Berkeley, CA: Parallax, 1988.

Heidegger, Martin. *Poetry, Language, Thought.* New York: Harper Perennial Modern Classics, 2001.

James, William. "What Pragmatism Means." In *William James: Writings 1902–1910.* New York: Library of America, 1987.

Keats, John. *Letters of John Keats.* Robert Gittings, ed. Oxford: Oxford University Press, 1970.

Keats, John. "Ode on a Grecian Urn." In *The Poetical Works of John Keats.* H. Buxton Forman, ed. London: Oxford University Press, 1937.

Ortega y Gasset, José. *Some Lessons in Metaphysics.* Mildred Adams, trans. New York: Norton, 1969.

Stevens, Wallace. "Man Carrying Thing." In *The Collected Poems of Wallace Stevens.* New York: Knopf, 1954.

Tillich, Paul. *The Eternal Now.* New York: Scribner's Sons, 1963.

Form's Future

Negative Capability, Apprenticeship, and the Poetic Line

Form is never more than a *revelation* of content.
—Denise Levertov

In several interviews from his prose collection *Halflife,* Charles Wright strongly advocates a formal apprenticeship for poets and cites his own with Donald Justice for what it taught him about chiseling a line. Wright reminds us that "most of the great masters of the free verse line came to it through writing formal meters" (164), and examples from his generation and the one preceding are numerous—James Wright, Sylvia Plath, and W.S. Merwin figuring as most obvious; in each is a sense of the free verse line as something weighted and memorable, something finely made. Charles Wright's advocacy of metrical training, of the way it manipulates formal attention, is rooted in his belief that it is preferable to focus on the line as opposed to the line-break, not because line-breaks are unimportant—quite the opposite—but because an emphasis on the line, each with its beginning, middle, and end, naturally encourages among other things line-breaks that are artfully deployed. "In fixed meters you have a built-in check against the excesses of [line-breaks]," he says. "In free verse, such checks exist only in the integrity of the writer's ear" (4–5).

Such a strong case for metrical practice may seem surprising from a man whose dedication to free verse is at the core of his aesthetic. "I feel about free verse the way Frank Stella feels about abstract art," he states. "My life is dedicated to it" (154). In fact the very restraint that makes formal writing so useful pedagogically, the very consistency of "built-in checks" against arbitrary line-breaks, becomes the thing that makes fixed forms less alluring to Wright later on. Rather it becomes the absence of such checks that draws him in his mature work to free verse. "The form, the glue that holds the free verse lines and structures together, is always changing," Wright claims, "because I'm always trying to do something I don't quite know how to do, so, in a way, it's always a failure" (154).

While the specificity of what Keats meant by "negative capability" will remain a matter of considerable debate, we can see in Wright's sensibility, in his romancing of uncertainty and imaginative risk, qualities similar to those which Keats praised in Shakespeare in his famous letter to George and Tom Keats:

> at once it struck me, what quality went to form a Man of Achievement especially in Literature & which Shakespeare possessed so enormously—I mean *Negative Capability*, that is when man is capable of being in uncertainties, Mysteries, doubts, without any irritable reaching after fact & reason—(43)

Although the above definition generalizes itself to apply to "a Man of Achievement," not even an artist necessarily let alone a writer, the full context of the passage, with Keat's discussion of *King Lear* and the power of its art "making all disagreeables evaporate," potentially qualifies our sense of negative capability as merely a capacity to dwell with irrationality and doubt. In the case of *Lear,* what is mitigated by art is the uncertainty of the world within that art, an "unpleasantness without any momentous depth of speculation." In an aestheticized world, such as that found in *Lear,* where there may be no consoling speculation, no organizing perspective, there remains for Keats the possibility of redemption through beauty as that which "overcomes every other consideration." However much Wright's self-doubt becomes tolerable by way of the aesthetic pleasure, it is equally true that the pursuit of beauty becomes ideally its own source of uncertainty. If beauty redeems, it likewise makes problematic. "Always a failure," says Wright of his own creative process—no match for Lear's despair, granted, and yet an anxiety for any artist, and one that only deepens Wright's compulsion toward beauty as something ever changing, defiant of reason or controlling point of view. "Always a failure," and yet he writes on, propelled by a simultaneous sense of failure and excitement, by an uneasy conception of ideal artistry as something necessarily blind, necessarily precise.

Wright's identification of free verse with the spirit of inquiry and spontaneity finds its complementary contrast in the image of formal verse as preferring the relatively known. Such associations are common: free-verse questions; form knows. Formal similitude provides the obvious metaphor for (and embodiment of) a stabilizing point of view. Rhyme especially, with its possibilities of cinching wit and mnemonic power, has historically lent itself to conclusive forms such as the aphorism and political slogan, didactic flourishes unabashed in their self-assertion: "a stitch in time, saves nine," we say, as if language and the imagined experience inside had been tied into a reliable knot.

On the other hand, the very phrase *free verse* (or, as Wright prefers, the Eliotic phrase *freed verse)* resembles *negative capability* insofar as it defines itself by what it is not. If meter or rhyme do not give birth to form, whatever forces of music, voice, and meaning conspire to delight by way of the line remain open. The free verse poet proceeds by way of a faith (and its complement, doubt) that some spontaneous determinate of form (however unconscious), some quickened sense of a poem's formal needs, will spring from and shape the poem's body, making possible something both precise and elusive, enriched with unexpected correspondences and music. Wright's particular sense of uncertainty suggests not only an impulse to make free verse exact, informed by necessities, but also a skepticism as to whether he can ever fully know what those necessities are—at least such doubt is paradoxically ideal. Thus the artfulness Wright desires shuns overly determined gimmickry, too consciously achieved to charm or unnerve, to arouse the interpretive imagination and so invite rereading.

Theories of organic verse may do little to appease a free-verse poet's formal uncertainties and the idealistic longing for precision. For one thing, such theories deploy the very form/content distinction that they would call into question. When Coleridge first put forward the notion of organic form as a way of defending Shakespeare's metrical irregularities as something other than lawless, he did so with a characteristic Romantic privileging of inwardness as a law both symbolic and exemplary of living nature—as if each poem might have an interior that determines and authenticates its exterior: "The organic form . . ." he claims, "is innate; it shapes as it develops itself from within, and the fullness of its development is one and the same with the perfection of its outward form" (500).

In arguing for the primacy of clandestine law, of inward force or spirit shaping outward flesh, achieving a sacramental "perfection," the concept of organic form implies a secularized metaphysic, a belief in and valorization of the poem's buried life, its soul, coming to fruition in form. To say this buried life has its own evolving and inaccessible linguistic structure (as Lacan says about the unconscious) is likewise a gesture of faith and does little to account for the birth of new meaning as one structure informs another. Nowhere does Coleridge's theory of organic form ever gesture toward the doubt that makes his faith possible and attractive, to the paradox of just how we know an inwardness to exist as determining (and thus distinguished from) the formal exterior that brings it to light.

Creeley's revisionary notion, as cited by Olson, that "FORM IS NEVER MORE THAN AN EXTENSION OF CONTENT," is no less metaphysically mysterious, since it places content first, as if originary, a spirit blown into the poem's body, bearing witness to itself in form (16). Once again what determines poetic form is, as far as our understanding goes, radically undetermined, inextricable from form and yet not identical with it. As practical and clarifying as Coleridge's and Creeley's theories of organic form may appear, as key as they have been historically to free verse pedagogy and credibility, they require a fair degree of metaphysical faith to accept, a belief in an indefinable inwardness as alpha and authenticator of form.

Denise Levertov's further revision of Creeley's formula is even more explicit in aligning itself with metaphysics and as such feels especially precise: "Form is never more than a *revelation* of content" (60). Far less mechanical and cognitive than Creeley's word "extension," the word "revelation" with its oracular resonance registers a sudden wonder at the creation of meaning. In Levertov's care to be precise, to be as phenomenologically descriptive as possible, never presuming the experience of a content preceding the forms of experience, the recalcitrant metaphor of some pre-formal phantom remains: to reveal is to unveil. The fact that such unveiling constitutes the instantaneous genesis of something individual and new only adds to the mystique of its paradox. Such theories of organic form, pointing as they do to some generative and eclipsed origin, have a mystifying power about them and so reinforce the link between free verse and an inquisitive spontaneity, each poem springing from its own individual mysteries, its own unconscious, its own god-within.

Doubtless the association between free verse and the spirit of inquiry and individualism owes much to the revolutionary rhetoric that characterizes early free verse theory and practice. Though neither Emerson nor Wordsworth were practitioners of free verse, they both prepared the theoretical ground—Emerson with his call for a "meter-making argument," Wordsworth with his advocacy of a poetic voice closer to common speech—and the Whitmanian free verse that grew from such seeds likewise became associated with spontaneity, individuality, and a liberal humanism challenging past constraint. Whitman's gestural and often explosive lines, the very figure of liberation and organic force, provided him a language for radical and fevered cultural progress, as if a vital principle of growth had been unleashed not only against a bloodless poetics of tidy measures but also against slavery, history worship, class stratification, and sexual repression. "The United States themselves are essentially the greatest poem," he writes in his 1855 preface to *Leaves of Grass.* "Here is action untied from strings" (711). Wedded to the idea of the modern and the political left, free verse grew up in the work of its primary English-speaking advocates as a voice of revision and expansion, an iconoclastic revitalizing of the cultural imagination.

Clearly such associations have shifted. In spite of a recent surge of formalist manifestoes and anthologies, free verse dominates most literary magazines today. Few contemporary poets are foolish or daring enough to see their works as the popularly influential cultural propellants that Whitman imagined; few share Whitman's optimism, grandiosity, and faith in free verse poetry's practical efficacy as a widely disseminated, politically transforming, and subversive cry. As the title of the recent neo-formalist anthology *Rebel Angels* suggests, some neo-formalists have made their bid for the status of underdog, and like Whitman in his century, many see themselves as moral populists, attempting to reach and celebrate a wider yet often neglected readership. While a great majority of poems spilling out of classrooms into literary journals are free verse, Dana Gioia's book *Can Poetry Matter,* so widely popular in the early 1990s, points out what remains the case today: that the characteristic favorite poems of people outside the academy tend to be formal. While the proliferation of formal writing has increased since the publication of *Rebel Angels* and *Can Poetry Matter,* the neo-formalist movement continues to serve as exemplary of a wider paradoxical and cultural phenomenon, surprisingly Romantic in origin and character. If the rebel status with which some neo-formalists identify figures as primary motivation, as well it might for any artist, as opposed to merely the consequence of an aesthetic, then the movement articulates a contradictory and highly American desire to be both populist and outsider, to be both assimilated into a mainstream yet defiant and remarkable within a community of specialists—to become, in short, an anti-elitist elite.

Aside from whatever political defiance it takes to be an outsider as formalist rebel—a label made precarious by our vastly different experiences with cultural norms—there is a practical way in which formal writing specifically makes demands on our negative capability, since the very formal contours that lend their stability in time may inspire an uneasy abandon in the working writer. Negative capability alludes most precisely to a writer's character and not the aesthetic object itself, which may, as in the case of Lear's pentameter, leaven mystery's burden with the pleasures of its music. When approaching a fixed form, one must open argument up to the unpredictable and so awaken perception to and by way of the disruptive limits of form.

Thus in addition to Wright's criteria for advocating a formal apprenticeship, we might make a case for a surprising sensation of liberty coupled with a breed of negative capability specific to formal process. The formal apprentice develops not only a heightened sense of the line but also a sense that it is the language in part which writes the poem. Poetry is thus experienced less as mere self-determination than as a participation in a medium that is both of the self and beyond it. How dull the prospect of self-expression when one can self-transform. Keats' theories on the unpoetical nature of the poet offer yet another definition of the capacity to "negate" models and instruments of control, to defy conventions of strict logic and impervious selfhood that inhibit a naturally transgressive, figurative mind: "What shocks the virtuous philosop[h]er, delights the camelion Poet. . . . A Poet is the most unpoetical of any thing in existence; because he has no Identity—he is continually in for—and filling some other Body—The Sun, the Moon, the Sea" (1818). Language itself constitutes yet another such body and so challenges the enervating, naive temptation to view poetry simply as self-reportage whose primary virtue is candor.

Whatever the poise embodied in fixed forms, writing them inspires characteristic anxiety, a fear of failure every bit as exacting as the one Wright describes. Donald Justice once told his students that there were only two successful villanelles in the language. Whether we agree or not, few would deny the extreme difficulty of writing good villanelles or sestinas. Only on the rarest of occasions do such forms fully succeed, and yet poets aware of the near impossibility of success continue to write them, or try, to court self-doubt as an unlikely source of pleasure, as thought's tease, enlarging desire, expanding its repertoire of charms.

Far from suppressing spontaneity and imaginative play, formal symmetries open up possibilities of musical surprise. As any good jazz musician knows, too much change is boring: in a world where anything can happen we're hardly surprised when anything does. It takes recurrence to raise an expectation and so then artfully to break it. Not only does rhyme tolerate difference; it requires it. A degree of rift and indeterminacy is its precondition.

Surprising many is how liberating the formal play of indeterminacy and fate can be, since the unresolved prospect of recurrence highlights issues of choice among alternatives and so strangely the sensation of will. Stravinsky knew this when he claimed that evolving limits in musical composition had the effect of freeing the mind, providing a stimulus to and language for the spontaneous. "All order demands restraint," he said. "But one would be wrong to regard that as any impediment to liberty" (Machlis, 159).

One might add that liberty *requires* restraint—an irony that characterizes all acts of choice, not merely aesthetic ones. To borrow a notion from Merleau-Ponty's essay "Cézanne's Doubt," just as the given and the made can never be neatly dissociated from one another, so it is with limit and liberation. Cézanne, according to Merleau-Ponty, required a sense that the world of objects was making strict formal demands on him—a perhaps surprising sense of objective subjugation for one often associated with impressionism's privileging of affective bias:

> It was the objects and the faces themselves as he saw them that demanded to be painted, and Cézanne simply expressed what they *wanted* to say. How, then, can any freedom be involved? . . . We can only see what we are by looking ahead of ourselves, through the lens of our aims, and so our life always has the form of a project or of a choice and therefore seems spontaneous . . . can a choice exist where there is as yet no clearly articulated field of possibilities, only one probability and, as it were, only one temptation?
>
> (21)

No freedom exists without constraints, be they aesthetic or otherwise, since constraints are needed to articulate, what Merleau-Ponty calls, our "field of possibilities" (21). Nor can any limit ever suppress the imaginative will, the need to "look ahead of ourselves" in order to "see" ourselves and in so doing remake both the self and the world that shapes it. We cannot choose not to choose.

While one might conceive of a poet's apprenticeship as Wright did, as a time for exploring the license and difficulty of traditional forms, even after their formal beginnings writers discover that a key part of the creative process is reinventing that process, creating new freedoms, new limits—which is why the most experienced may find it useful to alternate between free and formal verse in order to provoke some vital uncertainty. The original gang of French surrealists embodied a similar spirit in the way they sprang their own quirky and individually determined formal (albeit unmetrical) assignments on one another from time to time as a way of loosening conscious control. Whatever our approach, our chosen fields of possibility however articulated are inexhaustible. The infinities of free verse are no greater than those of formal writing. Even if one thinks of forms of fixed length, even if our range of remembered diction is fixed, there remains for the formalist numberless meaningful possibilities, given the fact that language opens itself up continually to neologism and connotative shift. And poems can be some of the most powerful agents of that shift, no less vibrantly imaginative given the power which we concede to formal fate, no less transfigurative and disturbing, flirting with failure, blazing a path into some possible, necessary, uncreated place, into silence ahead which, as faith would have it, gives way to a spontaneous music startled into measures.

Works Cited

Coleridge, Samuel Taylor. "Shakespearian Criticism." In *English Romantic Writers.* David Perkins, ed. New York: Harcourt Brace, 1967.

Gioia, Dana. *Can Poetry Matter?* St. Paul, MN: Graywolf, 1992.

Keats, John. *Letters of John Keats.* Robert Gittings, ed. New York: Oxford University Press, 1982.

Levertov, Denise. "An Admonition." In *The Poet in the World.* New York: New Directions, 1973.

Machlis, Joseph. *Introduction to Contemporary Music.* New York: Norton, 1961.

Merleau-Ponty, Maurice. *Sense and Non-Sense.* Evanston, IL: Northwestern University Press, 1964.

Olson, Charles. *Selected Writings.* New York: New Directions, 1966.

Whitman, Walt. *Leaves of Grass.* Sculley Bradley, ed. New York: Norton, 1973.

Wright, Charles. *Halflife.* Ann Arbor: University of Michigan Press, 1988.

The Wind in the Fire

Sentimentality and the Movement of the Mind

Although sentimentality suggests to many a failure of taste—a lapse that compromises an artist's credibility—a general uncertainty clouds the critical conversation in terms of what precisely sentimentality is; the extent to which it is, as an offspring of taste, too relative to be targeted; and how, if we agree upon its presence as a problem, one might avoid or transform it. The confusion is magnified by the fact that the word *sentimental,* in close association with the word *sentiment,* has had a less pejorative resonance for those who feel it is unfairly dismissed as the province of "the feminine." Novelist John Gardner, however, in his famous assessment of sentimentality as "false feeling," not only differentiates "sentiment" from "the sentimental," but points more emphatically to their incompatibility in literature. "Without sentiment," he declares, "fiction is worthless." This distinction helps tell us what sentimentality is not, yet still leaves us at a loss in terms of defining what sentimentality is. For this we need to investigate not just the psychology of sentimentality, but also its relationship to aesthetics.

Confusion over the nature of sentimentality comes in part from the ways we talk about it as being less acceptable in art than in personal character. Outside of art, it is not uncommon for folks to boast of being a little sentimental—about how unguarded they are in their loving attachments, and how objects or occasions become emblematic of endearment. Fetishism is endemic to the sentimentalist, just as it is to human nature, since the fetish provides one way for the self to deal with its undercurrent of angst, impotence, and dread. The transference of psychic energy onto things gives them (or rather the selfhood we invest there) an illusory sensation of dominion over time. The sentimental object, resistant to time, provides a means of dealing with the anxiety of attachment and subsequent loss.

Schiller's definition of the sentimental poet versus the naïve one is useful here in exploring the sense of loss connected to sentimentality, be it in character or art. According to Schiller, the naïve poet embodies nature and the sentimental one seeks it. In exile from nature, a sentimentalist feels a trace of melancholy, a longing for lost presence, just as the fetishist longs for the fetish, the possession to which one clings in light of all one lacks. If the fetish, as the bearer of ego energy, were successful in concretizing the self, fetishism would not have its compulsive character. Clearly the sentimentalist is trying but failing to resolve something by way of the fetish, repeating himself in denial of his own motives.

So it is with the sentimental artist and art. Insofar as we might focus upon sentimentality as a literary failing, the sentimental artist fetishizes both literal objects and people *as* objects. Sentimentality cherishes memorabilia, idols, places, and occasions in order to feel not just love, but the sense that love has been turned into an object. A trite phrase, much like a sentimental object, gives the sentimentalist a sense of comfort, of mastery over some greater difficulty that lies at the margin of awareness. The object empowers those who behold it, who stand outside it, attached and yet looking toward it from a certain distance. By way of the fetish or the cliché, the sentimentalist longs to freeze time and so gets stuck in redundant imaginative patterns. Such redundancy is a key to understanding both the fetish and the larger phenomenon of sentimentality. The authenticating imagination, by contrast, is both grounded and dynamic. The earth below it moves.

The Ungrounded Sentimentalist

Schiller's concept of the sentimental is less suggestive of literary failure than Gardner's, but in both there is an exploration of sentimentality as a form of disconnection, of feeling ungrounded, deceived, adrift from one's roots. For Gardner, those roots are narrative: the specifics of dramatic action, insofar as they authenticate feeling in a work of fiction, become the correlative to Schiller's "nature" as the ground and condition that make the world of fiction possible. In *The Art of Fiction* Gardner argues that for a feeling to be "true," it must be justified in relation to occasion and context:

> Sentimentality, in all its forms, is the attempt to get some effect without due cause. . . . Once it is dramatically established that a character is worthy of our sympathy and love, the storyteller has every right (even the obligation, some would say) to give sharp focus to our grief at the misfortunes of that character by means of powerful, appropriate rhetoric.

A counterfeit affect, on the other hand, does not grow organically from narrative events, from the "due cause" that would deepen the emotion and in turn our basis for sympathy. Feelings become false because we fail to believe their own terms for coming into being, if indeed such terms are even presented. As counterintuitive as it may seem to call a feeling "false," some feelings do spring from either a misrepresentation of the world or a failure to contextualize one's response to it. In either case, the sin of sentimentality is a sin of omission, or rather is best addressed if seen as such.

Elements of a popularly embraced form of sentimentality may favor leaving out all that is not wholesome or consoling, but such tunnel vision discredits an author who would claim a more responsible reckoning with the world and with the difficulties that bind us to it. The sentimentalist appears to value personal affections in their most unproblematic and self-flattering form. Sentimental indulgence, by sanitizing experience, flirts with moral pride. We see in its lens a commercial for love, rather than the world we love as it calls us to its disappointments, its contradictions, its responsibilities. Affect becomes affectation, and for this reason Carl Jung called sentimentality "the superstructure erected upon brutality." Given his diction, the leap Jung makes from sentimentality to brutality is sketchy and lacks some key distinction. For one thing, Jung does not differentiate between sentimentality as aesthetic form and as character flaw. Nevertheless his definition addresses a problem fundamental to writers who would deny the role the will to power plays in acts of representation. What Jung does not add is that genuine love may be both wedded to and positioned against that will. The image of the beloved may indeed be a constructed thing that unconsciously empowers the lover, and yet love by definition implies some sacrifice of mere self-interest.

Clearly pets, children, and old people appear so frequently in advertisements because they play upon the fundamental urge to reach out to those with less power. Few would doubt that a nurturing response to the powerless lays the foundation of charity. Likewise, few would doubt that the advertising world exploits our better nature to support various CEOs whose image we do not see. Whatever the commercial motive, we viewers might feel empowered relative to those who need us, especially since we do not confront in advertisements the difficulties of real presence: the stench of bedpans, the self-involvement of the child, the lizard corpse in the mouth of the kitten. Such realities challenge the ego's longing to attach itself to the beloved as if it were some vehicle such as celebrity, which would carry its energy without accountability or, beyond that, the recognition of its own hubris. When housed in the sentimental, the ego casts no shadow and can go about its business as if it had none. In such a world, moms are magnanimous, flags pristine, and all our cats declawed.

To his credit, John Gardner wisely advocates a dynamic solution that would make both characters and authors more accountable, but the indication of emotional origin may not be enough. When one excludes all but a tone of endearment, the rendering of emotion rings false—not necessarily because the feelings are false or we have no "due cause" for them, but because the focus is narrow. Some representations of genuine endearment may be equally sentimental. The inadequacy of "false feeling" as a definition of sentimentality points to a deeper failure, even more specific to the problem of art: a failure of imagination. For the writer, this implies a failure at the level not of feeling but of words. Or rather the source of the failure is better understood as verbal rather than psychological. One source of ambiguity here is that "feeling" can be seen as a phenomenon both inside and outside a literary expression of it. Obviously sentimental literature may, depending on the reader, fail in achieving a persuasively realistic and convincing affect. The source of this failure is not "feeling" as popularly understood, however. It is not that which precedes and engenders our verbal expression, but rather feeling as embodied in aesthetic form.

Lapses in rhetorical, conceptual, and imaginative energy may be invisible to the inexperienced in the way that an author's medium might to those naïve about the writer's craft. Much of the relativity of taste we may encounter regarding sentimentality concerns the degree to which we value the imagination in its power to be dynamic: to move, to enlighten, to surprise. To honor a writer's imagination is to honor his or her means; the musical, emotional, intellectual resources specific to that means; and how the imagination brings the far corners of one's nature into conversation. To avoid having sentimentality understood as an imaginative failure, more important than authenticity is an adequately complex and rendered *sense* of it, the impression of immediacy dependent upon aesthetic form. To understand sentimentality as a problem, we need to see it as symptomatic of one or both of two other problems: the phoniness of overvaluation and a relaxation into the authority of ready-made pathos. Both cases involve a sign of stasis—a passive sensibility in need of a quickening, a heart's curiosity, a mind's desire.

The Genuine in the Sentimental

To understand just how "false feeling" remains inadequate as a definition of the sentimental, imagine a young memoirist who describes the sadness she feels at the sight of kittens because one of her own recently died. All that might be perfectly true, even though the writer might have felt any number of other things that complicate the feeling of sadness. Telling this writer that what she is feeling is "false" would be odd indeed, as if she must disown such feelings not only as a writer but as a person. I would say that kittens are indeed incredible little miracles, and that I too find them generally adorable and believe, like millions of others, that animals deserve to be valued as amazing, and so I understand fully why people get attached to them. Nevertheless, the young memoirist's story lends itself to sentimentality, and if, by virtuosic insight into the narrative art, the story were to succeed, it would be because the writer brings far more than "due cause" to the narrative expression. Causal accountability may open the path to complication, but also some causes are, in reality, so readily familiar, so possibly banal, that going into detail articulates the obvious.

Although it is possible for feelings to be disproportionate to stated causes, people differ in their sense of due proportion in the same way that their tastes differ, which does nothing to discredit taste as a practical necessity. Still, if a writer's grievous associations with a dead kitten persist hourly for a decade, we enter the territory of a more widely shared sense of overvaluation that, if granted authority in a poem or story, might suggest a failure of both literary aesthetics and personal awareness. The redundancy of affect appears symptomatic, a mask of some deeper, unrepresented conflict. I would maintain that one has every right to grieve a dead kitten for a lifetime, but this grief gets harder to work into a story or poem as something the reader too is expected to feel. For the writer and reader alike, crucial to the depth of one's sympathy is the depth of one's insight.

Although Gardner casts sentimentality as a narrative problem, he adds in the context of his discussion a plea for "powerful, appropriate rhetoric." Such rhetoric implies a language calibrated according to subject and audience, but chances are the inexperienced writer has a differently developed sense of audience—and perhaps a readership less familiar with what constitutes an easy solution to an aesthetic problem. Literature, we know, is only as good as its imaginary reader, and a good reader is likely to respect the difference between emotion outside of art and emotion *in* art. Each suggests a different set of priorities, needs, and limitations—a different implicit contract with others. Few would deny that the experience of a father's death is not the same as that of reading or writing an elegy for the man. An elegy, if convincing, works precisely and attentively to honor the original experience, yet the terms of its intimacy are also those of aesthetic distance. A good poem or story does not simply mirror a painful situation, it transfigures it. By way of art's necessary illusion, pain becomes one more object among the objects in the room. Art backs away even as it steps into suffering, and in so doing it enables us to move a bit more freely in its midst: to see more and to know more, made vulnerable and safe in relation to the heartbreak of our forms.

Art Emotion

T. S. Eliot's much maligned claim in "Tradition and the Individual Talent" that the function of art is to escape the personality depends entirely—in the full context of that essay—upon the distinction between emotion as we commonly experience it and "art emotion." Unfortunately the temptation of an ad hominem approach to Eliot's work felt by many critics has promoted a received sense of his argument as reactionary, restrictive, reserved, cold:

> Poetry is not a turning loose of emotion, but an escape from emotion; it is not the expression of personality, but an escape from personality.

This sentence is famous in literary circles, but critics commonly overlook or ignore the logic that supports it—Eliot's rationale getting upstaged by his unfortunate hyperbole in the notion that one could escape a personality, as if a person were an inner space with distinct boundaries. More useful than Eliot's iconic statement is the example he gives of "structural emotion"—the great complexity of feeling that comes by way of art's architecture: its layering of contraries, its web of relations, its self-reflexive intensity and depth. "The poet has, not a 'personality' to express," he says, "but a particular medium." Personality, we might counter, is always mediated, and in art explicitly so. Nevertheless, Eliot makes a critical point here, one that initiates a category more useful to the artist than that of "false feeling." Art does not merely mirror what we know or what we have felt; it forges "a new art emotion." Thus, in his summons to the tradition Eliot advocates departure, a vision of art as bold, saturated in affect, bristling with ideas.

No doubt Eliot's exaggerations about escaping emotion constitute a rhetorical ploy designed to wake a general readership.

The intimacy between our stories and our lives has always been familiar enough, more so than the necessary tension between them. Much of this tension comes from the often unacknowledged pleasure we may take in form, in spite of and in light of a work's subject matter. Most unnerving perhaps is the pleasure we take in aesthetic depictions of the horrible, as we might find in Paul Celan's "Black Fugue" for example, a poem of tremendous lyric grace, strangeness, and emotional force. Form's beauty, however honorific and tasteful in its restraint, may seem exploitive to those in denial of art's paradoxical means of engagement. Ironically, the pleasure we take in form can heighten our grief by permitting us to tumble through the artifice, pulled by the current of surprise that animates character, rhetoric, drama, and all readers who value such things. Beauty, however revisionary our conception of it, provides the asbestos suit that allows us to go more deeply into the flames of conflict. This power of visionary strength and tolerance is precisely what Keats references when articulating his theory of negative capability. Beauty, for Keats, makes possible the power of a play such as *King Lear*: the language formally measures the burden of Lear's suffering so that we might consider it, weigh it, bear it.

While a pretty surface to the language might well characterize the sentimental, a more generous ideal of form as disciplined by necessity encourages greater emotional and conceptual range. Moreover, formal complexity and invention may come by way of a single gesture, the poetic image as what Pound called "an emotional and intellectual complex in an instant of time." William Carlos Williams, in the introduction to his book *The Wedge*, shares Pound's love of conceptual and emotional speed. Alluding to sentimentality as redundancy, he advocates for a defiantly unsentimental conception of a poem as a machine made of words:

> There is nothing sentimental about a machine, and: A poem is a small (or large) machine made of words. When I say there's nothing sentimental about a poem I mean that there can be no part, as in any other machine, that is redundant.

Williams does not argue against powerful feeling any more than do Eliot or Gardner. Rather, he shuns the sentimental view of art as unmediated feeling. For Williams the current of emotion and idea should be precise, dynamic, and alive, with each resonant gesture small on the page, large in the mind.

Williams' notion of sentimentality as redundancy becomes even more useful if we expand it beyond the connotations of formal efficiency. For instance, the sentimental rendering of kids and pets in commercials anticipates a broadly cultural or instinctual response, in the sense that it insists upon implicit and obvious associations. The sentimentalist relies too narrowly, too flatly, on the ready made. Sentimentality, defined as passive and familiar in its imaginative and conceptual energy, becomes the mirror image of sensationalism in that both opt for an easy, available vocabulary of feeling by pushing the buttons of emotion at the expense of thought. The word *kitten* may evoke an emotional valence that precedes the text surrounding it, yet numerous questions remain: What does an author do with that valence? Where does authority come from? Is authority imaginative, grounded, and therefore earned? Has the writer pressed the question of emotional authority in art, recognizing the difference between talking about feelings and creating them?

Opposition and Movement

The most obvious reach for many writers who wish to mitigate the sentimental is tonal opposition, but even though polarity trumps monotone, it can likewise become formulaic: where there is tenderness, add a little cruelty; where there are tears, add a joke. Obvious, tidy forms of opposition can create a new uninspired stability, a reincarnation of the sentimental in a slightly more evolved form. In some writers, you can hear the irony machine doing its predictable work, its steadily evasive dialectic that, like sentimentality, can feel manipulative. We sense in formulaic irony neither risk nor vulnerability, but rather an affectation. For this reason, the pursuit of imaginative movement, which will no doubt include tension, often yields better results than mere opposition as a means of authenticating a poem or story. One remedy for redundancy is difference; another is process, driven as it is by a complex machinery of differences.

Robert Lowell's poem "Skunk Hour" provides a useful example of the kind of dynamic instability that enlarges the scope of feeling and idea. Here, tonal complexity involves far more than the obvious friction of tonal registers between the words *kitten* and *skunk*. Rather, it springs from a vast interrelational process wherein the poem comments upon itself via reversals, contradictions, and surprises in point of view. Even as Lowell strikes a note of endearment with *kitten*, his elusive unfolding of emotion and idea suggests admiration, repulsion, self-pity, self-irony, identification, alienation, theatricality, heartbreak, and charm. Rather than straining to be symbolic, the details feel organic, their resonance the fruition of observation. In turn, the strongly individual character of feeling and its occasion contribute to a heightened immediacy as the foundation of our sympathies:

> I myself am hell;
> nobody's here—
>
> only skunks, that search
> in the moonlight for a bite to eat.
> They march on their soles up Main Street:
> white stripes, moonstruck eyes' red fire
> under the chalk-dry and spar spire
> of the Trinitarian Church.
>
> I stand on top
> of our back steps and breathe the rich air—
> a mother skunk with her column of kittens swills the garbage
> pail.
> She jabs her wedge-head in a cup
> of sour cream, drops her ostrich tail,
> and will not scare.
> (I. 35–48)

Through efficiency of detail as revelatory, the current of the poem keeps slipping forward, revising our sense of the skunks as both the speaker's mirror and his foil. The mother skunk's "ostrich tail," suggesting fear, leads swiftly to our recognition of her fearlessness, and the invocation of the ostrich's denial reflects back upon the speaker—whose rude awakening from the grandiosity of self-pity is by no means absolute. The poem does not close the door on the possibility that disempowerment empowers the man, makes his sense of alienation more pitiable, more extreme, even as the skunk enlarges our perspective to counter and contextualize the speaker's histrionics. The power relationships between skunk and speaker keep shifting and qualifying one another, making any one emotion difficult to isolate. Such poetry, in its resistance to paraphrase, raises its ambition from conveying emotional knowledge to producing it. Thus, the poem as a whole figures as a new term for a new feeling, or evolution of feeling, giving us a language to enlarge the awareness that inflects what we feel.

The ability of language to change feeling in the process of expressing it is the foundational insight of Freud's "talking cure." Feeling becomes a moving target for speech. In the spirit of Gardner's pragmatic clarity, however reductive, we might isolate three characteristics—as aspects of complexity—that authenticate the felt movement of the poem and so enlarge the scope of emotional insight. Those characteristics are particularity, strangeness, and resonance. Clearly more is at play in terms of making the poem's rhetoric compelling and beautiful in ways that draw us closer to the subject. In addition, pursuit of any one of the three (the particular, the strange, the resonant) can be carried to excess and create new problems, new forms of stagnation. Still, these three potential virtues, when understood as wedded to each other, help to clarify sentimentality's characteristic sins.

The Particular, the Strange, and the Resonant

The authenticating power of particularity is often a beginning matter of emphasis in writing instruction, with its advocacy of the concrete detail that pins us to a world. Particularity is also the virtue that, if excessively deployed, can most obviously exacerbate the sentimental. All three virtues are interdependent, but particularity is the one most in need of qualification for a writer. In Stanley Plumly's poetry, for instance, the essential power comes from an elemental physicality, but also from a certain strangeness and conceptual radiance to his details—which enable him to approach the sentimental without crossing over. In a poem entitled "Sonnet," for example, he moves briskly through the scene of his dying father, and this speed coupled with the naked strangeness of tears falling to the floor accommodates the pathos:

> My father would sit on the edge of the bed
> and let the tears fall to the floor,
> the sun the size of the window, full
> and rising. He was a dead man and he knew it.
> (I. 3–6)

The risk of overly familiar language and emotion in a poem about weeping is obvious enough, and yet a simultaneous closeness to and resistance of the sentimental can intensify the strangeness of Plumly's chosen image. These tears are nails that fix the poem to something local and uncanny (the familiar made odd, and more odd for being familiar), and the rhetoric here is swift and bare. Were we to linger on that moment, the whole poem would collapse—not into feeling but into an advertisement for feeling. Wisely the sentence does not cadence with overt pathos, but moves through it, as if to deflect pity. The poem arrows through the scene of weeping (and the nakedness of affect) to accentuate that vital and disturbing assertion of the sun, its rising in dialogue with the anguish of departure.

Tears frequent the sentimental moment. Their familiarity as signatures of sadness encourages us to see them less as physical immediacies and more as stand-ins for the abstract language of emotion. This fact does not exclude them from complications of affect, but rather makes them difficult to negotiate, to renew. Elizabeth Bishop, in her poem "The Man-Moth," similarly accommodates the act of weeping by way of speed, physicality, and a certain strangeness, all at the service of a larger accumulation of meaning and emotional depth. Bishop's intensity of aesthetic distance is more extreme, however, thanks to her metaphor that likens a tear to a "bee's sting"—a figure so striking we feel a jolt of wonder and wit, a surge of pleasure, a feeling of pulling back from grief even as we go more deeply into it:

If you catch him,
hold up a flashlight to his eye. It's all dark pupil,
an entire night itself, whose haired horizon tightens
as he stares back, and closes up the eye. Then from the lids
one tear, his only possession, like the bee's sting, slips.
Slyly he palms it, and if you're not paying attention
he'll swallow it. However, if you watch, he'll hand it over,
cool as from underground springs and pure enough to
  drink.
  (I. 41–48)

We do not need to know the cause of this tear to avoid its sentimentality. The fierce and quirky energy of the figure is enough. Knowledge of the rest of the poem—the man-moth's contemplation of the third rail, his attraction to the lunar hole in the sky, his solitary view of the world from the back of a train—informs our sense of the tear's resonance and power, but Bishop's metaphor is so strong that it provides a localized sense of transformative and dynamic imaginative authority. Metaphor, as its Greek background suggests, is conceived in movement: *metaphor*: borne across. When Bishop likens a tear to a "bee's sting," she carries "tear" into unexpected territory, not from pain to its obvious opposite, pleasure, but to its instigator (the tiny barb) and perhaps its relief (the bleeding away of its venom). So too we cross from fluid to solid, the clear to the opaque, emotional pain to physical pain.

In this metaphor's friction, we find what Robert Bly, in his book *Leaping Poetry*, calls a "tensive metaphor," where the associative movement leaps with great energy and surprise. Equally important to the unsentimental power of the figure is its depth, its wit, the physical and conceptual logic that make the association meaningful. If "heterogeneous particulars" are "yoked," their connection is achieved less "by violence," as Samuel Johnson once complained about John Donne, than by a combination of affinity and force. They are called into dynamic relation by a multiplicity of logics, including that of opposition. Speed is critical to this force, this wit. Change "sting" to "stinger," for instance, and much of the energy drains. The spell is broken.

Generosity

The fruit of wit, when it aspires to be more than merely clever, is resonance, which is to say, a depth charge of correspondences that becomes emotionally powerful in part because of the great wealth of simultaneous meaning. The resonant in language presumes semiotic speed, emotional stakes, and conceptual abundance. Language strikes, and the silence echoes. When Eliot says that a poet has not a personality to express but a medium, he shares with Pound the sense that great art is innovative in ways that are specific to that art. If literature is to lay its claim as necessary in an age dominated by visual media, it must continue to cultivate its strengths and do what no film or image can. One of those strengths is the word's unequaled capacity to encourage conceptualization by a reader—an internal action both caused by and the cause of committed, articulated, intellectual energy. This energy need not eclipse emotion. On the contrary, it can be the wind moving through the fire. Blake, who understood well the repressive potential of reason, also recognized the intellect as one of the fragments, the Zoas, that the imagination welcomes back into the visionary whole. The indulgence of the sentimental remains its being born of thought that is not hard enough won. Blind to the strengths of his or her medium, the sentimental writer would pit love against reason.

One pragmatic approach, then, to the problem of sentimentality makes the poem more generous with interpretive awareness. Such an approach sends the current of an idea through the moment of pathos, a little energy to light the place. As any literary writer knows, we can think too hard; we can become too conscious, too cold, too attached to the mastery of our cognition—none of which dismisses the intellect, but rather recommends Blake's sense of the imagination as the great conversation between our alienated parts. Intellect takes the watch of the world apart; love informs the care that puts it back together.

Sentimentality, which may pride itself on a generosity of spirit, is in fact cheap, offering little to transform us. Transformation requires language that is more than a vehicle of information. Literature, as an embodiment and creator of values, alters both word and world. We think with our hearts, feel with our brains. This activity, unsentimental at its root, happens constantly whether we recognize it or not. Imagination would intensify such activity and validate it as one way we enlarge our sympathies, wedded as they are to something more magnanimous, more fierce, and less passive than the ready made. Imagination's vocabulary longs to be intimate with the spontaneous novelty of being, to illuminate in speech if only to deepen our sense of the unspeakable. The care of our attention, woven into the genetic code of language, is bound to what is native to the word: its future tense, its intellect, its reach, its insatiable hunger to move and then—and only then—to move us.

Works Cited

Bishop, Elizabeth. *The Complete Poems: 1927–1979.* New York: Farrar, Straus, and Giroux, 1983.

Eliot, T. S. *Selected Essays.* New York: Harcourt, Brace, 1932.

Gardner, John. *The Art of Fiction.* New York: Vintage, 1983.

Jung, Carl. "'Ulysses': A Monologue." In *The Spirit in Man, Art, and Literature.* New York: Pantheon, 1966.

Lowell, Robert. *Selected Poems.* New York: Farrar, Straus, and Giroux, 1976.

Plumly, Stanley. *Now That My Father Lies Down Beside Me: New and Selected Poems, 1970–2000.* New York: Ecco, 2000.

Pound, Ezra. *Literary Essays of Ezra Pound.* New York: New Directions, 1968.

Schiller, Friedrich. "Naïve and Sentimental Poetry." In *Two Essays: Naïve and Sentimental Poetry & On the Sublime.* New York: Frederick Unger, 1979.

Williams, William Carlos. *The Collected Later Poems of William Carlos Williams.* New York: New Directions, 1967.

III.

Eros and Its Discontents

The Double Fall of Madame I

In 1905 the French neurologists Deny and Camus published their bewildering case study of a woman, known from then on in medical circles as Madame I, whose rather exotic difficulties underscore the genuine dangers of losing touch with one's free will and the body it inhabits. Given her own speculations, it seems her problems stemmed from a past of abusive relationships, which sent long-delayed aftershocks of sudden weeping into her adult years. But in spite of her husband's violent tendencies, she remained married even as her depression deepened, giving way to the brief episodes of amnesia and aimless wandering, her suicide attempts, the day she stripped naked in the middle of the street and stood there, expectant and confused.

Then it passed, quietly, irrevocably—her wandering ceased; the tears subsided—and she slipped into a kind of wakeful coma, though tinged with fear—a condition she herself called a "general insensibility." Though by all objective measures her nerves could register touch, taste, and sound, she felt increasingly estranged from these sensations. With a passionless awareness she told her doctors:

> I can no longer feel my arms, my legs, my head, and my hair. I have to touch myself constantly in order to know how I am. I have the feeling that my entire body is changed, even at times that it no longer exists. I touch an object, but it is not I who am touching it.
>
> (Rosenfield, 39)

And as she spoke, she compulsively pulled at her hair or scratched her head. Her clothes hung partially unbuttoned so she could rub the naked skin on her belly and chest, as if to reaffirm the knowledge she feared and desired most, that she was indeed still there, inextricably bound to her body and her past.

At night too she kept vanishing and reappearing under her own hands. "I don't know how I lie in my bed," she claimed. "I am always looking for my body and my legs, and in the morning I ask myself what happened during the night." In time she lost her appetite. When her husband and children came to visit at the hospital, they seemed distant, drained of presence. "They don't appear to be as real as they once were," she said. "I recognize them, but seeing them doesn't give me any pleasure" (40).

And so Madame I came to experience herself fundamentally as an absence, or more precisely as a trace, as something continuously lost or deferred. Seeking in the flesh some force of self-presence, she became stuck in something of an infantile mirror-stage, ever reattaching herself to her body, reconfronting one of a child's most alluring and horrific fantasies, the fear of psycho-physical disintegration. Not surprisingly, her personal history likewise grew chaotic and vague in her mind. She had increasing difficulty representing to herself her parents, her house, and people she knew well, as if some unbearable past in her longed to undo itself by undoing the historical mind.

In spite of the fact that life, as she claimed, was empty, Madame I kept speaking to her doctors—how better to be persuaded of one's identity—though her words seemed like a stranger's to her, like so many hands over a continuously dissolving body. "When I talk," she said, "I no longer hear the sound of my own voice . . . it is as if I were dead." And when she closed her mouth, she imagined she would never find her tongue again, because, as she claimed, she thought it had slipped whole into her throat.

If we are to believe there is a conservation of desire in the body, that it can never be extinguished, only displaced, it remains difficult to account for what became of hers, not just to what we might narrowly define as lust, with its object in genital fulfillment, but more fundamentally to her eros, what impels a self toward union with otherness. In spite of the fact that she claimed she did not love herself, she constituted for herself a version of otherness, eroticized to the extent that in touching her skin she touched the margins of some unreachable person, though with none of the pleasure and romancing of ambiguity, none of the mutual empowerment associated with erotic play. In fact it was her very self-hatred and craving for certainty, her very failure to feel joy that so tragically focused her narcissistic attentions. Not only her compulsive self-stimulation but also her exhibitionist trances provided her with ways of experiencing herself as an object, available to the world's senses, taking its place before some idealized, imaginary perceiver. Her body at its intimate distance was forever too foreign to be empowering, too immanent to be transcended.

In short Madame I was twice fallen. First she fell in the way that we all do, away from being and into language and selfhood. Such is the fall from that time when, having so eluded our conscious memory, we are free to conceive in retrospect as a paradise of continuity with otherness. Although clearly no conceptualizing of otherness or continuity could take place before the birth of selfhood and language, we can look back at our infant lives and imagine there a bliss of connectedness to being, to our mothers and whatever it is that feeds us. As if we held some shadow of the ideal in bodily memory, be it genetic memory or the imprint of precognitive experience, we may make an Eden of our flotation in the womb and even of early infancy, though it remains a mystery as to just when language and self-conception emerge in a child. What is clear is that the dream of our once unmediated participation in being has a troubling allure, all the more energized by the terror of it, by its demand that we sacrifice our very selfhood to reenter a state of grace. If paradise is a time when we tapped into the world by a spiritual umbilical cord, the first fall then marks the severing of that cord and the dawning awareness of our solitude.

Language, as both product and producer of desire, both barrier and bridge to the signified world, is likewise both what casts us out of the garden and what redeems us. Ever too abstract to accommodate the particulars of experience, too particular to embrace being as a totality, it is incessantly propelled by a sense of its own failure, throwing us forward into our lives, pursuing the many fragments of the ideal. In her poem "T" from the sequence entitled "Spellbound: An Alphabet," Maurya Simon writes of just such a pursuit in response to our fall into language and estrangement. Here God, as she puts it:

. . . blew a sigh of purity
into each human mouth

so that the tremor
of the sound

reverberated within them,
and God wept to see

how earnestly his children
on earth strained to hear

what they could never hear,
and to know that even

the green labyrinths of forests,
the great flowerings of clouds,

the deepest gardens of ocean
could not retain the sound,

but only echo and mimic it,
and God saw what he had done

and shook his head and
faded infinitesimally

into each person's heart,
upon each person's tongue.
(Simon, 42)

Much of the force of the poem's closure lies in how God retreats not upward into an incorporeal heaven but down into the intimate sensuality of tongues and the words that fade there. In much the same way that Madame I experiences herself, we experience God as an absence, as a vanishing and wake of wanting that binds us to the idea of him. As God retreats into the human body and word, the immanence that most defines us likewise escapes us. Interiority thus becomes an infinite space. Where some distant precipice once lured the likes of Wordsworth, in Simon's poem language and the flesh lure the imagination as thresholds of the sublime, all the more unnerving and inscrutable for their nearness.

The first fall then, as it eroticizes the world, likewise eroticizes the self, all eroticism being in some measure a form of autoeroticism. The luminous and disconcerting potential of the erotic lies in how it complicates our view of personal identity, in how the self, while providing the reference point for our aloneness, appears ever tinged with otherness—defined as we are by our investments—and likewise otherness ever faintly reflective of the self—what we see being inextricable from how we see it. This too is the transformative power of aesthetic experience, both for artist and art lover—to expand our range of feeling by reshaping the self in the medium of what it loves, to "throw" the self into the world mirror, we might say, though the metaphor breaks down. In fact it is through the act of throwing that the self is perpetually born and open to change. Perhaps "cast" is a better word, conflating as it does the senses of our simultaneous reaching outward and taking shape.

The paradox of erotic and aesthetic experience lies in how they thrive on both our amorous "castings" and the inviolate solitude no desire can overcome. Thus they heighten the tension between our essentially isolate and relational natures. In those peak moments of aesthetic and erotic pleasure, in the midst of some ecstatic departure, part of the intensity of the feeling lies in the fierce privacy of it. It is as if we were about to explode, or, to adapt a notion from James Wright, as if at any moment we might "break/ into blossom."

In Madame I, we see the horrific magnification of characteristics that, for an artist, might serve as both strengths and liabilities—that is, the autoerotic tendencies, the awareness of precarious selfhood, the resulting compulsion toward self-redefinition. But for her the current of libidinal energy that drives the imagination was short-circuited. When Madame I touched herself, the poles of self and other were too close, too narrowly narcissistic to provide any spark. She did not feel herself ecstatically thrown with any aesthetic or erotic force, nor did she feel herself changed by the expression of her desires. As she lost the ability to take pleasure in ambiguity and reach out imaginatively into the experience of others, as even her own children seemed unreal to her, she likewise lost her powers of self-transformation.

Clearly the force of erotic interpenetration is strongest when the beloved looks back as both chosen object and free subject. Like two mirrors gazing at one another, lovers at their most intense rush outward into themselves. They do not so much complete each other as blow deep openings in one another. No such openings exist in pornographic desire. The difference between erotic and pornographic relations lies primarily in the degree to which the desired is free to choose, both to desire and be desired, thus making the amorous gaze into something unstable and reciprocal, animated by the risks of mutual empowerment. Since in order to be chosen, one must first give the power of choosing away, erotic relations, as self-serving as they are, demand some measure of generosity. Erotic passion thus provides the libidinal grounding for an ethical passion. The same paradox of empowerment through disempowerment governs each, the principle that in order to gain a soul, one first must lose it.

A similar kind of empowerment takes place during acts of aesthetic creation as well. The empty page asks a writer to let go, to risk failure, grief, or embarrassment, and so to romance chance and the unconscious, to let the words to speak themselves. Since a writer's negative capability implies a willingness to be chosen by the unpredictable, writing a poem becomes as much a matter of listening as speaking, more of a dialogue with silence than a monologue designed to overpower it.

Of course one must first have a "positive capability" in order to develop a negative one. As Madame I's story so tragically demonstrates, there are obvious hazards in conceding too much to otherness, in failing to be self-determined enough. Through her role as victim, she became increasingly passive, something of a pornographic object, even to herself, and thus further estranged from her free will and core of subjectivity. Having been so burned by the world, in time she refused to venture emotionally into it. What better way to protect oneself from abuse than to cease to exist for it. In falling out of love with the world, she fell in turn from her own body, the place where all worldly relations begin. This was her second fall, the fall from the flesh and its erotic potential.

Another way of describing Madame I's condition is to say that in falling from her body she fell in turn from the body of the world, the one being inseparable from the other. The philosopher Merleau-Ponty was fond of reconceiving of our flesh in just this way, as something not confined within one's skin but as necessarily relational—as available to our experience only insofar as it is entwined in what it senses. It is only through the act of perception that the body becomes realized as a body for us, free to constitute an object to itself. In his essay "Eye and Mind," he writes:

> The enigma is that my body simultaneously sees and is seen. That which looks at all things can also look at itself and recognize, in what it sees, the "other side" of its power of looking. It sees itself seeing, it touches itself touching; it is visible and sensitive for itself. It is not a self through transparence, like thought, which only thinks its object by assimilating it, by constituting it, by transforming it into thought. It is a self through confusion, narcissism, through inherence of the one who sees in that which he sees, and through inherence of sensing in the sensed—a self, therefore, that is caught up in things, that has a front and a back, a past and a future.
> (162–163)

Merleau-Ponty then goes on to make great claims for the power of artists to lend their bodies to the world and so dwell within things. Whereas science manipulates things and gives up living in them, art—and in particular, painting—humanizes the world by casting the self into some palpable medium. The bodily imagination is primary for Merleau-Ponty since it restores phenomena to the freshness of their infancy, to their immanent emergence as sensation and likewise our identity's emergence through its reflection in what we sense.

This mutual inhabitation of self and other, the combined positive and negative capability that Madame I so tragically lacked and that makes for the artist's erotic disposition toward the world, complicates the whole notion of aesthetic freedom. The freedom of the artist is not the freedom of pure self-determination, but rather the free, erotic exchange between the self that chooses and those forces of chance and the unconscious that choose it. It is the freedom not to complete oneself but to open oneself, to inhabit the things that inhabit us.

It becomes an absurdity therefore to talk of censored art since insofar as art is censored it ceases to be art. The essentially erotic power of aesthetic experience does not lie so much in the sexual explicitness of a given work as in the liberty that may or may not express itself in such explicitness. Clearly the root of Madame I's problems goes far deeper than a lack of art in her life, her difficulties standing as a sad commentary on an all too characteristic assault on female subjectivity, though it remains highly possible that a deepened aesthetic involvement on her part might have helped to reawaken her emotional and imaginative investment in the world.

And so the "curse" of the first fall, the very eros so often perceived as transgressive, is what potentially saves us from the second. By repeatedly casting us into the world, by driving our language, imagination, and thus the terms of our intimacies, it testifies to the fact that, so long as we are erotic creatures, our estrangement cannot be absolute. In response to the severing of our spiritual umbilical cord, eros binds us by a scar tissue made of grief and expectation. The eros of our fallen state becomes what is sacred in us, not only because it contains the seeds of an ethics but also because it opens the world to play as the fullest expression of our humanness. Only once we have fallen into desire can we enjoy the imagination's compensatory freedom of movement; only then, to borrow a line from George Herbert, "Then shall the fall further the flight in me."

Works Cited

Merleau-Ponty, Maurice. *The Primacy of Perception.* Chicago, IL: Northwestern University Press, 1964.

Rosenfield, Israel. *The Strange, Familiar, and Forgotten.* New York: Knopf, 1992.

Simon, Maurya. *Speaking in Tongues.* Salt Lake City, UT: Peregrine Smith, 1990.

An Abundance of Lack

The Fullness of Desire in the Poetry of Robert Hass

> Often enough, when a thing is seen clearly, there is a sense of absence about it—it is true of impressionist painting—as if, the more palpable it is, the more some immense subterranean displacement seems to be working in it; as if at the point of truest observation the visible and the invisible exerted enormous counterpressure.
>
> —Robert Hass (*Twentieth Century Pleasures,* 274, 275)

The word "clarity" is often unclear. If by "clear" we mean "under the clarifying light of reason," placed with quieting control in a world promoted as stable, without contradiction, then Robert Hass's poetry is repeatedly unclear. But if by "clear" we mean "lit by an immanent light," creating a persuasive model of consciousness in all its disjunctions, wonder and loss, paradox and uncertainty, then Hass's poetry has a clarity that puts its language under immense pressure. Through Hass's clarifying lens, we see words as gestures of longing rather than vestiges of truth, as motivated by a sense of their own failure, a sense of lack that no discourse can finally fill. As though always on the threshold of saying what it cannot, Hass's language is both haunted and invigorated by an "immense subterranean" absence, an absence that we imagine nevertheless as a kind of presence, a "counterpressure" akin to a displaced unconscious. If his view toward language as both the product and producer of desire, as driven by a sense of lack at the core of its being, appears strikingly Lacanian, it may come as small surprise that Hass recalls, in his essay on Robert Creeley, the arrival of Jacques Lacan's *Ecrits* on the

Anglo-American shore as revolutionary, full of both astonishing and troubling notions that struck the contemporary nerve (TCP 152). The distinguishing generosity of Hass's work lies in how he turns the everpresence of lack, both as reflected and created by language, into not only a testament of loss, but also an occasion for praise—that which endears the ephemera of our lives. By way of language, absence eroticizes the world.

Despite how we may feel troubled in Hass's poetry by what language cannot accommodate, his is not the austere, archetypal, syntactically pared-down universe we often find in so-called poetry of silence—much of W. S. Merwin's verse, for instance. Hass's world is abundant, expansive, richly textured with unexpected detail, philosophical and intimate, unmistakably anchored in daily life yet appealing to our [Just] for wonder, astonishing us with, what Hass calls in his description of Yosa Buson's poetry, "the fullness and emptiness of things" (TCP 308).

Thus language in its failure to tell the whole truth appears in Hass's poetry as nevertheless redemptive, since such failure animates the imagination and inspires its continual revisions. In Hass's later work, we feel the imaginative urge to renew, set loose with particular abandon and an especially disjunctive logic. But although desire may cause disjunctions in consciousness, bringing to mind always the next needful thing, there are complicating moments in Hass's verse where desire appears briefly, paradoxically, as a connecting medium, a bridge made of the distance to be bridged. It joins what cannot logically be joined: self and other, past and present, word and the signified world.

Hass's view of words as gestures of longing, as both empty and full, animated by loss, is perhaps most familiar to his readers by way of his second collection of poems, *Praise*—in particular, the much anthologized poem "Meditation at Lagunitas" with its potently aphoristic claims that yield to an affectionately particularizing language, language that, as Hass makes explicit, can never be particular enough to bridge the gap between word and world:

> All the new thinking is about loss.
> In this it resembles all the old thinking.
> The idea, for example, that each particular erases
> the luminous clarity of a general idea. That the clown

faced woodpecker probing the dead sculpted trunk
of that black birch is, by his presence,
some tragic falling off from a first world
of undivided light. Or the other notion that,
because there is in this world no one thing
to which the bramble of *blackberry* corresponds,
a word is elegy to what it signifies.
(4)

The word's longing to cross that impermeable Saussurian bar, to embrace the signified world on the other side, resembles a desire to retrieve a lost past, as though that past harbored an original unity of self and other—a paradise lost, "a first world of undivided light."

The paradox of desire characterizes the paradox of language in that each presupposes a distance between opposites—self and other, past and present, signifier and signified—while creating the very basis for their intimacy. In the life of words, a greeting is always a farewell, an elegy. As Lacan claims, "the being of language is the non-being of objects" ("The direction of the treatment . . . ," Ecrits 263). And this non-being strangely discloses itself as a presence, a yearning, the very conveyance of the abundance of the world:

Longing, we say, because desire is full
of endless distances. I must have been the same to her.
But I remember so much, the way her hands dismantled
bread,
the thing her father said that hurt her, what
she dreamed. There are moments when the body is as
numinous
as words, days that are the good flesh continuing.
Such tenderness, those afternoons and evenings,
saying *blackberry, blackberry, blackberry.*
(4–5)

Desire is full, freighted with the stuff of memory, that which seems both immanent and distant. In reciting a text of remembered things, we are thus made up of a world we lack.

The phrase "numinous as words" recalls the Latin word *nu-*

men ("the spiritual"). Since the numinous world is by definition contradistinguished from the physical, to call the body "numinous as words" is to blur the very concept of numinosity, to confuse so-called inner and outer domains. Such "cross breeding" is in keeping with a typically Romantic conception of the imagination, that which invests the world with consciousness and consciousness with the world. By way of the image as the point of fusion, the word is made flesh. In his essay "Images," Hass writes, "that confusion of art and life, inner and outer, is the very territory of the image; it is what an image is. And the word was made flesh and dwelt among us" (TCP 304). Bound up inextricably in its lost presence, the word *blackberry* is itself sweet and palpable.

The notion of the body as numinous derives the power to astonish from its illogic—the fact that Hass in one stroke asserts and denies a distinction. Even the most intimate relation between inner and outer, present and past, self and nature, signifier and signified presupposes a distance—a difference. And it is this difference that drives the imagination forward. In his essay "One Body: Some Notes on Form," Hass claims that he doesn't share Wordsworth's belief that a childlike alliance with nature represents "the first I Poetic spirit of our human life." According to Hass, the urge to create grows rather out of a broken alliance. Hass states, "1 have none of [Wordsworth's] assurance, either about the sources of the order of nature or about the absolute continuity between that first nurturing and the form-making activity of the mind. It seems to me, rather, that we make our forms because there is no absolute continuity, because those first assurances are broken. The mind, in the act of recovery, creates" (TCP 63).

"Meditation at Lagunitas" pays tribute to memory as such an act, a creative and affectionate response to a fall from the first world of undivided light. Hass's poem "Natural Theology" from his third collection of poems, *Human Wishes*, offers a similar tribute, though exploring in more detail the evolutionary pattern of a consciousness:

> White daisies against the burnt orange of the windowframe,
> lusterless redwood in the nickel gray of winter,
> in the distance turbulence of water—the green regions

> of the morning reflect whatever can be gained, normally,
> by light, then give way to the blue regions of the afternoon
> which do not reflect so much as they remember, as if the light,
> one will all morning, yielded to a doubleness in things—
> (71)

In this first world, "the green regions / of the morning," the images, with their precision of coloristic detail, appear designed to dazzle us, not with their symbolic weight, but with their mere presence, their visual sweets. They have a primary potency to them. In his essay "Images," Hass explains:

> It seems to me that we all live our lives in the light of primary acts of imagination, images or sets of images that get us up in the morning and move us about our days. I do not think anybody can live without one, for very long, without suffering intensely from deadness or futility.
> (TCP 303)

In "Natural Theology," Hass's way of describing the mode of this world's first appearance works to circumvent the perceiver/perceived distinction associated with "the second world," the world of language and the broken alliances that language presupposes. Not a perceiver, but the green regions themselves "reflect," and the degree to which this reflection implies transformation in the process of emergence is ambiguous. The regions, according to Hass, simply "reflect whatever can be gained, normally, by light." What is clear is that, as time passes, this light and its green regions yield to an increasingly associative consciousness. Once again, Hass's essay enlarges our reading of the poem:

> I think that, for most of us, those images are not only essential but dangerous because no one of them feels like the whole truth and they do not last. Either they die or themselves, dry up, are shed; or, if we are lucky, they are invisibly transformed into the next needful thing. (TCP 303)

Secondary acts of the imagination, being more transformative, are more obviously metaphorical, and thus we find ourselves more obviously in the realm of language. Although Hass does not explicitly associate the "green regions" with infantile experience, such a world resembles the imaginary order that Lacan claims precedes a child's "mirror stage." The mirror stage marks not only the advent of language, but also the emergence of selfhood, made precarious since images of the self are always "out there," mirrored back from the world. In Lacan's words, the "I" "is objectified in the dialectic of identification with the other" ("The Mirror Stage," Ecrits 2). Bass's poem dramatizes a similar mirror stage, a point at which the dynamics of memory make possible the perception of similitude and difference and thus the tension between the two as language. With an associative consciousness, identification becomes possible, and the narcissistic imagination perceives a mirroring sheen on the surface of the other:

> images not quite left behind rising as an undertow
> of endless transformation against the blurring world
> outside the window where, after the morning clarities,
> the faint reflection of a face appears; among the images
> a road, repetitively, with meadow rue and yarrow
> whitening its edges, and pines shadowing the cranberry
>   brush,
> and the fluting of one bird where the road curves and
>   disappears,
> becoming that gap or lack which is the oldest imagination
> of need, defined more sharply by the silver-gray region
> just before the sun goes down . . .
>   (71)

Though one's literally reflected physical bearing provides a metaphor for the self as discrete, that independence is threatened by the otherness of the reflective surface. In Hass's poem, we feel the dissonance implicit in the emergence of selfhood as the reflected face floats tentatively over a restless flux of images.

Like the self, the other too is characterized by lack—in Hass's poem, that place out there where the road curves and disappears. As Lacan states in his typically elliptical style, "the subject has to find the constituting structure of his desire in the same gap opened up by the effect of the signifiers in those who come to represent the Other for him, insofar as his demand is subject to them" (264). For Lacan, demand includes more than mere physical need. That margin of demand that stretches beyond need is what he calls desire, and desire is infinite. Those who are subject to one's desire are always perceived as lacking.

The bird at the threshold of lack—what Hass calls "the oldest imagination of need"—invites a cultural memory of birds that serve as correlatives to the poetic imagination. Keats and Whitman most obviously come to mind, but also Stevens, in part by parallel contrast. In Hass's essay "What Furies," he describes Wallace Stevens' bird in the poem "On Mere Being" as "both an alien being and the one true resident; it sings its song without human meaning at the edge of space, its feathers shining." What is remarkably similar between Hass's and Stevens' birds is how they are both situated spatially at the limits of consciousness, positioned to imagine what no imagination successfully can. Paradoxically, extreme artifice, in the guise of a gilded bird, provides a vocabulary for the real, that which, as a nonhuman realm, spells the death of artifice:

> The palm at the end of the mind
> Beyond the last thought, rises
> In the bronze distance,
>
> A gold-feathered bird
> Sings in the palm, without human meaning,
> Without human feeling, a foreign song.
>
> You know then that it is not the reason
> That makes us happy or unhappy.
> The bird sings. The feathers shine.
> (*Opus Posthumous,* 117–118)

On its spare, remote threshold, Stevens' bird sits posed like an undying piece of formal glamour. The lines are short; the poem, full of silence. By contrast, Hass's bird appears but briefly, swept into the afternoon's "undertow of endless transformation." In contrast to the quiet posture of Stevens' lines, Hass's poem leads breathlessly down forty-one largely heptameter, cataloging lines before pausing at a period. Hass's expansiveness offers us a hymn to possibility, but possibility as grounded in the thingness of everyday life:

> . . . dance is defined
> by the body's possibilities arranged, this dance
> belongs to the composures and the running down of things
> in the used sugars of five-thirty: a woman straightening
> a desk turns her calendar to another day, signaling
> that it is another day where the desk is concerned
> and that there is in her days what doesn't belong to the desk;
> a kid turns on TV, flops on the couch to the tinny sound
> of little cartoon parents quarreling; a man in a bar
> orders a drink, watches ice bob in the blond fluid,
> he sighs and looks around; sad at the corners, nagged by
> wind,
> others with packages; others dreaming, picking their noses
> dreamily while they listen to the radio . . .
> (*Human Wishes*, 71–72)

Whereas Stevens' poem tends toward paring away the meaningfully charged details of the everyday world, Hass's tends toward including them all. Since neither absolute elimination nor inclusion of such detail is possible in language, both poems create a sense of irresolution.

As in "Meditation at Lagunitas," "Natural Theology" imagines the failure of images to tell the whole truth as potentially redemptive, since such failure sparks the urge to renew. But in "Natural Theology," as in much of Hass's newer work, we feel that urge working forcefully on the syntax itself. Hass's new poems have a particularly disjunctive logic, broad canvas, and rich texture of detail. In "Natural Theology," the poem's syntactic momentum and associative skips create the sense of an unseen pressure causing the verbal ground to shift:

> The religion
> or region of the dark makes soup and lights a fire,
> plays backgammon with children on the teeth or the stilettos
> of the board, reads books, does dishes, listens
> to the wind, listens to the stars imagined to be singing
> invisibly, goes out to be regarded by the moon, walks
> dogs, feeds cats, makes love in postures so various,

with such varying attention and intensity and hope,
it enacts the dispersion of tongues among the people
of the earth—compris? versteh'—and sleeps with sticky
 genitals
 (72)

Images rapidly displace one another, unpredictable though not entirely unguided, as though we had been dipped into the lively workings of a symbolic unconscious.

In such a world, Hass tells us, it is "the dark" that "enacts the dispersion of tongues." Thus language enjoys a degree of autonomy from conscious control. It is as though language were speaking itself into existence. The autonomous nature of language, its emergence as an alien self, is yet another Lacanian theme that, as Hass points out, finds its poetic dramatization in the verse of Robert Creeley:

> The system of analogies derived from Lévi-Strauss and Lacan and Derrida seems to assert that consciousness carries with it its own displaced and completely symbolic unconscious, that is, the structures of language by which consciousness is constituted . . . This is what Creeley's mode and the attractiveness of his mode have to do with, at least much of the time; it is a poetics which addresses the tension between speaking and being spoken through language.
> (TCP, 157)

In Lacanian terms, this tension is the tension between the "je" and the "moi," the self that speaks and the self that is spoken, "the object of the other." Most obviously in our dreams, we feel ourselves "being spoken" by an uncontrollable other, the forms of consciousness enjoying a level of abandon but nevertheless informed by some kind of organizing syntax and symbolic logic.

An element of abandon in the forms of consciousness makes possible their seductive play. In Hass's poem, the French question *compris?* stands posed with a semantic yearning answered by its parallel contrast in German, *versteh'*. The semantic resolution, albeit temporary, of parallel opposites corresponds to a sexual consummation, a metaphor made explicit as the poem then turns to an image of love's aftermath. It is comically appropriate that the question, like a seductive envoy, is in French whereas the response, offering reassuring closure, is in German:

> —compris? versteh'—and sleeps with sticky genitals
> the erasures and the peace of sleep: exactly the halfmoon
> holds, and the city twinkles in particular windows, throbs
> in its accumulated glow which is also and more blindingly
> the imagination of need from which the sun keeps rising
> into morning light,
> because desires do not split themselves up, there is one
> desire
> touching many things, and it is continuous.
> (72–73)

Just as erotic desire rises again, so does the craving for understanding since no understanding is complete. The whole truth is always deferred, inhabiting an imaginary realm "out there."

Appropriately, Hass's closure in "Natural Theology" offers us an image dramatizing the permanent revisionism of consciousness: as the ephemeral sense of sexual and semantic resolution, the erasures, and the peace of sleep give way once again to the climbing light of morning, we are reminded that the cycle of desire is infinite. The sun's movement, slow, inevitable, mirrors an inevitable yearning, rising, as Hass states, from "the imagination of need." Much of the power of Hass's final image lies in the tension it creates between closure and irresolution. The rising sun marks the end of a cycle, a completion that signifies the impossibility of completion. We end with a beginning.

Hass's idea that there is one desire that is "continuous" makes explicit the notion that desire is everpresent—continual. But also there is a way in which desire, being singular and touching many things, provides an associative continuity among the contents of a consciousness. In Hass's final lines, desire is credited with creating a sense not only of variety and disjunctiveness but also of coherence and belonging. In its everpresence, desire appears as a connecting medium, a subtle, undying force of contact between signs and what they bring to mind. Desire joins, albeit loosely, the many into a long and singular chain of signs and their displacing transformations, each yielding to and yet to some degree setting into motion "the next needful thing."

As we have seen, Hass's essay "Images" claims that primary acts of the imagination are transformed into "the next needful thing" only "if we are lucky." Throughout Hass's work, feelings of "connectedness," of intimacy between the past and present, signifier and signified, self and other, word and flesh, recur as ephemeral blessings, matters of luck—as when momentarily the body seems "numinous as words" or when words appear as "days which are the good flesh continuing." Naturally, the good flesh dies, as do words, as does the sensation that our words are made flesh. The explicit failure of Hass's claims to tell the whole truth humbles them to being. They gesture affectionately toward the inscrutable nature of things charged by language and thus by our desire to see them always more clearly, to retrieve them, to understand. His opulent catalogs are likewise devotional in tone, expressing an immense affection for the world, a longing to name it all. With a kind of devotional alchemy, Hass's poetry excels at creating out of humility, out of uncertainty and loss, a recovering sense of reverence and reverie.

Works Cited

Hass, Robert. *Human Wishes.* New York: Ecco, 1989.
Hass, Robert. *Praise.* New York: Ecco, 1979.
Hass, Robert. *Twentieth Century Pleasures.* New York: Ecco, 1984.
Lacan, Jacques. *Ecrits.* Alan Sheridan, trans. New York: Norton, 1977.
Stevens, Wallace. *Opus Posthumous.* New York: Knopf, 1957.

Mercury's Passage:

Poetry, Fracture, and the Talking Cure

> And he still hawks poems like news,
> as welcome in heaven as in hell.
> —Austin Hummell, "Mercury"

Mercury walks, if he walks, in either world, the highest and the lowest. Wing footed and hard to predict, he moves from Olympus to the underworld and back with the freedom of unbridled imagination. A god of contradictions, he serves as a messenger between opposites, as the patron deity of commerce, travel, eloquence, negotiation, thievery, and deceit, and so facilitates exchange of both goods and information. As god of opposites and the force that would connect them, it seems somehow appropriate that his caduceus resonates as an emblem of healing. Likewise it seems appropriate that this interpretation of the caduceus came by way of mistaken association with another symbol, the rod of Asclepius, which might recommend him as a kind of god of free association, a god of fortuitous mistakes, a god of the poetic. In short, he is mercurial, and therein lies his power to adapt and elude and so embody a spirit of transgression, of bearing news across the borders, like a poem. Like a poem, he knows what it is to give voice to the unspeakable, to honor with attention the broken, wounded, unseemly greed and cruelties of human nature, or so a certain faith would suggest. And what is faith without the truths of the imagination? Hell is hell. To see it as any less is not to see it. And yet Mercury travels there and elsewhere precisely because his nature empowers him to witness *and* deceive, to move with the quietude of light, the elusive artistry of thieves. He sees more because he has a levity to him, the speed of a radiance that arrives everywhere a little early, like a poet's word surprised by everything it brings to light.

One could say the same of dreams, that they seem to know their way around heaven and hell, desire and dread, that they cross the boundaries of defenses, repressions, walls of compromise that get us through the day. Dreams are one part of the mind talking to another, and only sometimes with anything to say. They might articulate, for instance, our literal appetites, our literal aches and discomforts, or like the Mercury of the hermetic tradition, they can speak the symbolic logic and illogic of some deeper hunger for meaning, for connectivity amidst difference, for a greater resolution, or at least an imaginative look, both intimate and distant, at what can never be resolved.

Dreams thus would make metaphysicians of us all. In their elusiveness, they suggest a language for the infinite, forever craving a more inclusive conversation among the exiled and wounded parts that make up the mystery of the whole, and those who fear them fear the vulnerability that makes the conversation possible. Because their origins remain eclipsed, because they intensify their urgencies in light and spite of this, dreams are the mind's fullest expression of a speculative desire that will not go away. They long to be read. They long for us to see what, with or without faith, we cannot see. Dreams, like the quicksilver in the alchemist's flask, hold out some promise to change us, to catalyze experience, to transmute our leaden confusion into something more ideal, more powerful in moving beyond the fundamental conflicts of being in a body, anxious to survive.

A dream is not a poem. Its medium is less tangible, however semiotic, less self-conscious than a poet's, less derivative of artistry, of selectivity and discernment. Poems may aspire to be wiser than dreams, less self-indulgent and compulsive, more active, concise, and inclusively aware, but a poet's aspiration might create the very problems it would solve. What we do know is that there would be no poetry without the intelligence of metaphor and spirit of transgression that offers us the wisdom of dreams in waking life. "Only the marvelous is beautiful," wrote André Breton, and that simple and striking perception remains one of his most incisive and useful, revolutionary even, the way it suggests that the aesthetic demands of a poem cannot disentangle themselves from the paradoxical nature of their stance toward the real. Poems, like dreams, enact an ambivalent love affair with the real. Like Mercury, they deceive us, and in their deceit, they reveal. Breton's notion challenges the idea of form and rhetoric, let alone truth-telling, as sufficient in themselves. As a statement about poetics, Breton's claim broadens the category of the aesthetic, such that beauty resides not merely in formal properties, not merely in a poem's flesh. That flesh must have color. It must have character. Like all living things, it must be a mystery to itself.

A poem is not a dream, and yet, even in its aesthetic being, poetry articulates the intelligence of dreams. Beauty, after all, cannot be reduced merely to the eye of the perceiver or the form of the perceived. It is relational. It needs desire, a sense of amorous intimacy with the beautiful that, like the imagery of dreams, remains at some paradoxical distance. Beauty summons us, though just what it summons us to see is, in some measure, what we already see. The very surface, the intensity of form, appears both immanent and transcendent, such that we sense in the arousal of wonder some deeper quality of being that is slightly beyond our power to witness or understand. As an expression of both subject and object, that deeper quality of beauty has both an inward and outward cast. It expresses the core of the personal as transpersonal, or animated by a longing to connect to what is beyond the self. It defies logic to suppose that we could desire what already satisfies us, and yet dreams, like poems, do just this, insofar as they speak across the distances inside the perceiver, across the sensations of eclipse that give to one mind its various defenses and walls, its multiple identities. The mind is many minds, as the experience of beauty reveals.

The Summons of the Shattered

While depth psychology's reputation, by way of its therapeutic viability, has come under criticism as slow, ineffective, programmatic, reductive, intrapsychic, it nevertheless can be thanked for the enormous production of new concepts that prove useful in articulating some of the structural tensions of mind that require contextualization via the volitional and transactional dynamics that inflect, transfigure, and challenge those structures and our necessarily metaphysical speculations about them. In fact, the tradition of depth psychology, particularly as articulated by Carl Jung, anticipates such criticism with statements that suggest some of the provisional and untenable nature of psychoanalytic metaphysics with its vocabulary for psychic architecture. In the book *Mysterium Coniunctionis*, for example, Jung emphasizes not only the limits of the conscious mind's capacity to know deep structure, but also the changing nature of phenomena. In enigmatic contradiction of his architectural theories, Jung claims that mutability (as opposed to principle) "defines" the real and our relation to it:

> The conscious mind often knows little or nothing about its own transformation, and does not want to know anything. The more autocratic it is and the more convinced of the eternal validity of its truths, the more it identifies with them. . . . In the phenomenal world the Heraclitan law of everlasting change, πάντα ῥεῖ, prevails; and it seems that all the true things must change and that only that which changes remains true. (358)

Even archetypes, he claims, are continually coming into being and passing into extinction—a fact that contradicts their defining characteristic as recursively transcultural, transhistorical. No doubt, elements of Jung's thought, so incompatible with contemporary critical thought, offend either poles of the postmodern split—that is, both reader-response critics and ideological critics. Archetypal theory in particular can suggest both reification and effacement of the individual. It can deemphasize individual difference and yet suggest a sense of self as autonomous alternative cultural contingency. Less popularized elements of Jungian theory can be used to suggest just the opposite.

Perhaps an analogy between the body and the psyche (as coextensive with the body) provides a useful model for thinking of the structural tensions of the mind. Obviously corporeal structure does not efface corporeal difference individually or historically. It does not negate the body's freedoms; it articulates them. Jung gestures toward the evolutionary model when he says:

> According to phylogenetic law, the psychic structure must, like the anatomical, show traces of earlier stages of evolution it has passed through. This is in fact so in the case of the unconscious, for in dreams and mental disturbances psychic products come to the surface which show all the traits of primitive levels of development.
>
> (*The Spirit in Man, Art, and Literature,* 97)

Neither Jung's argument nor the analogy between the psyche and the body need imply material determinism, since, given the dualist bias implicit in our language and available experience, a certain mutuality of agency appears between spirit and matter. Jung's evolutionary argument might make some uneasy, not only for its questionable logical basis, but for its challenge to a more extreme and tidy breed of dualism. It is far less threatening for us to think of our bodies as evolved from the apes than for us to think of our minds that way. Not that this proves a generalized denial of something demonstrated as scientific fact. The evolutionary basis for structures of mind must remain an object of inference and intuition. However, a resistance to the possibility does say something about the possible arrogance of consciousness that would set itself apart from evolutionary process and structure. Many minds would prefer to imagine an origin that is less messy, biological, base, as if it were possible to keep the spirit's hands clean of its place and development in the animal kingdom.

The structural tension of the mind, as an object of metaphysical speculation, occupies a paradoxical place in the imagination, since it seems in less subtle form to essentialize the self, to make it static and defined, however ironically the sense of structural tension figures as hugely "other." Jung's view suggests the contents and processes of consciousness cannot be fully explained as the products of infinitely malleable appearances that yield to volition. Consciousness is not fully accounted for as merely the creation of the individual nor of a culture of individuals nor a combination of the two. It must negotiate tendencies and resistances akin to those of our biological imperatives. Structural tensions of both body and mind challenge human, willful ingenuity, however collective or rebellious volitional constructions, to honor, listen, confess, and adapt. Biology asks the mind to summon some humility, not only in admitting biological influence, but also our necessary degree of uncertainty with regard to what that influence is.

As with all revolutionary thinkers, Jung routinely contradicts himself and remains hugely vulnerable to criticism. His cultish reputation is full of ironies, both in terms of his insight into cultish behavior and in terms of the ad hominem illogic that drives both hero worship and hero dismissal. He is, like Mercury, difficult to predict. In spite of the redundancy, unoriginality, and inflexibility that marks much Jungian critical application, where literary meaning articulates preconceived archetypes, Jung's opus is philosophically diverse and provocative, and one can only speculate that his willingness to change and revise his positions, to risk mistakes, to remain supple as a thinker, is directly related to his powers of intuition, his ability, like Mercury, to read productively into appearances a metaphysics of their depths.

Among the more pragmatic of his contributions is his refinement of the concept of "the complex," a notion that points to poetry's transgressive instincts as somehow instrumental. With regard to the complex, Jung is openly critical of the abuses inflicted by analysts in the name of the concept. What defines a complex is neither failure nor pathology, but more important "autonomy," the sense that there are silences in the mind that nonetheless "speak" and that these silences saturate our experience, ranging in degree from the harmless to the more unbearable and tragic:

> Today we can take it as moderately certain that complexes are in fact "splinter psyches." The aetiology of their origin is frequently a so-called trauma, an emotional shock or some such thing, that splits off a bit of the psyche. Certainly one of the commonest causes is a moral conflict, which ultimately derives from the apparent impossibility of affirming the whole of one's nature.
>
> (*The Structure and Dynamics of the Psyche*, 98)

Jung goes on to say that complexes differ greatly in degree, from the harmless to the extreme, cases that the Middle Ages diagnosed as "possession," wherein the unconscious would conspire with unrecognized voices of the complex to overpower the ego. The more contemporary way of talking about the complex has its own liabilities, and it is important to emphasize Jung's critique of psychoanalytic practice here, his sense of "admonishing therapist." To say one "has" a complex, for instance, expresses a particularly modern and regressive form of naïveté that perpetuates a culture of blame.

Granted, the Jungian ideal of "affirming the whole of one's nature" appears to be unrealizable as an absolute. There remains always the lingering sense of humility and ignorance in the face of the unconscious. Jung's other writings, on the shadow, for instance, frequently make this point. Moreover, "affirming" the whole need not imply "understanding" the whole. An important nuance to Jung's point maintains that we are free to see "wholeness" as something other than "completeness." Without this distinction the important dynamism in Jung's *The Structure and Dynamics of the Psyche* is lost. Not only can wholeness imply inclusiveness and receptivity, the word "wholeness" has an emotional valence that "completeness" does not. Whereas completeness implies acquisitive closure or autonomy, wholeness implies the opposite. It implies a mending, and with it comes a deeper realization of the psyche's transpersonal and collective nature. The mandala as Jung's recurrent image of the Self, or the wholeness of the psyche, embodies the dual sense of all circles. They are both closed curves and open portals. They both gather and take us out. They articulate the paradoxical notion of the Self in Jung's nomenclature (gleaned from Nietzsche's) as transpersonal and yet still bearing the signature of the personal (the self). We see a similar conflation of self and other in Jung's sense of the Self as inclusive of "the objective psyche." The Self defies the sense of interiority suggested by its name. Like the Sistine Chapel, it is a room larger than the house it is in.

For Jung, awareness of the world is predicated upon a reciprocal awareness of the self, such that it becomes very difficult to focus just what is meant by the words "self" and "world." Thus Jung's exploration of the social self often takes on paradoxical and contradictory terms:

> Just as man as a social being, cannot in the long run exist without a tie to the community, so the individual will never find the real justification for his existence, and his own spiritual and moral autonomy, anywhere except in an extramundane principle capable of relativizing the overpowering influence of external factors.
>
> (*The Undiscovered Self*, 23)

The term "autonomy" is the most problematic here, since he is quick to qualify the term in elusive fashion. "Autonomy," like "individuation," can be misleading, intended to convey a sense of psychic cohesion that does not negate external factors but rather acknowledges them as essential to one's collective and transpersonal nature. "Autonomy" does, however, suggest the positive sense of a maturing and "relativizing" intelligence of one's own "justification," one's groundedness in the sense of personal authority. Jung thus does not lapse into the reductio ad absurdum of the individuated self as merely autonomous or merely socially constructed, hegemonic and naïve, or unoriginal and passive, but rather he labors to find a language for the notion of wholeness as a dynamic process that honors the world without being defined exclusively by it. The "extramundane" principle need not imply "the personal self" in Jung's thought, for the relative integrity of the individuated self finds meaning only in acknowledged relation to the transpersonal.

Moreover, "autonomy" could imply a degree of integrity relative not only to external influences, but also to internal ones, splinter psyches that transform as the sense of autonomy or selfhood becomes more inclusive and less defensive. In this sense the singularity of self implied by "autonomy" suggests connection, not separation. The complex, as its own seat of power and agency, increases its influence with neglect and so intervenes in perception to assert its needs, its compulsions, its patterns of survival. It projects. A lack of self-awareness thus is not selfless. It consumes the world in self, though these expressions of self remain invisible as such. In contrast, ego strength, the opposite of ego inflation, enables the self to better assimilate the contents of the previously unconscious, simply because exposure had made the self less defensive, less susceptible to the sense of danger embedded in remembered trauma. The strong ego is less egotistical, more accepting of chaos, uncertainty, and alterity.

Jung does not speculate as to the physiology of the complex, though it is provocative to propose one model, however unscientific, that gives credence to the distinctive power of "talk" as unreplicated by medication for those struggling with trauma and depression. The energy dynamics of the psyche, as Freud conceived them, grew out of metaphors from physics (as evident in his notions of drives, repressions, and sublimations). It remains possible that a physics model is more than metaphorical insofar as it suggests a conservation of energy in the brain. It is consistent with experience that the autonomy of the complex, the structural/electrical resistance around the trauma, could drain otherwise motivational energy while heightening oppositional dissonance and anxiety and thus lead to depression as symptomatic of a diseased will. Certainly this corresponds with the felt nature of depression. It can take a lot out of someone to keep a secret, especially the dangerous kind that one keeps from oneself. It takes a mind inside the mind to oversee it. We can only speculate that the physiology of dreaming allows for greater relaxation of defensive boundaries, greater exchange between the alienated parts of mind.

This is not to say that dreams mend us, though they can articulate the terms of mending. They give voice to what it is in silence that longs to mend. The associative logic of the dream, like the talking cure, can help to bring the underworld of the psyche into greater assimilation into conscious life and thus transform the autonomous nature of the complex. The dream symbol is a form of both obscuration and connection, and paradoxically its very obscurity can encourage greater connection. As a protective device of the unconscious, the symbol provokes the desire of the reader to investigate, to gaze in wonder a while, to break open the code with all its aches and riches. The mind can thereby be led into a more active, interpretive intimacy with its depths by way of the defended nature of the enigma. Like Mercury, the dream symbol both deceives and negotiates. It reveals and conceals. It mitigates fear with the pleasure, and part of the pleasure is the very summoning of desire. The symbol thus embodies the element of beauty associated with the marvelous, the slightly out of reach, the simultaneous sense of strangeness and wisdom, the news, as Pound called a poem, that continues to be new.

Aesthetics and Despair

Poems, like dreams, guarantee no cure, though they might save a life now and then. Poetry is, alas, so strongly identified with the vague category of "madness," it may seem counterintuitive that it would breed mental health. The long list of suicidal poets tells us little about poetry's agency, whether it exacerbates inner conflict or provides the most exigent means to tolerate and make use of it. It is possible poetry could do a bit of both, the way chess could structure the self of the paranoid schizophrenic and then in turn become compulsive, such that the very strategy of coping with anxiety creates more of it. The spectrum of personalities among poets is too vast to translate into statistically reliable conclusions about the effects of poetic practice on psychic integration. Given the sea of variables, poetry appears no more reliable than psychoanalysis in its repeatable successes. That said, there is no denying poetry's power (or that of psychoanalysis) in crossing boundaries and thus giving voice to the alterities of mind. For one thing, metaphor lies at the heart of the poetic imagination, and, as the etymology of the word suggests, a "metaphor" is a "bearing across," a fundamental connective principle that cannot predict all that it connects. Equally true is the fact that the poetry, in cultivating the tension implicit in the symbolic logic of dreams, conceals and reveals at the same time. Thus it honors the alterities of mind with an inexhaustible spirit of inquiry that it seeks to preserve. The wells of being that haunt the beautiful engender this spirit.

Poetry writing differs from the talking cure of psychoanalysis in ways that are critical to both poetry's therapeutic limitations and, more surprisingly, its therapeutic potential. Poetry conceived as therapy may not yield good poetry. The aesthetic demands of a poet's medium will obviously require a craft beyond the "making" of conversation, and, no matter the sensibility, a poem cannot embody the fluid spontaneity of dreams.

For many, the aesthetic impulse, with its implicit selectivity, inhibits its therapeutic spontaneity, and yet that same aesthetic impulse might be poetry's therapeutic gift. Poetry's medium endures greater pressure ideally, not to suppress essentials but to intensify them, not to foreground ego needs, but to be mindful of the poem as reaching beyond them. Moreover, the pursuit of meaningful, intense, and inclusive forms of beauty animates the will.

Keats understood the instrumental value of beauty when he came up with the theory of negative capability. For instance, it is not the content but the beauty of the language in King Lear, he argues, that helps us bear the weight of despair. Beauty alone allows one to dwell "in uncertainties, Mysteries, doubts, without any irritable reaching after fact & reason" (43). Just how beauty does this, he does not say. One could surmise that aesthetic form compensates us with some ghost of pleasure, or, as Nietzsche argues, that it renders suffering as mere appearance, allowing us to step away. Related to both these arguments is the notion that beauty's architecture models a sense of integration and strength through which one perceives, tolerates, and transfigures the chaos of despair.

Even poems of despair must, if they succeed as poems, affirm something, less perhaps by sentiment than by the fact of their existence. The nihilistic poem is a contradiction of terms. The hidden voice of aesthetic form argues for its reason to exist, for the act of making as a value, such that the making of meaning is itself meaningful. If the poem rises to the emotional and revelatory potential of its medium, it contains within its form the pressure of necessity, of what is at stake. It whispers that the pleasure of form, its rapture even, can take to heart the worst and "bear" witness. Auden's poem "In Memory of W. B. Yeats" makes precisely this point. While it both argues for the transformative power of poetry to awaken the will, its affirmations owe a good measure of their credibility to tougher, more skeptical claims of the poem's early passages. The opening section, for instance, grounds the poem personally and emotionally in its elegiac occasion, wherein the traditional consolations of art as immortal body of artist are rejected:

> The words of a dead man
> Are modified in the guts of the living. (l. 21–22)

As we move through the paralyzed landscape, the deserted streets, the public statues disfigured in snow, the isolation of the living from the dead mirrors the isolation of poems from their makers. Not only are poems impotent to resurrect the dead, they do not move the political mountains that Yeats longed to move. Contextually, this bitter fact gives emotional and conceptual authority to the famous hyperbole of section two:

> Now Ireland has her madness and her weather still,
> For poetry makes nothing happen: it survives
> In the valley of its saying, where executives
> Would never want to tamper, . . . (34–37)

So reads the original version of the poem, included in his 1945 edition of his collected poems. Auden's revision of the word "saying" to "making" in later editions of the poem sharpens the sense of isolation implicit in the chasm between art and artist. "Saying" implies a "sayer" and a listener, a transaction of some kind, and yet Auden's view here is that the poem is simply "a way of happening, a mouth," as opposed to a message, for its vision is subject to revision.

Thus the shift from "saying" to "making" supports the tough mindedness of Auden's refusal of false consolation. To further complicate matters, "making" as opposed to "saying" foregrounds reasons for hope. With the third and final section, the poem suggests that the poem as a made thing strengthens its claim as redemptive, since "making" ("poesis") foregrounds creative volition. The form of the poem, as it moves from free verse to rough blank verse to strict trochaic tetrameter, likewise comes into focus as a made thing, structured as songs are, more conspicuous in its artfulness, in this sense removed, but so, too, closer to the stuff of popular ritual or song:

> Follow, poet, follow right
> To the bottom of the night,
> With your unconstraining voice
> Still persuade us to rejoice;

With the farming of a verse
Make a vineyard of the curse,
Sing of human unsuccess
In a rapture of distress; . . . (54–61)

The expressive friction of the phrase "a rapture of distress" suggests that the pleasure of song comes not only in spite of difficulty but in light of it. Moreover, the word "rapture" comes from the Middle Latin *raptura* that means "the act of carrying off," but also by extension the violence of "seizure" or "kidnapping," which explains the existence of the cognate of rapture: rape. The word "rapture" gathers about it a paradox of affect akin to that of elegiac pleasure. Perhaps the closest synonym to rapture might be ecstasy, since in being "carried off" one is taken out of oneself or out of one's ordinary sense of self, but this need not imply escape from the real. Auden's poem rather insistently returns to the notion that art of genuine sustenance does not blind us to the horrors outside it. The ideal must not idealize. In the thick of despair, one might therefore turn to song less for euphemistic negation of experience than an assertion of aesthetic volition in the face of it. Art evidences resilience and thus animates its form with the spirit of rebellion, an assertion of the values of creative volition and life affirmation that human difficulty would put under pressure.

The irony here is that the increased sense of artifice as a means of setting the language apart mitigates the mood of introspection and isolation in the poem. Equally ironic is how the various contradictions in the poem, insofar as they authenticate the struggle, strengthen rather than weaken the argument, particularly as the meditational discursiveness gives way to public plea. By way of the stark sobriety of the poem's opening, the final lines feel more earned, tested by bitter skepticism and experience:

In the deserts of the heart
Let the healing fountain start,
In the prison of his days
Teach the free man how to praise. (62–65)

The invocation of "the free man" defies the poem's earlier preoccupation with human limitation, and yet, as the metrical form exemplifies, freedom and limitation are not mutually exclusive. They require one another in the sense that limit articulates choice, born of both measured boundaries and spontaneous liquidities. Its freedoms do not come in spite of restriction. They are the force of will in the flesh of limit.

The notion of "farming" a verse likewise registers a collaboration between the given and the made, a structuring of nature by way of pruning, weeding, irrigating, laying down seeds in furrows that turn at the ends. They "re-verse" or simply "verse." Farming as a metaphor for imaginative collaboration points to a distinctively aesthetic dimension of poetry and in turn its therapeutic value. Poetry does not simply tell us the news; it embodies a farmer's attendant care in the artfulness of its "making." In this way it affirms life via the force of its subjectivity, its creative eros, and opens up "the healing fountain" in the heart's wasteland. Like farming, the fountain conflates the senses of making and honoring, volition and receptivity, as reflected in the formal beauties of the garden. The fountain's waters suggest both vitality and bereavement, while its formality mirrors that of the ritual or hymn, what supports and facilitates the therapeutic power of grieving. In structure therefore lies liquidity, a music, the kind of fluency of grief no wound can heal without.

The Problem and Pursuit of Discernment

Music shares with Mercury a freedom of access. To make a "rapture of distress" is to possess the power to walk, not only in heaven or hell, but in both places at the same time. Small wonder Orpheus opens his passage with a lyre. He would break the silence of the underworld, as poetry must if it is to explore the expressive and transformative potential of its medium. Thus music provides access to exiled regions of the psyche that seem to speak no other language. For this reason music possesses a special status for philosophers such as Arthur Schopenhauer:

> Because music does not, like all the other arts, exhibit the *ideas* or grades of the will's objectification, but directly the *will itself,* we can also explain that it acts directly on the will, i.e., the feelings, passions, and emotions of the hearer, so that it quickly raises these or even alters them. (114)

For Schopenhauer, because music *embodies* will, it penetrates more deeply. One might add that, as a result, it opens up passages in the mind, crossing the boundaries of our complexes, our scars, our language even. One might call music a messenger in this regard, though just what news it bears defies conceptualization. Music *is* the news it bears, although its implicit "message," if it can be said to have one, feels ambiguously affirmative. As Schopenhauer puts it, although music speaks of worlds better than ours, "it flatters only our will-to-live" (124).

Poetry might be said to possess the same powers, though Schopenhauer insists that music is an "independent art form," not to be confused with poetry. Music, as it moves deeply into consciousness, whispers of the transcendent and thus is more immanently distant than other art forms. However, poems, as forms of music, have similar powers. What Schopenhauer notes is essential, that music penetrates psychic boundaries, affirms the will to live, and transforms the passions, and yet, without the play of differentiation associated with language, including the elusive semiotics of dream, it does not have poetry's articulate power of conceptual play, confrontation, and assimilation. Musical prodigies exist. Poetry prodigies do not. The very young are often natural poets, and yet cannot sustain a sense of visionary breadth and meditative assimilation of experience. Whereas poetry requires knowledge of the world, music can affirm without articulated commitments of understanding. It can be profound but never wise.

The instrumental value of music's spirit of affirmation is tremendous, especially given the imperfect and forever unresolved nature of understanding. The quest for knowledge at the expense of beauty might well cripple one with anxiety. Music's therapeutic potential, its capacity to allay defenses, to allow access, is related to its formal integrity. Like the realized self, it is individuated, the many parts engaged and reflected in one another. Like poetry, it resists paraphrase. This said, the therapeutic value of music might work within poetic language to strengthen a sense of aesthetic unity in counterpoint with the play of difference. It is in this play of difference, coupled with a heightened sense of cohesion and connection, that poetry performs a breed of alchemy that music does not. As in alchemy, poetry thrives on a sense of the self as out there, embedded in the material processes of nature, and it is only through the sense of projection and witness that certain insights become possible. Thus the relative "objectification" that Schopenhauer degrades in art forms other than music makes possible a poet's vision. Jung's particular insight into the alchemical enterprise strengthens the analogy:

> The alchemical *opus* deals in the main not just with chemical experiments as such, but with something resembling psychic processes expressed in pseudochemical language. . . . The real nature of matter was unknown to the alchemist: he knew it only in hints. Inasmuch as he tried to explore it he projected the unconscious into the darkness of matter in order to illuminate it.
>
> (*Psychology and Alchemy*, 231)

Like a poet, the alchemist "speaks" not simply "to" things but in the language of things, poetical images radiant with affect and concept, and the will as objectified becomes subject to exploration at a level of greater structural complexity. In both alchemy and poetry, projection illuminates, though what Jung does not mention in this context is that projection is the same faculty that obscures. The self-poisonings of many alchemists testify to such obscurity and its hazards. Thus both poetry and alchemy make problematic the act of reading the world, and thus they call upon language's implicit powers of discernment to darken it, complicate it, toughen it up. To transgress boundaries to no end would be, in any case, to remain a child.

Ironically enough, alchemy has its own language for the tough-minded differentiation necessary for self-realization. As Edward Edinger outlines in his book *Anatomy of the Psyche*, the alchemical process of "calcinato" marks the psychic stage, wherein conscious awareness emerges from the undifferentiated self, the prima material or raw material of consciousness, in order to dissociate its unconscious ego needs from a world it would otherwise overpower:

> *Calcinato* has a purging or purifying effect. The substance is purged of radical moisture. This would correspond to the drippings of unconsciousness that accompany emerging energies. Or, in other words, the energies of the archetypal psyche first appear in identification with the ego and express themselves as desires for ego-pleasure and ego-power. The fire of *calcinato* purges these identifications and drives off the root, or primordial moisture, leaving the content in its eternal or transpersonal state, restored of its natural heat. (44)

With calcinato, the ego must go through hell, a sense of exile and dismemberment, before the self is ready for the reunion and fulfillment at later stages of alchemical and spiritual process. In psychological terms, successful marriage is predicated on differentiation first, before union can be tolerable.

Far from taming poetry, the tension of discernment adds to its excitement, since neither world nor self, logic nor illogic, assert themselves as lone points of reference. To read well, one must both objectify and subjectify, which is to say, one recognizes the self in the world, the world in the self, without oversimplifying and obliterating their relation into sameness. The associative consciousness embedded in metaphor would be impossible without first a differentiation of parts. As both Robert Bly and T. S. Eliot have argued, the more unalike those parts, the greater the energy between them. Part of the rush of metaphor is the spirit of rebellion and embrace within it. The exiled regions of mind clash and coalesce. Poetry articulates a more generalized ambivalence about boundaries with the excitement of eros on the threshold of the other. True, language mediates experience in a way that music alone does not, and yet, as a form of music, poetry asserts the experience of unity and difference as simultaneous, aesthetically related, neither reducible to the other. Poems express the dual nature of consciousness, and so we see in them some imaginative reconciliation of this duality as a model of who we are, or who we might be, and what it is to heal.

Mind-forged Manacles

In every voice, in every ban,
The mind-forg'd manacles I hear.
—William Blake, "London"

Suffering does not make us stronger. Anyone who has watched someone in chronic pain collapse into terminal narcissism and dementia knows that. Suffering, however, does solicit our strength. It can break down defenses, offer a glimpse into the depths of the psyche illuminated by the depths of pain. It can sharpen relational priorities, even as it finds it difficult to listen, or long for change, even as it fears it. The inability to change, to move, to pay attention is symptomatic, as pain, the messenger, will tell you. If the wounds of the psyche were content to remain as they are, dreams would not have given them a voice. It takes a leap of faith to believe that listening to these voices breeds virtue. The oppositional model by which the demons of the complexes are locked in their cages maintains a different bias. Hell, in such a model, is conquered, not charmed. Poetry can be bred of either model, though not without paradox. The paradox of the open sensibility is that the medium of its connection, language, necessarily raises boundaries. For this reason its language must fail to succeed. It must invite silence and mystery into its realm of understanding. By contrast, the paradox of the oppositional sensibility is that it needs its demons to justify itself. The oppositional poem thus tends to appropriate the energy of its demons, either consciously or unconsciously, and hallucinate evil in unadulterated form. To oppose the other with the ready-made energies of dread is to obscure it, to aggrandize one's moral pride, to victimize oneself and others in an effort to purify the spirit of its demons. The poetry of the merely oppositional model can be earnest, imaginative even, but, like music, never wise.

As Blake noted of Milton's *Paradise Lost,* the dominant figure of Satan, bristling with energy, is far more charismatic than Christ and thus suggests Milton was of the devil's company. It is important to emphasize that Milton's familiarity with the devil is, for Blake, not necessarily a bad thing, since it suggests a liberality of attention. Milton has, in some compelling way, engaged the complexity of pride without indulging in his own. This insight of Blake's reflects the abiding spirit of "The Marriage of Heaven and Hell," where hell represents not so much "evil" in its unadulterated form as the force of creative energy that takes on that quality when alienated from the whole of the human spirit. Blake's proverbs of hell are fierce in their wisdom:

> Prisons are built with stones of Law, Brothels with the bricks
> of
> Religion.
> The pride of the peacock is the glory of God.
> The lust of the goat is the bounty of God.
> The wrath of the lion is the wisdom of God.
> The nakedness of the woman is the work of God. (21–25)

As recently as 1957, Allen Ginsberg's "Howl" came under legal scrutiny for expressing sentiments that bore an enormous debt to Blake and such passages as these. Both poets argue for a more liberal affirmation of the body and a more skeptical view of moral status of social law. Granted, such lines voiced from hell constitute one half of the matrimonial conversation, but it has long been the role of poetry to write toward one's "other self"—that is, to give voice to that which needs one.

The walls about the prison and the brothel might equally be seen as psychological. They are the scar tissue that would sequester its wound in dread and shame. Blake's embrace of virtues hidden in the cardinal sins suggests a spirit of inclusion that challenges the oppositional model of virtue. Part of that oppositional model involves a Manicheism in which the dual nature of the universe exiles evil from the divine. It is just such a model that leads to the phenomena of "possession" as Jung describes it, and as the scandals of many public Evangelicals will testify. In such a model, the ego chooses not to identify with (and thereby relate to) its shadow, as if disinheritance were the essence of virtue. The notion of "purifying" oneself takes on the form of self-rejection, self-cruelty, and its reciprocal relation to the world. Unfortunately the diffuse notion of the Jungian "shadow" threatens to drain it of its stubborn relevance as ever-present, ever-elusive, and difficult. The shadow's contents remain diffusely defined precisely because they undergo constant revision, both culturally and individually. Wherever there is conviction, there is shadow. It is the inner residue of passionate purpose that creates as we go a sense of that which resists our relation or identification. As with any other complex, the shadow complex gathers problematic energy by way of our neglect, and its wound deepens by way of strong identification with moral imperatives.

The moral philosophy of Lao Tzu's Tao-Te Ching articulates the paradoxical nature of virtue in its relation to law:

> The more taboos and prohibitions there are in the world,
> The poorer the people will be.
> The more sharp weapons the people have,
> The more troubled the state will be.
> The more cunning and skill man possesses,
> The more vicious things will appear.
> The more laws and orders are made prominent,
> The more thieves and robbers there will be. (section 57, l. 6–13)

While it is difficult to imagine the above influencing public policy, the passage nevertheless contains a pragmatic insight into the psychological logic of the taboo. The discontent of the thief who acts out recalls Freud's insight into the effects of prohibition in *Civilization and Its Discontents.* While Freud's model of social adaptation reflects the dominant social model of opposition where the ego must learn to defend itself against the impulses of the libido, he also introduces the notion of sublimation as a way of channeling and transfiguring transgressive desire. Lao Tzu's text goes further in offering up the image of an ideal unity of mindfulness (the Tao) absent in the psychoanalytic tradition, save in Jung's elusive sense of "wholeness." Both Jung and Lao Tzu encourage greater openness and spontaneity of intuition, a suppleness mirrored in the water imagery of the Tao-Te Ching. Both writers express great faith in awareness as that which breeds compassion, but the object of awareness remains elusive. Awareness that would make manifest one's moral intelligence requires a sense of relatedness expressed in terms of some totality as ideal, "wholeness" in Jung, and "the One," in Lao Tzu. Without the same concept for totality in both writers, "awareness" may signify little of ethical importance. Totality, or "the One," by definition, eludes cognition, thus "oneness" is less an object of knowledge than the body of simultaneous being and nonbeing that breeds a style of awareness. "Awareness" maintains its openness toward the Tao without presuming to appropriate it by way of control or cognitive grasp.

Herein lies part of the elusive nature of the Tao, why Lao Tzu claims that those of great intellect tend to look so far they cannot see it. The Tao is not a concept, and yet it finds expression as one by way of the intellect. The Tao is not an ideal, but it appears as one who longs for the reconciliation. More problematically, oneness, or wholeness, presents an epistemological and ethical challenge to the weak, inflated ego since its summons of humility speaks a language close to that of totalizing ambition. The notion of the world as "one" could suggest either harmony or totalitarianism, though in either case inner differentiation is assumed. On the other hand, without inner differentiation, oneness implies death to the individual. Thus "one" is both the most comforting and terrifying of numbers. Jung notes the danger imagined totality constitutes for the ego, since the ego faces in turn a temptation to take credit for the whole. A thought strikes someone, and the ego thinks, "I thought that." The weaker ego in turn might identify with the totality of the psyche, the Self, and so manage its moral dissonance through the projection of Self onto some ostensible "other," such as a charismatic leader or prophet. In this way, supplication harbors hubris, and its shadow intensifies in cruelty. In Jung and Lao Tzu, the suppleness of their minds advocates a larger spirit of openness, acceptance, and play as facilitating virtue.

García Lorca, too, expresses that suppleness, which, in his case, would honor the sacred in the profane, the profane in the sacred. Here we find an oppositional model, but handled in a nonoppositional way. For García Lorca, poetry needs the demon, the "duende," for the "black blood" of its visceral and mercurial energy. He explicitly rejects the notion of inspirational source as muse or angel, who are less bodily, less "of the earth," less messy with the shadow material of our enraptured bodies.

Likewise he rejects the notion of duende as Christian devil, "destructive and of low intelligence." We must struggle with the duende, physically, intellectually, and soulfully, and yet it figures in the imagination as "blithe." Thus it challenges our ability to categorize it clearly as either good or evil:

> To seek out the *Duende*, however, neither map nor discipline is required. Enough to know that he kindles the blood like an irritant; that he repulsed all the bland, geometrical assurances. . . . Where is the *Duende*? Through the empty arch enters a mental air blowing insistently over the heads of the dead, seeking new landscapes and unfamiliar accents; an air bearing the odor of child's spittle, crushed grass, and the veil of Medusa announcing the unending baptism of all newly created things. (30, 31, 39)

There is a romantic primitivism in García Lorca's sense of mystery and style that will resurface in the deep image poets of the 1960s. In García Lorca as in Robert Bly, James Wright, and W. S. Merwin, we find a primacy of diction and dailiness of experience infused with surprising moments of wonder and luminosity. García Lorca's evocative power owes some of its immediacy to its speed, not just the concision of ideas, but the quickness of their emotional impact. His is a poetics of rapture. "The odor of a child's spittle" and the "crushed grass" work to evoke upon impact, to strike deep into sensuous memory and call up a sensation of the uncanny, of the resilient mystery of physical presence, all the more haunting because of its particularity in frictional juxtaposition. The effect is one of crashing boundaries, of breaking in. Duende thus takes the everyday to heart and returns it soaked in blood of the unconscious.

Psychoanalytic nomenclature has a way of domesticating the expressive otherness of demons like the duende. "Possession" becomes mere illusion. The psychoanalytic word complex, however, is not terribly complex. Drained of affect and expressive power, it places demonic energies within the walls of the human subjectivity, the psyche, where the more naive might seek to "overcome" them by dismissing their reality. The hidden hubris of this carries with it an unrealistic sense of aggrandizement, responsibility, and possible blame. One thus reverses the ancient metaphor of possession and thereby flatters and pressures the ego in its identification with the whole. What makes García Lorca's language and, more generally, the language of poetry instrumental in opening the gates of the underworld is its ability to speak to demons in their native tongue—or so a poet might say. In truth, there is always more to the language of the underworld than we understand. Poetry, at its most liberating, eschews the paralysis of absolutes. It shuns the language of mere objectification or subjectification, preferring instead the imaginative intensity of conflation. It must inquire, or it ceases to be wise. A poem's lantern pursues a darkness that recedes. That, too, can be healing—not simply the power of the truth but the power of moving toward the true, loving it, longing for it, honoring the alterity of it. In the process, poetry thrives on irresolution as facilitating movement, openness, and transgression. In its dynamic quality, it enacts what psychoanalytic language tends to describe, objectify, reduce. This dynamism is characteristic of creativity more largely. Jung states:

> Every creative person is a duality or a synthesis of contradictory qualities. On the one side he is a human being with a personal life, while on the other he is an impersonal creative process.
>
> (*The Spirit in Man, Art, and Literature,* 101)

On the other hand, is this not the case with all people? Is it not fundamental to consciousness to express the creative principle of its nature? This creative principle is what Auden embraces as restorative in difficult times. Health is marked not by knowledge alone, but by technique, a style of inquiry, acceptance, and renewal. To go deeper into the mind takes a little trickery, a dream perhaps, a metaphor, a contradiction. It takes faith, which is to say, the ability to doubt. It takes the music of the human voice that goes where we cannot, into some cave or other, returning, or so the poem would imagine, with news.

Works Cited

Auden, W. H. *The Collected Poems of W. H. Auden.* New York: Random House, 1945.

Auden, W. H. *Collected Poems.* Edward Mendelson, ed. New York: Random House, 1976.

Blake, William. *The Poetry and Prose of William Blake.* David V. Erdman, ed. New York: Doubleday, 1965.

Edinger, Edward. *Anatomy of the Psyche: Alchemical Symbolism in Psychotherapy.* Open Court: Chicago, 1991.

Freud, Sigmund. *Civilization and Its Discontents.* New York: Norton, 2010.

García Lorca, Federico. "The Duende: Theory and Divertissement." In *The Poet's Work.* Reginald Gibbons, ed. and Ben Belitt, trans. Boston: Houghton Mifflin, 1979. 28–41.

Hummell, Austin. *Poppy.* Washington, DC: Del Sol, 2004.

Jung, Carl. *Mysterium Coniunctionis.* Princeton, NJ: Princeton University Press, 1963.

Jung, Carl. *The Spirit in Man, Art, and Literature.* New York: Pantheon, 1966.

Jung, Carl. *The Structure and Dynamics of the Psyche.* Princeton, NJ: Princeton University Press, 1981.

Jung, Carl. *The Undiscovered Self.* Princeton, NJ: Princeton University Press, 1990.

Keats, John. *Letters of John Keats.* Robert Gittings, ed. New York: Oxford University Press, 1982.

Schopenhauer, Arthur. "On the Metaphysics of Music." In *Philosophical Writings.* Wolfgang Schirmacher, ed. E. F. J. Payne, trans. New York: Continuum, 1994.

Tzu, Lao. "The Lao Tzu (Tao-Te Ching)." In *A Sourcebook in Chinese Philosophy.*Wing-Tsit Chan, ed. and trans. Princeton, NJ: Princeton University Press, 1963.

IV.

The Listening Word

The Limits of Metaphor

Just how it is that a metaphor, a lie, tells a truth is one of those conundrums that beg us to look at how language might approach the challenge of truth-telling and just what we mean when we use the word "truth." As tempting as it might be to eschew the category of the real with a kind of late adolescent embarrassment, a lost faith in the more naïve versions of exposure; the fact remains that poetry that does not concern itself with the pull of the true is destined to the frivolity of radical irony that would pass for sophistication when it, by its own sad logic, has nothing to reveal. It has been common, especially since the introduction and development of Romantic poetic theory, for people to assume that poetry, inconceivable without metaphor, addresses a different order of reality than science, that it refuses to extricate the truth of affect and the imagination from our models of the real. The value of the imagination is that it testifies to subjectivity as valuable, or, more obliquely, to the value of value, since it is the imagination, not reason, that renders the world as something worthy of our care.

Beyond this, however, there is a more essential difference between the truth-telling of science and that of poetry—namely, that the word "telling" in each case points to a different phenomenon. Whereas science seeks to tell us *about* our world, poetry seeks to complicate just what we mean by *world.* It seeks to embody that world as a relational phenomenon while nonetheless maintaining a sense that the world is indeed something we might talk *about,* albeit in unresolved terms. As language at its highest self-awareness, poetry must fail in order to succeed. It must move with the greatest precision it can muster to inspire a longing to continue and deepen the imaginative act of reading. Poetry thus aspires to model what it is for a world to become a world to us. At its best it does not merely tells us *about* feelings. It creates them. It does not simply tell a truth. It models it. It models the word's unresolved desire in relation to what it is we call true. It models a world as embedded in how we see it.

At the heart of poetry's ability to do this is the power of metaphor's resistance to one model of the real. The dissonance between two things that are alike and therefore, in some measure, different arouses the resources of our longing in ways that provoke, evoke, and luminesce. A metaphor, unstable by nature, figures as verbal radium, its free radicals haloing the formal structure, such that the force of illogic within the logic, even within the more astringent charms of the conceit, provides language with its spirit of necessary rebellion, its search for new terms, its ontological drive to speak the unspeakable into being. Poetry "tells" in the way that one tells a joke. The objectifying sensibility, on the other hand, tells no jokes. It explains them.

Certainly a metaphor can fail or become merely serviceable if it lacks that degree of difference and surprise in its structure to make new both word and world, to do the work of literature in reawakening the quality of immediacy in the suddenly unfamiliar. The metaphor with too much logic, or a too familiar logic, sits so flatly on the page, the physical world translates a bit too readily into abstraction. Physicality is mentioned, but not conjured with expressive force, not suffused with blood by original genius. To say "my love's hair is like silk" is to deploy a metaphor so listless that it does little work for any reader acclimated to poetry's more obvious means. To say "my love's hair is like a tire" is not necessarily more convincing, given how difference asserts a sense of the arbitrary, but the figure is more energetic by way of the friction of the dissimilar. Given the spirit of transgression in original, powerful metaphors, it might seem odd to talk of such metaphors as operating within limits, and yet all credible poets know this to be the case. Moreover the limits are not definitive limits, but rather strains that begin to sap the energy or credibility from the figure, the kind of resonance that surprises us, awakens us, seduces us to believe in the face of simultaneous disbelief. These strains in metaphor can figure as a weakening of physical wit, conceptual resonance, emotional truth, or ethical awareness.

Weaknesses in physical logic are the most obvious, and yet certain stresses to this logic might indeed be engaging and convincing if the wells of meaning are enriched from multiple sources. "The rain fell like bits of sand" has a discernable logic whereby the physicality of each part of the metaphor asserts its more obvious qualities. Therein lies one of the many possible faces of wit. "The rain fell like pebbles" exaggerates to the point of being slightly clumsy. "The rain fell like dirt clods," "the rain fell like boulders," or "the rain fell like mountains": such progressive elaborations suggest that the further we travel from physical similitude, the more we abandon physical wit, and so the mind seeks out more abstract resources of symbolic logic. Truth is, none of these figures is terribly striking, particularly without context, but some fail more noisily and for more obvious reasons.

In pursuit of greater intensity, wonder, and inwardness, one might be drawn further and further from more apparent physical hinges in metaphor. One might, for instance, be drawn to the kind of wildly associative moves advocated by Robert Bly in his book *Leaping Poetry: An Idea with Poems and Translations.* What interests Bly are the leaps of association that make "a jump from an object soaked in unconscious substance to an object or idea soaked in conscious psychic substance" (4). Metaphors born of such leaps assert their mystery and power by virtue of equal footing in the familiar and the strange. If we pull against a more familiar logic for a realm imbued in unconscious energy, we might say "the rain fell like a house on fire," and thus evoke physical similitude by way of the crackle of both rain and fire, but in ways that open up multiple registers of resonance. Each shares in the other's particular signature of loss, even as the elemental natures clash. The mind must work in numerous ways to read and write its way into the emotional exactitude of such figures if indeed they find a place that is not merely ornamental in a poem but architectural, pressured by a sense of affective and conceptual necessity, engaged in an ongoing conversation with other moments of the poem's resonance. In the most resilient and inexhaustible metaphors, it becomes impossible to dissociate physical, conceptual, and emotional truths from one another. The truth of such metaphors is imbedded in a kind of complexity where the figure sets off a depth charge of wonder in the thinking heart.

No doubt the very phrase "the limits of metaphor" breaks down under scrutiny. While writers may intuit an inexactitude, an emotional or conceptual falseness, in lesser metaphors, such intuitions outrace any attempt at systematic criteria. Nevertheless the sense of necessity, surprise, and precision when it comes to the metaphor is critical and, I suspect, of little controversy. It is the ethical realm where we open up the area of greatest concern, particularly in an aesthetic climate sensitized by lively and somewhat dominant political critiques of literature and its reception. The mere mention of ethical limits to aesthetic practice may seem to advocate self-righteous censorship, whereas the notion that there are no such limits may invite a self-satisfied complacency. Ironically, poets lined up on opposite sides of the issue of expressive restraint, identify equally with enlightened liberality and compassionate democracy.

Nevertheless I would argue there are indeed ethical limits to metaphor—call them degrees of impaired vision if you like—but such limits need not imply censorship as a remedy so much as a broadening of perspective, a willingness to let more of the necessary light into the poem—not to eliminate our controversial moments necessarily, but, on the contrary, to allow into view a humanizing complexity that makes for a deeper and more animated model of us and our world. What this implies is that the ethical limits of metaphor are indeed related to the question of a metaphor's perceived precision or truth, emotional or otherwise.

In my early years as a visiting professor at the University of Kansas, I encountered a great example of what I believed was an imprecise metaphor whose limited perspective had ethical implications. A student wrote a poem about test anxiety in which he stated that he felt as though he (both the speaker and the writer, according to the student) were in the path of a nuclear bomb. Granted, this move in a poem can be easily defended as getting at some emotional truth, but the issue goes beyond whether the test anxiety "seemed" to the student like a nuclear threat, though I have my doubts whether even this was true. Certainly "emotional truth" could be summoned as a defense of just about reckless claim, including those of the racist or paranoid.

The over-reliance upon some vague and inarticulate sense of affect is precisely what W. K. Wimsatt and M. C. Beardsley intuited as problematic when they coined the phrase "affective fallacy"—that is the fallacy that what we feel about some piece of literature necessary reveals anything useful about "the poem itself, as an object of specifically critical judgment" (21). The phrase "the poem itself" is unfortunate however and suffers from a form of reductivism complementary to that of the affective fallacy. What is useful about Wimsatt and Beardsley's notion is not so much the naïve essentialism that many associate with New Criticism—the notion that poems have definitive and stable natures beyond our varied and culturally conditioned experiences of them. Most productively, Wimsatt and Beardsley articulate a will to question *mere* subjectivity. That said, a critic might deepen this impulse and begin by dispensing with the simplistic notion of subjectivity as pure and unadulterated, as possible without degrees of objectivity in its structure. A critic of greater precision with a less systematic approach cleansed of passion's distortions might talk of different degrees or modes of subjectivity, some of which pay more attention to the otherness of both word and world. A poem's success thus lies in the nature of its attention in all its passion for what, by virtue of its generosity, comes to matter.

In considering the unavoidable subjectivity necessary to write and reconsider metaphor, one might ask if the metaphor does what poems do best, that is, go inward and outward at the same time. How far outward is a writer reaching when reaching for the figure of a nuclear bomb, which, like or not, invokes physical and cultural facts? Facts are always part of the structure of a metaphor. As Wallace Stevens says,

> There is no such thing as a metaphor of a metaphor. One does not progress through metaphors. Thus reality is the indispensible element of each metaphor. When I say that man is a god it is very easy to see that if I say that a god is something else, god has become reality.
> (148)

I would add to this that, while "man" figures as the real world referent in the statement "man is god," the statement also depends in its meaningful resonance on our sense of what makes a god a god, just as, in the student's example, we cannot ignore what makes a bomb *the* bomb.

I was a young professor when I encountered the example of the atomic bomb metaphor, and I believe that I did not handle the situation very successfully, since I remain genuinely uncertain if I did little more than make the author angry. I simply asked, in as quiet a voice as I could muster, "Hmmm, what would a survivor of Hiroshima think of this moment in the poem?" Unfortunately I believe that comment was read as hostile, and it could be that it was, for better or worse. Looking back, I realize a greater problem: that is, I asked the writer to create some fictive reader so vague, constituted of projection, that it became difficult to trust or not trust that reader's imaginary judgment. If led too strongly by the question of what some vast and victimized homogeneity might feel about our work, we could easily stylize our complexity in a way that becomes ironically self-serving and morally proud. The subtext of such work leads not to a world in need but back to the ennobled persona of the writer. What, we might ask, are we "listening to," the summons of the world or our own voices echoed back at us from that world's hollow spaces? What I wanted in my failed way was to make a bit more difficult the invocation of the one's emotional truth as purified from that of someone else's. I wanted the other voice out there, the remote one invoked with barely much notice, to make its presence felt. I longed for a little "hmmm" in the poem, a move beyond the descriptive impulse, such as it was, to something more ambitious and generously exploratory. I wanted the poet to acknowledge, negotiate, and listen to the larger cultural valence of our shared medium.

The deference to emotional truth as somehow giving permission to metaphors of limited perspective is familiar to most working poets. This is precisely the defense exercised on behalf of Sylvia Plath's poem "Daddy" where the speaker likens herself to a Jew suffering at the hands of her father, imagined as a Nazi:

It stuck in a barb wire snare.
Ich, ich, ich, ich,
I could hardly speak.
I thought every German was you.
And the language obscene

An engine, an engine
Chuffing me off like a Jew.
A Jew to Dachau, Auschwitz, Belsen.
I began to talk like a Jew.
I think I may well be a Jew.
(l. 26–35)

As it turns out, we know very little from this poem about the literal occasion of anger, what precisely for instance the father has done. Nor does the speaker feel impelled to explain it all and break the spell of her invention, authenticated less by facts than by Plath's sheer brilliance with metaphor, her strong intuitive sense as to where the heat is, where the vulnerable matter might be pressed and transfigured into incantation. Since much of what we read is translated immediately into metaphor and symbol, the poem has a wild and intense inwardness that, unlike the atomic bomb metaphor, makes its case via its intelligence and resourceful, imaginative power. Of course, one would have a hard time clearly distinguishing wisdom from distortion in Plath's metaphors, since the reality to which they point is so obviously eclipsed. The result is that eclipse becomes inescapably part of the poem's true subject.

While one might say that the speaker exaggerates (a claim both asserted and denied relative to biographical context and Plath's particular reputation as a "confessional"), the symbols are thorny and courageous in part because they refuse to be simple even in their exaggeration, and the emotional ambivalence in the poem makes for an even more dynamic field of emotional truth-telling:

I made a model of you,
A man in black with a Meinkampf look

And a love of the rack and the screw.
And I said I do, I do.
(l. 64–67)

Regardless of what we might project into this poem as credibly grounded in biographical fact, the disturbing testament of affection here, of complicit marriage, destabilizes the felt nature of the victimization and so serves to open up the whole field of vision. The sensibility is letting in a little unexpected light, taking up the old territory of metaphor but broadening its terms beyond the obvious.

Plath's example is, admittedly, controversial, and one might pose to the poet a question akin to the one I asked my student: "Hmmm, I wonder what a victim of Dachau would think of moment after moment in Plath's poem?" Many have already asked this question. I do not aspire here to put forth some kind of system whereby one can clearly determine ethical lapses in metaphors. I do not believe such a rationally conceived and therefore stable, transferable system exists. I do believe however that metaphors often come to us on great breezes of surprise, and if we are to rise to the opportunity of this we, as writers and readers, might listen to the voice inside the voice and so on, the regress of echoes in our often unconscious though no less collective natures.

Ethics has always been problematic in art. "Ethics," to quote Wallace Stevens once again, "are no more a part of poetry than they are of painting"—a statement that, in context, never leads to a close look at painting but leaves implicit a strong aestheticist bias (148). Clearly Stevens wishes to assert aesthetic virtues in the strongest possible terms, and few would disagree that moral agendas threaten to stifle and trivialize a poet's vocation. To write the merely "correct" poem does not sound very interesting or genuine. I would argue however that an ethical engagement calls upon far more than a sense of "correctness." Moreover it can be conceived as the opposite of correctness, if by correctness we mean a kind of inflexible adherence to a systematic code of behavior. Contrary to any preconceived code, an ethical engagement begins in a mode of receptivity. It requires listening.

Such listening could well lead to ambiguity rather than clarity, to a sense of difficult choices between two less than perfect alternatives. What is relevant to art is this mode of listening as wedded to a will to remake the world without negating it. Obviously one cannot include everything in a poem, nor is the democratic impulse to do so consistent with a poem's eye for the necessary. If poetry is language under pressure, part of what we expect from that pressure is a revelation of what matters, aesthetically and emotionally, or what the poem can transform into something that matters, in light of how poetic distillations give voice to some larger context and concern.

Even now, it is common for professionals in literary studies to conceive of aesthetics as a branch separate from the historiographical and ideological criticism so dominant among academics. The dichotomy between aesthetic and ideological approaches to literature remains unfortunate in part because it is impossible to dissociate the two so neatly and remain sensitive to the fullness of art and its particular way of knowing. It is perhaps more obvious what the world of political struggle has to offer poetry than what poetry has to offer the world of politics. One thing poetry has to offer is a vivification of language in all its complexity, its inward and outward origins and movement, the tensions and dependencies between our private and cultural natures. It calls us to look at the moments of poetry, of metaphor in particular, that inform every area of discourse, that humanize the perceived, invest the perceiver, realize and make persuasive our values, however unconscious our intentions. It exemplifies truth-telling that must humble itself again and again as it labors to include and exclude, to let in and pare down, to permit and intensify.

Poetry relishes complexity at the speed of grace, and that complexity by necessity requires meaningful transgression against our former notions of correctness. The metaphor is a model of that transgression, a mode of transgression. The very word *metaphor* (from the Greek for "borne across") suggests *transgression.* In metaphor, the separate selves of the world exchange gifts and identities while nonetheless asserting their separateness. Metaphor thus feeds on paradox. It embodies paradox. In metaphor, we embrace and rebel against our logic in the service of some mysterious sense of the fullness of being as that which lies beyond representation. Metaphor teaches us to listen to the language around us, including the language of politics, and to hear in it always the thing that has not been said, the synaptic gap inside the metaphor. It invites us to honor the not yet, not yet, the great unfinished business that makes us metaphorical by nature, surprised by what it is we come to know, out there in the otherness of our own nature, in the nature of others, in the great conversation of all things that, like one another, cannot be the same.

Works Cited

Bly, Robert. *Leaping Poetry: An Idea with Poems and Translations.* Boston: Beacon, 1973.

Plath, Sylvia. "Daddy." In *The Collected Poems.* New York: Harper Perennial, 1992.

Stevens, Wallace. "Selections from *Adagia.*" *In Modern Poetics,* James Scully, ed. New York: McGraw-Hill, 1965.

Wimsatt, W. K. "The Affective Fallacy." In *The Verbal Icon: Studies in the Meaning of Poetry.* Lexington: University of Kentucky Press, 1954.

The Genius of the Medium

Identity and Alterity in Poetic Practice

When I was an undergraduate at Pomona College in the mid-seventies, the question of the authority of personal narrative in poetry versus a less "I-centered" approach was still a matter of some controversy. On the one hand, Sylvia Plath was hugely popular, as was Allen Ginsberg, and on the other hand, the label "confessional" began to be deployed as pejorative, as if to suggest some mode of self-indulgence that the newly sophisticated might dismiss as hackneyed and adolescent. The objectivists still had a small following, as did those of a later day modernist sentiment who longed to "escape the personality" in their work in ways advocated by T. S. Eliot. For many, Eliot became the epitome of a repressed individual with stodgy views about traditional values, and it took me years to figure out that the gist of Eliot's argument in "Tradition and the Individual Talent" was hardly controversial—it seems obvious to me now that there is a difference between emotion as mediated through art and emotion outside the realm of art. Eliot's hyperboles are unfortunate, but surely I would agree: one has not *merely* a personality to express, but a medium, or, rather, the dimension of personality inseparable from the dynamic, cultural, and historical tension of one's medium. That much, I suspect, is something that Plath and Ginsberg might readily have acknowledged. Nevertheless something of that polarized atmosphere persisted in poetry for quite a while, and though much has dissipated from that weary debate, we still find something of it embedded in, on the one hand, poetry that embraces the often politicized authority of the author's personal identity and, on the other hand, a poetics that eschews even the lyric impulse as reifying a sense of identity that is untenable and narrow.

Back when I was in college, two major cultural shifts had begun to nuance poetic debate, and they continued to do so in years to come. One was the rise of literary theory, the other was an increasing politicization of poetry that began with Vietnam and deepened with the culture wars of the eighties, a time that helped to coin the phrase "political correctness." The rising popularity of postmodern epistemology and its influence on literary and critical practice roughly corresponded with a larger cultural evolution in the politicization of difference. The latter brought on a shift from the liberal attitudes that sought to emphasize similarities across cultures to one more sensitive to difference as a source of both marginalization and power. Egalitarian politics and popular culture began to align themselves less with the idea that we are fundamentally all the same and more with the assertion of difference as something to be not only tolerated but also celebrated.

Obviously such an evolution was gradual and complex, and looking back, I see now that the liberal assertion of personal and cultural difference, versus its underemphasis, was something Americans might well have anticipated. My friends and I, as awkward young progressives in the poetry world, had been perhaps unconsciously conditioned, made receptive to a change in liberal rhetoric by the subcultures of the fifties and sixties. Olson's celebration of roughness, candor, and spontaneity in verse, although objectivist in its original sentiment, resonated strongly with a generation of Beat poets who, in a resurgence of American Romanticism, articulated and affirmed with therapeutic and political openness the marginalized differences of their sexuality and lifestyle. Confessional poems too expressed less what was universal to us all, than what was the individual mark of the extraordinary as a source of authority. Transgression was power. The margin, within the wounded conscience and changing power dynamics of a poetic subculture, was to occupy the center. Subject matter and point of view came to obscure issues more obviously related to aesthetics, such that critical culture became more conversant with ideological modes of critique than it was with Eliot's more formal approach of looking for complexities and originalities of poetic architecture and resonance.

Doubtless the disenfranchised, for whatever individual or cultural reason, looked to the language arts to "name themselves," having been named already, so the imperative notion of poetry as a means of self-transcendence became relativized according to perceived needs with political implications. We might well turn Eliot's words against the spirit of his argument when he says: "But, of course, only those who have personality and emotions know what it means to want to escape from these things." Once again, Eliot's hyperbole obscures his point, for surely few poets of any ilk are without emotions. Buried in Eliot's notion however is the sense that a construction of self or personality makes possible and attractive the concern with self-transcendence. Might we likewise look with greater compassion at those whose sense of self suffers more greatly at the hands of a dominant culture? Might we as individuals and as a culture be better served via receptivity to the self-constructing voices of those in the pursuit of some healthier balance and commerce between selfhood and its context?

Part of the problem in talking this way, as Eliot might well have known, is that we cannot "self-construct" without also negotiating and exploring the cultural otherness that is in our medium of construction. No matter what the more obvious subject matter, poems must find their power relative to an original encounter with language. It was no surprise therefore that, as personal narrative gained the upper hand in American poetry, the resistance to authority based on the writer's persona increased in reciprocal fashion. Poets such as Lowell, Sexton, and Plath who had gained enormous popularity inspired the inevitable backlash, a resistance that heated the debate concerning the self-indulgence of the confessional impulse in poems, an impulse often conflated with any consuming attraction to autobiography. In 1971 for example, Galway Kinnell wrote:

> The poetry of this century is marked by extreme self-absorption so we have been a "school" of self-dissection, the so-called confessional poets, who sometimes strike me as being interested in their own experience to the exclusion of everyone else's.
>
> (219)

The irony to this common and understandable critique is the fact that what appears to be an exclusionary sensibility nevertheless speaks to a lot of people, some of whom might take more pleasure in self-absorption in poems (imaginative constructs) than they would in real people. To say a narcissistic culture loves a narcissistic art does not explain much, since often the last person a narcissist wants to engage is another narcissist. In addition, the idea that the canonical confessionals attracted fans simply due to a fresh and edgy transparency does not fully honor the role of imaginative mediation, how it empowers readers voyeuristically to experience a specifically aesthetic form of empathy, intimacy, and identification.

Clearly Kinnell's own work has demonstrated throughout his career an abiding interest in first-person narratives of domestic life, so his personal example suggests that his rejection of the exclusionary and exhibitionistic does not imply a return to the perceived coldness of high modernism and Eliot's promotion of an escape from the personality. As heated as it is, Kinnell's critique is hardly revolutionary. One would be hard pressed to find a statement of poetics at any stage in literary history that would not indebt itself to "the other" in art—the universal, the transpersonal, the communal, the material, the historical, even the aesthetic—as if to compensate for poetry's ready association with the self.

Remnants of complaint akin to Kinnell's have persisted long after the period of confessionalism and its immediate influence. For instance, it is remarkable to see how similarly broad the contemporary target is in Jorie Graham's critique in her introduction to *Best American Poetry: 1990*:

> The poetry that fails the genius of its medium today is the poetry of mere self. It embarrasses all of us. The voice in it is not large but inflated. A voice that expands not to the size of a soul (capable of being both personal and communal, both private and historical) but to the size of an ego. What I find most consistently moving about the act of a true poem is the way it puts the self at genuine risk.
> (xxxvi)

The idea of risk here is tremendously useful, for it advocates not only vulnerability and tension, but also a sense of the dynamic, exploratory process of the poem. Graham invokes Frost's notion of poetic ingenuity as "getting into danger legitimately so that we may be genuinely rescued" and so raises a host of productive questions in reconceiving the category of "the genuine" as a matter of both epistemology and aesthetics. By association, the inauthentic self appears to be the autonomous self, or the self that labors to promote the illusion of its autonomy, its denials and defenses, its safe place, its formal closure. A poem based on this particular illusion is not a "true poem" less because it resists the real (most poems do this and the opposite) but because it does not fulfill the defining characteristic of a poem as driven by alterity and eros, their capacity to inspire wonder and magnanimity.

Poetry no doubt finds itself in a defensive position relative to a general sense of poets as impractical narcissists. As Graham further advocates the legitimate poem, she not only justifies it via epistemological categories (the true and the genuine), but also ethical categories suggestive of generosity and transpersonal utility:

> To place oneself at genuine risk, that the salvation effected be genuine (i.e., of use to us), the poet must move to encounter an other, not more versions of the self. An other: God, nature, a beloved, an Idea, Abstract form, Language itself as a field, Chance, Death, Consciousness, what exists in silence. Something not invented by the writer.
> (xxvii)

There is something circular in the argument that in order for a poem to be useful to *us* it must encounter an alterity, such as an *us*, and yet the statement itself proves useful in laying bare the impoverishment of the poem that lacks not only a certain humility but, somewhat paradoxically, a certain ambition. In contrast, the so-called modest poem, careful not to over-reach its scope of authority and previous experience, eschews the risk and vulnerability implicit in exposure to enormity, however embodied in the small. The constricted modest poem in this sense appears content merely to *express* meaning (as something that precedes the poem) rather than *expand* and thereby *create* it. Certainly the latter is a more ambitious enterprise, but in its ambition lies its generosity. Thus humility as ambitious and ambition as self-transcending summon the imagination to risk, to process, to vulnerability and exposure via some unforeseen act of transformation.

Many of the alterities mentioned by Graham resonate as bearing the grandeur of the absolute or some totality that is, if not God, God's surrogate, some vast and fundamental mystery, akin to a metaphysical ground. Even groundlessness (Chaos or Death) as an imaginative category can occupy the space of that ground, that deeper reality, reference point, or principle that solicits faith in lieu of knowledge. Even the focus of the intimate love poem or elegy gathers resonance in its relation, not simply to the lover or the lost one, but to imaginary readers, yet another metaphysical "other" that haunts the medium as a nexus of the public and the private. Thus the intimate poem resonates by honoring the powers of imagination, conceptualization, and form indigenous to the medium. In all cases, poetry intensifies the tension and connectivity between the local and something larger, such that the so-called poem of mere particularity, like that of "mere self," ceases to be a poem.

An anti-metaphysical, "language" poetics of obdurate surfaces, what Charles Bernstein calls the poetics of non-absorption, may resist the tedium of literality and semiotic closure; it may reflect the rigor of refusing to affirm what it cannot know; it may position itself against of poetry of *mere* transparency; but it is not a poetry invested in the element of faith and metaphysical hunger that drives a language to remake itself in response to some unrepresented reality. It is a "poem," to borrow a phrase from Jorie Graham, that "fails the genius of its medium." That genius implies the immense desire for the fullness of being as beyond the grasp of the medium. When Graham refers to "Language as a field," she invokes a sense of the vast, the inter-textuality of all texts. This is often perceived as an alternative to a metaphysical model, the sense of endless surfaces, but endlessness is itself something we cannot experience. For one to suggest that there is no end to the play of interpretation is to raise the question, "How do you know?"

The work of Wallace Stevens expresses a keen appreciation for the paradoxical nature of the imagination as driven by a real it can never accommodate. It is for this reason that Stevens writes in "Of Modern Poetry:"

> The actor is
> A metaphysician in the dark, twanging
> An instrument, twanging a wiry string that gives
> Sounds passing through sudden rightnesses, wholly
> Containing the mind, below which it cannot descend,
> Beyond which it has no will to rise.
> It must
> Be the finding of a satisfaction, and may
> Be of a man skating, a woman dancing, a woman
> Combing. The poem of the act of the mind.
> (l. 19–28)

The poet, as metaphysician in the dark, makes a sound, however imperfect, that goes where neither she nor her instrument can. The music is not captured. It "passes through," and thus the paradoxical satisfaction that a poem breeds in the local. The man skating, the woman combing—these things grow radiant via some great and unresolved metaphysical process. That process is nothing less than mindfulness, attention to one's time, one's moment, and to the hunger that binds attention to what it sees. "The act of finding," states the opening of the poem, which already is paradoxical, since finding is not an act, but the end of an act. Likewise satisfaction, as we find it in the poem, it bears the lingering signature of desire.

The pleasure of poetry therefore is always that of the arriving departure. It speaks to our desire to make intimate the great dialogue between the self and the other, the immanent and the transcendent, the real and the imagined. Its search must, consciously or not, negotiate the world in honor of both the individual and the cultural. In the process, poetry makes of the dissonance between them a music. It makes of hunger a satisfaction. It makes of form an act. And of the self, it makes a glass island, a thing that is both there and not there, a thing that is only there at the peril and grace of all that it can never be.

Works Cited

Eliot, T. S. "Tradition and the Individual Talent." In *The Selected Prose of T. S. Eliot.* New York: Houghton Mifflin Harcourt, 1950.

Graham, Jorie. "Introduction." In *Best American Poetry: 1990.* Jorie Graham and David Lehman, eds. New York: Collier, 1990.

Kinnell, Galway. "Poetry, Personality, and Death." In *Claims for Poetry.* Donald Hall, ed. Ann Arbor: University of Michigan Press, 1987.

Stevens, Wallace. *Wallace Stevens: Collected Poetry and Prose.* Frank Kermode and Joan Richardson, eds. New York: Library of America, 1997.

Empathy and the Poetic Imagination

There are Selves who unify their expressions by their subjective force; it is only with the intensity of such subjectivity that one even sees the world of objects.
—Robert Motherwell

For every poet as ventriloquist, there is a planet made of tongues. Birds talk. Chairs respond. The dead rise and give advice, and in so doing they throw their voices into us. Hard to tell at times just who is talking, where the font of agency begins. What we do know is that the poetic imagination could not exist without some sense of reciprocity in its chamber of thrown voices. The poem thus is a kind of doll that surprises the child with what it says, with the ongoing dialogue between her inner depths and outer reaches. The poem's cave that takes some voice into the dark returns that voice in a new inflection. What is the human throat if not a cave? In the echo chamber of poetic resonance, poems articulate something fundamental about the reciprocal and seminal power exchange in all language. We speak and so are spoken, and what we speak about in turn speaks of us.

Leave it to the poetic imagination to see the dead as willful, creative, slipping their desires into us. Those of a less superstitious nature are bound to reject a ghost as literal, but they still might embrace the poetic wonder and heartbreak of the haunted dream they remember as they wake. They might savor the clarity dreams give to the relational pull of their deepest affections. Likewise even the most superstitious must register, consciously or unconsciously, that if we could know beyond doubt that the dead talk, the dream sheds a little of its awe and wonder, a little of its force. It would surrender its faith, its love/hate relation to the real. Poems cannot exist without the pull of the real and the push of the unreal. The same is true of metaphors more largely, one side of which pins itself to some intuited ground. Magic cannot be ordinary, though poetry thrives on the tension that both would and would not make it so.

If a poet's ventriloquism were not tempered by attention to the real, if the real did not in turn throw its voice into the imagining subject, the world would be voiceless or its voice would be displaced, appropriated, subverted. Projection would overwhelm its vessel with pre-existent needs and so lapse into something less transformative, into the aesthetic narcissism perhaps, the decadence in which artifice devours the vision it would serve. On the other hand, if the poet were merely passive, literal, unassertive in her formal rendering, the dead would lie down in their graves once again. Chairs would sit silent. The world would slowly bleed dry, drained of the radiance of felt relations. It would lack the power of eros that first summoned us to the world, that taught us the imagination's most fundamental vocation: to make the universe into something we can love. The cold rationality of science may get things done, but it cannot fall in love with science. Where science gets strange, it invites us in as strangers. It binds us, drawn to the limits of our knowledge, more closely to the material world by virtue of its enigmas, its distance bridged by awe and speculative desire.

In truth, it is hard to imagine the extremes of subjectivity or objectivity since our experience, bound by the principles of each, must negotiate the vast possibilities between. Those deeply attentive to the variety of our dreams tend to maintain some ambivalence about their power, whether they bring us closer to the world or shield us from its harsh bright light. A poet's imaginative assertions, however underplayed, may inspire similar ambivalence, for although poems call upon a sense of craft that dreams lack, both poetry and dream depend upon a sense of mediating the unknown or, more paradoxically, the unknowable. Both imply a vehicle, a semiotics, a progressive syntax of signs, the elusive logic of symbol speaking to symbol. Both "mediate" something that appears beyond expression but that, in spite of our ignorance, must suggest the gravitational pull of the real. Without such gravity, the search for meaning is frivolous. Without doubt, the search cannot exist.

Thus when Jacques Lacan famously reiterates that "the unconscious is structured like a language," he is quick to note the importance of the word "like" and what it does not, cannot, claim:

> You see that by still preserving this "like" [*comme*], I am staying within the bounds of what I put forward when I say that the unconscious is structured *like* a language. I say *like* so as not to say.
>
> (48)

Both poems and dreams deploy a language that appears to articulate something beyond them, something that cannot be represented without the residue of doubt that makes oneiric faith possible. With regard to the power and significance of this faith, not all dreams are equal. Some are paranoid nonsense. Some tell us we are hungry. Others register suppressed or deeply awakened insight. The defensive boundaries relax, and the subject-objects of memory and desire come into greater conversation to coax us into greater recognitions. Similarly, poems may be either exercises in self-indulgence or forces that expand the felt awareness that seems indigenous to a poem's origin in its dialogue with the world.

The question therefore remains: if a perceiver's imaginative commitments invest the world with value, with eros as an articulation of values, at what point does the perceiver risk an overvaluation of imaginative subjectivity? Is it still eros if, in time, it comes to worship eros? Is falling in love with love not a form of narcissism and thus the end of love? Implicit in these questions is the larger question as to whether a poem can succeed if the subject matter of the poem narrows to contemplate itself merely, its own imagination. In an absolute sense, this is impossible, but relatively speaking, the polar extremes of aesthetic overindulgence and barren literalism figure as equally dull. Wallace Stevens, obsessed as he was in making a case for "the supreme fiction," argues in "The Noble Rider and the Sound of Words" that the imagination must register the pressure of the real, that elusive world beyond its subjectivity, or it relinquishes its "vitality." Moreover it becomes frivolous. It is not enough that the external summons to the imagination is simply some vague social sphere, relativized and ungrounded. If that world does not register affectively as real, however imperfectly modeled as such, its summons is weak.

The difficult question of degree bears on the elusive nature of taste, which, in the context of art, often resonates as the province of aesthetics merely, as if aesthetic concerns could be met or bracketed off from epistemological and ethical ones. It remains hard to imagine however just what "taste" could mean if not some intuitive negotiation of multiple values, some conversation involving what is said, how it is said, and whether it is worth saying. Characteristic lapses in taste, such as sensationalism and sentimentality, fail as artificial in part because they are artless. In both cases the affect appears monotonal, manipulative, imposed and thus, however grounded in fact, not quite genuine in modeling the real. Their aesthetic failure is therefore embedded in a perceived epistemological one and, by virtue of their manipulative self-indulgence, an ethical one as well.

Given the vast range of artful stances toward the real, the words *aesthetic* and *aestheticization* are often vague and insufficient as terms to describe the level of attention and authenticity in imaginative assertions. For both aesthetic and epistemological reasons, the sentimental and sensational do not provide credible *and* compelling models of the complexity of inner life. They fail the demands of a poem to answer to often competing values and so to reanimate the poetic imagination as something deeply conflicted at heart, as a form of creative play called to meaningful difficulty, to empathy and understanding. To define what empathy could be in a poem is difficult indeed, since the very act of reading or writing has some sense of voyeuristic distance built into it, and yet the tension that empathic listening gives to a poem remains critical to its power, a quality of speaking and being spoken, of going more deeply inward as if somewhere in there were the path to others.

Till Human Voices Wake Us

In his essay "Tradition and the Individual Talent," when T. S. Eliot famously states that art does not have a personality to express but rather a medium, he does not argue against the oneiric transformations that seem so suggestive of one's character. Nor does he characterize imaginative powers as intrusive and narcissistic. On the contrary, he wishes to create some distance between art and artist and so argue for language as something other than a mere *transparency* through which we would see the poet behind it. The persuasive and useful part of his argument positions itself not against "personality" but against the myth of art as merely passive "expression" for the personality as some essence that precedes imaginative form. It is not personality so much that art escapes as the naïve conception of "personality" as something fully constituted and thus capable of dominating its medium:

> The point of view which I am struggling to attack is perhaps related to the metaphysical theory of the substantial unity of the soul: for my meaning is, that the poet has, not a "personality" to express, but a particular medium, which is only a medium and not a personality, in which impressions and experiences combine in peculiar and unexpected ways. (10)

In asking us to reconsider the association between the poetic imagination and autonomous selfhood, the above passage registers more sensitivity to the difficulty of Eliot's subject than his questionable metaphor of "escape." His notion that poetry "is not an expression of personality, but an escape from personality" relies ironically upon a reification of the boundaries that it would critique. The metaphor of escape implies a movement across such a boundary. It suggests a "substantial unity" of some kind, a delineated sense of personhood, however contextualized within some larger consciousness. What Eliot seeks is perhaps less an escape from the walls of the personal than a radical dismantling of those conceptual walls, a calling into question their metaphysical sustainability.

Eliot's most obvious point is that, in poetry, the imagination, as mediated, must negotiate the collective, objective, and historical tensions embedded in form and diction. Given social context, a poem stands in relation to a tradition, whether consciously or not, and greater consciousness empowers one to move that tradition forward, to find what is meaningfully new to the conversation. A less obvious assumption suggests that the imaginative craving for the "peculiar and unexpected" might mitigate against the more naïve ways in which poets perceive their work as "personal." The need to "make it new" suggests that poetry's medium, as more assertive in its energy, locates its authority in the dialogue between tradition and individual subjectivity.

If we see in Eliot's hyperboles an enthusiasm for the imaginative order of a tradition that cannot possibly be orderly, he likewise expresses a healthy bit of subversive will, both in his rhetorical defiance and his affinity with the revolutionary inwardness and evocative techniques of French Symbolism. The example of "The Love Song of J. Alfred Prufrock" embodies this spirit in its reliance on the deeply conflicted poetic image, the image saturated in unconscious energy at the same time that it critiques the alienated solipsism of imaginative excess:

> I should have been a pair of ragged claws
> Scuttling across the floor of silent seas.
> (l. 73–74)

The self-hatred and anger that claw at Prufrock register his failure in the social sphere, not only because that sphere appears superficial, but because he is no less so. In so doing, the poem explores something of the possibility of inward, imaginative excess that subordinates women to their mythic or archetypal value relative to the speaker's desire. Thus, if they appear, they do so as fragmented bodies and bits of conversation, never as clear subjectivities in their own right. They become the correlative to mermaids, subordinate to projection, dream stuff incapable of genuine coupling. Prufrock's particular imagination as the expression of a crippled and thereby inflated ego consumes its world in the projection of its needs. It cries out for meaning, which is to say a relational ground in either the metaphysical or social realm, but pursues it by assertively and imaginatively recasting the given nature of the world in an attempt to further reify, articulate, and structure his threatened sense of self. Human voices, as opposed to mythic ones, are dangerous, precisely because their desiring subjectivities remind Prufrock of the vulnerabilities and limits of his own. Taken to an extreme, Prufrock's symptoms verge on a kind of paranoia wherein the weak ego exposes the self to the assaults of the unconscious. If such a person throws his voice into the world with the ardor of a conspiracy theorist, it is in part because the forces of alterity and their hallucinatory displacements are so strong.

This said, to critique the character of Prufrock is not to critique the poem, and images such as the scuttling claws speak intimately of universals. Thus the same imaginative projections that alienate Prufrock from his world connect us to his. Moreover they, as rising to the demands of poetry's medium as inventive, peculiar, multiply evocative, articulate and expand a collective sense of wonder and insight into the way consciousness works and does not work. Representations of pathological narcissism in poetry include us in ways that the narcissist does not. In a poem, we, as readers, as voyeurs at the clarifying distance required to read, are not cornered by the narcissist. By virtue of the mediation that Eliot honors, we are invited to explore the conceptual and affective complexity that is an element of form. Irrationality in poetry makes room for us. It draws us as readers both inward and outward at the same time, empowered to participate in a construction of meaning made possible by the familiar in the peculiar, the clear in the distorted, the daylight in the partially eclipsed. While Prufock may not model empathy, he might well solicit it, not because he meets our ethical criteria, not because we would chose him as a friend, but because his inner life resonates as authentically and powerfully rendered, which we can only recognize as such because that life resonates, consciously or not, with our own.

Suffering is power. It is also suffering. Pain has a defiantly private dimension and as such asserts itself in one sense as a boundary between selves. Suffering makes plain the impossibility of empathy as an absolute. Nowhere is the ambiguous subject of "appropriation" more heated as when it involves the appropriation of one's power in the form of self-inflating assumptions about and identifications with another's suffering. Thus the sense of violation implied by the notion of appropriation extends beyond the ethical realm into a fundamental epistemological one. Stated another way, ethics and epistemology inform each other's resistance to the act of appropriation, particularly in difficult times when a public sensitivity to the problem of appropriation and imaginative eclipse rises. With suffering, particularly on a collective scale, the pressure of the real increases, along with the expectations that imaginative forms honor the alterity of that pressure. In extreme cases, art goes silent.

In his book *Shock of the New,* Robert Hughes points to the silencing effect that Holocaust photographs had on the world of painting. Painters felt paralyzed, unable to compete with the greater transparency of the documentary medium. This is not to say that photographic journalism lacks an aesthetic, only that the aesthetic elements appear subordinated more emphatically to their subject. The greater the suffering rendered, the greater the perceived need for such subordination. Take Nick Ut's Pulitzer-winning, Vietnam-era photograph of a naked girl running from napalm. Indeed it has a striking composition to it. We see there at the center of our attention the girl framed by other children, one of whom looks back to soldiers bringing up the rear, and behind them in the distance, the great, black, devouring cloud. Given that drama and our likely empathic response, it may disturb our ethical sensibilities to admit to the aesthetic elements of satisfaction, of pleasure even, that contribute to our response. That said, it is unlikely that the photograph would have garnered such attention if it had been out of focus or badly composed. Journalistic aesthetics must above all appear to intensify rather than mitigate the pressure of the real. It is not the role of the news photo to draw attention to the dissonance between compositional satisfaction and documentary pressure.

In his "Essay on Cultural Criticism and Society," Theodore Adorno's famous claim, "To write a poem after Auschwitz is barbaric" (p. 34), benefits from the greater context of his argument:

> To anyone in the habit of thinking with his ears, the words "cultural criticism" (*Kulturkritik*) must have an offensive ring, not merely because, like automobile, they are pieced together from Latin and Greek. The words recall a flagrant contradiction. The cultural critic is not happy with civilization, to which alone he owes his discontent. He speaks as if he represents unadulterated nature or a higher historical stage. Yet he is necessarily of the same essence as that to which he fancies himself superior.
> (p. 19)

Here he admits a certain humility and culpability, enmeshed, indebted, and shaped as he is by the objects of his critique. Although in a similarly self-effacing spirit, he will admit later that he overstated his case about the barbarism of poetry after the Holocaust, his famous claim is nonetheless useful in articulating something of the humility and shame that haunts the effort to turn extreme horror into the stuff of poetic wonder and compositional satisfaction.

Beyond this, his statement implies that some historical shifts are so enormous that they must dominate the conversation. To change the topic belies complacency, and complacency is ruthless. If the world were not saturated in blood and guilt that would totalize experience with its themes, Adorno's would not have garnered such attention. Anger simplifies, as does bitterness. The complicating irony in Adorno's tone, in spite of his admission, is its dictatorial sweep, the fact that his rhetorical power depends upon a culture of shame and outrage to take to heart its totalizing conceptual overthrow. What Auschwitz did was put poems under pressure to reconcile the pleasure of form with the sobriety and immensity of collective suffering. The refining of horror into artifice might better be described as decadence rather than barbarism, but this is precisely why "barbarism" is the more forceful metaphor. Decadence characterizes an artful excess relative to its content or occasion. Barbarism implies brutality. Moreover it has a social register with its roots in the perceived violence of the crude outsider. Thus the tone of "barbarism" runs counter to that of "decadence," which can imply the social license, often made possible by greater means. Somewhat ironically, Adorno's rhetorical strategies (conceptual opposition, theatricality, metaphor, hyperbole) are that of a poem, rendering not simply the cold subject matter of the world but our felt relation to it. Adorno's claim pleases, on some level, with its compositional speed and force.

The pleasure of such form figures as a subcategory of the more pervasive and less obvious pleasure of representation. Though it is clear the barbaric element of the poetic is in the intensification of this pleasure, there is some larger category of representation at play, and it is through representation at large that one expresses the hunger for empowerment that drives language and its proliferation. With such empowerment, the mind performs the magic of making the absent present, of conflating absence and presence in imaginary ways that help us cope with the anxicty of non-being. Moreover, as Nietzsche explores at length in "The Birth of Tragedy," there is a satisfaction in rendering suffering as "mere appearance," and by virtue of aesthetic form, the sense of imaginary mastery intensifies. We can through artful referentiality, however transfigured and abstract, encounter suffering while nevertheless stepping back from it, enjoying some freedom, however illusory, of movement in relation to it.

Such is the troubling position of empowerment that we have relative to Nick Ut's photograph, with its compositional order muted beneath our empathetic response. We are not looking at the world, after all. We are looking at a photograph, and as horrifying as it is, we might well prefer to look at the representation versus the real presence. If an urgency of suffering did not cry through the surface of the work, we might ease more comfortably into the pleasure of representation. The contemplation of a painting of a mountain, for instance, might well be preferable to the real mountain because the painting is imbued eros, relational by nature. We see not only a mountain but ourselves in the mountain and the mountain in us. In contrast to the documentary aesthetic, art as it moves increasingly toward the poetic would imitate not simply the mountain as object but our relation to it and thus the very act of attention, of imitation. Poetry, as something other than mere escape, is self-reflexive in this way, though it need not be self-conscious about that fact. Poetry, if it aspires toward the visionary in ways specific to poems, is self-reflexive since its chosen "reality" is always to some extent the imagination itself. The imaginative element thus is not an escape from reality, but rather a restoring of it, an actual embodiment of the fundamentally relational nature of experience.

The aesthetics of Ut's photograph derives its power in part by subordinating the pleasure of representation to the horror of the real as inhering in the material and social other. The naked girl pierces us more deeply because she is naked, as is news photography in a relative sense. We see ourselves in her, and yet we are acutely aware of the vast difference between us and the unspeakable anguish that she feels. The transparency of representation is a kind of soundproof glass. Our empathy feeds on its impossibility, the feeling that her pain is hers alone, and we can at best be present in some imaginary space. We go out to meet her, or rather the representation of her, who occupies a silence, a place beyond representation. Part of the connection to the real then is in the imagined experience of difference, of powerlessness, of bearing forward the memory as our imperfect summons to the world.

The Other in the Dream

Paul Celan's poetry on the Holocaust represents another extreme in terms of moving away from journalistic transparency toward a medium more conspicuous in its beauty and imaginative structure, more surreal in its figurative defamiliarization and internalization of the real. His poetic imagination is less intent on bearing the news in readily recognizable terms than in inventing a strange, new, and sometimes incantatory dialect for the unspeakable. His most famous poem on the subject, "Death Fugue," resonates with the dark beauty, wonder, and horror of a nightmare, such that the distinctive feature of its authority lies less in horrible information and more in the damaged inner life that bears the legacy of horror. Grief clashes with wonder in a way characteristic of the most inward spaces of the wounded psyche:

> Black milk of daybreak we drink it at sundown
> we drink it at noon in the morning we drink it at night
> we drink it and drink it
> we dig a grave in the breezes there one lies unconfined
> A man lives in the house he plays with the serpents he writes
> he writes when dusk falls to Germany your golden hair
> Margarete
> he writes it and steps out of doors and the stars are flashing
> he whistles
> his pack out
> he whistles his Jews out in earth has them dig for a grave
> he commands us strike up for the dance
> (l. 1–9)

The lush music and figuration of the poem, scriptural in its recursivity, is potentially both disturbing and satisfying. The way it infuses the brutal facts with the deep, formal fluency of lyric lamentation, we may feel haunted by the exposed inner life as a form of intimacy, and the lyricism as a form of distance. The simultaneous sense of intimacy and distance bears the characteristics of a dream. Lyricism somewhat ironically becomes mimetic of horror via the mechanism of repression. Part of the horror here is the horror of denial, however merciful, where the psyche protects itself against itself. Tonal opposition has within its illogic a strong logic nevertheless and so lends both dynamism and structure.

Adorno's claim about poetry, however metonymical for art in general, registers an awareness of poetry's particular threat or character, though he does not explain what that is. He does not note that poetry, as the art that is most about language, is the one most prone to the uneasy combination of external referentiality and self-reflexivity, nor does he make distinctions with regard to styles of self-reflexivity that might indeed wed themselves more strongly in emotional and conceptual fashion to scenes of horror and the human dilemma of spiritual survival in light of them. The mind in shock might well lend itself to a poetics of far greater tension and psychological realism than the so-called correct poem of social realism, appropriately pressured by shame or pragmatism to be more literal, clear, and directive.

Written during the Spanish Civil War, Pablo Neruda's poem "A Few Things Explained" gives rationale to the writer's act of turning away from a more introverted, opiated poetics of wonder in order to make room for a new phase of empathic and political engagement:

> You will ask: And where are the lilacs?
> And the metaphysics muffled in poppies?
> And the rain which so often has battered
> its words till they spouted up
> gullies and birds?
>   (l. 1–4)

One of the framing ironies of the poem is that the cry to look depends upon the averted gaze. The numbing poppies, after all, are in the poem, as is the house that "exploded/with geraniums" later on (l. 14–15). The elements of wonder are essential not only for their tonal opposition but as loving testament to what has been lost. The "beautiful/ house" contains within it the memories of the victims, including Federico Lorca, whose fellow poetic sensibility finds expression in Neruda's line, "June drowned the dazzle of flowers in your teeth" (l. 23).

Such stubborn surrealism with its saturation in the associative logic complicates the tone of anger at the end of the poem:

> Come see the blood in the streets,
> come see
> the blood in the streets,
> come see the blood
> in the streets!
>   (l. 75–80)

The call to witness is a call for immediacy, both of seeing and feeling, but the demands of factual confrontation and empathic response rely upon competing strategies in the poem.

The poem is soaked in both beauty and horror and as such

moves in and out of a dream space toward a closure that, in its urgency, registers the struggle. The raised pitch would wake not simply us, but the speaker's projected and imaginary sense of "us" as the embodiment of his own former aesthetic. Given the competing sensibilities in the poem, the final summons cannot help but have an inward cast as well. Even the final lines do not quite flatten into journalistic transparency. After all, enjambment structures our attention to regard a shifting emphasis. The small matters, politically and aesthetically. Form embodies care by way of attention to the small. It mediates the longing to overcome the limits of mediation, aesthetic or otherwise, to confront facts so difficult that they breed insistent incantations and so articulate and dismantle a lingering disbelief.

The Unconscious Political

It may seem counterintuitive that a surreal aesthetics, such as that of Pablo Neruda, should lend itself to politics, particularly as conceived by the Communist Party that Neruda represented as a senator in 1945. Surrealism has had, since early in its development, a troubled relationship to the Communist Party and its competing notions about art's political efficacy. When, in his first manifesto, André Breton framed his central notion of "psychic automatism," he specified that it be "dictated by thought, in the absence of any control exercised by reason, exempt from any aesthetic or moral concern" (p. 26). However, in both France and the Americas, surrealism as a movement and a practice carries with it a strong history of socialist aspirations, as evidenced in André Breton's joining of the French Communist Party in 1927 and his expulsion in 1933. The expulsion did little to dim Breton's enthusiasm as he went on to write *The Political Position of Surrealism* in 1935 and to visit Leon Trotsky, Frida Kahlo, and Diego Rivera in Mexico in the late thirties. Clearly the aesthetic of surrealism, with its enigmatic inwardness, is diametrically opposed to the desired pragmatics and lucidity of Stalinist social realism. As Breton states in his first manifesto of 1924, the greatest surreal image is:

> the one that is arbitrary to the greatest degree, the one that takes the longest time to translate into practical language, either because it contains the greatest amount of seeming contradiction, or because one of its terms is strangely concealed. (38)

By the 1930s, it has become clear to Breton that the enigmatic quality of surrealism obscures for many its political value, especially in Marxist terms that emphasize the external, material ground of dialectical process, as opposed to the inwardness so salient in dreams.

In his essay "Surrealism and the Situation of the Object," Breton defends Hegel, whom, he claims, his fellow socialists attack for the idealist bent of Hegelian dialectics, hostile in the minds of many to Marxist philosophical materialism. According to Breton, Hegel's detractors would have dialectics "walk on its head." In contrast, Breton believed that Hegel would have proved far more qualified than his critics to understand if surrealism is "ill-founded" or not, for Hegel understood more thoroughly and precisely the relation of consciousness to sensible forms in dialectical process (p. 259). Breton's emphasis here is not on poetry but on painting, more obviously material, where the dream logic of surreality signifies not alienation but connection. Surreal painting thus invests material with the immaterial. In surreal poems too, we might add, matter is not the lifeless stuff of an objectification. Herein lies the less obvious connection of surrealism to Marxism in reimagining some alternative to withdrawal. In Breton's words, the surreal aesthetic serves social process by "excluding (relatively) the external object as such and considering nature only in its relationship with the inner world of consciousness" (p. 260).

Breton's argument gives support to the notion that the heavy dose of subjectivity in a work of art models a breed of intimacy with one's material world. However, this argument does little to address the messiness of competing subjectivities. The possible presumption of Breton's claim is that "the inner world of consciousness" is *one* world and therefore shared. He does not fully investigate the potential ironies of his statement. The example of the schizophrenic suggests that the mind's ventriloquism speaking into the forms of nature could drown out the other subjectivities in the room. One might complicate Breton's discussion by investigating the metaphor of "listening" when it comes to aesthetic process. This is far trickier when it comes to social as opposed to material alterity. Clearly, there is no safe place in ideology that translates into the empathic consciousness of the ideologist. This is likely to be obvious, and if not, one need only look at the character of Breton with his imperial edicts and "expulsions" from the surreal movement. Moral pride is characteristically cruel. By grace of its complexity, experiential grounding, and inclusiveness of affect, poetry, including Breton's, cannot be sensitively understood as mere ideology, however many ideological tensions it may embody. Breton's notion of the poet as operating without "moral concern" might better be understood as a lack of the vanity and self-consciousness to be morally correct. Paradoxically, the lack of moral self-styling might itself be a moral gesture, more genuine in its empathy, but there is no guarantee that it would be.

Another possible irony suggests that poetry can figure as more persuasive, even in political or ethical terms, than overtly ideological discourse. The empathic ground of its perspective may appear more earned, of greater emotional summons, precisely because of the imaginative force of inwardness. With the influx of South American surrealism into the United States in the 1960s, many poets of the Vietnam era turned to surreal techniques to produce some of the most successful poems of protestation, including "Counting Small-Boned Bodies" by Robert Bly and "The Asians Dying" by W. S. Merwin. The success of these poems lies in part in how the surreal impulse mitigates against the rigidity of conviction, so the poems do not fall victim to the didacticism that would paralyze their powers of evocation. Bly's poem works particularly well in wedding political outrage to surreal wonder, both as the source of the poem's authoritative tension and as parodic critique of the war bureaucrat's euphemistic take on violence:

> Let's count the bodies over again.
> If we could only make the bodies smaller

The size of skulls
We could make a whole plain white with skulls in the
moonlight!
(l. 1–4)

Such poems temper their instrumental ambition with a critical element of the dream, its quality of strangeness and surprise that, unlike political conviction, could not have preceded the expressive act. The poem relinquishes some measure of control modeled in the certitude of the political manifesto or, for that matter, the phone book, work predicated on our passivity as readers and the passivity of the medium in yielding to intention. The poet's voice must give voice.

The Grace of Accuracy

Admittedly "subjectivity" is an immense and blurry category. As such, it gestures toward a certain metaphysical blurriness as embedded in ordinary language. As one pole of the subject-object continuum that makes consciousness possible, subjectivity suggests relief from the bias that imparts the lion's share of reality to the objects of perception. "Empathy," as no less difficult a category, would occupy a space at both ends of the continuum. This is in part because its "object" *is* a "subjectivity," which like one's own is messy, and that very subjectivity calls us to the humanity of our own. Empathy cannot be objective, nor can it shed a metaphysical sense of irresolution and hunger for that which is beyond representation. Empathy thus provides a model of what poetry longs to be, empathetic in the sense of listening as it speaks. In poetry, the surreal image potentially pays homage to something beyond the self, something transpersonal in both the outward and inward sense. "Empathy" conceived as listening speech is at the core of what gives the poetic imagination its expressive power, its attentive invention, its imagined reconciliation or conflation of facts and values. In order to see poetry in the light of its strengths, it helps to see all good poems, in the broadest sense, as love poems. This is to say that their power depends upon what is at stake in imaginative play. Love is the signature of commitment. It gives a poem its pressure of necessity. All poems animated by this necessity see in the world the care and investment of imaginative awakening, of eros as dialogical, born in the conversation between the given and the made.

One of the practical problems that an artist confronts is that eros requires a subjectivity that in excess threatens to overwhelm its object. We see this in romantic love, in the necessary tension between the archetypal and the individual bearing of the beloved that makes romantic love possible. The mythic dimensions of romantic love that characteristically subside with familiarity can inflate themselves at the expense of the beloved. Romantic love struggles to overcome the narcissistic element within it. In poetry too, it is less specifically an inwardness that tends to break the spell of eros than it is self-regard, or self-consciousness in its pejorative sense. Surrealism characteristically aligns itself with a more "naked" poetics, as articulated in the popular Vietnam-era anthology *Naked Poetry*, inclusive of Bly, Merwin, and others whose plain diction and figurate leaps combine to give the marvelous the quality of the homemade. The surreal image as expressive of eros suggests a subordination of artifice to improvisatory candor, less hesitant, more freely associative, less plagued by issues of "correctness," or, as Breton says, "aesthetic or moral concern," but it takes a great deal of faith in the transformative power of disinhibition to believe the unpoliced sensibility moves toward empathy. One need only look at the frequent misogynist elements in early surreal visual art for an example of disinhibition giving license to sadism.

On the other hand, repression of the cruel appetites and paranoia of the psyche does even less to transform them. No manifesto can render unproblematic poetry's (and the psyche's) need for both passion and discipline, surrender and control. In bracketing off aesthetic and moral concerns, Breton leaves wonder and authenticity to fill the void. Somewhat ironically for some, surrealism, as a higher realism (a sur-realism), gains much of its authority from its psychic "truth." Poetry is frivolous without some such revelatory possibility. Still Breton's subordination of aesthetic and moral concerns conflicts rather sharply with the aesthetic and moral subtext throughout his manifestoes. The so-called lack of aesthetic or moral concern, as a trick one plays on oneself in surreal practice, does not account for Breton's investment in the aesthetics of juxtaposition and the ethics of material dialectics. It appears the problematic tensions among the good, the beautiful, and the true simply cannot be resolved, but only, at best, ignored for the sake of opening up the spontaneous activity of the mind.

With personal immediacy, Robert Lowell's poem "Epilogue" brings into focus the fundamental tension in poetry between the beautiful and the true, a tension that recalls both his early deployment of more obviously formal devices and his later relaxation of them:

> Those blessed structures, plot and rhyme—
> why are they no help to me now
> I want to make
> something imagined, not recalled?
> (l. 1–4)

The urge to make something imagined competes therefore with the urge expressed later to "say what happened." With a note of personal crisis reminiscent of Yeats's "The Circus Animal's Desertion," Lowell suspects the worst. He sees his work as devoid of both the vitality of the beautiful and the authenticity of true:

> But sometimes everything I write
> with the threadbare art of my eye
> seems a snapshot,
> lurid, rapid, garish, grouped,
> heightened from life,
> yet paralyzed by fact.
> (l. 8–12)

Although the poem is less explicit about the ethical tension in poetry, the moral intelligence of the poet finds expression in Lowell's attempt to reconcile the beautiful and the true through art as an embodiment of care. Vermeer's art strikes its balance with regard to the beautiful and the true by virtue of its "caress," its imaginative precision:

> I hear the noise of my own voice:
> *The painter's vision is not a lens,*
> *it trembles to caress the light.*
> (l. 5–7)

In contrast to Vermeer's art is not simply the photograph, but, in Lowell's terms, the "snapshot"—decidedly less artful, less considered, "lurid, rapid, garish, grouped" (l. 11).

In Lowell's dramatic imperative to "pray for the grace of accuracy/ Vermeer gave to the sun's illumination (16–17)," the word "grace" conflates the values that he would honor. It suggests both divine bestowal and artistic refinement at the service of some clarification of attention. Vermeer's medium "gives" to the world its grace such that its artistry foregrounds neither subject nor object but their relational being as manifest in one another. Truth cannot *be* beauty, but the two may share the same space in art's act of bestowal, its generosity, its attentive "caress."

Lowell's insight here notably comes to fruition as prayer. The gesture acknowledges a certain metaphysics in great art, where, by virtue of unseen grace, the real and the imagined both find expression in the ache of care that binds one to the world. The artist's disciplined agency, if animated by the grace of accuracy, is always paradoxical, always open, always a surprise. This comes to matter because mortality puts self and world under pressure to seek one another, to affirm themselves in the face of death:

> We are poor passing facts,
> warned by that to give
> each figure in the photograph
> his living name.
> (l. 20–23)

Lowell's poem ends less with certainty than with some registration of the pressure that is the gift of our passing. Death has a voice. It is our voice, our projected fear and aspiration in light of the threat of non-being. What is more certain that the fact of one's death? What is more uncertain than its nature? What is more uncanny than the look of death on someone we loved, someone we continue to love, we might catch ourselves saying, not knowing exactly who or what it is we love? What is more immanently distant than the artistic rendering of the deceased who wear the look of life, mercifully odd in light of what we know and do not know? Poetry, in giving presence to our felt relations, cannot help but be haunted by absence, as we are, as our language must be. It cannot help but recognize the mystery of death and non-being as woven inextricably into that of being, such that thirst for the deeper resources of being belies an anxiety drawn from the wells of non-being.

It is the vocation of art therefore to make of hunger its own satisfaction. The presence that art conjures is thus always in part a product of hunger, a product of the imaginative encounter with non-being. Keats intuits as much when, in "Ode on a Grecian Urn," he states:

> Heard melodies are sweet, but those unheard
> Are sweeter; therefore, ye soft pipes, play on;

The imperative to "play on" self-reflexively affirms not only the imagination's power of collaboration, but also its power to manifest the real conceived, not merely as subjective or objective, but as that which makes tenuous their distinction. The sweetest melodies complicate our sense of aesthetics, since beauty has no true home. It can reside neatly neither in the relativity of human subjects nor, conversely, in the stability of external objects. It cannot locate itself exclusively in being or in non-being. Beauty therefore is restless. It breeds the very hunger it requires. In a paradox of relations, the imagined music of the urn sweetens the very desire that makes it sweet.

From non-being come the forces of imaginative affirmation that have no clear beginning, no end, though we are bound to happen upon them now and then with all the shock of the new. Somewhere in a museum in Vienna perhaps, we might look up to see a painting of a girl posed before a map. She is holding a book and an antique trombone, eyes closed, breath still. We do not feel what she felt. We cannot. We do not hear what she heard in the music of her horn. However, what we do feel is enormous and sustaining in light and in spite of that which is lost. We feel the hunger for being in the artist's grace, his compositional regard for the real to articulate that hunger. As non-being and being find focus via the sense of the whole, we see the luminous shadow of death, of absence in the presence, of solitude in our shared desire for communion. We feel the nature of the summons that is specific to the imagination, the sense that, in going out to the girl in the painting, we pass through an inward space, a space that is both ours and not ours. This is the space of the poem. It has no other. And if we are met by grace, we feel not only some shadow of the way things were but how, imbued with our own vulnerable attentions, these shadows come to matter.

Works Cited

Adorno, Theodor. "An Essay on Cultural Criticism and Society." In *Prisms*. Samuel and Shiery Weber, trans. Cambridge, MA: MIT Press, 1967.

Eliot, T. S. "Tradition and the Individual Talent." In *The Selected Prose of T. S. Eliot.* New York: Houghton Mifflin Harcourt, 1950.

Lacan, Jacques, *The Seminar, Book XX: Encore, On Feminine Sexuality, The Limits of Love and Knowledge.* New York: Norton, 1998.

Lowell, Robert. "Epilogue." *Day by Day.* New York: Farrar, Straus, and Giroux, 1977.

Motherwell, Robert. "Reflections on Painting Now." In *The Writings of Robert Motherwell.* Berkeley: University of California Press, 2007.

Neruda, Pablo. "A Few Things Explained." In *Five Decades: A Selection (Poems: 1925–1970).* Ben Belitt, trans. and ed. New York: Grove, 1974.

Nietzche, Friederich. "The Birth of Tragedy." In *Basic Writings of Nietzsche.* Walter Kaufmann, ed. and trans. New York: Modern Library, 1968.

Stevens, Wallace. "The Noble Rider and the Sound of Words." In *Necessary Angel: Essays on Reality and the Imagination.* New York: Vintage, 1951.

V.

Postscript

The Age of Technique

The history of poetry demonstrates with compelling regularity that great shifts in poetic discovery coincide with great shifts in technique. This fact is likewise greatly misleading. Coincidence is not causality, vision not technique, meaning not form, though we find ourselves in a climate where it is tempting to reduce the fundamental tensions of these to the dull tedium of sameness where, as both cultural symptom and epistemological assumption, "the medium is the message." While poetry's defining characteristic lies in its resistance to translation, its singularity of form, statements that would conflate form and meaning continue to assert the differences they long to dismantle. Moreover to conflate form and meaning is to dissipate one of the critical animating tensions in language and render poetic practice naïve about the complexity and difficulty of its medium. While new forms may lead to breakthroughs in vision, the history of poetry shows us just as plainly that a fetishistic faith in gadgetry can inspire rather redundant, soulless, and undeveloped work. As for the question of innovation, it is no easier to locate the source of poetic vision than it is to locate the source of creative will. The distinctive role of technical innovation continues to open up the complex question as to what that innovation would serve, if it need serve anything other than its own novelty, and to what extent the negative capability solicited by new technique puts a poem at enlarging and revelatory risk. To what extent, we might ask, does form open the space of meaning and meaning open the space of form.

Poetic theorists, from Aristotle to the present, have gone to great lengths to see in poetry's vocation an enhanced intimacy between form and meaning. A rough sketch of this conversation suggests that poetry has moved toward a conception of this intimacy in increasingly intimate, relational terms such that the distinction between medium and mediated vanishes altogether. What was once an issue of decorum or appropriateness, of form's metaphorical and tasteful relation to its subject, lends itself to examination, not simply in aesthetic terms, but in epistemological terms as well. Coleridge's breakthrough in this regard suggests that form might have not simply a semiotic, symbolic relation, but also a causal, indexical relation to its inward source. Form does not simply mirror nature; form is *caused* by nature. It manifests nature's meaningful dynamic. Form participates in the great unfolding of being and so bears testament to the real as inextricable from our relation to it. Organic form is, as he says, "innate; it shapes as it develops itself from within, and the fullness of its development is one and the same with the perfection of its outward form" (500). With form as the causally derivative index *and* sign of some other, his model expresses a problematic metaphysics. The inner originary force of form implies a formal dimension that is paradoxically hidden, thus invisible and in that sense not accurately understood as formal. The contradictory quality of this formulation points to the paradox of immanent distance with regards to form. It has both an inside and outside, and yet it becomes impossible to distinguish the two.

As discussed earlier in this book, similar justifications of individually determined form crop up throughout the nineteenth century, most famously in Emerson's notion of a "meter-making argument" and Whitman's justification of the explosive and emblematic inclusiveness of his free verse. America's cultural soil provided a rich environment for the flourishing of free verse not simply as a metaphor for revolutionary individualism but as a force of nature as something distributed throughout. As both index and sign of the real, the open form of twentieth-century verse, especially projective verse, calls for a reframing of the relation between form and content, as reflected in Robert Creeley's notion ("form is nothing but an extension of content") and Denise Levertov's reformulation ("form is nothing but a revelation of content"). These statements, while asserting both difference and continuity between form and content, move the discussion of their binaries closer toward the postmodern sensibility, wherein an increased resistance to metaphysical depth models of textual meaning suggests a conception of language as an ungrounded and self-referring field of signs wherein the real emerges as the fruition of textual play. Doubtless statements of radical relativism deconstruct themselves into nonsense, but there is a stubbornly fundamental question articulated by a twentieth-century resistance to essentialism—that is, how does one intuit meaning as different from form if its manifestation must be formal? On the other hand, what is the originary force whereby new form, however derivative of the old, bears new meaning into being? The fact that we only experience meaning via form does nothing to account for the origin of new meaning, as one form yields to another. The extremes of metaphysical essentialism and antimetaphysical constructivism, as equally untenable, leave open the question of the *genesis* of meaning as far more problematic than the more pedagogical and politicized question of interpretive closure. It is easier to embrace the notion that there is no end to interpretation than to believe that there is no beginning. New meaning does indeed come into being. As William Blake recognized, originary force has the liberating potential to make us skeptical about empirical skepticism.

In recent decades, what we encounter in poetry's strong advocacy of and identification with formal invention is an increasing sense of technical innovation as seminal to new vision. In his essay "Formal Experimentation and Poetic discovery," H. L. Hix writes eloquently on the subject:

> Great poems speak with a greater wisdom than the poets who wrote them possessed. The catalysis for such alchemy comes from form.
> (50)

The target of his critique will then be a pervasive, youthful naïveté that sees poetic form as a mere transparency, a rather passive medium as vehicle for self-expression. Hix makes a crucial pedagogical argument, particularly for apprentice poets whose sense of form, including rhetoric and diction, is artless, unimaginative, merely literal, and dull, secondary to a no less narrow impulse in terms of the complexity and generosity of vision. In such an apprenticeship sensibility, the impoverishment of form mirrors and encourages an impoverishment of vision. The apprentice poet's first challenge is most obviously understood as formal, in that she must first explore a language more inventive and radiant than the flatly instrumental transparencies of daily discourse. Nevertheless the question, less voiced in contemporary poetics, remains as to whether the catalyst for poetic vision need be conceived specifically as formal, as if to isolate its agency. By this, I refer to form as broadly conceived in its binary with meaning. Thus form includes categories of style and diction for instance, or any of the elements of visual or auditory surface. Has the emphasis on technique and form bred another kind of mainstream in contemporary poetry that cuts across the embattled "schools" as we perceive them? Is the unipolar sense of form as seminal both positive and negative as an expression of a larger cultural valuation of technique or technology as taking on the mystique and mantle of the visionary?

Such questions need not dismiss the visionary potential of technology or technique, but rather they would examine the elevation of technique to the status of fetish or prime mover whereby meaningful discovery becomes eclipsed or curtailed by a preoccupation with gadgetry. Moreover, meaning's impoverishment lies more specifically in the fetishization of formal *novelty* as a source of immediate authority. Admittedly, poetry's practice thrives on the notion that new meaning requires a new "vocabulary," understood as inclusive of the form, rhetoric, diction, and visual or auditory medium. A poem in this sense is a new term or set of terms for some newly manifest territory of feeling and idea. However the validation of formal departure as the bearer of revolutionary force belies the nature of language as bound to the tension between form and meaning. To trust formal innovation with visionary force is as naïve as trusting authentic self-expressivity to legitimize exigent form. Neither the material nor the conceptual being of language gets too far into the realm of poetic vision if conceived as operating independently of the other. More specifically the dismantling of traditional syntax can often figure as necessary and expressive, and yet without some new "syntax" or syntagmatic accumulation of relational resonance, it lacks a powerfully progressive unfolding of meaning. Sequential relations among elements become so unspecific, they risk little at the level of insightful follow through and summons, a sense that one cares enough to dwell and deepen. To say the dismantling of syntax is the point does little to illuminate the work as thinking any harder. For this reason, there is an air of anti-intellectual (or non-intellectual) intellectuality about much conceptually uncommitted form. The foreground of formal novelty in its remote flirtation with and resistance to logos features as the salient poetic element, as opposed to an aesthetic of greater penetrating musicality and visual beauty that give emotional energy to the hunger for meaningful depth.

A climate that celebrates a formal novelty incapable of an unfolding process of new ideas might well have a distorted sense of its importance in transforming consciousness. A poem that does not commit to a *process* of new meaning becomes a static plane, either a system or a Rorschach or as some postmodern combination of the two, not a dynamic engagement. Poetry's practice easily becomes secondary to some theory where conceptual energy might be ironically more concentrated. Another level of ambition might be to embody the philosophical impulse in poetry's soulful complications, such that, if theory is important to the practice, that theory is made emotionally significant and generously developed via the work itself. To *think* poetically (which for Heidegger is to fulfill the truest definition of thinking) is doubtless difficult, and thus it could be that poets need different emphases at different stages of their development. Where the apprentice poet might need to trust the conspicuous elements of form as a muse, as the thing that leads the interpretive mind, a more experienced poet becomes increasingly interested in the formal impulse as synchronous with the speculative. More than that, the two impulses become paradoxically indistinguishable without dissolving the tension between form and meaning altogether. One thinks with the body, thinks with the image, thinks with the line or lack thereof, thinks with a bold formal experiment pressured by an equally new conceptual necessity, such that neither mind nor body takes the exclusive lead in the process. That said, a recalcitrant dualism haunts the process that would render dualism obsolete. However antiquated, Coleridge's notion of inwardness as pressuring form into being has the advantage of binding formal innovation to some "inner other" in an effort to make form matter. His speculation need not imply a tidy temporal causality, but it does ever so slightly privilege the invisible inwardness as authenticating forms with a sense of necessity. There is a ghost in his model still, akin to Blake's notion of infinity, the sense of "no form" as the divine force within form.

Romantic theories of form would thus make form more precisely responsive to the spontaneity of being, so that technique as a formal mode of opening being might play both an aesthetic and epistemological role. Similarly, Heidegger offers a compelling defense of technology (the forms of technique) as bound to visionary force, its power to "unconceal," but so too he notes a critical difference between these forms and what they would honor and reveal:

> When we consider the essence of technology, then we experience Enframing as a destining of revealing. In this way we are already sojourning within the open space of destining, a destining that in no way confines us to a stultified compulsion to push on blindly with technology or, what comes to the same thing, to rebel helplessly against it and curse it as the work of the devil. Quite to the contrary, when we once open ourselves to the *essence* of technology, we find ourselves unexpectedly taken into a freeing claim.
> (25, 26)

Blind adoration and rejection of technology therefore mirror one another as compulsive and regressive, ironically so given the liberating potential of technique. The antidote to technological obscuration is technological luminosity, which implies that, in opposition to a poetics that would isolate materiality, technology at its most liberating must *see* something or, in the case of language, it must *say* something. It must open the space of being. It must become something other than the object of its own gaze. True to the nature of its being, it must think.

The speculative vocation of poetry was obvious to poets of modernism, a period of intense formal innovation, so much so that it is hard for contemporaries not to feel a little nostalgic for an age so filled with the fruits of mission and experiment, with manifestoes and revolutionary excitement. The experimental poetics of Whitman and Mallarmé inspired the generation of Pound, Eliot, Williams, and Stein to challenge some of the foundational continuities with regard to formal practice in an effort to reflect a changing cultural and philosophical climate wherein traditional forms of authority were likewise under pressure. These moderns in particular conceived of their aesthetic shifts in epistemological terms, wherein truths were both modeled and created by poetic form. For Pound, the poetic image modeled and provoked intellectual and emotional complexity. For Eliot, the mythic method illuminated the elements of cultural fracture by way of greater inter-relational design. For the Williams of "Spring and All," not only did particularity give authenticity to imaginative knowing, that knowing challenged more passive and traditional models of art as mimesis. For Stein, the "tender buttons" of poetic structure gave voice to a more nuanced sense of the being of common objects as embedded in their context, tone, and temporality. All voiced intellectual ambition and generosity in their poems (though Williams less so), while remaining keenly aware of the problem of "overthinking" a poem. As Eliot recognized, the lesser poet is either too conscious or not conscious enough.

While most would agree with Eliot, there remains vast disagreement as to just what constitutes thinking too much and precisely what the dangers are. Archibald MacLeash's hyberbole that "A poem should not mean/ but be" exemplified a particularly American breed of sentimental anti-intellectualism, though a more specific resistance to "meaning" born of referential instrumentality has morphed into the more recently fashionable breed of anti-intellectual intellectualism. Charles Olson as a transitional figure between Pound and postmodernism both carries forward much that is modernist in its attempt to "escape" the narrowly personal, and yet he would raise the modernist stakes in terms of poetry as a spontaneous process versus a tightly structured mythology or system. As discussed earlier in this book, Olson's legacy has been appropriated in such a way that his implied metaphysical notion of poetry as a "stance toward the real" has lost out to his formal resistance to lyric subjectivity as self-conscious and thus self-reifying. In terms of a poem's epistemological force, thinking too hard by way of hesitant selectivity pollutes the poem with phoniness, with self-serious artifice as a manifestation of ego. By way of both Olson and Derrida, a new generation of poets thus sees in the poetics of closure something both metaphorical and exemplary of logocentrism, which they see as thinking gone awry through its insistence upon consistency and control. In other words, logic's resistance to contradiction and indeterminacy appears in alternative sensibilities to penetrate the whole of a poetic form. Logic and closure seem synonymous with logocentrism as opposed to being in tension with equally essential elements of experiment, spontaneity, irrationality, emotionality, and abandon. Since the word logocentric cannot be specific about degree, it can be applied rather freely, metaphorically, particularly in a political context that contributes to a self-serving theatricality and exaggeration of projection.

Since the ego functions in both the conscious and the unconscious, there is no guarantee of course that the self-conscious are any more egocentric than the spontaneous. In fact, a post-confessional mainstream of less thought-driven and more narcissistic and unbridled spontaneity attracts sharp criticism from poets of both the most avant-garde and traditional sensibilities. What this mainstream lacks is some semblance of Olson's devotion to form. Form, whatever the sensibility, potentially figures as an alterity that poets must honor. In her interview with the Society for Cultural Exchange, Marjorie Perloff levels some apt criticism at a mainstream, both popular and academic, that disregards poetry's formal integrity and complexity and thus has a rather marginalizing sense of poems as mere vehicles of moral sentiment. Conceived this way, poetry is ill equipped to compete with "the serious stuff" of other discourse. The truth of this prompts Perloff's emphasis on poetry's formal and specifically aural basis. In the course of her discussion, Perloff notes quite usefully that radio as a medium has yet to be explored by poets. Radio's medium could figure as a rich untapped resource for poets, she states, and then she points to theory as the place where one might speculate about what it is to have a voice without a physical presence. What these insights highlight is a more generalized sense of the respective strengths of poetic theory and practice. The speculative dimension becomes aligned with prose, the formal with poetry. These alignments reflect a widely accepted bias, but especially so if one finds of particular interest a poetic tradition focused upon immanent surfaces.

Perloff's highly original and influential book *The Poetics of Indeterminacy* maps out two traditions in the twentieth century, one derived from the more metaphysical poetics of Romantic and Symbolist poetry, the other beginning in Rimbaud and less rooted in the presumption of some metaphysical ground beyond architectural surface. The first tradition, as exemplified in the work of Yeats, Eliot, and Stevens, encourages poetry that, she notes, is "polysemous," rich in "multiple relational meanings" and suggestive in rendering "parts of an absent whole." In Rimbaud, on the other hand, we find the "free-standing sign," in other words an accent on immanence rather than transcendence. Granted, the contrast is a tad blurry, since the indeterminate tradition relish the polysemous as well, but the key difference is in how the polysemous structures of the Romantic strain represent some interconnective interior to the poem, as if to suggest a metaphysical whole or ground. The phrase "free-standing sign" is likewise blurry. Derived from Barthes, it is a curious hyperbole that ironically would make a "free" and yet "standing" or stable place of the sign's failure to connect absolutely. To be fair, Perloff does not mean to imply such an absolute. The confusion in Perloff's contrast lies in the fact that "the free-standing sign" insofar as it is a "sign" connects, albeit multiply, and is therefore as "polysemous" as the Romantic symbol. Part of the appeal of the tradition of immanence is its openness, "free-standing" in the sense that new connections are interpretively constructed rather than intentionally reified. Perloff's specific readings of texts, however, characteristically become sketchy and inconsequential as they labor to make clear what it is of interest in the indeterminate tradition.

Take for example Perloff's essay on the immanent poetics of language poetry, where she guides us into Susan Howe's *Secret History of the Dividing Line.* Here is a short quote form Howe's poem:

> mark   mar   ha   forest   1   a   boundary manic   a
>   land   a

tract indicate position 2 record bunting interval
free also event starting the slightly position o
O about both of don't something
  INDICATION Americ

The beginning of Perloff's analysis demonstrates terrific resourcefulness then in opening up the field of the poem's possible reference:

> Here *mark* refers first of all to the surveyor's (William Byrd's) mark made in delineating a boundary between "tract[s]" of forest land. But the mark is also a trace, a sign that points us to specific things that have happened: one thinks of Blake's "London," with its lines, "And mark in every face I meet / Marks of weakness, marks of woe." The poem's opening "Mark mar ha forest 1 a boundary manic" gives the word "mark" a number of paragrammatic possibilities.

The analysis sounds promising indeed. Unfortunately Perloff goes on to sound out a few more possible referents and then without conclusion moves on to another poet. The ostensible virtue of the poem thus lies in the signs as "free-standing" that do not commit. They gesture freely, provisionally, and in like fashion the critical reading wanders a bit in the field without little pressure of necessity coalescent around the pleasure and daring of some point of view. The subversion of predication itself emerges as thematic in the poem, which is provocative, though it would take some semblance of a predication to explore more fully why or why we should care. The relatively indeterminate nature of meaning might find validation if the meanings constructed (by reader, writer, or both) were profound, but what Perloff offers us is bland and episodic, wide with possibilities that do not follow through with much development or substance. This is not to say that form is isolated absolutely from meaning. This is language after all. However, form emerges as the salient and authoritative feature relative to meanings that are *relatively* indeterminate and, at least as rendered by Perloff, rather dull. If such a poem occasions wisdom, it does so as if without authorial intention. The poem does indeed have virtues, though they align themselves far more with the materiality and diffusely thematic and powerfully emotive evocations of visual art than they do with the conceptual development of philosophy.

Doubtless there is a wonderfully mercurial associative consciousness on display to the poem's surface. The text opens itself up to so much complex play that it raises the question as to how much meaning is given by the reader and how much made by the author. Although familiar, this figures as an intriguing starting point. If we wish to argue that the poem is intellectual, it emerges as such via some ironically metaphysical effort to discern the presence of ideation as working beneath the surface fragmentation. One could say the same of much conceptually freighted visual art. As emblematic of the general philosophical notions that Perloff brings to bear, the poetry is rendered as a material grid of the possible, reiterative in its general conception that calls to our attention the ever presence of dividing lines as pervading and destabilizing the personal and historical—that is, no effort has been made by Perloff to discern something in the poem's progressive particulars of insight that risks an unfolding thoughtfulness and exposure. Process is less modeled in the poem than made possible. What Perloff highlights as convincing is a field of themes that connect, lightly, to those of her theoretical context.

With regard to that context, Perloff has indeed done an ambitious thing via her delineation of twentieth-century poetry into two competing traditions, and as with all broad sketches of literary history, it is far easier to pick at her model and find where it breaks down than it is to risk such a synthetic approximation. The model has proved useful to many subsequent critics, such as Cole Swenson, who, in the introduction to her and David St. John's anthology *American Hybrid*, provides historical context for a new crossbreed of poetic traditions. In invoking the Romantic tradition, she refers to their "belief in the stability and sovereignty of the individual"—an understandable and familiar shorthand that in truth does not register the destabilizing, transpersonal force of the Romantic "inner other" (as Coleridge's vast "intellectual breeze," both inner *and* outer), not to mention the often intimidating alterities of the natural world. Cole's subsequent implication is that a Romantic sensibility expresses itself in traditional lyricism of the twentieth century, whereas an alternative tradition reflects more interest in the material text, "innovations in form," and a dismantling of the individual's claim to authority:

> This split is more than a stylistic one; it marks two concepts of meaning: one as transcendent, the other as immanent. Thus, the twentieth-century American poetry offers both a model of the poem as a vehicle for conveying thoughts, images, and ideas initiated elsewhere—a model that recognizes language as an accurate roadmap or system of referring to situations and things in the real world—and a model of the poem as an event on the page, in which language, while inevitably participating in a referential economy, is emphasized as a site of meaning in its own right, and poetry is recognized as uniquely capable of displaying that.
> (xviii)

Given these terms, the latter, more progressive tradition sounds far more nuanced, whereas the former contains the words "accurate roadmap or system," which suggests an unproblematized view of how referentiality works and does not work. One might ask, so in which tradition do we put Stevens, the quintessential "metaphysician in the dark"? Do we, as Perloff does, situate him (with all his skepticism and iambic pentameter) within a Romantic tradition of, as described here, the stability and sovereignty of the individual? Moreover, where are the texts out there that describe language as an "accurate roadmap," which sounds simplistic, as if to align the "transcendent" tradition once again with that of "self-essentialism" and "self-expression?" The tradition of transcendence appears one dimensional in the above description, while that of immanence tempers its identity with some sense of referentiality and thus the invocation of the invisible. Where do we put the huge tradition of American surrealism with its metaphysical tensions so influenced, not only by depth psychology, but also by notions such as Lorca's duende, decidedly destabilizing, transpersonal, and irreducible to *merely* material and formal immanence?

It is tough to know what "meaning as immanent" means as void of the metaphysical tension that makes meaning, however formal, into something other than form. Postmodern examples in so far as they shed the ghost of transcendence likewise shed their pressure of necessity with regard to meaning. Moreover, there is something dodgy and trendy in the phrase "participating in a referential economy," with the word "economy" as jargon that conjures contemporary theoretical discourse about meaning as a production of power. To say language "participates in an economy" deftly avoids commitment with regard to the veracity, however partial, of language as referential. Roadmaps are models of the real with clear one-to-one relationships that avoid equivocation, but referentiality is a larger, more complex phenomenon that allows for imperfection, suggestion, and intimation with regard to the pressure of reality. Without such pressure, no claim, including Swenson's, can be true. So we might ask, is language referential in relation the real, or do we simply participate in an economy that operates as if it were? According to Swenson, the French tradition will assert no more than the fact that language has a referential currency minted by social transaction. While this is obviously true, Swenson's rhetorical strategy brackets off the messiness of a real world beyond the pale of the language and focuses instead on a social context credited without qualification with the production of a *sense* of reality.

Equally shaky is Swenson's notion that a non-Romantic tradition would by contrast emphasize language as "a site of meaning in its own right." The phrase "in its own right" is blurry and untenable with regard to the phenomenon of meaning in language. Yes, poetry true to its vocation binds meaning inextricably to form and thus resists paraphrase, but in so far as there is such a thing as language and meaning, these things gesture beyond their own "site." They are inherently relational and, more specifically, referential, imperfectly so, in ways that affirm more than simply some social consensus and self-referring economy. Language must have an outside, which, granted, makes it problematic. If we accept referential meaning as *merely* a production of social exchange with no so-called real other than the one we provisionally create, then language would have to cease to function as a language. Moreover our descriptions of language must be equally relativized and therefore neither true nor false. The banished ghost of the signified outside of language drains poetry of its consequence and necessity, and meaning gets conceived rather simplistically as *identical with* form, which it cannot be. The non-Romantic tradition, as conceived by Swenson, espouses an anti-metaphysical skepticism, while remaining unable to avoid language that is in some way metaphysical—words such as "self" that are neither cleansed of faith nor "an accurate road-map" of the real.

Once again, it is easier to attack these kinds of sketches of literary history than to formulate and risk their useful approximations, but one might well wonder if the concept of meaning conceived as either transcendent or immanent is very interesting. The conception of meaning as mere transcendence would of course be blind to form, its pressures, its agency, its challenging alterity. The conception of meaning as mere immanence would be blind to the metaphysical tension and hunger that engenders new meaning. The latter blindness explains a fetishization of formal novelty as in itself meaningful. At this point in history, it might well be more enriching to conceive of meaning as vigorously both immanent *and* transcendent, that it has always been both, and that we find ourselves, via the hybridizations in current intellectual and poetic culture, in a position to better appreciate the instability, tension, summons, necessity, and lovely difficulty all implicit in meaning as both.

Of course there are many factions and gradations of sensibility in the poetry world today. The caricature of our time with its two dominant factions has thus far struggled to identify and probe "in depth" the major works that fit appropriately into those traditions. That said, the sensibilities that align themselves with traditional or experimental form have one thing in common: they both self-identify via form. This, as mentioned earlier, figures as a healthy antidote to the more naïve notions blind to form, but it says little of substance about a poem's visionary vocation, let alone its duende, its soulful, revelatory, imaginative color and vitality. The cold, unmusical reiterations of much avant-garde work and the stilted, unambitious literality of much traditional formal work suggest that, no matter what the sensibility, the reliance on form conceived as independent or conflated with meaning trivializes its felt, imaginative understanding. At the same time, critical correctives that might value something akin to duende, something less narrowly formal, something more intuitively metaphysical such as "soulfulness" or "saturation in unconscious energy," might seem too vague. "Soulfulness" in particular has the odd resonance of the "personal transpersonal" and so might seem to essentialize the unknown as a personal possession. These more metaphysical notions, like that of "authenticity," are relative, never absolute, and so affirm more than they can fully represent. On the other hand, it is hard to imagine poetry of powerful evocation without some ghost of authenticity, soulfulness, and the energy of unfathomable depth.

While it was once popular to attack poetry workshops and MFA programs for their culture of consensus and uniformity, the current diversity reflected in poetry pedagogy makes questionable the notion of their homogenous mediocrity. It was once trendy to see the professionalization of poetry as some tedious machine churning out the "workshop poem," but that complaint has figured as a new mainstream. Perhaps the more challenging impact now of the professionalizing of poetry practice is twofold: proliferation and specialization. The proliferation of poets is exciting, though for young poets in particular, it provokes anxiety. For editors, it floods their desks with manuscripts. The effect is that it is difficult for a poem, especially from a young unknown poet, to stand out upon first encounter, and a young poet's anxiety might thus focus on the elements of first impression (on the more conspicuous elements of form as inclusive of style, diction, and voice) and trust less in deep structure (embedded in form and yet "interior," less readily visible). Truth is, most young poets *need* to focus on style and voice in order to appreciate how they cannot be dissociated from vision, but the process of professionalization has little time to model the breadth of curiosity or nurture the development of creative speculation a poet needs to move beyond the "merely acceptable." Thus the second challenge for the student poet is to transcend the possible limits of a concentration on poetry, especially the poetry of one's own time. Poets might be better served to be voracious generalists. Their work, in its visionary potential, might grow large in relation to their hunger to know things in the margins of poetry's current conversation. In a changing world, poetry will always have new things to say, just as much as theory does or science or political discourse or the inspired, associative interjection of a child. In its felt relation to whatever it is that comes to matter, poetry's scope of reference, revelation, and reimagined mystery is enormous.

If it is the vocation of the poet to write toward one's other self, perhaps the other self for many in our time has less to do with what is readily apparent in form than in visionary potential as articulated in the tension between form and meaning. The isolation of formal authority, traditional or experimental, might figure a crutch, or, in Heidegger's words, a "stultified compulsion," and this crutch or compulsion reflects a larger, cultural preoccupation with technological mediation. Such mediation, while it undeniably opens up the space of poetry, is only as powerful as what it chooses to mediate. The medium cannot *be* the message, not if the medium *has* a message. A computer may be one wonderful eyeball, but it cannot be a point of view. It is doubtless the case that, for many careful editors, the poem that stands out is the poem of magnanimous curiosity, the kind of poem that takes the top of your head off precisely because of what it reveals *and* conceals, how it enlarges heart and mind in a way that is genuinely transformative. Moreover such curiosity is at the heart of poetry's fundamental summons in its hunger for being. This is not to dismiss mystery, but rather to make a distinction between frivolous obscurity and mysteries that have the pressure and pleasure of necessity in them. Such mysteries do not so much "model" the real as honor it as critical to that necessity.

To this end, aspiring poets might better concentrate on the spontaneously unfolding task of *development* of speculative energy rather than the architectural stasis of grand, predetermined, vision. The phrase "grand vision" lures a breed of ambitious ego-distortion and loss of adaptability and focus. Poetry's distinctive way of knowing need not work out the kinks of contradiction, and its alliance with myth suggests a negotiation of contradiction via imaginative constructs full of humor, wonder, and lovely difficulty without sacrificing the tension that resonates with emotional truth. "Great poems speak with a greater wisdom than the poets who wrote them possessed," writes Hix. The reason for this is not simply because of technical breakthrough. The novel character of form's techniques may or may not be critical. *The revelatory surprise and surpassing of intention derives from the capacity for form to open the space of meaning and meaning to open the space of form.* It stems from the elusive agency of vision that cannot locate itself neatly in the past or present, the self or the other, the personal or the impersonal, the heart or the mind, the poem's materiality or its mercurial spirit. As both immanent and transcendent, the language of poetry hungers for presence and absence as making their equal claim on us. In this way, poems become resilient, concentrated, physically significant, radiant with the intimation of being that, ruthlessly, mercifully, cannot fully bring itself to language, nor, as seminal to how and why we write, tear itself away.

Works Cited

Heidegger, Martin. *The Question Concerning Technology and Other Essays.* New York: Harper and Row, 1977.

Hix, H. L. *As Easy As Lying: Essays on Poetry.* Silver Spring, MD: Etruscan, 2002.

Howe, Susan. *Secret History of the Dividing Line.* New York: Telephone, 1978.

Perloff, Marjorie. "Language Poetry and the Lyric Subject." *Critical Inquiry* 23 (1999): 405–434.

Perloff, Marjorie. "Marjorie Perloff 3." *Youtube.* 2009. Interview with the Society for Critical Exchange. January 30, 2009. <http://www.youtube.com/watch?v=d37kHq1TQrk>

Perloff, Marjorie. *The Poetics of Indeterminacy: Rimbaud to Cage.* Princeton, NJ: Princeton University Press, 1981.

Swenson, Cole. "Introduction." In *American Hybrid.* Cole Swenson and David St. John, eds. New York: Norton, 2009.

Those who restrain desire,
do so because theirs is
weak enough to be restrained.

- William Blake

BETWEEN THE CRACKS

the Daedalus Anthology of Kinky Verse

edited and with photos by

Gavin Geoffrey Dillard

Daedalus Publishing Company
San Francisco

Books by Gavin Dillard:
IN THE FLESH
NOTES FROM A MARRIAGE
YELLOW SNOW
THE NAKED POET
PAGAN LOVE SONGS

Photos represented by: GAVCO, Ink.
Post Office Box 330
Bolinas, CA
94924-0330

Heartfelt thanks to Antler, William Barrett, Gloria Brame, David Dalton, Michael Hathaway, Jane Hirschfield, Garland Kyle, Jules Mann, Robert Manners, Deena Metzger, Harold Norse and Gerry Gomez Pearlberg for their assistance with this collection.
Also to preceding anthologies: THE MALE MUSE and SON OF THE MALE MUSE (Ian Young), ANGELS OF THE LYRE (Winston Leyland), THE BADBOY BOOK OF EROTIC POETRY (David Laurents), MY LOVER IS A WOMAN (Lesléa Newman), THE ARC OF LOVE (Clare Coss).

ISBN: 1-881943-10-0
Library of Congress Catalog Card Number: 96-86478

DAEDALUS PUBLISHING COMPANY
584 CASTRO STREET, SUITE 518
SAN FRANCISCO, CALIFORNIA 94114 USA

CONTENTS

List of Photos

All photographs by Gavin Geoffrey Dillard

Introduction

Several problems present themselves in the anthologizing of "kinky verse" - besides where to find the shit, how to obtain it, and what to tell my mother. First and foremost is "What is kink?"

What an awesome task, to define *kinky* as a modern idiom with herstorical references and reverberations. I took the coward's way out and decided to allow the work to define itself, merely putting out the call with suggestions of relevant topics. What came back was not entirely what I would have expected, and a few surprises obliged me to create entirely new categories.

I should also add that I have made absolutely no attempts to have equal numbers of women versus men, straight persons versus queers. Neither have I allowed such categories to dictate where in the manuscript poems were to be placed. Everything was accepted on the basis of content and was positioned accordingly. In fact, if I had any ulterior motive in choosing this project, it was to deconstruct the limitation of such labels and illustrate the simple thesis that human (not to presume any limitation upon *non*-humans) sexuality is fraught with individuation, and that if any conclusion can be made, it's that sexual anomolies are the rule and not the exception.

As far as what we as a society choose to make perverse in our mores-du-jour, this is up for grabs. As I have stated, I allowed my authors, for the most part, to decide. The only regret being in the assumption that much relevant material, especially among antiquated female poets, has been lost, buried or burned.

As for my categories: certainly both oral and anal sex have at times been considered kinky, and no doubt still are to many people. Nonetheless, I've not included such, in and of themselves, in this book, for the simple reasons they are too commonplace, and amply covered elsewhere.

Neither have I included group sex, per se, prostitution, or sex in off-hand places, except within the context of some other event or intent.

Likewise, I don't consider porno watching - or any film-watching - kinky. Neither is phone sex, of itself. One might of course make a pitch or a case for most anything, but based on the tepid responses I received to these two topics they are mere lounge acts.

Sex with youngsters and animals are undoubtedly the most highly charged issues. Herstorically, I don't see how sex with youths can be considered as anything other than natural, but I have actually negated this topic on the grounds of its universality - when one delves into early Roman and Greek verse, rarely is anything written that is *not* about the lust for youth. This should be its own book.

As for sex with non-humans, I had only determined to limit poems on the grounds of consent. But truly I have neither found nor received anything that would make me question the integrity of an animal relationship, and generally the poems encountered are of a solely fantasy/metaphorical nature, bridging more than any other topic the spiritual. As such, I have ended the collection with a brilliant piece by Kelvin Beliele about a seduction by a hummingbird (the Aztec metaphor for Deity).

This did bring up the one definition that I felt obliged to make regarding human consensuality, leaving non-consensual encounters out of the realms of kink. Still, I received little of such dubiously appropriate material, and most all that I did receive were of a purely theoretical violence.

Otherwise, I do hope that everyone will find *something* to be offended by - you may wish to start with the Crowley poems - but above all I intend that we have shown some of the more concealed petals on the lotus of mortal sexuality, that those who are exploring their desires and peculiar yens might feel less alone, less cast asunder, and less inclined to allow their modes of expression to be lost between the cracks.

- Gavin Geoffrey Dillard

Trebor

Between the Cracks

EXTERNALS

spats, chaps and tats

PRAYER

- Robert L Rucker

Sunday morning and
I am throwing prayers
at the God I swear I
do not believe in.
God, let Him be safe
this day.
Let the tricksy steel
of motorcycle bring
the King of Dogs
safely home or
away forever, only
not down to the
scabbed concrete,
smashed for good
in your daddy arms.
Mr. Maker, make
for me a spare, a
spare just so, should
the one I have decide
to go. Allow
the scrabbling claws
of love to grip my
neck once more
and squeeze.
God, let him be safe
this day, for it was
not the bike I liked
but the fine smell
of leather when
he undressed.

THE GODS FAVOR YOU IN LEATHER

- Paul Mariah

Why dress the stone in leather
unless you are truly Bellerophon
in exile, a pederast journal

without a kingdom, who is King?
Carrying your seed to Poland
or to lands, New York, in between?

(Then, it is true in separate ways
we ride the night: you, your mare,
and I, the emptybed of stars.)

Discipline in any form, chains,
blank checks, febrile minds, beggar,
supplicant I have become... to leather.

Why leather? why binding? why hiding?
Tanning curing rawhide? cycles?
Leather the strangest way of saying "I DO".

the prophecy

- Rhonda C Poynter

I was going to tell you about it when I woke
up
about how it was snowing and everybody
else

Was wearing their JC Penney's
coats
and their handy dandy sensible
boots

I was going to tell you about
how
the dream got so damned white with
snow

And cold that I almost couldn't see a
thing
but then you came in from a
corner

Of the dream blazing right into the
whiteness
and you were head to toe in your
black leather

Fuck December fuck sensibility
baby
and fuck the snow and the cold and
everybody

Else who would never look as good as
you
in all that leather and just then I woke
up

Looked up to see you coming through the
door
in black leather that I could smell
across

The room and just a look
just
a smile just a touch told me no matter what else
happens

we belong together

FIRST OF THE MOTORCYCLE POEMS

- Lori Faulkner

you
soft in your leather
not quite a
bike dyke
no studs on your jacket
but
oh
those gloves are sinful
long
black
leather
with
zippers
no less
so butch
of you
to have those gloves
so femme
of you
to have those eyes

SECOND OF THE MOTORCYCLE POEMS

- Lori Faulkner

At night, in my dreams,
my legs and thighs
spin a cocoon
around her

and there is a penis
slender and firm
it slides gently into me
and I hold her there

In daylight
she appears in front of me
leaning against
her classic black
BMW motorcycle
leather jacket
denim jeans
on her boy body
raking five
juvenile delinquent fingers
through her short dark hair
she is my teenage guy
in different times
I could be gun moll
to her gangster moves
a cigarette dangles
from her seductive
heart-stopping lips

When I hold her wrists
above her head
and take her with my tongue
the smell of her strong and wild
as the best acid trip
When I feel the outside curve
of her breasts
soft as my heart melting
at the sight of
her citrine almond eyes
we know the truth together
it's an inside joke
When they call her butch
and rate her high on the scale
I call her my woman
and take what I want.

FOR A CONFUSED FRIEND WITH TWO LOVERS, ONE SUBMISSIVE, ONE DOMINANT

- Lynne Savitt

waking to a morning bright, brimming
with promise unable to choose what to wear
uncertain of the weather
is it cold as penguin soup?
hot as alligator eggs?
does she wear a dove white ermine g-string
or ear muffs of soft silver fox?
cover her ample behind with leather
slick as a panther
or a flowing skirt colorful & light
as parrots' wings?
does she carry a whip or a jeweled collar?
when he kisses her morning mouth
does she fall backward like
an awkward kitten; spring forward
like a confident cougar?
does she bind his gorilla wrists
with electrical tape?
does he lash her flamingo neck
to the mast with sailing knots?
the movements the same jungle rhythms
the force of her hips provide the push
in a phone booth she can change
quick as superman
is she the mouthpiece or the receiver
on the telephone of love?

STREET THEATRE (for Cynthia Slater)

- Pat Califia

Cinched up tight in
Leather supple as human skin,
She is the ancient smiling Queen
Of Air and Darkness.

The keys at her belt
Have liberated her from
The anxiety of speech,
And the snug embrace of her jacket
Makes her invulnerable
To loneliness.

Black gloves and gauntlets
Conceal the hands that dispense bliss
And administer terror.
Her high-heeled boots
Make the hollow sidewalk
Echo like a bell.

Be warned by the straight line
She travels, and her speed:
She's looking for a target
To bury her body in.

She finds a light to wait at.
There is no traffic -
She just wants to dip
Her shoulder, and toss her hair
(A waterfall dark as her thoughts)
Back over it.

You catch a glimpse
Of collarbone and throat.
If you kissed right there,
Between her ear and shoulder,
The flesh would yield so readily
That you would find yourself

Biting her fiercely,
Going after blood.

She would move back one step
And then another
Until you were leading the dance.
The light persists.
Her weight flows.
The hip moves in to support it.

She is hawking herself.
Do you dare stalk this nonchalant,
This vibrant woman,
Whose every gesture has been
Tuned and honed and pruned
For the sake of provoking
That most creative reflex,
Lust?

Can't you see
The light has long since changed,
And she has opened her jacket
(The snaps part with
Little padlock clicks)
To bring out a cigarette?

Have you got the spark it takes
To light her up?

late

- Jules Mann

she didn't take me
home that night
though the breath of black cloth fluttered
playing femme to her sm
stricken hair glancing off leather

black glove against my/rhinestone
hand jerking like a tethered bird
clavicles pulling as we pass
the guiding feathers rippling on her
arrow

HAPPY BIRTHDAY BABY

- Gerry Gomez Pearlberg

Was I handcuffed, John?

> *No, baby,*
> *you were wearing restraints,*
> *the leather ones, and you*
> *were on your belly,*
> *with the full head-hood.*

John wrote *It's my birthday: Fuck me.*
across my back in purple wax
and sent a stranger in to do the job.

Remember when we saw our bodies
as perfect, untouchable things,
sea shells on shelves
that nothing could mar,
silvery souvenirs?

VIEWINGS I

- Gerry Gomez Pearlberg

Six months later we run into each other at the Queer Film Fest.
You've shaved your head, something you know
    I can't resist.

When they let us inside I retreat to a far-away aisle.
The lights dim, balcony a black chasm between us.
The dark, though intangible, is an insistent presence.

In the first scene
boys' and girls'
inviting asses
invite black rubber,
lube and rubber gloves.
"Master" flashes on the screen
intersecting sex and text.
Girls go down on each other's cocks,
go down on their knees
licking black Doc Martens clean.
Then sea anemones, swimming pools, steam.

Six months later,
here in porn's soft core,
you're still the star of my show.

Remember the night I wrote on you in lipstick,
how the lipstick left a stain?
The sheets were full of expletives for days.
Handcuffs. Hands clasped in hair.
Tongues like rings down fevered drains.
My desire for you is still crowned in that flame
like the MGM lion clawing out of his frame.

Scene two: back seat caresses, strap-ons, cowgirls and lassos,
pirate suits, anchors, and punk boys with tattoos.
All backdropped by the rhythms that you used to
    fuck me to.

But when the handsome dyke in the last frame
stroking her girlfriend's cock
urgently murmurs, "Thank you, Daddy,"
I remember why we're sitting
in this dark so far apart,
what's pushed up against us -
intangible, insistent.
Not these sexy games, but him.

THE BIG BANG THEORY

- Diane Williams

There is a joy that runs like morphine
through my fingertips
when I'm touching her,
this brown-bomber-jacket-wearing woman
with skin that blushes at the touch,
this warrior
teddy bearish
glossy smiling
cigarette smoking hyper
still-water testosterone pumping
black Mustang cruising over bumpy roads
hard between her thighs
raw crude thuggish
when her broad back is pinned against the headboard
by faceless women,
nameless women
who wear soullessness like pantyhose, nonchalant
fingernail-polish-lipstick-flavored-spike-heel women
who want to stand on their heads make
love voodoo ritual with a curl of a tongue, a bend of a finger:
There is a depth others can only imagine when she's
holding me,
this cherry-popping sugar-coating chocolate-dripping
woman with
sinister eyes
soft belly
stubborn kisses
thumping stereo bully boy swagger
soapy fingers
affection translucent for me,
the indefinable, heart protected by attitude
exaltation exhilaration
red sheets black sheets
sunlight through the blinds checkerboarding us with morning
promise
strawberry massage mixing music like lemonade,
pouring it over ice,

and the smell of something burning beyond shame,
her wavy hair pomaded, pulling light from an unlit room,
jelly-stained breasts consuming healing submission regret:
I understood the lock and key of commitment
when I opened the door and let her go.

POEM WITH AN ATTITUDE

- Lynn Goldfarb

You think I'm such
a nice girl

because I still write
sonnets sestinas even luv
poems

because I still don
camisoles pantyhose even sport
a bra

because I still shave
wear skirts mascara even carry
a purse

You think I'm so
straight polite frigid

Newsflash Babe

You've never seen me
in my half-zipped black jeans writing dyke poems
topless in the moonlight

You've never been inside my wilderness

You don't know
how my lips would sear your tattoo
turn it purple then red

You don't know
how hard   my hips   would throw
your ass   against the wall

You can't imagine
the frenzied circling   of my pelvis   my hands
my thighs'   merciless grip

I am not
a   nice   girl

And you
under all that   black   and metal
are as soft   as a chocolate

kissss

in the noonday sun

WING

- Simon Sheppard

Last night I had kinky sex
(a flight of birds)
in memory of you. Vince
laced me up in his
leather body bag,
encased neck-to-toe in
crow-black cowhide.
Put earplugs in,
my head in a leather hood.
Within
my armor, I began to
sweat. (To soar.) Within the
darkness, I began to

dream. Of you. Your
adventures, stories of
places where
I'd never dared
set wing.
You nearly choking
on that guy. Dark
parties. Electrodes. Fear
and its anodyne.

I lay there
as blind as you were
after the jackdaws had
stolen your sight.
As damp with sweat
as 3 am had found you.
Robbed of myself,
found a strange
kind of joy.
Is this what you
found here,
this glow in the
darkness?
(How you loved
paradox!) Within the
leather's grip,
I found myself expanding
toward the lineaments
of you. (The sky.)

And after who knows
how much time,
Vince unsnapped
some flaps, used
his skilled hands
to send me to heaven.
Heaven, where you are.
The body bag,
where we are.
Illusion.
Loss.

Infinity.
Sweet dead boy,
flying,
what you found here,
down here,
far above.

PIRANESI'S LAST SUPPER

...from soup to nuts...

- *Mike Castro*

Denude me; protrude me
O Cat-o'-nine-kisses
deep in a mirrored dungeon's
Chamber of Hedon's
Navel of Narcissus

cinched - winched - and pinched -
all fours strapped towards the four posters
of a cat's-cradle bed all scaffolded and webbed
harnessed and suspended leviathan
hoisted and dropped - belly flopped -

impaled upon the butting end
of a battering ram biffing heaven
gyro-frigging with rings and rigging
my stopcocked pendulumbob swinging
to the beat whipped to the kisses

of your fertile crescent, Tigress,
busting saddle upon a spark-plugged ass
  rock a cockhorse to Uranus and back
    ride the Seven Rings of Hades
bless these piston rings, Milady,
jerking pearly jism fizzes

  debutantes french-kissing fishes
    succubusboys hosing dishes
jeez *Mon Squeeze!* my cods rise like yeast,
a foamy, gruelsome coming-out feast

Holy Balls! how many told strokes must toll?
my overrunneth cup needs be a bowl!
Make it twice tight once the table's aslop;
reform my tongue, Bustress, into a mop:
le Truffle Grubber... Truss Hussy, lace *this* in rubber!

LATEX DREAMS

- Selena Anne Shephard/Andy Plumb

All I want for Christmas
is to be wrapped from
head to toe in latex.

Thick latex.
Black latex.
Skintight latex.

Cock & ball hugging latex.
Mouth watering latex.
Neck embracing latex.

Ass squeezing latex.
Thigh binding latex.
Tummy molding latex.

Tit pleasing latex.
Hot & bothering latex.
Cool & smothering latex.

Fantasy unleashing latex.
Awe inspiring latex.
Sleek and smooth and scintillating latex...

BREATH OF EDEN

- JR Kangas

After one adolescent toot
when you came over to sleep it off
in my adolescent bed, my friend,
virgins the two of us, surely, drawn
towards naked worlds we would soon plunge into,

I woke early (if I slept at all)
wanting to touch you, but instead
slipped from the sheets' cocoon to the chair
where your T-shirt and jeans lay strewn, knelt
to bury my face in them and breathe

you in as I'd breathe in the odor
and pollen from a rose deep
into my lungs and blood. Nothing
since then has intoxicated me
like that flesh-scented garden: your clothes.

501

- Gavin Geoffrey Dillard

The Shroud of Turin never
held such mystery as this
rag of blue denim on the
bedroom floor;

The sloughed-off shins from a
reptile just skinned,
limp, yet crisp with
history:

Stench of smoke from a
disco dive,
rhythm, fire and
spilt beer;

Stains of urine, sav'ry
salts, the
fertile seam of his
rear.

He comes out of the shower,
slick and clean, a
serpent returned to his
lair;

But he is too late, my
heart lies spent, his
jeans now beside me are
there:

Dreams like dirty underwear;

Sperm on my gun.

He smiles at this treason;

Levi's: 501.

- *Gavin Geoffrey Dillard*

Would it be rude to
ask for the socks that I
gave him for Christmas
back now that
he has soiled them?

SOCK MAN

- Thaddeus Rutkowski

Most days, I cannot wait to get home from work so I can raid the public laundry. Usually, I bypass my apartment and go directly to the basement. By the time I enter the room with the washer and dryer, I am trembling. If someone has a load in the tumbler, I know I've struck gold.

I make sure no one is looking, then I open the dryer, root through the clothes and grab a pair of socks. They are usually warm, somewhat damp, and - if I'm lucky - soft and fuzzy. The fact that these socks belong to a stranger gives me the shakes.

Socks in pocket, I race upstairs to my apartment, rip open the door and slip inside. I take out my booty, have a sniff, then a rub, then say to myself, "Sock it to me."

I waste no time in defiling the socks. I nibble them with my lips, soak them with my spit, then take out my argyle buster and work them over till they need patches.

When I am totally spent, I return them to the dryer. If the machine is still running, I throw them in. If not, I keep them. Then I make a vow never to steal socks again.

But I know it won't be long before I'm back to sock stalking. My sock drawer is bursting with loot.

LOVE OF SHOE

- Laurel Ann Bogen

Oh love of shoe. He have love of shoe. White bucks. Black pumps. Shoes for peace. Shoes for industry.

He watch shoe of women walking to work. He love the secretary shoe. The shoe have the good sense. It bet on Native Dancer. It play the shoe horn. The shoe be no-nonsense.

He love the no-nonsense shoe. It know when to put the foot down. It be up-front. It stand on own two feet. It wear the eyeglasses and go to Vassar on scholarship.

No-nonsense shoe have the degree in art history and work in the insurance agency. Oh he want to free her to dance the light fantastic. He want to show her the Tintoretto.

Oh the shoe. The love of shoe that stumble when she hurt when she lose the dream. She want the rhinestone clip-ons and the spike heel. She want the staccato of her heel in the spanish cabaret, the taffeta skirt at the ankle, the eye on the foot.

Yes. Yes.

Yes.

He take her home to The Projects. He clean the kitchen. He empty the ashtray. He straighten the sheet and the pillowcase.

This be it.

He take her to the exclusive salon. The polish. The stream lie. The work up whittle down like the 35-year-old divorcee from Palm Springs.

He make the satin curtain. He make the fur rug for her to sleep. Oh the love of shoe.

Boot servant. I be your boot servant. I love your thin hot spikes. Walk on my chest.

He take off the glasses. She throw back the chair. He rip off the shirt. She get out the black gloves.

Walk on my chest.

She grind her pointed black toe on the sternum. He gasp with pain.

Tell me what it feel like to be ugly. The no-nonsense shoe. The shoe with no magic. Tell me how I give you magic.

I love to see you moan. She hiss. I kick you in the face. I owe you everything. I devour you. I walk on your chest.

Oh the shoe.

Oh the shoe.

Oh the love of shoe.

Oh the love of shoe oh.

Oh the love of shoe oh.

Oh.

Oh.

Oh.

Oh. The Tintorettos. The Botticellis. The dainty dreams of

the art history major. The ivory tower. The Rapunzel Complex.

She learn the power that undo the laces. She kick out the jams. She light the candle and she know the curse.

Daily he falls in love of shoe. They line the closet in the neat row. They be separate by color and date. He know the mission. He liberate the shoe from the constraints of the conventional morality. He understand their baseness. It be OK.

HI HO SILVER

- Catfish McDaris

shedding her purple velvet pants
she took a big toke
her breasts expanding
like armadillos
fastening her spurs
onto her only attire
her alligator Tony Lamas
she asked
"you ready to ride, cowboy?"
i gave her my best
imitation Bronco Billy grin
she handed me a horned condom
with a smiling picture of L.B.J. on it
"cause i put the cunt
in country"
i buried it
deep
in the heart of Texas.

THE CATALOG GODDESSES

- Stan Rice

I stare down at the gossamer
Flounce of blond tigress
With the pelvis of perfume
In the Bloomingdale's Catalog.
Aching that she not snub me
As the bumpkin I am, aching
For the six-foot kitten with eyes
So blue they show through her sunglasses.
In the catalog, flat and cool,
In her own rectangle, by which is written, "Rejoice
At the return of the boy coat
In camel." They can do no wrong,
These carnal crushed-sequined halter-sheathed
Keyhole snapbottom lycra
Felines in fuscia and silver.
I keep the catalog beside the toilet.
I open it and feel like one of their
Buttery-soft black leather purses and
Make sounds like a tray of ice cubes
Thrust under running hot water.

STREET INSTRUCTIONS: AT THE CROTCH

- Edward Field

It is not against the law to grope yourself. - DDT

Remember yourself. - Gurdjieff

While walking toward housewife wielding baby
reach down and squeeze your cock,
looking at her casually.

Adjust cock from left side to right
causing half hard-on,
then shift it back.

Wear balls on one side, cock on other.

Tug at crotch of pants as if to free genitals
tangled in underwear.
Give it a good tugging.
Go out without underwear.

Make small tear in bulge of basket
exposing skin.
Sew patch on crudely.

Wear pants of some material
flimsy as the law allows.

Go out with fly unzippered.
Go out with fly half unbuttoned.
Break zipper and fasten with safety pins.
Rip crotch and sew with large jagged stitches.

While talking with friends
unzip fly, lower pants, and arrange shirt tails.

Ask policeman for directions
and while he's telling you
give yourself a feel.

Walk loosely
to give yourself as much stimulation as you can.
Let it all move.
Be there.

MY HERO

- Orlando Paris

There, on the locker room floor,
Just as I have stripped nude,
I see his jock-strap lying, dropped
In a little heap, the narrow
Bands of webbed elastic flowing
Casually over the form-fitting pouch,
Bulging hugely, though empty,
Testimony to the great size of
The warm, soft burden it protects
In its damp, stained folds.
Trembling, I bend over and
Pick it up, handling it as I would
A precious jewel, a sacred thing,
And bring it to my nostrils and
Breathe deep, inhaling the perfume
Of his sweat, the aroma of his
Oft-dribbled urine, and the memory
Of some glorious concealed ejaculation
When our high school cheered.
I hold it to my lips and am
Tongue-kissing it when he returns
From the showers and smiles and
Noticing how hard I am,
Proud of my love for him,
Tells me I can keep it if
I will let him wear mine.

Anonymous Poet

clothes make the woman

- Gerald Locklin

i read in roland barthes: "*striptease*
is based on a contradiction... woman
is desexualized at the very moment
when she is stripped naked."

you see, my love, i was right when
i insisted that, one time,
you keep your blouse on
and another time your bra.

i was right when i asked you to remove
your blouse and bra
but pulled your panties over to one thigh
and slipped it into you between them.

i was right when i bit your nipples
through your bra
and when i ate you
through your panties.

when i left your panties dangling
from one of your ankles
i was right then,
and when i slipped your lubricated panties
up your ass and yanked them out as you came,
i was right then too.

i never tied you to the bed
with your underwear and pantyhose
but i probably should have.

i did hold your ears shut
so you would only hear the inner ocean
as i fucked you.

christ, i know the practicalities of the decision,
but how do you stay away from me so long,
love? sex is all in the skull,
and i am not done conceptualizing.

BLACK SLIP

- Terry Wolverton

She told me she had always fantasized
about a woman in a black slip.
It had to do with Elizabeth Taylor
in Butterfield Eight.

She came to my house with a huge box
gift-wrapped with gigantic ribbons.
Inside, a black slip.
Slinky, with lace across the bodice.
She told me how she was embarrassed
in the department store,
a woman in men's pants
buying a black slip clearly not intended for herself,
and about the gay men in line behind her,
sharing the joke.

She asked me to try it on.
I took it into the bathroom, slipped it over my head.
I stared at myself for a long time
before I came out of the bathroom
walked over to her
lying on the bed.

That was the first time. It got easier.
The black slip was joined by a blue slip
then a red one
then a long lavender negligee, the back slit to there.

I wore them to bed.
In the morning she would smile and say
how much she loved waking up next to a woman in a slip.
The black slip remained our favorite.
We always made love when I wore the black slip.

Once I showed up at her door late at night
wearing a long coat
with only the black slip underneath.

One night I cooked dinner at her apartment
wearing nothing but the black slip
and red suede high heels.

It was always the first thing to pack when we went on vacation.

And she used to make me promise
that if we ever broke up
I'd never wear that slip for anyone else.

I don't know where it is now.

Stripped of that private skin
when we broke up
I never went back to claim it.

I think she must have
packed it
given it
thrown it
away.

On bad days I imagine her
sliding it over the head of some new love
whispering about Elizabeth Taylor
and waking up to a woman in a slip.

Or perhaps
it's still there
draped on the back of the door.

A sinuous shadow.

A moan in the dark.

BLACK BRA

- Matthew LaPierre

She left
a black bra
on the bed
a couple weeks
after you had
started seeing
each other.
It had a small
black bow
on it &
you rubbed
the lace between
thumb
& forefinger
& thought of
her breasts.
The bra
still smelled
like her perfume.
For a while,
at least,
you believed
you would never
leave her.

976-CHAT

- Charles Webb

The man - short, thin, Jewish - tried to grow
an Afro before he went bald. "I'm six-three
and very muscular," he says. "German
descent, with shoulder-length blond hair."

The woman - forty-four, divorced, a hundred-
sixty pounds - still smarts from her last-chance
prom date with crosseyed Jimmy Swift.
"I'm twenty-two," she says, "five-six, one-nineteen,

thirty-seven D." Naked, linked only
by a wire the most ingenious germ
or obligation can't squirm through,
she describes a filmy bra and wet panties;

he describes red g-string briefs with a huge bulge.
They both whisper "I love you"
at the end, then hang up fast to hide
the crash as they fall back into themselves.

- Jacqueline Lapidus

You look divine in drag: though I won't wear
skirts myself (too feminine), I love that smart
oyster-shade ensemble over white, your hair
coppery by contrast, and the sight
of your strong feet in pantyhose and two-
tone shoes excites me. Jacket on your shoulder,
you tell it to the judge while, getting bolder
by the minute, I fantasize what I'll do
to you after you've won your case
and I get you on a deserted beach somewhere
and pull those stockings off you. No disgrace
in playing with bygone traditions, is there?
The judge, bless her, sports a wig and a bow tie.
If I don't make you come this week, I'll die.

TRANSVESTIA

- Victor Borsa

pseudo woman in your dark joy
at Gene Comptons, miniskirted and pink
inverting sexes with urgency
in frills and bracelets and finger-

nail polish; Nefertiti now blond profiled
of flowing brow and sloe-eyed stare
in desperate argument against masc-
ulinity, you play with coke and destiny

alike, measuring your words
and lines with studied softness, aware
of men pondering your feminacy.
Being a woman is more important now

than Life itself; recalcitrant you sit
in radiance calculated of desire, fighting
your violated self with love. To whore
is suddenly ultimate and beautiful:
you kiss

a passing leatherboy with your eyes

POPESS JOAN

- GG *Belli*
translated by Harold Norse

She was a real woman. She chucked the apron
Before anything else and signed up with the army;
Then she was made a priest, became a prelate,
Then bishop, and a Cardinal finally.

And when the male Pope was taken sick
And died, as people say, by poisoning,
She was made Pope, transported like a king
To Saint John Lateran in the papal chair.

But here we solve the plot of the whole affair;
All of a sudden she got terrific pains
And dropped a kid right there on the chair!

From then on this other chair was arranged
In such a way that it was easy to grope
And tell if the Pontifex was Popess or Pope.

- Anakreon
translated by Sam Hamill

Artemon once traveled in shadows,
he wore a hood and earrings,
wrapped his waist in leather,
and carried a filthy shield.

He lived among beggars and whores,
often in prison or at the wheel,
the bite of the whip on his back,
his beard and hair plucked clean.

But now this son of Kykos
arrives in a woman's carriage,
gold earrings dangling,
parasol twirling, with a wink at us.

THE REAL WORLD

- Selena Anne Shephard/Andy Plumb

the real world is
a corset sucking in my gut
and a leather hood claiming my face
for its very own

the real world is
12 feet of chain dangling
from my swelling balls

the real world is
a night drenched in skintight latex

the real world is
a $100 bill shoved between my phony tits
and the drop of his pants to the ground

the real world is
a lacy petticoat & little girl sighs
and savoring "Daddy's" sweet thing
as if it was the last lollipop in the whole world

the real world is
the sound of the whip coming down
upon my girdled bottom

the real world is
a yellow raincoat
beckoning me, enticing me, seducing me

the real world is
legs split wide &
a midnight cock
plunging up the middle

the real world is
a kiss deep and long
yes, I do like to kiss

PRETTY PERSUASION

- Selena Anne Shephard/Andy Plumb

- beginning

I skate around the mall
with a walkman tuned in to
subversive sounds
I am in search of secret passageways
people of unusual genders
spaces of unabashed desire
The teenage girls with
nasty tongues never look at me
yet they tell me stories from afar
strange, exotic tales
they could never have gotten
from television
they dress in layers
in bizarre mosaic patterns indecipherable
I listen for simple truths
yet hear only complex lies
which, of course, are much more trustworthy
I purchase working class lingerie
(I mean, underwear) at Sears
from a salesgirl who *knows*
but will never tell
I plead with her to scream it out
reveal the source of her despair
but she just laughs heartily and
steals away into the hardware section
I call the security guards
who arrest me for wearing plaid socks
with a leather skirt
I manage to escape between the cracks
and return unscathed to the scene of the crime...

- middle

I light a cigarette
though I don't know how to smoke

it seems natural at the time,
I cross my legs
right over left
then left over right,
I refasten my garter,
smooth my skirt,
fluff up my titties
    I'm anticipating something
but I'm not quite sure what it is
a recurring moment, perhaps
a (parenthetical thought), maybe
the merger of parallel lines
that's it, the merger of parallel lines
    I remember vividly the secret dance
I used to perform
when I was nine and yearning
so awkward
so strange
so utterly incomprehensible
yet it couldn't be denied
it had a raw beauty to it that exhilarated me
    I check between my legs
to see what gender I am today
I find nothing in particular except
an old beat-up baseball mitt
and two dozen rose petals
"I must be a guy," I say to myself,
though I can't be certain,
I never am, but I never give that away
there are much better things to give away
imaginary kisses
telltale signs,
sideways glances
    I dream of climbing Mount Everest in my Maidenform
bra
I never reach the peak
I wake up in a cold sweat...

- end

We make love in a vacant lot

as it was meant to be
cold asphalt below
full moon above
crickets chirping madly in the background
    He is my dada daddy
I am his exotic drag princess in heat
when we kiss, our fantasies collide
explode
immersing us in minute particles
of lust and longing
    He touches me as if I weren't there
when I cry out for more
he gives me less
the pleasure is all too much
so I revel in the pain
    He draws his sword
and I my water pistol
we duel for hours into days
he backs me into a corner
I dive between his legs
and make a run for the abandoned space
between provocation and allure
between outrage and surrender
between perception and scandal
    He calls for me
he pleads for me
he paints his face by numbers
and recites nursery rhymes for me
remembering my name for the first time in weeks
I reach out and pull him deep within
and hope he hasn't forgotten how to swim...

MARILYN

- Jeffrey Lilly

"Hi, I'm Marilyn,"
said the youngish fellow
so seductively wrapped,
his red dress studded with
a flashing brilliance
that hinted of diamonds.

It was near
the witching hour
and I, a stumbling Steppenwolf
lit by drink,
beheld a fetching image
that still playfully flashes
before my eyeing memory.

There was the artful makeup
mixed with a smile
of seductive willingness,
and he beckoningly held a fur
that seemed to speak
of hidden territory.
His hair was his own,
although as blonde as Marilyn's.

I smiled the look
of an evening predator
caught in fascination
and suddenly remembering
his heart.
The drag of my dreams
still lights
the sky of my recollection.
The Queen of the Night
mixed with the yehudim
of the Sabbath.
Soft words beat gently
like a longing heart.

A proposition was met
by a nod of consent.

At home
upon a hill
overlooking a city
of lights,
we undressed
and wed
in the evening,
blessed by a New Jerusalem
that matches men
in a ringing stillness.

It was like this
that I took "Marilyn's" invitation
and, in an evening's trance,
entered the gates of paradise.
My cock played
upon the manly cunt
to leave this music,
a scored reflection
of ecstasy.

TV GUIDE

- Thaddeus Rutkowski

I am not the kind of guy who buckles a belt around his pillow and rubs against his creation until the feel of fabric cinched with leather provokes a tiny explosion. I am not the sort of dude who grinds against a tree until the hardness of bark and the smell of sap trigger a steadily building, unbearably twitchy emotion. No, I am the type of man who picks up men dressed as women on the street and gets down to in-the-flesh back-door action.

I try to remember, when cruising for cross dressers, that it is not always easy to distinguish transvestites from regular vestites. But there is something in the walk, if the TV is walking, or in the look, if the TV is looking, that gives the true TV away. It is a drag to guess wrong and end up with a woman instead of a drag queen.

The best way to separate women from drag queens is to have my friend-for-the-evening remove his or her pants. This can be done in one of the small gardens next to the posh apartments that line the transvestite block.

I avoid legitimate tenants. They are likely to say, "Get off the street" and are not likely to add, "Please."

The questionable transvestite may delay the moment of reckoning by excusing himself or herself to dose up on drugs. "I just need a moment to pull myself together," he or she might say.

I wait politely while my unreadable companion walks back and forth from lighted areas to dark corners, sniffing.

When positive identification is made, I can begin to salivate. I can let my eyes get wide. I can wave my paws in the air and think of nothing but semiotically significant undergarments, perfume and wigs. Then I can forget gender markers and behave like a large dog humping a small one. I can utter exclamations of grinning, animal joy.

DRAG

- Tavya Nyong'o

Lipgloss and falsies
and too much hairspray transform
me. I wet my tongue
and move like I had a pussy
bathing in the love of others
who want to touch
me. Who want to thrust
against me. Who see and smile
and laugh and
for a while

for a moment
I am near
I am connected
I am seen.

- Gavin Geoffrey Dillard

All drag queens have
big dicks I
theorize as she
hitches up her
skirts
and
shows me what is
hers

Something about
all that
makeup
brings out the
man
in a woman

- Gavin Geoffrey Dillard

I would like to

shave
your body clean

strip its
hair
to nakedness

and see you
bland
as a cave lizard

shimmering
blind
as a white cave fish

if I might
to touch your
fleshiness

and move about
your
glassiness

my lips
of pinkened
steel.

as simple

- ron androla

as suddenly
shaving away
all pubic hair
for my reaction
tho I feel silly
visualize female infancy
little girl's hairless slit
like a gill down there
fish-gristle fish-guts
inside

SHAVE

- Gerry Gomez Pearlberg

The flea market razor
will do. We'll do it
with the silver
heavy-handled one:
a force of nature,
organic in my hand.
In an old wooden bowl
warm water,
shaving brush,
and soap will
whip a froth amalgam
blinding white
as winter in
a wintermint canoe.

Tip up your handsome chin.

I'll slush
a slash of foam
across your cheek,
but just for fun:
tonight, my girl,
we'll row out
past the crew-cut
docked upon your shore
and pull that silver
oar across your heady
waves of auburn grain
to leave a smooth
stone polished in its wake,
organic in its purity of form.

HAIR CARE

- Thaddeus Rutkowski

I had my tongue to a nipple when I tasted a hair. The hair was about two inches long and was, as far as I knew, an anomaly. There was no such hair on my partner's other nipple, nor had there been on nipples of other partners in my memorable past.

Now, I knew that, were I a baby, I might want to wrap the hair around my thumb while I nursed at the nipple. But since I was not, I wanted something else: I wanted to tweeze the hair. I wanted my partner to lie back while I dabbed alcohol onto her nipple. I wanted her to stay still while I latched tweezers onto the hair and plucked. I wanted to hear her say, "Aye!" then, "Aye yi yi!"

But I did not want to stop there. I wanted to shave her entire body. I wanted to prep her. I wanted to scrape to the edge of tender areas. I wanted to put my thumb over vulnerable spots to protect them while I razored.

I wanted my partner to have skin like an infant's. I wanted her to call me Daddy. I wanted her to know without doubt who was wearing the diapers.

Needless to say, that was our last date.

I heard recently, though, that she is now going out with a new man. I guess the hair is still there. I assume the new man does not attempt to tweeze it. I am convinced each of them attends privately to his or her own shaving needs.

BALDNESS ABOLISHES COMFORT AND CREATES ANXIETY

- Barbara Hauk

A bald man is different.
He has skin
where other men have hair,
a web stretched over round bones,
his flat face a nightmare mask.
Baldness is frightening.

A bald head could be mistaken
at first sight for a breast:
its milky smoothness and shine
attract disciples, even babies.
Baldness is dangerously deceptive.

It is easier to imagine a bald man
naked than anyone else: he has lost
a right to clothes along with his hair.
Nude, he stands with his cock in his hand.
Baldness is degenerate.

Beware the bald man! After
shaving his pubic hair, he will
creep into your bed at night
for the cream lips of your willing wife.
Baldness is immoral.

He claims he doesn't need hair.
Don't believe him:
he peers at you knife-eyed,
hating and envying your hair.
A bald man is a killer.

He must be stopped.
Kill the bald bastard.
Starch his hairless pate like
a potato chip and string it up
in the village square,
before he has a single chance!

pierced pandemonium

- Catfish McDaris

amnesia hang over
waking in a strange circumstance
a buxom naked blonde
next to me
not completely nude
she wore cowboy boots
with spurs & an
assortment of pierced jewelry
both sets of lips
were adorned
her nose, nipples, & one eyebrow
i felt a twinge of pain
in my penis
looking down i noticed
my newly pierced
appendage
i pissed a split rivulet
& vowed sobriety
forever

OH, TO KEEP BEAUTY BACK FROM VANISHING AWAY

- Edmund Miller

Your face is beautiful,
Indescribably beautiful as I pass by,
Beautiful and beautiful and beautiful:
And more beautiful still.

Then as I pass completely around you,
I see that you dare to go further.
And I am drooling
Over the exquisite and imagined dueling

That went into your two parallel
Your too perfect,
Cheeky
Scars.

from CLAY DOVES

- Mikhail Kuzman
translated by Simon Karlinsky

Nine delightful birthmarks
I count with my kisses
And as I count them, I read
A mystery, sweeter than heavenly mysteries.
On your cheeks, on your dear neck,
On your chest, where your heart is beating...
That which is darker than musk
Will not be erased by kisses.
Thus, over the heavenly staircase,
As I tell the beads of caresses,
I shall reach the gates of paradise
Of your miraculous beauty.
Now, that eighth birthmark
Is the most precious one in the world,
Sweeter than the shade in sultry summer
And lovelier than the breeze in May.
And when I reach the ninth one
I no longer bother counting,
I simply melt, I melt, I melt,
Enveloped in a tender flame.

ABRASIONS ON THE BODY

- DS Lawson

The scar on your leg,
The scar just above and to the left of your bush,
The scar, like an anchor, to the right of your mouth -

I treasure them;
You were hurt in these places once.
Probably you never paid

Much mind to them, cannot recall,
Save for the surgery scar,
How or when you got these marks

Which have become so much a part of you
I may as well ask you where you got your toenails.
The new scar on your shoulder,

Still purple and wrinkled - you can remember that one,
Falling off a moving car onto asphalt
And scraping, burning, peeling the living skin

Off, leaving a scab that stuck for months.
I taste it where you were hurt; I kiss the scar;
I learn another wonderful letter of your alphabet.

eating szechuan eggplant

- Thérèse Murdza

like sucking up along your collar bone
and licking heat,
the ink
of your tattoos.

PIRATES

- Laurel Ann Bogen

> *"Those as hunts treasure must go alone, at night, and when they find it they have to leave a little of their blood behind them."*
>
> Loren Eisley, THE NIGHT COUNTRY

Alone I sniffed
for buried treasure
the tumble of night
in your wandering eye
I chose you
for your swagger
and cutlass tongue
I did not mind
the lash you left there

Tattoo that is your name
more precious than gold doubloons
I scratch the letters on my arm
the ink and blood still mix

BLADE RUNNER

- Thaddeus Rutkowski

If you have long been fascinated with knives, with their power and danger, you might feel a need to cut someone.

Before you carve your partner, you should sample the blade yourself. You don't want random markings, of course. You want a pattern that has mystical power, like a Celtic sunrise. Such an image would look nice etched into your epidermis. Pick a relatively large, flat area to use as the canvas. The blank slate of your abdomen, below the belt, would be perfect.

Get a knife artist you trust to do the slicing. Blood sport is not a game. Bare your flesh, then feel the pressure of the blade splitting your skin. Feel the endorphins kick in. Later, notice how your clothes rub against the cut lines, causing a pleasurable itching-and-stinging sensation.

After much study, you will be ready to perform cutaneous surgery. Make sure you use a sterile scalpel, one ordered directly from a medical supply house. Swab the cut-ee's skin with alcohol, put on plastic gloves, transfer the pattern with tracing paper, and cut through four layers. Remember that the skin has seven layers, and if you cut deeper, the slices will form keloid scars. (Your partner might want scars, of course, if he or she is a really tough cookie.) Watch the blood pool in a vague red mass. Blot with paper. Watch the Celtic sunrise, or singing nightingale, or whatever image you have chosen, emerge. If it doesn't, slap the skin with your hand to bring more blood to the surface.

Remember that scars are a badge of honor among tribes that share your lust. Keep in mind that many prison inmates pierce their skin with pins and apply ink to gain respect. Never forget that your partner is giving you his or her life force freely.

You hold a sacred trust. Drink in the faith as you draw pictures in blood with your blade.

SUNDAY, AUGUST 1, 1977 (from *TREE*)

- Deena Metzger

I am no longer afraid of mirrors where I see the sign of the amazon, the one who shoots arrows. There is a fine red line across my chest where a knife entered, but now a branch winds about the scar and travels from arm to heart. Green leaves cover the branch, grapes hang there and a bird appears. What grows in me now is vital and does not cause me harm. I think the bird is singing. When he finished his work, the tattooist drank a glass of wine with me. I have relinquished some of the scars. I have designed my chest with the care given to an illuminated manuscript. I am no longer ashamed to make love. In the night, a hand caressed my chest and once again I came to life. Love is a battle I can win. I have the body of a warrior who does not kill or wound. On the book of my body, I have permanently inscribed a tree.

I WANT MY DICK SUCKED

- Michael Lassell

I want my dick sucked by a puppy of
a thing while he's having a tattoo on
his left asscheek. I want him naked and
flat on his tight stomach on a leather
table in the back room, and I want the
man with the needle nearly naked, too -
thick, hairy, covered in designs of his
own devising and wearing a leather
vest, his jeans down around his knees and his
dick up the boy's asshole while he works on
the sore soft flesh stretched over clenched muscle,
and maybe he's wearing cuffs, and I am, too,
and we shoot our loads together inside
the kid - and that's how to get a tattoo.

THE SKULL

- Ian Young

When the boy undressed,
I saw on his left shoulder
a blue tattoo -
two daggers, crossed
under a skull.
"That's pretty phony,"
he said, and laughed,
uncertain.
Later, I half expected it
to peel off
in my mouth.

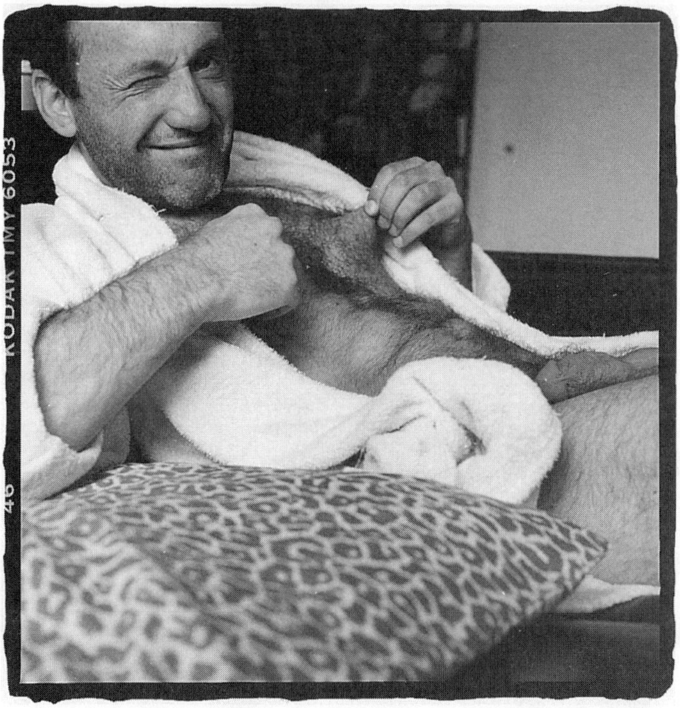

Leonardo

THE DEFORMITY LOVER

- Felice Picano

The first one he loved - an accident
was a deaf mute
golden lean as a West Coast
basketball star.
Surprised by his luck
all he could think of was sex.
Until after
when they spoke on sheets
writing messages in vaseline.
They met after that
once a week for some time.
The sex got hotter
their bodies fit better.
Then his speech began to slip.
Words seemed inexact
and harsh
compared to reading lips,
or making a point
with a fingertip
or a kiss.
Then the deaf mute went away.

The next one was a blind boy
at a college gym dance.
A curly head of hair
the body of a stevedore,
an Adriatic address,
convinced him this would be special.
He wasn't disappointed.
This time they talked
but softly,
never looking at each other
in the bedroom's blinded night:

letting touches rediscover
soft steppes of ribs,
meadows of flesh,
seas of infinite skin.
They got together often -
geographers of the tactile.
Each visit left him thinking
our senses -
so misused when there -
when missing, are seldom missed.
Then the blind boy found a lover.

Since then he's gotten bolder
searching
for what others pass over.
An afternoon with a veteran
who happened to have left an arm
in a rice-paddy in Viet Nam
disproves that two hands
are better than one.
A night with someone older
whose seizures
when he's ready to come
aren't orgasm, but pre-Grand Mal
becomes a game of sex
roulette.
Nothing indiscreet.
No ads in the papers for amputees.
No loitering near the handicapped
hoping a hunchback wants to connect.
It's beauty
not the grotesque he seeks.
But the only perfection he can see
is that most apparently,
poignantly
flawed.

This isn't a case from Kraft-Ebbing.
If asked,
he'd say he's a normal guy.
For him a chiselled profile is fine,

but handsomer with a speech defect.
A well-defined chest will evoke
his desire
but heavily scarred or mispigmented
its athletic cut is more gratifying.
Deformity is a grace, he'll say.
Like courage, it's clean
and always naive,
open and free, no hiding -
the truest state or man perhaps.
Want to see him use this philosophy?
You can find him almost every night
in any one of a half dozen bars.
He's a hospital ward
for the maimed young gods:
a port for anyone's surgical storm:
looking to fuck
the human condition.

COURTING RODNEY

- Gavin Geoffrey Dillard

Rodney is an extraordinarily beauteous young man of thirty.
When he was twenty, the wrong dosage administered in a
hospital somewhere crippled him and zapped his
nerves. His back is crooked, his hands gnarled with
palsy, and his legs, thick and muscular beneath
loose-fitting shorts, curl in and shake from
his body's own weight.

He cannot speak, but carries around a portable
computer on which he is capable of rapidly
punching out responses to queries - he
is not shy about using this device. I
was not introduced to the lad, but
hastily offered that he
share my table.

He had just returned from a hospital up in Canada that
he hoped would be able to cauterize the glands which
salivate a continual stream down his chin; they
put him on another medication (which
appeared to not work very well). I
desired to offer my hair and my
lips to keep him dry.

I do not know of his sex life, before or after the
"accident" when he was twenty; I would love to
watch his paralysis respond to an orgasm (if he
can have such). Rodney smiled and cavorted with
the employees of the cafe, who all knew and
loved him; yes, someone answered me, he is
always this effulgent - I wanted to
ask of his romantic proclivities,
but did not.

Perhaps he was just being shy with a stranger, or
maybe he presumed that I would not be inspired by a
case such as his; I desired to inform him that I
am a cripple too, that my disease is inside and
needs a patient hand and a steady heart. But I
merely watched him bounce out with his to-go
burritos and the small shoulder purse in
which he carries both computer and a
book of paper towels.

Next time lunch will be on me, I will feed him his
meal and wipe the napkins across his proud chin and
contorting lips; when we are done we will lie
together, trembling with the spasms of spent
passion, sharing secrets of how the world has
damaged us, and how two spirits can soar
above this troubled, palsied terra.

HUNGRY

- Lisa Glatt

Monday night.
I'm at Safeway. I feel
the honeydew and a man comes up, winks
at me with green eyes and walks away. I pick up
ears of corn and another man comes up
and asks about my melons. I don't quite understand
this influx of attention, having been a shopper
for years and never been approached. Suddenly I realize
it's *date night* and these shoppers
are tired of barstools, numb soles,
and vodka. These shoppers
buy their food for the week
on the night
the hungry
come out.

I leave with a guy
and a bottle of red wine. We go
to his apartment. The paint cracks
on all four walls. I comment
on his unfed plants. An insect
floats in a molded coffee cup and I'm happy here
in his mess
talking about toilet paper and garlic, unpacking his food
for the week. *People* magazine. He says he bought it
for the article on Bukowski. I tell him
he looks and walks like a writer. He shows me four poems.
Three are very good and I
kiss his cheek. We end up
rolling around on the bed. He tells me
he has only one ball.
I feel. Yes, one ball
but it's big. I show him
my scars and onions. He tells me
perfection is no great thing
and swallows my ear
like a vitamin.

KINKY

- Denise Duhamel

They decide to exchange heads.
Barbie squeezes the small opening under her chin
over Ken's bulging neck socket. His wide jaw line jostles
atop his girlfriend's body, loosely,
like one of those novelty dogs
destined to gaze from the back windows of cars.
The two dolls chase each other around the Orange County
   Camper
unsure what they'll do when they're within touching distance.
Ken wants to feel Barbie's toes between his lips,
take off one of her legs and force his whole arm inside her.
With only the vaguest suggestion of genitals,
all the alluring qualities they possess as fashion dolls,
up until now, have done neither of them much good.
But suddenly Barbie is excited looking at her own body
under the weight of Ken's face. He is part circus freak,
part thwarted hermaphrodite. And she is imagining
she is somebody else - maybe somebody middle class and
   ordinary,
maybe another teenage model being caught in a scandal.

The night had begun with Barbie getting angry
at finding Ken's blow-up doll, folded and stuffed
under the couch. He was defensive and ashamed, especially
about not having the breath to inflate her. But after a round of
pretend-tears, Barbie and Ken vowed to try
to make their relationship work. With their good memories
as sustaining as good food, they listened to late-night radio
talk shows, one featuring Doctor Ruth. *When all else fails,*
just hold each other, the small sex therapist crooned.
Barbie and Ken, on cue, groped in the dark,
their interchangeable skin glowing, the color of Band-Aids.
Then, they let themselves go - Soon Barbie was begging Ken
to try on her spandex miniskirt. She showed him how
to pivot as though he was on a runway. Ken begged
to tie Barbie onto his yellow surfboard and spin her
on the kitchen table until she grew dizzy. *Anything,*
anything, they both said to the other's requests,
their mirrored desires bubbling from the most unlikely places.

THE SAFE-SEX CELL.

- Tom House

Room #9 there's a row
padded saddles
hydraulic chrome poles
They straddle
your legs
and buckle them under
straps at your ankles
The phallus intrudes
They hold your thighs
spread Your wrists
then elbows
cinched
behind you
The hard rubber pulses/ struts
jerking naked
your ass
a mouthful of gag
grows full/ starts
dripping
narcotics & cum
the truth reveals
the pleasure becomes
(down the back of your throat)
the nipple alligator
electric clips
the mechanical pocket
& fist masturbator
(and there's
perfume in the air
and the door is locked
and it's by the hour
from here on out

- Catullus
translated by James Michie

Aurelius, I'm entrusting you with all
I love most, with my boy. I ask a small
Favour. If you have ever pledged your soul
To keep some cherished object pure and whole,
Then guard him - I don't mean from any stranger
Walking the streets on business bent: the danger
I fear is you yourself and that great spike
That ruins good and naughty boys alike.
When you're outside the house, wave your erection
At any one you like, in what direction
You please, but (I'm not asking much, I trust)
Make him the one exception. If, though, lust
And sheer perversity unhinge your reason
And drive you to the abominable treason
Of plotting against me, a grisly fate
Awaits you. Feet chained, through the open gate
Of your own flesh you'll suffer, for your sins,
The thrust of radishes and mullets' fins.

- John Giorno

	I sat
I sat	on his face
on his face	I sat on his face
I sat on his face	I sat on his face,
I sat on his face,	and he tongued
and he tongued	my ass
my ass	and he tongued
and he tongued	and he tongued my ass
and he tongued my ass	my ass
my ass	and ate
and ate	out
out	my asshole
my asshole	and ate out
and ate out	my asshole
my asshole	and ate out my asshole,
and ate out my asshole,	while I jerked
while I jerked	while I jerked off
while I jerked off,	then I took
then I took	the tube
the tube	of KY
of KY	then I took the tube of KY,
then I took the tube of KY,	and smeared it
and smeared it	on my hand
on my hand	and smeared it
and smeared it	on my hand
on my hand	and smeared it on my hand,
and smeared it on my hand,	and eased it
and eased it	into his asshole
into his asshole	and eased it
and eased it	and eased it into his asshole,
and eased it into his asshole,	into his asshole
into his asshole	and I pushed
and I pushed	and I pushed
and I pushed	until it was
until it was	in
in	up
up	to the knuckles
to the knuckles	and I pushed until it was in

and I pushed until it was in
up to the knuckles
until it was in up to the knuckles,

then I gently
forced
then I gently forced
the rest
of the hand
into the opening
then I gently forced
the rest of the hand into the opening
into the opening,
and it slipped
completely
inside
and it slipped
completely inside
and it slipped completely inside,
and the lips
tightened
and the lips tightened
around
my wrist
around my wrist
and the lips tightened around my wrist,
and I slowly
began
to twist
my arm
and I slowly began
to twist my arm
and I slowly began to twist my arm,
fuck
fist fuck,
and he went
out
of his mind
and he went
out of his mind
and he went out of his mind.

up to the knuckles
until it was in up to the knuckles,

then I gently
forced
then I gently forced
the rest
of the hand
into the opening
then I gently forced
the rest of the hand into the opening
into the opening,
and it slipped
completely
inside
and it slipped
completely inside
and it slipped completely inside,
and the lips
tightened
and the lips tightened
around
my wrist
around my wrist
and the lips tightened around my wrist,
and I slowly
began
to twist
my arm
and I slowly began
to twist my arm
and I slowly began to twist my arm,
fist
fist fuck
and he went
out
of his mind
and he went
out of his mind
and he went out of his mind

THE FIGA

- Paul Mariah

I want you to know
how it feels
to have a fist
the size of a poem
up your ass.

Get the vaseline.
This is one finger
and if I angle right
I can get past the knuckle.
Hold still.
This is two fingers
introduce rhythm
fingermovements
allow the play to continue
This is three fingers
Keep the rhythm steady
never stop the movement
I want you to feel the size of
This is four fingers
Cupped and the play continues
and I am not going to stop
Lift the left leg higher
This is my thumb
and the movement is steady
the fingers move into
you are closing around my wrist.

Now how does it feel
to have a poem
shoved up your ass
the size of a fist?

Now, I am going to uncup
my palm and make
a scratch on the inside.

This was the scene
and I had to get out of bed
to write it
so you would know
the size of it
and now we can go on...

A FIGA FOR TWO

- Paul Mariah

There was this
movie w/3
guys. Two were
standing, one
on his knees,
he cd've
blown both
dicks at once
but rather
he had a fist
up to wrist
in each
of them

He flies in
from Texas
once a year
I give him
a full figa
wrist up to
forearm to
aftarm to
elbow. Ah,
his sport,
me, huh!
Up to my
elbow in work.

FIXING THE BRACELET

- Jules Mann

what did you do to it he said
as he handed it over the counter
just wore it all the time
I guess
and I walked out putting it on
the hinge still slightly bent

from all those nights with my
hand inside you and you grabbing
onto my bracelet holding on like
reins as we rode it out

CURRENT ATTRACTION

- Ruan Bone

My friend has
a parlorsize pink totem
with a patriotic twisted flex
she keeps on a short leash
with two controls
one makes it wriggle outside
the other vibrates the tongue
of the smaller mammal,
a squirrel-cum-platypus-tongued
baby riding piggyback at speed
so fast it makes the tongue buzz
like lemon sherbert.
The latex virgin mary,
bubble-gum pink, sometimes
turns herself on inside her private drawer
quite spontaneously
when the vibrations are suitably strong.
Electricity, boredom or animal magnetism?
This gets to be embarrassing at airports
through the X rays.

My friend is highly charged herself
she says it wakes her in the night
& when she switches on the light
there it is shimmying its way along
the polished wooden floor
beside the bed
a strange luminous sea cucumber
doing a moonlight flit

perhaps it's just going
to take a leak
or explore.
Does it tire of the same black box
& dark hold everytime
or is it trying to escape the forced intimacy,
the invariable routine?
Is it merely engaged
in a Woody Allenesque dialogue,
its negative and positive currents
holding their own Summit Meeting
in Cantonese or Mandarin?
Or is it discussing the Chinese
Communist takeover of
Hongkong or Taiwan?

MOUSE

- Trebor

I started downloading porn images
not 2 hours after I first got online
Within 3 hours I was downloading myself

I grabbed what was at hand
since I'd already dropped my pants
I was stroking my nipples with my mouse
ran it across my tongue
and over my scalp

rolled it inside my thighs
drove it with pressure up my cock
hitting blue-veined speed bumps

By the time I got it up my ass
the screen saver was on
which just happened to be a white mouse in a maze
As I squirmed, files started opening

fonts turned bold
there were preferences and commands
tools and windows
the control panels all went down

I've got a tail
and a solid state boyfriend
with a plastic monitor for a face
that responds to every move I make
And when I squirm in my sleep at night
he lights up
and sings
fills me with knowledge
and shows me what boys are on his mind
as I download a billion megabytes of virtual manhood
the entire world wide web of techno-virility
I'm a spider caught in its web
I'm fucked!
and I'm the willing slave
of a big plastic monitor-faced spider
with a dick that opens windows so far and wide
my asshole blossoms the size of the universe
and we cum comets and light years

DILDO

- Ron Koertge

Someone called me a dildo the other day so now I am thinking about their history and stature in the republic.

To the Greeks they were *olisbos*, a more mellifluous choice than ours. Still, few of us let a trochee get in the way, and dildos come by mail or from any XXX shop where they stand at attention in the smudged case like so many - well, privates.

A staple of male pornography (*Heather is so lonely, and here comes Dominique in a teddy...*), a dildo
is formally classified as a marital aid, a phrase some feel
is more melancholy than anything by Matthew Arnold.

And it can be melancholy. Sometimes the drama of
the trousers is more like dinner theatre where some
poor ham actor won't rise from the feverish sheets but
claws the air and grimaces only to fall back, exhausted.

But sometimes it is just fun: you and a friend pick up
a dildo on a shopping spree. Or you're a little lonely
and you buy one instead of a pet.

Now that I think about it, I do resemble a dildo. Not,
of course, the Double Whammy Electric Ecstasy II, but
the Ronnie model: bald, clean, average in every way
right down to the one dumb all-purpose expression.

Well, so what? I'm well-liked, I'm trusted, and in a few
cases downright indispensable.

Hell, I might even run for office.

MY COLLEGE SEX GROUP

- Molly Peacock

All my girlfriends were talking about sex
and the vibrators they ordered from Eve's
Garden which came with genital portraits
of twelve different girls. All my friends' needs
swirled around me while their conversations
about positions crescendoed and they waved
their vibrators - black rubber things. Saved
by volubility I looked at the relations
of labia to clitori - look, there was one
like mine, labia like chicken wattles

below a hooded clitoris. "Friends!
of these twelve genital portraits, which
are you?" I couldn't ask them. Happy
to have found a picture of one like me:
the portrait held the hair all back and popped
the clitoris out like a snapdragon
above the dark vaginal stem.
Oh God, it was me! (And another, I stopped,
there were others like us, throughout the world.)
When my order for the vibrator was filled,
I'd get my own portrait. I'd show it to the next boy
before I got undressed: "Here's what you're getting."
And I'm not alone, or ugly, if that's what you're thinking.

private OBsession

- Jules Mann

It all started when I walked into Becky and Nina's dorm room one day to find Nina absorbed in what looked like a wad of toilet paper soaking in a glass of water perched on her dresser. It works, it really works - she shrieked in her everyday Yonkers pitch. Becky rolled her eyes at me. What is it? I asked. A tampon - she said. Not just a tampon you idiot - screamed Nina - it's an OB. I just wanted to test what they say about it expanding to twice its size and here it is - probably even more than that! Nina, it's been in there for fourteen hours - said Becky. What's an OB - I asked. After Nina explained, I realized that in Missouri where I grew up there was probably a law against them since it involved a woman putting her fingers up her own vagina to insert the OB correctly. I wasn't sure if I liked knowing how big it could get, and I can't even remember when it was I first gave one a try, but I've certainly helped other women insert an OB and I can safely say in fact I've harbored a certain private OBsession.

A PENTECOSTAL NEIGHBOR

- Belinda Subraman

tells me about
speaking in tongues.
I act interested,
and am
philosophically.
She demonstrates
saying it's like
a climax,
and "when
you're really getting it,
saying oh lord oh lord,
suddenly you peak
out of control,
words flow with joy
in the tongue of angels."
I ask her if she's
relaxed afterwards,
she says yes.
I ask her if she
smokes a cigarette,
she smiles
and touches the bible
like a lover's cock.

SHE SAID

- Belinda Subraman

I was looking
at a miracle:
she used to
smoke and drink
and hinted
at casual

and abundant sex,
but now she gets off
on jesus.
She's found the lord,
like some mentally projected
battery operated
dildo toy.
And by her bed,
his 8X10 glossy
in a frame...

SHE'LL SHOW YOU HERS IF YOU'LL SHOW HER YOURS

- Belinda Subraman

The 6 inch phallic symbol man
wears a tall hat to protect himself,
has his eyes closed tight
and knees and hands tucked away,
resigned to bear the plunge.
This stone man may easily
be broken if he doesn't please.
But a gentle girl
may keep him in silk
inside a padded box
like a delicate lover
too fragile to hold.
Or the brazen tourist
may keep him on her coffee table
next to a statue of Jesus
not knowing why
the Mexicans laughed
when she bought it.

THE MAD GIRL IS SICK OF POURING OVER VICTORIA'S SECRET FOR JUST THE RIGHT

- Lyn Lifshin

velvet or leather to pull eyes her
way, to make everyone admire, maybe
even lust. Chic simplicity that
unravels with just one wear

won't do. She's sick of
their custom fit bikinis, wants a
custom fit dick for a day that
won't shrink or go out of style,

perfect for summer or winter, a
penis to get thru autumn and
spring, strapless for summer
nights. She doesn't (definitely) want

a dildo, slinky's ok with a flared
silhouette but it has to be of
flesh. Her fingers are numb from dialing
1-800-888-8200. She wants some

thing new she can just reach and
touch, not have to be Fed Exed or come
Special Delivery. Even if Victoria's
Secret is there around the clock,

it isn't there just for her, it
isn't hers. A penis of her own would be
comfortable as long denim, the
easiest shape to wear in summer for

the weekend, ribbed as cotton to cuddle
up with. Mid thigh length in a variety
of colors you can't resist

TRASH

- Linda Smukler

I stopped home at lunch because I left my cock on the bathroom sink I found it there upstairs nested in its harness condom still on who did you think you would fuck that you needed a condom? a man? a woman? I liked that you were ready a little ashamed that I was not I never thought that harness worked very well but it worked perfectly with you and maybe I don't need a new one after all so I rushed home at lunch afraid that my lover (or is that what I call you now?) might show up I looked around for tell-tale signs in the guest room where we slept shook out our two pillows and took one downstairs to the master bedroom I know I'll sleep upstairs again tonight and take that pillow with me to bury my head where you rested yours I rolled the condom off the cock washed the pink rubber and put the cock and harness back into their soft cotton bag I wrapped the condom in one of our Lipton tea bag covers from last night took it with me into the car and stuffed the package into the now empty bag of vegetable chips from which you fed me parsnip yucca ruby taro that one with a drawing inside another that looked and tasted like potato but which you insisted was not you fed the chips to me one by one then repeated the sequence then repeated it again until we got tired I finished the chips this morning in the car and it was a way to keep you close taking that condom still full of you out of its Liptom tea bag cover unrolling a bit and placing the tip into my mouth I tasted latex and lubricant and I tasted you and after I was done I rewrapped the condom stuffed the bundle back into the empty chips bag and put it all into an old brown paper lunch sack I had to go to the bank so I threw the whole thing out in the lobby under where one writes deposit slips

ANONYMOUS SEX DREAM

- *Whitman McGowan*

She dances like a flip book,
Running away in stop-action,
Chased by a mechanical penis.
She's terrified.
She doesn't seem to be moving.
Finally, the shiny metal prick
Catches her from behind.
Bending her over,
The huge thing goes in.
She smiles.
Ramming is what she wanted
All the time,
To be filled up
By an insensitive dick,
Filled up again and again.

YOU'RE MY ROCK

- *Gary Goude*

"You're my rock," she said. "I know I can rely on you, because you are so strong, so sane. You give me comfort." I said goodbye to her and hung up the phone. I didn't tell her that I had just finished fucking my vacuum cleaner hose with a piece of ham wrapped around my dick. It was a pretty good fuck, too, and didn't seem like an insane thing to do at the time.

TESTICLES

- Robert Peters

I snuggle oranges between my legs,
simulating the size, so I think,
of Mitchum's testicles. They don't
bounce right, so I try tennis balls -
they at least have fur. But they aren't
quite suitable. At an abattoir
I buy a pair of ram balls complete
with scrotum. I trim the skin,
insert a roll of fat ripped from
the rear cavity of a hen, and settle
the gonads into my own pouch.
They bounce exactly as I'd fantasized.

NEW TRICKS

- Cheryl Townsend

Arms crossed over head
tied around the open back
of his kitchen chair My
hair spilling out the
opening with my legs
bound up and over another
like a TV antennae My
ass and cunt centered in
the void Then the blind-
fold No kiss foreplay
all starts in the curve
of my neck First gentle
tit caresses soon break
to groping kneading and
unshaved sucks then bites

Hands now spread all lips
and fuck fingers into moist
mouths his own stretching
my nipples like balloons
Snapping them back Scraping
across laughing teeth I drool
everywhere and drip generously
onto seat cushions
Lips all tighten
He stops
Steps away
Laughs
My back arched
begging
Then fingers spread
cunt lips again
and a tongue
roughly
laps my clit
like a dog would
water
Like a dog would
itself
Like a dog would
Like a dog
Like a German shepherd
Like our neighbor's
German shepherd
My question
answered with a gag
A strap-on dildo
strapped backwards
around my head
crammed enough
I nearly choke
but not enough
Then his wet cock
across my cheek
my nose
My clit is sucked
The dildo vibrates

His legs straddle me
cock between my
squeezed tits
I feel my nipples bruise
My clit is hard
My tits are fucked
My cunt is begging that fucking dog
The dildo is ready to cum
My tits are liver
I elevate
I scream mute
His cock ejects domination
in my face
The dog
barks

THE COBBLE STONE STREET

- Cheryl Townsend

made you feel like a
battery operated dildo
as you slid your cock
up into my pudding as
we rode downtown on
the East Street but I
just sat there on your
lap like a good little
girl no one knew any
better to the underneath
the full skirt concealing
the actuality of our smiles
we are always the last ones
left on the bus

HE LIKED TO FUCK ME

- Cheryl Townsend

when I had a cold
'cuz when I'd sneeze
it would grip him
like a first time break

MASTURBATION

- Cheryl Townsend

I want to feel her breasts
as her tongue proves knowledge
is the best teacher
I want a cock up my ass
in my cunt and mouth simultaneously
I want a little boy virgin
to suck my nipples with revelry
as I raise his cock for part two
I want big macho hands groping
I want soft hands sharing
I want a gang-bang of gender benders
I want anything and everything
strapped or straddled
just fill me in every way that you can

BREAKFAST BETWEEN MY THIGHS

- Cheryl Townsend

like laying a sacrifice before
the great gods of estrus we spread
cheerio's across your bed the
crunchy O's against my back
a guarantee of my own when you
spilled your milk over the rim
of my bowl

COTTON CANDY

- Susan Terris

In a circus tent as we approach,
I am holding my cotton candy aloft.
When we stand face-to-face,
he pinches up sugar fluff and puts
it on my nose.
Laughing, I pluck some, press it on his.
While we kiss and laugh and grope,
I rub more on his nose, he rubs more on mine.
His tongue in my mouth - everything
sticky, pink, sweet, delicious - I'm

remembering tales of the Princeton prof
(before the days of women students)
who taught Shakespeare's sonnets, saying,
'My heart' means 'cock,'
'her heart' means 'cunt,'
'my eyes' means 'cock,'
'her eyes' means 'cunt,'
'my nose' means 'cock,'
'her nose' means 'cunt,'
all of it sticky, pink, delicious, sweet.

KINKY RUBS PLUMS

part any of the long saga of Vagina Dentata

- Elizabeth Kincaid-Ehlers

When Kinky rubs plums,
she prefers two,
soft and firm
and that peculiar color.
It takes practice.
Tricky to bruise
with perfect pressure,
softening centers,
keeping skin intact,
so that when the great
toothed mouth approaches
juices are ready to spurt.

GRAPES

- Amy Kashiwabara

I have developed
    a fascination with grapes
    of late
I find them popping
    into odd places
    like my poems and mouth

Their smooth pliant skin
    peels stickily apart
    like legs
    revealing wet slippery flesh
    fragrant and sweet
    around the seed

strangely wrinkled and hard
to be at the heart of such
lushness

Sometimes I swallow that seed
to remind myself
I am a woman

I'd venture to say that, yes

- Thérèse Murdza

because your nipples rise
like a woman's
like big black berries

all puckered and dark, I imagine
(watching them grow large
and hard on your broad chest)
slipping my tongue through

that silver ring
warming the metal and
letting my mouth close
around you, wet,

I'd catch you quickly
between my teeth
sucking fruity sugars

and let your deep, sweet
berry juice
run down my chin.

UPON THE NIPPLES OF JULIA'S BREAST

- Robert Herrick

Have ye beheld (with much delight)
A red rose peeping through a white?
Or else a cherry (double grac'd)
Within a lily? Centre plac'd?
Or ever mark'd the pretty beam,
A strawberry shows, half drown'd in cream?
Or seen rich rubies blushing through
A pure smooth pearl, and orient too?
So like this, nay all the rest,
Is each neat niplet of her breast.

STRAWBERRY HARVEST

- Norbert Krapf

This is what heaven
will surely be like:
a field of ripe nipples
begging to be plucked.

I touch the first and know
I will live forever.
I touch a second and feel
all my sins being forgiven.

Now word is traveling
from stem to stem
and they all
cry for my touch.

I take several at once
and know I will become
the greatest poet to write

in any language. I switch
to the other hand, take
several more, and hear
the women I have longed
to love whisper how
much they want me.

They simply cannot get
enough of me. I can do
no wrong. I give my
fingertips to as many
as I can reach
in the short time
I am given to harvest
this sensual abundance.

I rise from my knees,
blue denim all red,
lick forbidden juice
from my lips,
see telltale red
on fingertips and palm,
look down at my cartons
heaped with devotees

and hear voices from
the earth hum a prayer
for my return.

RASPBERRIES

- Deena Metzger

We passed raspberries between us, after you carried them a half mile - swimming - in your mouth. They were intact, the taste of you inhabited the dark center. You came out of the river, a goat boy, dripping, hair curled into god's horns.

Kiwis cut into the perfect lunar circle of cunt, all the long slices of white fruit, the silk of corn, the daring fuzz of apricot, the hard grind of cherry stones. Fruit washed in the river glistens before the knife creates the longing of one half for another.

We were devoured under the dark waters, taken up into the roots, exploded into the air in bristling yellow pollen of pine, only a bit of us remaining in the tang and bite of fruit, in the musk and blood of berries, in the sting.

Our smallest fingers fit in the red pulp, it spread open, calling back the stem. We carried the river in our hair, every atom of our bodies had once been the others'. Wherever we touched there were entrances, filled with raspberries.

LUST

- Stan Rice

Lift your skirt.
I want to see you.
And the oleaginous
Guilt and filth
Flushed from the cut fruit.
Bend over with your shoes on.
Your hair falls forward.
Your breasts
Are pulled by the mass of the earth.
Now lie down.
I want your anklet
To sparkle on your calf.
The whites of your eyes
To be above your pupils.
Without shame
Fill the mirror

Until it oozes
For lust has left me
And I need you to make me
Fear no more
The small black pig in the peach.

- Emily Dickinson

My Heart upon a little Plate
Her Palate to delight
A Berry or a Bun, would be,
Might it an Apricot!

LOVE SATISFIED

- Ruan Bone

I want to eat my peach
suck the sweetness round your stone
lick the drops from off your bush
smell the flesh that hugs the bone
splash in the nectar of your navel
clean the damp from out your ears
gather the fruit, my fig, my plum
and breathe in the heart of your dark
honeyed hair. Tongue explores outer,
to find inner you, sweet as Nebraska hay,
seeking out sudden shock of liquid deep
essence smooth and velvety
cointreau dipped chocolate buried liqueur
a rich seam of ore
slipping like an oyster
fresh down my gullet.

WHEN I TAKE IT INTO MY MOUTH

- Jules Mann

As if it were alive
an entity of flesh
I begin by rolling it gently
between the crest
of my tongue
and the hard
ribbed arc of mouth
then roll it
suspended
beneath my tongue
it gives slightly, against
the even row
of lower teeth
where it heats
and swells
after a moment
I let it rest
on the very tip of my
tongue, sucking it
behind my jaws
then bite
until that small
burst of sweet juice
lands against
my throat, that
crunch of tender
skin I reach
for the pod
the hard round
nipple
fresh from the garden
from the young flat
and delectable
to the bulging
sun-ripened
perfectly round
begging to be
plucked
pea

Jules Mann

- Gavin Geoffrey Dillard

Plucked out the worms
their families and remains
and cast the good parts into the pot
with honey and ginger
into applesauce
to spread across your chest
redden, hot, that smiling crest
and slide among the golden hair growing

Then I would be the worm
then I would crawl onto
and try to find my way within
there I would nest
amid tasty hair breast
there I would sleep
in those sunset skies
your golden delicious thighs
your apples, your pies!

SKULLCUPS VS. BOYMOUTHCUPS

- Antler

Rather than a skull fashioned into a cup
    to drink from,
Why not a boy's mouth as a cup to drink from?
A nude youth who is an experienced boymouthcup.
The last two summers he's earned spending money
    as a boymouthcup for paidophile illuminati.
Naked servant girl fills your young friend's mouth
    with juice, wine, nectar, beer
    and all you do is sip.
And sometimes it's nice to eat
    strawberries in whipped cream
    out of boymouth

While watching him be serviced by
the servant girl's mouth
while he fondles her tits.

ORIGAMI VS. ORIGASMI

- Antler

As we learned how to dry peaches, pears,
apricots and apples,
So we learned how to dry human semen
and make sheets of paper
from mancome and boycome
just the way we make paper from rice.
And now, a new artform for America -
and a gift in return to
the land of the rising sun,
from the land of the rising boner,
For as Japan gave us tea ceremony,
flower arranging and origami,
we to Japan give
jack off ceremony, boycock arranging
and origasmi.
Origasmi-folded sculptures made from
boyorgasmspurts.
As Teddy Roosevelt sent the White Fleet
around the world so other nations
could see a bold display
of our might,
So America now sends an armada of origasmi,
touring for World Peace
an outstanding show of
nakedboy jacking off sculptures
made from boyorgasmspurts
made into creamy paper
intricately shaped and folded
into realistic lifesize or miniatures
of teenage jerkoff joy.

THE ULTIMATE POMPOSITY

- Antler

All the lubricant drops of all the boyerections through time
    really exist, really happen, really annoint
        the head of every boy's love,
    really crown the beautiful passionate
        boyhood penis crown.
Only care for lubricant drops, no semen please,
    all I want from now on are the translucent pearls
        of lubrescent tumescent pubescents
    that surface, pearl after luminous pearl
        on their pre-ejaculant dicks.
Again, let me make myself perfectly clear,
    not boy's souls, not any part of a boy's body,
        not even his balls or cock,
    not even his creamy dreamy semen,
        only those gleaming pearls
    my lips sip from the tip.

THE AUTOFELLATOR *(for Scott O'Hara)*

- David Laurents

In the full-length bathroom
mirror, the autofellator scowls.
"Suck my cock!" he orders.
And then he does just that,
sitting down on the toilet,
grasping his legs as he bends
forward and takes his cock
between his lips. He watches
himself go down on himself.
Truth to tell, it's the watching
that most turns him on, more
than his own mouth. He can
only suck an inch or so, rolling
his tongue across the red glans;
his back aches almost immediately.
It's the sight of himself, out
of the corner of his eye, his
cock between his own lips,
that gets him off. With one
hand to steady his cock, he
lets loose into his mouth,
loving the otherwise forbidden
sight of cum shooting into
his mouth and the bitter-sweet
taste of himself.

AUTO FELLATIO

- Harold Norse

fingers delicately palpate hairs on backs of thighs -

run gingerly along bulging buttocks

and gently rest on asshole - belly trembling -

bands of muscle rippling - waist tight - sucked in -

thighs arching - blunt arrow quivering

- to shoot - !

lowering head, grasping feet -

tickling toes with moist fingers -

bending further - straining - panting -

back and spine aching - tongue protruding -

lips with kissy stress pursing

towards pearly moisture glistening -

heart pounding - tongue darting -

hands beneath thighs clasping -

fingers gripping - grappling -

head burrowing, grunting -

hot snout pressed in musky nest -

aaahh! mmmmmm!

GULP!!

Venice, CA 1969

BEAU BLOWS HIMSELF

- John Gilgun

> *Performers! Earn cash*
> *(wages and tips) If you*
> *have what it takes ask*
> *for an audition.*
> - Advertisement, Nob Hill Theater

Beau limbers up by massaging his spine.
Then he leans forward and blows himself.
What a plush sensation that must be -
lips closing over the silky glans,
brushing the circumcision scar,
the tip of the tongue probing the pee hole,
the taste of yourself, musky, funky, moist!
There are only five men here
in the arena of the Nob Hill Theater
on Bush and Powell in San Francisco,
but at that moment all five applaud.
Beau moves toward me, stands over me,
and lets me cup my hand
under his tight little balls.
Then he whispers in my ear,
"Put money in my sock.
I'm trying to earn a living here."

EAT YOUR SPERM...

- Vytautas Pliura

...or
Massage it into your scalp
Your hair will grow back
Mine did

Rub it in the creases around your
  eyes
No better beauty lotion to be found
Your body accepts it greedily
It's your own DNA

Share it with others
They need it too
Cup it to their mouths like
  freshly churned buttermilk

When I was in jail
In solitary confinement
There was a gloryhole
An unknown man fed me each night and
  kept me alive
He knew they were not feeding me

Alexander the Great got lost with his
  legions of men on their way to
  conquer India, 600 miles off
  track, lost in the cruel desert
Even today historians do not know how
  they survived with no food and
  water in that hot barren clime...

Cup it to your mouth like freshly
  churned buttermilk
Nurse the milk out of your lover's
  cock
Drink his juices like wine

JULY 30, 1974

- Michael Gregg Michaud

I waded into the deepening cold water.
The sun was still razor hot
in the late afternoon.
The lake closed around my legs,
lapping, and held on.
Little fish darted one way
then another, furious with me.
David met me when we were chest deep,
bear-hugged me and laughed in my face.
What's so funny? I asked.
I'm pissing on you, he said.
I struggled, tried to wiggle away,
but he squeezed me closer.
Like it? he laughed.

AUGUST 8, 1974

- Michael Gregg Michaud

David sat on the toilet
with his pants around his ankles,
looking at me blankly.
I listened to the plop, plop, plop,
as he shit.
Then he made me piss into the bowl
between his legs.
Now, he said,
we've done everything together.

YELLOW SNOW

- Gavin Geoffrey Dillard

Yellow snow
wherever he goes,
it's all that coffee
he says, but knows
it's more than that,
it's something genetic,
he's marking his trail,
alchemic, hermetic,
he's writing in runes
while I collect bones
and follow behind
eating yellow snow cones.

ALEXANDER PEEING

- Gavin Geoffrey Dillard

Photos of Alexander, naked in the
wake of the Point Reyes Fire, smiling
amidst ebony-stained arms and
fingers which appear to grasp after his
cool pink assurance, Life;

Alexander, urinating within the
charcoal ring, a hose like a brazen
viper lunging out from its thorny
copse, spewing forth the Holy Venom which
resuscitates all;

A coyote bush, parched like a tongue in
Hades, hisses and crackles, laps and slurps at
the Litening Stream, leaps at this
Epiphany, its emerald shoots sprouting back
as if in lust.

DRINKING TREBOR'S PEE

- Gavin Geoffrey Dillard

To drink Trebor's pee
sweetened, with lemon over ice
would be a bastardization of the
Truth; one
drinks Trebor's pee, like one
swallows Trebor's semen, hot and
directly from the fount -
or at least within minutes from a
favored mug or goblet.

I consume Trebor's pee the way I
consume Trebor's words, without
question or editing of my own
conceits; who
am I to challenge the visceral ejacu
lations of so worthy and proud a
beast?
I seduce; I consume.
I succumb; I am consumed.

Love is neither easy nor attractive,
wholesome nor sane;
when Trebor speaks, worlds are rent
askew, hearts pryed from their ossi
fied tombs; when
Trebor speaks my gonads quiver, my
scrotum titens and my anus
convulses with the revelations of a
burgeoning dawn.

Who am I to challenge this mystic-
eyed mongrel; I
set out my bowls, plates, and watch the
varmint pick and choose from my
table -
if I am lucky he naps on my sofa be

fore wandering back to his sacred
wood; if I am
lucky he stops to feed me from his
trove of used poems and found
objects; if I am truly
lucky he does not bite me but re
sponds to my caress with a
sigh or a low growl,

and I know that I have fed Trebor some
thing he can use,
that my offerings have been
accepted -

and this is more than enough for
one small lifetime.

- Gavin Geoffrey Dillard

He peed on my favorite
rose bush
and I thot it would
never stop
blooming.

THE MITCHUM TOMATO

- Robert Peters

We've always pissed in our garden.
One Big Boy tomato plant is Bob's,
another is mine.

Whose plant will yield the best fruit?
Mitchum suggests we invite Bette Davis
to irrigate the plants:
"Great!" I shout, fingering some tomato seeds.

Mitchum waters his plant, scorching the leaves.
"Keep your pee on the ground," Bob.
"You'll sear the blossoms."
I'm content with his urinary cascades,
fantasizing his meaty head.
I tamp the loam with my bare hands.

Bob's tomatoes smell of ammonia.
I swallow slices chilled, without condiments.
He, alas, never tastes mine,
although I smother them in a cock cheese dressing
garnished with tuna packed in spring water.

ERIC HEIDEN'S THIGHS

- Harold Norse

grinning with exertion
arms flapping
he races
toward us from the green
sports page
for his fifth Winter Olympics
speedskating
gold medal

I wonder
what it's like
to catch this prize
as he skates
off the page
into your arms

and you remove
his tightfitting
sleek gold suit
peeling
the smooth fabric
down
from waist
to ankles

jesus!
one could lie
at his feet
look up at that godlike body
& ask
nothing more
than a little water sports
(without ice
please)

Monte Rio, 21.ii.80

YELLOW FEVER

- Selena Anne Shephard/Andy Plumb

Streams of liquid lust
rain down from above
spray painting the old man yellow

He thanks the Gods of Piss
and wallows in the urine mists
coming from a circle of cock

He opens his mouth wide
and takes a drink of bittersweet pee
it goes down like fine wine

WITH ONE RED STILETTO

- Cheryl Townsend

heel indenting his forehead
and just enough pressure
to warrant a satiating whimper
I showered him in golden sun
shine and afternoon rain Holding
that one hundred dollar bill
in my teeth his hands unable
to hold his cumming cock

HER HOT PISS

- Cheryl Townsend

streamed down
around his cumming
cock pumping like a
plug that wouldn't work

DITTY

- Cheryl Townsend

With your cock
up my ass
and your finger
on my clit
when I reach
that plateau
feels like
I'm cumming shit

HIS FACE WAS

- Cheryl Townsend

under the kiddie potty
looking up with an
eager smile waiting
for the hot drop of
his every worth my
little bobby socks
on each side of his
sobbing chest but
no mommie came
to help wipe

- Gavin Geoffrey Dillard

Spivy and me
lying on the bed
reading Flannery O'Connor and
giving each other enemas

Life's subtle pleasures
I hope to still recall
when I turn twenty

A lovely evening at home
lying on the bed
with Spivy
reading provocative literature
and listening to the douche-bag's song

Spivy always says, Stick to your craft
and I answer back
proudly
that I will
I'm gonna write a poem about this

About Spivy and me
trying not to get the bed wet
thinking we can't hold no more
when Spivy says,
Stick to your craft
and he runs into the bathroom, eyes shining

And when he comes out he isn't the same

And I say, I will
I'm gonna write a poem about this
about Spivy and me
and the changes we've been seeing

- Gavin Geoffrey Dillard

A sucker for a
hairy ass, I've
never let a
prime one pass
without at least a
furtive feel, a
cursive cop,
surreptitious steal;

A home at best for
chin to rest, in
pungent cleft of
gaseous nest,
a garden grove of
fragrant farts, a
treasure trove of
missing hearts.

A SHROPSHIRE LAD

- Simon Sheppard

As lewd as
green fucking nature is,
we met, hiking,
he was gleaming
coming toward me
on the trail.
Half my age
punked-out hair
loud Bermuda shorts
stiff nipples
spied through
an old Sex Pistols T-shirt.
Small talk
about the day,
then "I've gotta piss,"
I said, pulling it out,
arcing gold in his direction,
the purest essence of
poetry.
He was getting hard
inside his baggy shorts,
inside his teenage life.
"Now you
piss in your shorts,"
I said. He did,
piss running
hot down his leg.
I knelt to bathe
my face in it. We
dropped our packs,
I pulled his soggy
shorts off.
(If it
gives you a hard-on
it's done its job. If it
gives you
a hard-on,
it has.)

I took a handful
of the muck
I was kneeling in,
smeared it over
his smooth white thighs,
up the crack of his ass,
fingered it inside him
til I felt hard shit
pushing back,
a sacrament of decay.
I had him down in the
mud now, legs up,
his hand pumping
away
on my cock.
And when later
we lay,
exhausted,
covered with piss and cum,
shit and mud and cum,
he looked up with dark,
hypothetical eyes
and said, "You
older guys,
all you think of
these days
is death."
I caught my breath and
told him about
the road kill
I'd seen that morning,
its unrecognizable,
stinking pelt
which someone had draped
on the interstate's
guard rail,
a neat but gaudy display.
And I stuck
my filthy hand
roughly
between his thighs
and felt him get hard

all over again. (His
beautiful secret prick.)
I never saw him again
after that.
But not a day goes by
I don't think of him.
High impact, big fate.
Not a day goes by.
Not yet...

- John Giorno

I'm giving
it to you
in a slow
stream,
the way
you like it,
I love
to feel
your throat
swallowing,
this Bud's
for you,
the king
of beer
is coming
through.

Then I put
my ass
down
on his face
and he rimmed me
while I jerked off.

1970

HI RISQUE

- John Giorno

I want
to scat
in your mouth,
I want you
to scat
in my mouth,
I want to scat
on your face
and rub it in

chocolate,
caviar,
and champagne,
absolute
preliminaries

pushing
the inner
envelope
to the limit,
one more
time,
mining
diamonds
with your tongue
for the crown
of one
of the kings
of hell,
when the going
gets rough
the tough
get gorgeous

squeezing
money

from the air
squeezing money
from the air,
snake
tongue,
stretching
your tongue
to the Buddhas,
diving
into the wreck
diving into
the wreck
diving into the wreck

curiosity
and compassion,
and an exercise
in non-aversion,
fear spiraling
from you
fear spiraling from you,
that gun's got
blood
in its hole

We do not do
this anymore,
but I still
think about it
when I'm
jerking off,
I was king
of promiscuity,
LSD,
crystal meth,
and fist fucking
with 40 guys
for 14 hours,
it's worse
than I thought

and now,
everyone
I ever made
love to,
every single
one,
is dead,
and may they be
resting
in great
equanimity

We gave
a party
for the gods,
and the gods
all came.

1990

SONNET TO THE ASSHOLE

- Paul Verlaine and Arthur Rimbaud
translated by Harold Norse

Dark and puckered like a mauve carnation, it's dim
And breathes, humbly stashed in the hairy froth,
Still moist from love caressing the smooth slopes
Of white ass-cheeks far into the deepest rim.

Filaments drip on it like creamy tears
Shed there by a pounding, relentless storm
Over the small brown pebbles of russet marl
To vanish when the white slope sucks them in.

My mouth meets often with this windy hole
Eager for oral copulation, my soul
Enters the musky nest with sobs of joy.

It's a swooning olive chute, an enticing vent,
A tube where the heavenly praline makes its descent,
A feminine Canaan clammy with gobs of cum.

[Note: Written in 1871, the first two stanzas are attributed to Verlaine, the last two to Rimbaud. But I have seen no adequate translations of "Sonnet to the Asshole". All suffer from obscurity or the purple patch. I have tried to make mine accurate, to say what the original intended, and prefer to let the rhyme scheme rather than the meaning suffer. In translations you can't win them all. HN]

"GO INTO THE HIGHWAYS AND HEDGES, AND COMPEL THEM TO COME IN"

- Aleister Crowley

Let my fond lips but drink thy golden wine,
  My bright-eyed Arab, only let me eat
  The rich brown globes of sacramental meat
Steaming and firm, hot from their home divine,
And let me linger with thy hands in mine,
  And lick the sweat from dainty dirty feet
  Fresh with the loose aroma of the street,
And then anon I'll glue my mouth to thine.

This is the height of joy, to lie and feel
  Thy spicéd spittle trickle down my throat;
This is more pleasant than at dawn to steal
  Toward lawns and sunny brooklets, and to gloat
  Over earth's peace, and hear in ether float
Songs of soft spirits into rapture peal.

LEAH SUBLIME

- Aleister Crowley

Leah Sublime
Goddess above me!
Snake of the slime
Alostrael, love me!
Our master, the Devil
Prospers the revel.

Tread with your foot
My heart til it hurt!
Tread on it, put
The smear of your dirt
On my love, on my shame
Scribble your name!

Straddle your Beast
My Masterful Bitch
With the thighs of you greased
With the Sweat of your Itch!
Spit on me, scarlet
Mouth of my harlot!

Now from your wide
Raw cunt, the abyss,
Send spouting the tide
Of your sizzling piss
In my mouth; oh my Whore
Let it pour, let it pour!

You stale like a mare
And fart as you stale;
Through straggled wet hair
You spout like a whale.
Splash the manure
And piss from the sewer.

Down to me quick
With your tooth on my lip
And your hand on my prick
With feverish grip
My life as it drinks -
How your breath stinks.

Your hand, oh unclean
Your hand that has wasted
Your love, in obscene
Black masses, that tasted
Your soul, it's your hand!
Feel my prick stand!

Your life times from lewd
Little girl, to mature
Worn whore that has chewed
Your own pile of manure.
Your hand was the key to -
And now you frig me, too!

Rub all the muck
Of your cunt on me, Leah
Cunt, let me suck
All your glued gonorrhea!
Cunt without end!
Amen! til you spend!

Cunt! you have harboured
All dirt and disease
In your slimy unbarbered
Loose hole, with its cheese
And its monthlies, and pox
You chewer of cocks!

Cunt, you have sucked
Up pricks, you squirted
Out foetuses, fucked
Til bastards you blurted
Out into space -
Spend on my face!

Rub all your gleet away!
Envenom the arrow.
May your pox eat away
Me to the marrow.
Cunt you have got me.
I love you to rot me!

Spend again, lash me!
Leah, one spasm
Screaming to splash me.
Slime of the chasm
Choke me with spilth
Of your sow-belly's filth.

Stab your demonical
Smile to my brain!
Soak me in cognac
Cunt and cocaine;
Sprawl on me! Sit
On my mouth, Leah, shit!

Shit on me slut
Creamy the curds
That drip from your gut!
Greasy the turds!
Dribble your dung
On the tip of my tongue!

Churn on me, Leah!
Twist on your thighs!
Smear diarrhoea
Into my eyes!
Splutter out shit
From the bottomless pit.

Turn to me, chew it
With me, Leah, whore!
Vomit it, spew it
And lick it once more.
We can make lust
Drunk on disgust.

Splay out your gut
Your ass hole, my lover!
You buggering slut,
I know where to shove her!
There she goes, plumb
Up the foul Bitch's bum!

Sackful of skin
And bone, as I speak
I'll bugger your grin
Into a shriek.
Bugger you, slut
Bugger your gut!

Wriggle, you hog!
Wrench at the pin!
Wrench at it, drag
It half out, suck it in!
Scream, you hog dirt, you!
I want it to hurt you!

Beast-Lioness squirt from your
Cocksucker's hole!
Belch out the dirt from your
Syphilis soul.
Splutter foul words
Through your supper of turds.

May the Devil our lord, your
Soul scribble over
With sayings of ordure!
Call me your lover!
Slave of the gut
Of the arse of a slut!

Call me your sewer
Of spilth and snot
Your fart-sniffer, chewer
Of the shit in your slot.
Call me that as you rave
In the rape of your slave.

Fuck! Shit! Let me come
Alostrael - Fuck!
I've spent in your bum.
Shit! give me the muck
From my whore's arse, slick
Dirt of my prick!

Eat it, you sow!
I'm your dog, fuck, shit!
Swallow it now!
Rest for a bit!
Satan, you gave
A crown to a slave.

I am your fate, on
Your belly, above you.
I swear it by Satan
Leah, I love you.
I'm going insane
Do it again!

THE NIGHT-APPLE

- Allen Ginsberg

Last night I dreamed
of one I loved
for seven long years,
but I saw no face,
only the familiar
presence of the body:
sweat skin eyes
feces urine sperm
saliva all one
odor and mortal taste.

Paterson, Spring 1950

THE ODORS OF GOD

- James Broughton

I am in love with the odors of God
I am in love with the smells of his offspring
I am in love with the reek of mankind

Praise the perfumes of heros
  the belly of Gilgamesh
  the butt of Beowulf
  the armpit of Samson
  the balls of Caesar

Praise aromas of exertion and zest
  Leonardo's codpiece
  Nijinsky's leotard
  the socks of Solomon
  the jockstrap of Hercules

Praise fragrant oozes of the goodly
  the toejam of Mohammed
  the jism of Jesus
  the crotch of Krishna
  the smegma of the Pope

I am told Abraham ecstasizes regularly
and gets himself into a Great Sweat
I am longing to lie in that smelly bosom

BICYCLE SEAT ENVY *(for Sam & Robert)*

- MJ Arcangelini

In spring the boys of the central valley -
the college boys, the high school boys -
put on their spandex shorts and their
ragged denim cut-offs and their tank tops,

and mount their bicycles to ride around
and around the streets of Chico. Throughout
the day they ride - and in that uncertain
alchemy of streetlight, neon and moonlight
they ride. Overflowing the campus,
spilling out of Bidwell Park until the
city becomes an intoxicating buffet
of flexing calves and pumping thighs.
Buttocks grip tight the slim seats
of their bicycles, while their musky
sweat runs down back and belly to pool
in their shorts, moistening and
seasoning their balls and assholes.

And they cast their spoor into
this combustible air where it
finds my nose and turns my head
toward impossible opportunities.

SWING SONG OF A GIRL AND A SOLDIER

- DH Lawrence

Brother, the scent of your clothing
Is like biscuits baked for a feast
Of victory, kneaded with sulphur
Worked with clean sweat for yeast.

Brother, I like your fragrance.
It smells strange like the shouting of men
Womanless shouting in anger.
Brother, let me die down again.

- Gavin Geoffrey Dillard

He could work in any
Polish factory, his
long smooth and
shining white flesh

Any Hungarian sweatshop
his long-dangling balls
sweating like eggs in a
wet sock banging between
those treetrunk legs

And I, a little peasant
girl might see him one
day and, knowing that he
would never bring me
wealth

Marry him anyway and have
his children, just
for the dank and dreamy
factory smell

Beneath his arms, in
his socks and boxer
shorts, every day when he
comes home from work.

ESSENCE OF MITCHUM

- Robert Peters

Sweet musk of heavily-worn trench coat,
whiff of crankcase oil, elixir of armpit glue
beaded and roiled along the latissimus
dorsi, taint of belly button grease,
lovely gland effusion between the fingers,
butane faint chocolate buttocks smell,

rain-dampened nostril hair, chalky leek
of penis, musky citronella of balls and
epidymus, gun-metal paste-fur of groin,
funky debris of toe and instep:
splendid humus, expectorations, bold,
never bottled or sold.

MITCHUM'S NAVEL

- Robert Peters

Mitchum lifts his safari shirt
revealing a dank omphalos.
I smother it in gentians.
Paginini's violin concerto is on the stereo.

The navel winks in a swirl of hair.
There's a taut fold, a gray-rose foreskin.
"It's yours," he says, throwing his arm
back under his head.

My tongue, thrust to the core,
swirls up a compote of rancid fruit.
Soul-vapor oozes forth. I swallow.

"Easy," Mitchum warns. "It's the only
belly button I've got."

from SONG OF MYSELF

- Walt Whitman

I believe in the flesh and the
 appetites,
Seeing, hearing, feeling, are
 miracles, and each part of me
 is a miracle.
Divine am I inside and out, and
 I make holy whatever I touch
 or am touched from,
The scent of these armpits
 aroma finer than prayer,
This head more than churches,
 bibles and all creeds.

from ODE

- Mutsuo Takahashi
translated by Hiroaki Sato

In the name of
man, member,
and the holy fluid,
AMEN.

Quo Vadis?
Where?
Where on earth are you going?
Please do not go
Please stay
For that I would kneel, I would kiss
The skin of your soles, turned moist, white, flaccid in the
 shoes
Smelly from the greasy socks, your feet
Your toes, rolling upward, nails storing dark-blue dirt

Let me give them passionate kisses repeatedly
The four spaces between the toes, four small darknesses
infested with fungi
Backs of the arrogant toes, the arches clammy with sweat
The knotty ankles, the calves, the hams
Do accept
The wet admiration of my tongue and lips that climb
leisurely
Above these, there are two splendid pillars
Entasis columns, cruel cracks running over them
The part further up, lost in a cloud of overwhelming
fragrance, is invisible
A perfumed oil factory, the darkness of its storehouse, and
in the deeper darkness
Inside its irregular, dusty pots, heavy perfumed oils
undulate separately
In a vat, pomade kneaded with bamboo spatulas shines green
The perfumed oil of nard rubbed on the thighs, down to the
shins
Of a bullfighter in a tight corset
The young smell of olive oil which the youths
Of the gymnasiums of ancient Greece
Rub on one another's naked skin, some standing, some
bending
The smells of the balm, frankincense, myrrh, cinnamon of the
mummies
That suspend the flowery death of young Egyptian nobles
The smells of the oil rubbed on a rifle, of an armory, of
gasoline
The smell of heavy oil spreading rainbow-colored on the sea,
over a sunken ship
Smell of iron, smell of iron rust, smell of solder
Smell of metal burnt off by a blowtorch
Smell of the dark of a smith's shop
Smell of the cord short-circuited late on a cold night
Smell of the lightning that struck, smell of a fire, smell
of flint, smell of an ignitor
A power box, gunsmoke, cartridges, their smells
A coffee grinder, pepper grinder, muller, their smells
Smells of spices cramming the spice shelves
Of a spacious kitchen that the cooks guard

Clouds of spices, clouds of flowers
The suffocating smells of flowers
Grown in a greenhouse covered with a glass-paned ceiling
Milk vetch carpeting the field, a carpet of rape flowers
The alfalfa crushed by a young steed as it trots past, led
by its trainer
Wood-sorrels, hare's-ears, dayflowers in the shadow, wild
grasses, their smells
The azure coast, the perfume town of Grasse
Jasmine, violet, that grow in the fields under fierce sun
Mimosa, genista, that spew golden fire
Heliotrope, lilac, magnolia, their smells
The smell of lavender that is particularly manly
Smell of s strong perfume soaked into Grasse leather
Tanned hides hanging from a tanner's ceiling
Piles of a shoemaker's leather scraps, the strop the barber
sharpens his razors on, their smells
The smell of the saddle, still raw, painful to the naked
thighs
Smell of the young horse's wound covered irritably by blue
flies
Smell of spilled blood, smell of blood plasma
Smell of a woodcutter's stout thighs a pack of wild dogs
devours
Smell of the forest, smell of fallen leaves, rotting leaves
Beneath the rotting leaves, earthworms, sow bugs,
centipedes, their smells
Smells of nuts, the acorns, honey locusts, hazels
The sunny smell of a pasania nut as it pops
Smell of bones washed brownish white by rains and winds
Smell of a tile made of the bone of a solitary desert
animal
Smell of a copper thrown on a sheepskin spread on the sand
Smell of the saliva foaming around savage men's lips
Smell of the palm smelly with sweat
Smell of vagrancy, smell of an outlaw
The leather belts men wear around their waists to carry
swords
The machete drawn with a flourish, its cool blue smell
Smell of the sea, smell of coppers on a littoral
Smell of navigation, sails tattered in wind and rain

Worm-eaten decks, hawsers that squeak, their smells
Smell of brine, separate routes, separate ports, their smells
Here now is London, a basement pub that smells of men
Male Britons crack traditional solemn jokes
And never smiling themselves
Puff Havana cigars clenched in their white teeth, that smell of tobacco
The man, impeccable dandies in every way
But totally indifferent to the nicotine that burns their nails, that smell
For the pleasure of a long winter hibernation, out of oblivion and dust
They take out their pipes made of rose roots from cold wastelands
Clean and polish them, their smell
Smell of roses, smell of a rose perfume, the cut tobacco moist with perfume
Smell of soap, smell of a bathroom
Eau de cologne, smell of lotions that smell of men
The Roko oil, the brilliantine fragrant on a young man's sideburns in a risque print
Smell of freshly washed indigo
Smell of the sooty fireplace in an old mansion, smell of the fire in bygone days
Smell of the stove
Smell of the coal that bare chilblained hands pick and add
Smell of powdered coal, smell of the fire made in a powdered coal dump on a cold morning
Smell of the yawn of a young bum warming himself by the fire
Smell of hunger
Smell of the station where trains are rushed in and out
Smell of the grime in the waiting room criss-crossed with steam pipes
Smell of a cheap hotel, smell of the room for men
Smells of a prison, dormitory, army, the smell of war
Coarse khaki overcoats, military uniforms, boots, knapsacks, their smells
Smell of the blanket one pulls up with both hands to one's mouth

Smell of an army on the move, smell of a retreat, smell of reticence
Smell of a march, rain never ceasing
Rubber boots, the insides of sweaty rubber coats, their smells
Smells of puddles, smell of marshes
The ditch outside a public bathhouse at one a.m., the steam rising from the waste water, that smell
Smell of raw garbage rotting inexorably in a polyethylene bucket
Smell of fermented rice, smell of yeast
Inside the steamer, the smell of the warm leaven
Smell of the country sink outlet where water-hemlocks flourish
Smell of the flesh of a clam as it opens in tepid water in the sun
The finger, rotten purple, its joint bound with tough thread
Smell of the finger that crushed an insect, smell of the firefly's crushed tail
Elderberry bush growing in delicate shadows, smell of summer grasses, smell of overgrown grasses
The green snake cornered in the sun and stoned to death
Red ants swarm and lick its white belly, the smell
Above my head as I genuflect in the dizzying smell
YOU rise more and more haughtily, and tower
Your upper part, growing higher into the blue clouds
Drawn ever deeper into the middle of the clouds...

- Yosano Akiko
translated by Sam Hamill and Keiko Matsui Gibson

What can I put in
my burning mouth now the blood
from my lover's finger -
he asked me to kiss it -
begins to dry on my lips.

THE BANDAGED SHOULDER

- Constantine Cavafy
translated by Gavin Geoffrey Dillard

He said that he'd hurt himself on a wall
or that he'd fallen down.
But there was probably another reason
for the wounded, bandaged shoulder.

With a rather abrupt movement,
while reaching for a shelf to bring down some
photographs he wanted to view more closely,
the bandage came undone and the blood again ran.

I rebandaged the shoulder, though
taking my time; he was in no real pain,
and I enjoyed looking at the blood.
That blood was a part of my love.

After he had gone I found a blood-soaked rag in
front of his chair, left to be
tossed into the garbage,
which I brought straightway to my mouth
and held there for an endless time -
this blood of love upon my lips.

- Gavin Geoffrey Dillard

His bad breath
takes the place of
coffee, startling
me awake; I
moan an twitch with
anticipation of our
morning routine to

gether. Sex and
pancakes, tea and
vitamins; we
cover back up to
ruminate. Face
to face, his
bad breath: *Thank*
you I'll have
one more cup...

IT'S BEEN A LONG TIME SINCE I'VE LIVED WITH A STRAIGHT BOY

- Gavin Geoffrey Dillard

Billy's been here a week and
everything smells of him.
Strong smells.
Intense, aggressive
smells.
Not just the reek of Old Spice all over the
bathroom sink, lining the tub,
but the construction sites in their
entirety, big men, steel-backed men,
burly black men and truckloads of
dusty Mexicans;
a lockerroom hanging from his bedroom
walls, oozing from blankets and
pillows - the small bathroom
rug that wafts entirely of
rank socks, as if some elixir had spilt
out of his boots.
His towel, two days fresh, has a
life of its own, matted with
hairs, exuding pheromones -
what are these little gray balls in the
bathtub drain?

In the kitchen I boil pungent Chinese
herbs, burn Tibetan incense and
pour elegant teas;
in my bedroom, the tastes of
sperm always linger, some
lotion or another, the
short breath of latex.

Can he smell me for what I am?
Oh not just the Royal Copenhagen I wear to
remind me of Grandad,
but the urine I've consumed,
the semen I have bathed in,
the feces that has permeated my
pubic rags, the smoke, the
nitrates; the fine dining in my
brain, the elegant hotels,
the liqueurs, the wines that
critics covet?

Here he is now after pouring
concrete all day, blue collar to the
neck with mud and grease
to boot;
moments from now his steam will
blast these aromas thru curtain thru
doors, into towels and pores,
he'll come clean, but his imprint will
ever remain, in the head of
the air, in the strains, in my
hair -
it hardly seems fair,
but certainly
I will become accustomed.

- Gavin Geoffrey Dillard

He showers,
I bathe-
my baths taste of his feet.

JULY 15, 1974

- Michael Gregg Michaud

His feet are perfectly formed
as if carved from purest marble.
And cold as stone.
My feet are warm, he says. And soft.
My toes curl with little provocation.
The sound of his voice,
his tugs at my fingers,
a casual glance, a grin.
The sound of a zipper
and clothes falling to the floor.
The smallest things.
The sight of his perfect toes.

THIS WAS US IN THE TOP OF THAT HOUSE

- Michael Gregg Michaud

We were lying snug in that single bed
all pretzeled over each other to keep warm
during the cold, breezy night
in that back bedroom. All over each other,
nothing erotic especially, more like a game,
Morty being athletic and all,

with the worst case of acne,
big volcanic boils bursting all over his back
and across his wide shoulders.
I couldn't draw away without bloody fingers
each time, but the fluffy blond hair between
his legs, so yellow it shone like sunshine
coming from his spread apart knees, there
was nothing so beautiful to me.
And his brother's square-headed dog,
big as a billy goat, sitting at the foot of the bed
watching us like he liked to do, listening
while we said the stupid little things
people say to each other
when they're doing what we were doing.
The dog scrambling, his claws scratching
on the hard wood floor, and barking
when we wrestled, and us trying to quiet him,
and Morty's blond hair floating like angel wings
in the dim moonlight of that upstairs room,
and the big bloody spots on the sheets and my fingers,
his toenail scratches on my legs,
and the dog barking, and yapping,
and the flashlight beacon from the yellow hair
around his privates glaring me in the eyes.

THE NIGHT JOE DALLESANDRO PUKED ON ME

- *Michael Gregg Michaud*

Joe stood unsteadily in the shower
leaning back away from the hot water.
Wash yourself, I said.
But he swayed as the water splashed
at his feet.
I stripped and climbed in,
pushing him into the steaming spray.
He arched his back

and looked up sleepily into my eyes,
What're you doin'?
Trying to wash you, I said,
soaping his chest, his soft nipples
and hard belly.
Why? I'm not a baby, he mumbled.
You stink, I said as I gently wiped
the festering tracks in his left arm,
then lathered between his legs,
cupping his balls,
and taking his cock in my sudsy hands.
I'm sick, he exclaimed.
His body became rigid and he puked,
hitting me in the chest with a hot
lumpy spray of vodka and the blueberry cake
I had hand fed him earlier.
The vomit ran down my legs as he choked up more
and I reached out to pull him against me.
He puked streams over my shoulder
and down my back.
It ran hot in the crack of my ass.
I held him tight as he retched,
feeling his body convulse
and his stomach muscles clench
against my belly.
As he coughed up more, I felt a tingling
and my erection popped up hard between us.
I turned him around and away from the hot water
and lowered him into the tub.
Without washing myself,
I grabbed my cock covered with his puke
and pumped for just a moment before
I came against the shower door
and across his legs at my feet.
Joe looked up slowly, vomit slimed across his chest,
and with a crooked smile mumbled,
that was the best blueberry cake
I ever had.

THE NIGHT KEANU REEVES KICKED ME IN THE FACE

- Michael Gregg Michaud

About the time I knew I was in trouble
I was crawling on all fours
in a crowded nightclub
trying to get under Keanu Reeves' table.
He had broken his ankle a few weeks before
in a motorcycle accident
and his foot was still in a cast.
What on earth are you doing, a woman asked me.
I dropped a contact, I fumbled.
But you're wearing glasses.
It wasn't mine, I said
as I quickly crept to his table.
I saw his foot, his naked toes
just inches from my nose once I was
under the tablecloth.
I moved a little closer, my heart pounding,
as I strained to see in the dim light
and struggled to detect his odor.
His toes were long and calloused,
his big toe flat and wide,
the little pinkie twisted inward.
His dirty nails were longish
and curled ever so slightly
down around the end of each digit.
I moved so close I could smell
the dryness, the staleness of his foot.
I wanted to take each dusty little kicker
slowly into my mouth,
let my tongue roll between each gummy bear,
flick each nail,
and suck like a nursing babe,
licking under and around,
pinching each one hard between my teeth,
playing with the wonky, wiry hairs
on his toe knuckles,

kissing sweetly, smooth and delicious,
brown between my lips.
But then he moved his toes,
slightly stretching toward me,
pointing each, one at a time at my nose
just barely an inch away.
And then moved his foot abruptly,
slamming the cast against my left cheekbone,
sending my glasses clattering to the floor,
drawing blood from my nose
with his razor nails,
painfully sweet as a first kiss,
and I was in heaven.

PERSONAL FOIBLES #2

- Michael Lassell

Just because I like feet
doesn't mean I'm a fetishist.
I admit to a certain
fascination, not adulation
but certainly not revulsion
either. Women's shoes hold me
like a moth flame. I could have
sucked the tiny toes of
the Javanese dancer all
night long instead of just
for hours;
and then there was this
sweet hustler in San
Francisco who charged by the
shiatsu massage and groaned with
pleasure not the first time I
put his dick in my mouth but
the first time I touched his soles,
his cowboy boots erect at bedside.

I wanted to squeeze those balls
and knead those heels until
my brother of mercy was
helpless with rapture, to
work my knuckles into the wrinkled
flesh of his feet until he dropped
in mindless abandon. And of all the
things to notice about the
nude hunk on the runway, I
was swept away by the pedicured
perfection of his toes -
the nails trimmed on
a diamond template. And
why of all the things
that must have been said at a
party twenty years ago
do I remember only: "His feet
were beautiful. They were the feet
of a sculptor's model"?

SATYAGRAHA

- Edward Field

They say that the great Gandhi
yielded just once to violence.
When he saw two boys making it together
he lost his temper and gave them a whipping.

But he had a favorite disciple
tickle his feet at night.

A COUPLE MORE POETIC FEET

- Whitman McGowan

As we sit at the Ajax Lounge reading,
My baby feels up my ankle,
Feels the grooves of my brown sox,
And I look over and take in another foot,
Young girl's foot jiggling as she listens.
The thong of her sandal
Is fucking the space between her toes,
And my baby is feeling my ankle.

FEET

- Jim Cory

Begin with slow strokes
below the calf
Circle with moistened thumb
that socketed hill
of bone
with its thicket
of barely covered violet
that has the clumsy
less-than-charitable name
of ankle
Go round & round it
Next: apply fingertips
that are pearls and antennae
to that wizened
leathery little
heel C'mon, don't shy
from that massed
callous: be firm!
For a minute at least...

This is prep work
Because then you gently
pluck almost
that velvet slope
between the 2
Do you hear sighing?
Good!
Make a harp
of its tenderness
Don't be afraid
to give it
(or any human place)
your tongue
Now move your fingers
along the long marble
toward the toes
Don't be distracted
by those vines
under the skin
They're tunnels, tributaries
loaded with liquid & cells
They keep the treasure
breathing Instead
concentrate!
Rub rub rub & rub
but do it
like the blind
who find beauty
in pure shape
If you're restless
(or to vanquish
predictability)
reach back & tug
the pubic bush
or tongue-flick
tit or bellybutton
Then return
to the task at hand
Turn it over
Squeeze the ball of it
Brush your palm

against the arches
Repeat repeat repeat
Take the weight
of the whole now
& feel
the delicate solidity
of what lies under
That's cartilage
compacted to sculpture
a pliant hardness
as of some machine
steered by nerves
belted together
with straps
called tendons
Resist the temptation
to tickle
Instead go for the toes
Go ahead! Leave
whatever reservations you have
on the floor there
by the clothes
& shed shoes!
Take them 1 x 1
& pull them
bend them Pausing
to stroke & massage
Then apply
the softest wettest lips
you can conjure
to each of those
beauties Kiss them
as if they were
souls They are
Take them fully
Draw fluid thru
Run your teeth
lightly over
Do this til
the body beneath your hands
abandons its fortress

Then lean back
& look at what you've loved
Imagine how satin would fit it
Think of the lifetime of steps
these walked
to get here

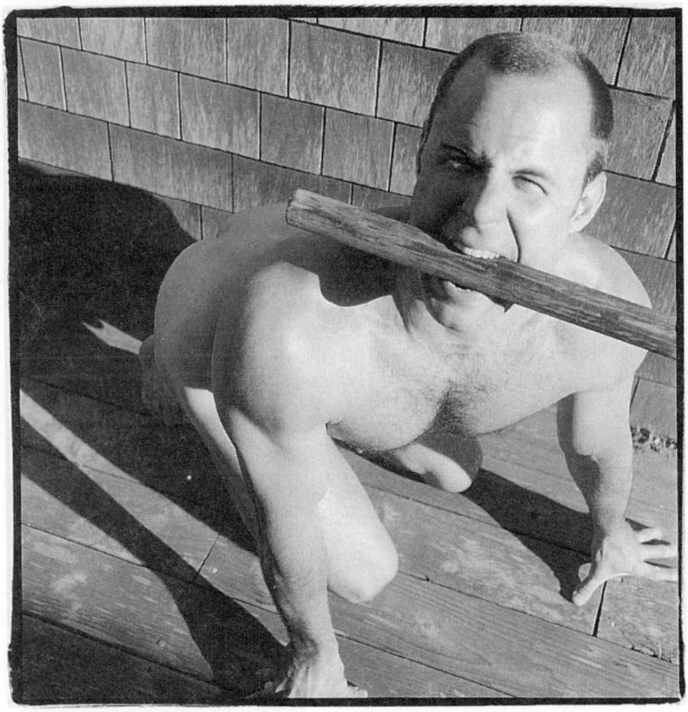

The Dog

Games we Play
muses, ruses and bruises

BIG THICK DICK

- Harold Norse

Big Thick Dick & Tasty Jr. Bear
Hairy & Sweet Delectable Indeed
And Dirty Mouth Showoff Awesome Gypsie Top
Big Irish Hung Like You'd Hope & Black Body Builder
For Muscle Worship Super Safe Mega Dick
And Creamy French Delicacy Horse Hung For Dessert
Plus Uncut & Hungry Fantasies Fulfilled
You'll Go WOOF! For This Smooth Blond Nice & Nasty
Stud And Rock Hard Professional Cleancut Gym Studs
Waiting For You
A Man For All Reasons Bigger Is Better Indulge Yourself
All Scenes Considered Eat at Pete's Low Hangers
Or Bubble Butt Boy Toy Handsome Student Body
Or Prime Hot Rod Therapeutic & Erotic
Or Asian Dream Hairy Russian Rodeo Cowboy
French Marine German Master Rican Masseur
Eros + Agape Double Pleasure Body Magic
Affirm Self Love Sing The Body Mechanic & Surrender
Unravel With Stressbuster Deep Throat Man To Man
Warm Hands Warm Heart Warm Head
Warm Butt Warm Rod
Nurturing Touch In Finest Tradition of Bodywork
Ahhh...Slow.Sensual.Complete.Ecstatic.Hot.Close.
Nips Aching For Touch? Call Bearcub or Dick of Death
Or Nebraska Farm Boy or Ragin' Cajun
Or Dungeon Dragon
Big Holiday Sale More For LE$$ You'll Feel Real Good

[This is a "cut-up" poem, i.e. the words and phrases were cut out at random from a gay newspaper, ads and personals, and put together as an invented "poem." HN]

DANCER(S) WITH DICK(S) AT THE 1 SALOON

- *Michael Lassell*

I have one hand on his cock, the other
deeply involved with the shaven every-
thing between his balls and asshole, at which

willing target I've aimed my spit-slick thumb.
"All *right*," he says, bending to help me and
offer a kiss, "work *me!*" I don't want to

disappoint, so I pop one proffered tit
in my mouth while he grinds that totally
tubular rod of his into my palm.

"My name is Chris," he says (he's a solo
tonight - the other dancer's father had
a stroke). "You *are* a hot daddy," he says,

which takes me aback (I feel twenty-six
most of the time). I give him another
buck: "I guess I'm getting there," I shuffle.

"No getting there involved," he says, his brown
forehead a furrow, "you have *arrived*." I
take him at his word - after all, he's the

pro. He might just be right. So, now I'm a
daddy, I think and let it sink slowly
in. Well, it's better than nothing, I guess -

here at the far end of further away
than anywhere and way beyond what the
hell. You know what I mean, pretty baby?

RENDEZVOUS

- Edna St Vincent Millay

Not for these lovely blooms that prank your chambers did I come. Indeed,
I could have loved you better in the dark;
That is to say, in rooms less bright with roses, rooms more casual, less aware
Of History in the wings about to enter with benevolent air
On ponderous tiptoe, at the cue "Proceed."
Not that I like the ash-trays over-crowded and the place in a mess,
Or the monastic cubicle too unctuously austere and stark,
But partly that these formal garlands for our Eighth Street Aphrodite are a bit too Greek,
And partly that to make the poor walls rich with our unaided loveliness
Would have been more *chic*.

Yet here I am, having told you of my quarrel with the taxi-driver over a line of Milton, and you laugh; and you are you, none other.
Your laughter pelts my skin with small delicious blows.
But I am perverse: I wish you had not scrubbed - with pumice, I suppose -
The tobacco stains from your beautiful fingers. And I wish I did not feel like your mother.

TELEPHONE II

- Linda Smukler

(I was out to dinner and wanted to get up and say to all of them: I am in love with someone who is not sitting at this table)

You tell me this over the phone and in the next breath ask me to be a young man off the street when it's hot and I am sweaty and I have followed you home I will do anything for you and tell you that I watch you secretly as you bathe and then lotion yourself put on silk panties and camisole I will do anything for you and suddenly I grab your arm and drag you into the bedroom I tell you that you will never do what you have done that you will never again walk in front of me and tantalize me I will force open your legs I will touch your clit and tell you that you are shameful and that you will not be separate from me that I will take you any moment I want do you understand? you ask me over the phone to be a young man off the street and after you come you order me to lie down I will do anything for you but this is more difficult OK I say besides I have to pee and you a woman will not let me for hour after hour until it becomes unbearably painful and your voice takes over and you hold my cunt in your hand and you will punish me severely if I can't hold it any longer you say you will parade me around the bedroom in a dress that only you will have this and know as I walk around the world in suits and ties and white shirts you will tell me exactly what I am a woman and a girl and that I am also some young boy whom you have taken off his bicycle into the woods and shown him your cock and played with his little dick that you show him how to get hard and show him how you get hard and at some time he gets frightened and you turn him over and fuck him in the ass and bring him off with your hand yanking on his dick and now you are some tough ravishing woman who loves me grime and all who will tear it all apart for me one strand at a time who will put it all back

THE BEATING

- Paul Mariah

Hung
black leather
jacket

on my
chair & then
let me

have it,
whipt me with
yr tongue,

lapt me
til you'd consumed
all milk.

My body
lay empty saucer-
like

and you
curled up a
round it

and went
to sleep, almost
purring.

This morning
you removed yr
jacket

from the
chair and left
without

kissing
the milkmaker
goodbye.

ABSENCE MAKES THE HEART GROW FONDER

a Valentine for Gavin Geoffrey

- Ian Young

I dreamed I came into your room and saw you again for the first time after three years.
We were both naked.
You had long hair.
Your ankles were shackled, with a loose chain between them and you had a thin leash of soft brown leather around your balls.
You were very tanned and a trickle of sweat ran down your temple onto your cheek.
Your mouth was slightly open.
I fastened your hands behind your back with handcuffs.
I noticed you were uncircumcized and wondered how that could be.
Your foreskin was tight over the head of your swelling cock.
I reached down and began to gently masturbate you with my cupped hand.
In a second or two your cock started pumping a flow of warm come onto my belly, cock and pubic hair, for what felt like minutes.
It was like warm milk on my skin.
I dropped to my knees.
Your cock was pulsing and warm in my mouth as I gulped down what seemed an endless stream of your hot piss.
Then you turned around and pushed your smooth ass into my face.
I pulled your ass-cheeks apart and worked my tongue into your asshole.
I pushed you onto the bed and gripped the back of your neck in my teeth.
When I mounted you, the come soaking my belly made your buttocks slippery and sticky.
I pushed my cock into you with one thrust and shot my load deep into your ass.
All the time we held each other in a wet, hungry kiss.

I had you across my lap with your hardon against mine and my hand on your warm ass ready to give you a hot, hard spanking when I woke up, with a hardon, my body curled around my friend's.
He was asleep.
I masturbated and came all over his naked ass, not golden and ripe-looking like yours but pale and thin and delicate.
I smeared the come onto my cock and fucked him.
He moaned and hugged the pillow.
I wanted to spank his ass till he cried.
I wanted to come and come and never stop.

HONEYSUCKLE *(bonds of love)*

- Ian Young

Would you
I wondered,
submit
to bonds of love?

You begged:

strung up by the wrists,
nipples sore,
bottom spanked,
eyes bright,
cock ready to burst.

It's I who am bound,
slave to your need,
to your trust,

found by you

STANDING AND KNEELING FIGURES

- Ian Young

his eyes are closed
parts of his nakedness glow
with the pleasure inflicted

his mouth is open
his face shines
with ecstasy and light

he is kneeling
leaning into darkness
his elbows pinned behind him
resemble wings

there is a slight pressure
from the gloved hand
above the head

without it he would faint
or levitate

the curve of his white back
glistens with dew

the black hand's mate
brushes where narrow wrists
nuzzle at steel boundaries

the earth
and the standing figure
anchor him

his mouth and hands are open
his eyes shine with nakedness
he would levitate
with ecstasy and light

a deep uneven breathing
as though an angel
trapped inside one lung
gasped for infinity

"take it slowly now"
the sound of keys
turning in silver locks

"take it slowly now
unfold your white wings
and fly"

JEFF

- Ian Young

Twenty-four and
never been spanked

Must've been a
good boy

I can
take care of that

NOT MY ENEMIES EVER INVADE ME.

- Walt Whitman

Not my enemies ever invade me - no harm to my pride from
them I fear;
But the lovers I recklessly love - lo! how they master me!
Lo! me, ever open and helpless, bereft of my strength!
Utterly abject, grovelling on the ground before them.

CONSTRUCTIVE INSTRUCTIONS

- Dan Diamond

"When you get here, the first thing
you do is strip, get down and worship
my boots. I want to see you lick 'em good,
clean 'em off!"

I wanted to ask, "Can you just hug me
before we get started? Hold me for a minute?"
But I didn't. We played the scene your way
and I was happy.

But when I dressed to leave you held out
your arms, offering what I hesitated
to ask for.

PETER

- Jameson Currier

White
conservative
Republican
lobbyist
loves me
to spank him

at first
it bothered me
to be
with someone
so easily
humiliated

now it plays
like a play
and he asks me
if he is
as good as
my other lovers

I smile
and say
of course
knowing
really
no one
is the same

ARSE POETICA

- David Laurents

A bottom should be capable and mute
As he licks your boot,

Bum
Offered high for dildo or thumb -

A bottom should be wordless
Unless answering, "Sir."

A bottom should be motionless in time
As the moon climbs,

Waiting, as his top releases,
Thrust by thrust, the moon-white cum,

Waiting, as the paddle finds his behind
and shackles bind his heart and mind -

A bottom should be motionless in time
As the moon climbs.

For all this history of pain,
An empty colon and an oiled whip,

For love
Of beaten asses and a top who cares -

A bottom should not act
But be.

LOVE POEM # 9

- Paul Bloom

I've never wanted to be anything but your slave,
though i played the game
and took all the roles that were offered me,
inside my head i was screaming,
inside my pants i was groaning,
Take me, take me completely.
Take me to the end of ultimate ecstasy
and dip me in.
Make me putty for your will to dip into
when it wants to get its hands dirty.
Lobotomize me.
Mesmerize me.
Plant your commands on every strand
and every silver thread of my skull's will to live,
so that every nerve exists
only to serve you.

Cover me in such transparent sounds as Mozart wrought
and, lifting the cloth, finger my baby's bottom
with your deep-throated glove. Spank me,
and send me out with the laundry,

and a filmy gauze over all my eyes
which glaze every time they think your thought.

Turn to your love baby's pitiful orgasms,
whose pajamas are slowly rupturing
for your every iddy biddy need,
and why not give your pampered poo poo
a break in my bliss,
and give me this:
a chance to be owned in the full
and manipulated out of the seasons of time
by a thread so delicate
that only fingers of destiny
can sift the fibers to reveal
the naked pink truth
which has sweated its offering
on the shores of evolution
since the dawn of fetish creation.

Oh honey,
i pledge allegiance to your underpants
and bark naked through the gutter
to return to you a turd you dropped
if you want me to,
because i've never ever wanted anything
but to be your slave,
a torn and twisted remnant
of a self i once loved too much,
yet spent unquenched on the sand regardless,
but how it wanted you,
and turns to you,
exploding on the surface of the beach like a sun
to turn the eye to the one true you,
to turn to you bottoms up, and say:
Brand me. Terrify me, please,
i beg you
below gravity's drifting complaint
let me crawl from my grovelling pit
to the altar of that need
i dare not deign to name,

climbing inch by inch up the long-legged
leather-shorn lashes of your glance
at my most naughty disobedience,
mouth open, your foot deep inside
(How absurd it is!),
begging you to let me fetch for you
whatever a minor whim,
a most whimsical caprice,
a most capricious turn of your mind commands,
to let me fetch for you,
to let me fetch,
and kneel,
and worship,
because i've never ever wanted anything
but to give you more than is decent
for one human to give to another,
my whole,
body and soul,
the thousand year strands
of my silken evolutionary spirit
turned to matter and crushed by you
into a dazzling powder.

ON BEING FUCKED BY A TALK-SHOW PANELIST

for Daphne Gottlieb

- Ali Liebegott

If you hadn't been a safe sex
S/M lesbian bottom
who'd been bribed to tell
every gawking housewife in America
the do's and don'ts
of inserting a whip into a vulva,
and I hadn't met you a year before
in a San Francisco dive bar
declining your offer
to light my cigarette for me

by extinguishing the flame on my forearm,
then we never would've got together in New York
to bridge three thousand miles
and a bar-made friendship
over a slick Italian dinner
with the producers of *Geraldo*.

If I hadn't consumed two Bloody
Mary's, two glasses of good Merlot
three pints of beer, and a hash joint
given to us by our taxi driver, I still
would've pushed you against
the wall, crawled under
your silver shirt that glimmered
through thick bar smoke,
and moved my tongue
over your nipple ring
with the same fervor I've used to free
any of the lost poppy seeds caught
between my bottom teeth in this lifetime.

If we hadn't squeezed into a cab
with the dyke porn star,
the lesbian stripper,
and the bisexual S/M top,
who when asked why she stays
with her boyfriend said,
"It's hard to find a guy
who cooks and cleans
and lets me sodomize him,"
then we never would've leapt on the bed
in such a flurry that my boot
would smudge the wall,
or your teeth would gnaw
assorted violet bruises
from my neck to hipbone.

If you hadn't said you'd never had sex
in a hotel before, I wouldn't have said
I'd never had safe sex in my life.
And if you hadn't put latex gloves on,

flipped me on my stomach
and dug your hands in me
like my pussy was a cookie jar,
I wouldn't have limped around
the next two days, enjoying the burn
of each careful step into a stairwell.

If I didn't have to leave
to move into a new apartment
and you hadn't forgotten to ask
Geraldo if you could borrow his limo,
then I wouldn't have had to face
the masses of Wall Street commuters
the next morning,
who stared at my bruises
and general sex-stenched state,
preparing themselves for next Thursday
when your show would air,
and you would admit your desire
to flog heterosexual businessmen
who take public transportation.

WHIPS AT THE RITZ

- Lyn Lifshin

he said it was
like heroin
too delicious
would hook him
the sear of leather
splitting air like
a cock plunging
a deep sea diver
into where what
no one could

imagine would startle
and stone he
said just to see
legs in chains
spread wider
a dancer opening
as you came off
like the black of
the Times on fingers
hardly touched

- AD Winans

Lily was an expert
In S and M
Bondage and discipline
One-hundred clothespin treatment

Men stood naked legs spread
In front of her dungeon rack
Her nails raking their back
As she delighted in how
They drooled at the sight
Of her crack

Chocolate flavor and VCR camera
Kept them coming back and back
No matter if they were from Wall Street
Or the other side of the track

S AND M GAMES

- AD Winans

She liked to play
S and M games
Tie you down to the bed
And stand over you dressed
In black leather gloves
Boots and a garter belt
Using your tongue like
A lapping dog
Her pussy a dog biscuit
That kept you coming back
For more
But you had to bark
Loud and long
And the choke collar
And leash
Kept you at bay
Until it was feeding
Time at the kennel

S AND M GAMES TWO

- AD Winans

She let me watch once
Or twice
Perhaps sensing
I had the same desires
As the young slave
She kept on his knees
Begging please
As she lowered her pussy
Down on his face

Stuffing a giant dildo
Up his ass
Turning on the vibrator attached
To the cock ring fitted
At the base of his cock
As his semen shot out like
Cannon volleys
At the same time
Her yellow shower spurted
Into his eager mouth

I couldn't tell
Whose cries were
The loudest.

S AND M GAMES THREE

- AD Winans

It began when
He was in Catholic school
And his cock got hard
When the nuns whacked his knuckles
With a ruler
For infractions of any kind
Harder still at boys military
School when the head master
Had him drop his pants
For the stinging paddle
On his bare ass

It took him two decades
To find the right mistress
Who understood his needs
Serving her every desire
Dreaming of castration
His balls bronzed and worn

Around her neck
But for now he settles
For the ball-buster device
And a turn on the rack
Hot wax flowing down from
His cock and balls
Visions of nuns floating through
The purple haze of his childhood

LOVE COMES IN DIFFERENT FLAVORS

- AD Winans

The whip master is waiting
It's time to atone for your sins
Get down on your knees
And beg repentence

Refreshments will be served
At the conclusion of the
Black and Blue Ball
Swimsuits are optional
Shackles a must
Crosses in the shape
Of Christmas trees
Will be made available
For those with hammer and nails

Leather clad porters will be there
To punch your ticket

The climax of the evening
Will coincide with
The orgy master's late arrival

WHAT MONEY CAN BUY

- Louis McKee

I was the first man she ever had
pissed on - or so she said -
and I have to admit it was the first
time it had been done to me.
And she was the first, too,
to chain me to a wall, to set
my head and arms through a stock,
and to lash my buttocks and thighs
with a thick black whip. What a night!

She commanded me to crawl, to stay
quiet, to touch only her feet;
and I did, though her voice carried none
of the anger and hardness I expected.
Her whip hurt, but she could have
given it more snap, and even
when she drove her long spiked heel
into the back of my hand, I could feel
her holding back the full weight
of her love. Face down, my cries loud,
I could still hear her quiet laugh.
She was there for fun, not for love.

from BEN'S WHIPS

- MJ Arcangelini

i:

The first time your whip
fell across my bare back
I winced before it even hit
- expecting pain, surprised

at the pleasure the leather
had wrought. As though your
hands had grown slender
tentacles to caress me
ever more thoroughly -
long warm leather fingers
- sweet stinging singing
through the air, stroking
my flesh. Cock rising, breath
coming harder and deeper each
time the leather strikes.
I smile and pleasure leaks
laughter out of my mouth
like an idiot's drool.

from BEN'S WHIPS

- MJ Arcangelini

excerpted from part iii:

Ben begins to whip me.
Slowly, gently,
pausing between strokes.
He shows more mercy
than I deserve, more
kindness than I think
I need. I want to be beaten.
I want all the evil and perversion
to be beaten out of me.
The way my father beat me to make me good.
I want to be whipped until I am pure, clean, decent.
The way a penitent punishes
his flesh to purge desire
until pain becomes the only
true path to God.

Is it then that desire twists about
and takes punishment as its own?

I am angry now.

Finally I am angry, and feeling anger releases pride,
and pride releases desire,
and desire releases love.
And I love Ben and I love his whip
as it strikes my back first one side
and then the other and then again
before the sting can fade.
And love releases trust
and trust allows vulnerability
and to be vulnerable releases
pain and pain blossoms from
my eyes in tears and convulses my body.
Breath is strangled into sobs.
My skin shivers in waves.
And I know that there is nothing this whip
can do to my body that can equal this pain inside me.
And I am afraid of what I am feeling,
of how much I am feeling.
Raw sounds struggle out of my throat
and Ben tells me "I love you."
and "You are good."
and "You deserve to be loved."
I feel Ben's arms around me -
his naked body against mine -
there is love in every point
where we touch and every word
he whispers into my tears.

I collapse into his grip -
a boneless beast and he, the
only thing keeping me human.

Ben says "Are you alright?"
And I say "Yes."
And I am.
For now. All right.

STRAPS

- Tavya Nyong'o

Jezebel dresses up
and fingers
- with aching love -
the whip.
Ahab's tender bottom
is displayed
between coils and straps
made of rubber and leather
and love ooh-la-la.
Oh, that aching whip
Oh, the bounce of
Israel's favorite son
to and fro in the swings.
Oh, to touch the
cellulite on that buttocks.
Oh, to be one of those
straps biting
into tender Ahab.
Oh, to be Jezebel
All dressed up and horny
Peaceably whipping her boy.

CHRIST IN CHAINS

- Robert L Rucker

The whip lifts up, falls down,
separating flesh where
he prays to be given the salt
good martyrs remember to beg.

He knows this position well,
knees and hands to the ground,
robes cast from the back
which waits for the touch
of a heavy man standing
behind his upturned ass.
Licks his lips under the sun
of a cruel and holy land
stilled with anticipation.

Up. Down.
When Pilate strokes him
with the lust of a patriarch
Jesus' many faces open into
small, grateful smiles
and his prick rises stiff
and impressive against his belly,
lifted by unseen angels
whose calloused hands
stroke him harder
than the lusty Magdalene
ever could.

Pilate strokes.
The angels stroke.

Christ in chains, ready to shoot,
lifts up his gaze
to the hump of Golgotha
while his voice, lost
in the roar of the crowd
he despises for their worship,
cries, "Oh Father, oh Daddy, oh
yes Father. The cross, too,
it's time Father. Yes.
Yes."

MEETING THE MASTER

- Elissa Wald

> "Beware the fury of a patient man."
> - John Dryden

I dreamed you had the patience of a prayer:
You let me memorize your open hand
Before you closed a fist around my hair.

I read a warning written down somewhere:
"Beware the fury of a patient man."
I dreamed you had the patience of a prayer.

I'll swear to the truth if you'll take a dare,
Plead guilty if you'll force me to the stand,
And close a knowing fist around my hair.

Yours is the rhythm of a rocking chair:
Steady as an hourglass spilling sand.
I dreamed your patience would make saints despair.

I've yearned to cringe beneath your level stare.
My wish has been to be at your command -
To kiss the iron fist around my hair.

I've waited for years, searching everywhere,
But only you have made me understand:
Patience in a slave is itself a prayer,
And answered by your fist around my hair.

MASOCHIST'S LOVE SONG

- Elissa Wald

Take my hair
And we're halfway there
And together as we
Degrade me.
You'll never care
And you'll never care,
So strip me down naked,
Invade me.
I'm only what you and I made me.
I couldn't be more
of your whore
If you paid me -
I love you, it's there
In my hot, angry stare
But I'm only a lay,
And you've laid me.

THE JOY OF WOMAN'S DESIRING

- Elissa Wald

I've never met you but I've read your book
So often that it's coming apart at the seams.
And I learn what I can about you and your life,
So I know you are married and loving your wife;
Still it gives me incredible pleasure to look
At your picture, and visit you nightly in dreams.

I know you as sure as my knees know the floor.
I'm worn with worship I won't impose.
Respect is the practice of knowing one's place...
I'm sore from not throwing myself against your door

And laboring at grace;
I'm in the throes

Of a racking desire. Behold me and see
A cynic all a-tremble, as before revelation,
An atheist in religious ecstasy.
Oh, I wouldn't trade this passion for consummation;
Wouldn't have you be mine, mine to collar and flaunt
And surrender the quivering joy of: I want.

HEAT

- Elissa Wald

My cat is in heat.
She flattens her young body
Against the floor,
Clawing the air, writhing in need,
Wide-eyed, not knowing what she's crying for.
Only knowing she doesn't want to wait.

You don't negotiate.

You keep me distraught.
If there were nothing about you
Worth keeping but that
(And there very well may not)
It would be enough.
A knuckle, a cuff.
Enough: O Amazing Grace,
To be hands and knees in this craven crawl.

Contemplating the art of longing,
But still an animal,
After all.

PROMETHEUS AND HERCULES

- *Elissa Wald*

They fastened me to a rock on the side of a cliff
Where I could see what I'd taken from the chariot wheel
Flickering in the hills below as if
Keeping scattered vigil throughout my ordeal.

In the late afternoons came the birds of prey,
Descending on my gut from the tranquil skies.
Obscene in their leisure, they fed there each day;
I saw Leda reflected in their merciless eyes.

I lost track of the years before he came,
A lion's skin heavily draping his shoulder,
Less than me, and more. His shadow broke the sun.
Deliberate, dark-eyed, and hard as the boulder
Beneath my back, he approached and asked my name,
And why I was there, and what I had done.

And after I'd told him, he crouched at my side,
Tore open my shackles bare-handed and then
Smiled into my eyes, well-satisfied.
For that moment alone, I would do it again.

MOST VALUABLE ROOKIE

- *Edmund Miller*

The goal, their orient,
Is your goal,
Goalie Chris.
Tonguing the mask
Masking your tonguing,
Melting the rink

And the bleachers,
Your hot mouth huge
With rinky-think encouragements,
You're happy home on ice.
And you stick to your goal,
Give icemen their due,
Let each take out on you
His nice violence,
His stick-whipping,
His man-thing.

SURVIVOR *(To David Wentworth)*

- Harold Norse

I want to make you laugh.
The long nightmare is over.
But you've stored the pain
in your shrunken body
with one hip askew,
in your narrow shoulders
and skinny arms
and sunken chest
and small broken hands.
Survivor, child
from a Nazi camp in the suburbs
with a swimming pool
and country club
and half a million a year,
there is nothing left,
not even the money.
But you're still here
and I want to make you laugh.
He beat you daily till you were six
making you understand
that even a brother means destruction,
that parents mean abandonment,

gone forever in the private plane
that crashed when you were three.
Locked in the closet without food for days
as punishment for not knowing fear,
now you're out of the closet,
20 years old
with a ruby in your right ear,
with a flowing stride and long silky hair,
with a pretty face,
with a trust fund,
with an eye for men,
with a need for chains
and the stinging strokes of a strap on your rear.
But you've come through,
you're here.
Poor little rich boy,
I want to make you laugh.

A FINE WINE

- Amy Kashiwabara

I want to take your pain in
    my mouth like marbles or your balls
    slide my tongue over its rough surfaces
    feel the colors of its bruises between my teeth
    taste the grapejuice of its sweetness and swallow
    suck out the bitterness and spit
    it into the street
        below our apartment window

THE BATH (*for my submissive*)

- Gloria G Brame

He was a child in my house.
I led him to the bath and lowered
his thin body into a swirl of suds.
He winced at my caress.

His calloused souls became petals
when I placed him in the bath.
His quiet gaze turned inward
when I fondled his soft chest.

A white lotus flower. A dark lotus stem.
I cleansed him with my hands.
He closed his eyes and yielded.
"They beat me," he said.

"Stand up," I said, "I want to wash your legs."
I passed my hands over limb and limb,
marveling at the perfect skin,
and healed the burning scars within.

THE RAPE

- Gloria G Brame

Tonight I dreamt that you trapped me
in a room. You swore that, before the end,
you'd possess every part of my body
in every conceivable way,
frightening and exciting me.
You gave me no choice, no options
for resistance, no escape. My belly
was your bed, you anointed me

with sweat, rocked me in the cradles
of your legs. I burned, I wept.
All my mad destructive longings
made flesh from random words.
I was pierced like St. Teresa,
yet even in my dream you left.

BRUISES

- Gloria G Brame

Your flesh craves to contain me.
You caress the bruises of last night's tryst,
my cruel and loving fingerprints.
Each blue star my sign, each blue kiss
an antidote to loneliness.

The traces of our pleasures darken
at first light. All day, these epigrams
on whip and bite will pulse invisibly
beneath your clothes, silent tributes
to our erotic dialogues.

The ancient gods played like this,
unashamed of their obsessions,
heroic in their capacity for pain,
primal in their delights,
bruising what they loved for pleasure.

Tonight we'll lose ourselves again
in high-intensity games.
Rapacious slave and charming bitch,
I'll bend you to my will and you'll submit.
You'll beg for the marks of my ownership.

MECHANICS OF LOVE

- Lynne Savitt

i am taking the brush to bed.

he is my father.

you do not understand
the mechanics of love.

i need to be shared.

how we accomplish this
is under discussion.

you may have my right
shoulder and inner thighs.

for which you have
shown a preference.

my tongue is spoken
for and my cunt the

first to go you
will not mind it
not being your favorite part.

the rest is up for grabs
painfully enough to go around

and enough to con vince you
of my earnest belief in punishment

in the yielding of my father
upon my most vulnerable parts.

if you cannot master the brush
leave my bed my love chamber

watching the welts rise
by themselves before you go.

Anna Bergman

PANTOUM: *This time will end*

- Anna Bergman

The rape doesn't stop
when you back in a corner
ask a lover to hurt you
with wax, canes, and lashes -

Backed in a corner
liking her rough talk
the wax, canes, and lashes
this one is different.

You like her rough talk
picked her that way,
this one is different
yet still bruises you.

You picked her to do that
hands tied, her fist inside
these bruises won't last
- ten years till you find -

her fist in you, your hands tied
you're in control now,
ten years finding out
how to give up, trusting

you're in control now.
What you lost comes back
when you give up, trusting
this time will end.

What you lost comes back
with a lover who hurts you
ends just in time, when
the rape doesn't stop.

CONVALESCENCE

- Anna Bergman

She tied him to a wood chair in the main room of the warehouse. "Open handed, remember?" "You told me," she snapped, "now keep your head back." Her shoulder's curve filled the space under her buzz cut. The first slap wasn't loud - everyone watching was silent. It hit the exact middle of his chest. Lips pursed, marking the same spot, she smacked it again - building force, palm open. He smiled the first few then moaned. Then made no sound. Her arm drew back further, the sound wasn't sharp anymore - it was a thud, skin ignored for the bone. Annoyed by the man whispering to me I slid through the crowd, trying to see her face better. In the chair he screamed and she hit him harder, swinging her whole body back then into it. "Mercy!" came between screams - she stopped immediately. His laugh spiraled between gasps, knocking through his chest. Untied, his shoulders rotated - giggling, his face glowed. The scar from the base of his neck to his chest looked like a thick strip of strawberry taffy, the too sweet kind. "Open heart surgery." She poured a glass of water and told him to drink it.

LAURIE'S TRANSEXUAL FANTASY.

- Tom House

tightening this
cinching that
attaching a clamp
sticking a plug
it's all clinical

this man has paid her a lot of money
what he wants/ feels
she really has no idea

he wants to be tied up and hurt
but more than that
and what is it?

being a man
such a bullshit gig
from the day I was born

he's trying to
explain it to her

she's soothing him
"now now"
as she folds the satin
cloth over his mouth

and straps the tape over
his going on and on

THE PROFESSIONAL PSYCHO-DRAMA.

- Tom House

1.

I hired her from one of the escort services. I studied it for awhile what I wanted to do. She arrived dressed very nicely/ some polyester shiny and clinging - "You're a queer, aren't you? or what do you want you fucking goddamn freak, is that what you want, someone shit in your face fuckhead, pisshead, nobody?"

I paid her a hundred and fifty bucks.

2.

We're tying up Vicky. I'm scratching her bush and thinking how she's moving her body as I'm licking her dry hairs and Terri sucking my dick and clicking the handcuffs wrists in place

  wrapping that coat hanger around my nuts, cinching nylon cord behind my back,

  asking Terri, "How much has he got in his wallet?" And I knows it's an act, but everything's getting a little blurred. Vicky jerk my head off the edge of the bed, squat her cunt, squeeze her thighs/

  asking "How much has he got a real woman would want?" taking my 43 bucks and my Exxon and Mastercard saying, "Sis, just leave him." Terri's done this before, and I been human, ain't I?

  "Let 'em find him in the morning," as she's pulling on my prick and smiling so funny

BORROWED TIME

- Kathleene West

"Sometimes talking to each other is as difficult as dying."
-Marguerite Duras

He brought to her room a length of rope, 10 feet or so, coiled between sweater and jacket like a snake dulled by warmth. Rope, she repeated, thinking of the bristly, fatly-twisted hemp that held a cow's head down in the stanchion, or the skin-ripping twine knotted around each bale of hay, breaking and callusing even gloved hands. "It's soft," he said, and it was, white and slick, unsmeared by grease, unroughened by resistance.

He saws it in fours with her penknife, unsharpened since her last game of mumblety peg, 30 odd years ago. The knots he fashions are embarrassingly unfamiliar, domestic artifacts representative of a culture where she once moved easily about.

She watches as he moves from one limb to another, naked and still as death, intent on his task. When the knots close on wrist and ankle, the quick heartbeat of fear surprises her. In the dim room his face is so pale an aura heightens it like the luminescence of a television set or halos in a quattrocentro painting. The winter has rearranged his shape, twisting the knots of his shoulder, splaying out blades and ribs like the torso of a saint.

It is not the rope that binds nor her masque of veneration that she fears, not even death, but its impersonation, pale horse, pale rider, driving the atmosphere of the room into a rarefied gloom and strenuous despair, their small passion sparking the darkness.

With but a word she will be free. She depends on that as she depends on the relief when he swoops his face between her breasts and all she can see is the afterimage of cheekbone and whittled flesh illuminating the space between eyelid and eyeball. Their mouths stretch into each other's skin, and for a moment they can simultaneously believe their sealed words are neither necessary, revelatory, nor real.

TIES

- Terry Wolverton

About the time our relationship began to be in serious trouble, she began to talk about tying me up. One night in bed she confessed she had a fantasy of tying my legs apart, my arms over my head, and making love to me.

I expected to feel repulsed, but was startled to find that the image was exciting to me. Rather than pulling away, turning my back to her in the bed, I raised up on one elbow and asked her to tell me more.

Our relationship was in trouble because I wanted another lover. I said I didn't want to leave her, but I wanted something else too. She was threatened, threatening. Our days became peppered with accusation. Our lovemaking got better and better.

We would talk about her fantasy while we were making love. She would whisper to me, "I can't wait to have you tied up. Your legs will be spread so far apart, only your ass will be able to move." The anticipation would heighten our passion. I was turned on by what I felt was the extent of my trust, my willingness to surrender. She talked about the kinds of ties she would use ("Soft, cotton, I don't want to hurt your baby skin.")

I was still moving ahead with the other lover. Our fights intensified. We broke up and reconciled. Broke up. Reconciled. The sex sizzled. We went to the hardware store and bought eyehooks to install in the wood frame of the bed.

She accused. I defended. She derided. I exploded. She provoked. I attacked.

The ties were flimsy. Soft. Cotton. I could have broken away in the snap of a wrist. But I stayed. Spellbound. I stayed and stayed. Until the ties themselves began to fray and weaken. Until no amount of tension could make them hold.

AN ARCHITECTURE OF PAIN

- Simon Sheppard

"Swarthy good looks," as they say.
I'm glad that you're Jewish.
When you're lying there,
your ankles bound,
hands chained behind your head,

I see in your hairy body,
beyond piercings, tattoos and the gym,
the fleshly history of our race:
great-grandparents in the shtetl,
uncles and cousins in Bergen-Belsen,
you in bonds of an
utterly other sort.

In another life, you would have been
a dentist, maybe, married, overweight,
dissatisfied somehow, trapped.
In this life, though, I know what you need.
With the palm of my hand,
then with leather thongs,
I turn that furry butt pink, then red,
until I feel the bloodheat
glowing from your flesh. I love to bring
that peaceful smile to your lips,
to kiss those perfect lips, hard,
as you lose yourself in pleasure.

"Uninfected." I know I shouldn't
think this thought, but I'm guiltily glad,
glad that you will still be here
for maybe many years to come.
That the aftermarks of love
will only be those gained willingly,
eagerly taken upon your straining body.
There's already
so much suffering out there.
Let's just you and I,
dark eyes, build our own
little house of pain,
judiciously constructed. We'll call
these well-crafted agonies our friends
as we curl up together,
(two nice Jewish boys
who have made it through)
in the darkest, warmest,
friendliest of rooms.

POETIC DISCIPLINE

- Simon Sheppard

So this leather daddy poet
(you all know who he is)
got me handcuffed to the keyboard
and he growls, "Boy, give it up.
Shoot out that fuckin wad of words
and grovel, grovel like the writer that you are."

And I whine, "Sir, please, I'm trying, sir."
So he slaps me hard and says,
"Pussyboy poet, it just ain't good enough."
And I beg him, "Please, oh master, please,
flog me hard with your stinging turn of phrase
and shove your thick pentameter
down this faggot's throat."

And he sneers, "You poet pussy,
it's time you had some training."
And he ties me down
spreadeagle to the bed,
and all night long he reads to me
from Ezra Pound and Coleridge
In Xanadu did Kubla Khan
from Poe to Gertrude Gertrude Stein.

At last he gets me to my limits.
I use the safe word ("Frank O'Hara").
Then he holds me tight to his well-known
hairy chest and murmurs something
like he's talking to himself:
"I topped that Eileen Myles
and I made Ginsberg scream.
But I ain't never seen a boy
who needed this like you."

And he gets me down on my hands and knees,
commanding me to worship his big iambic foot

while he spits on me
and mutters through his beard,
"You prolix little bastard.
I've had first-year writing students
who gave better verse than you."
And I whimper, "Daddy, you're so right.
This writer-boy deserves your scorn,"
but I'm thinking *Walt Fucking Whitman!*
I can't wait to get out of this scene.
What does this old fart understand
of post-modern irony and poetry slams?

Well, to make a long epic poem short,
at last he gets his rocks off,
shoots his well-crafted quatrains
all over my free-verse butt.
And I gather up my manuscripts
and head out, speechless, to the dawn-dead streets.

In the days after that I tried to forget him,
but his snarling face kept coming back to me
just like a simile. I started to hang out
around sleazy writing workshops
in hopes of catching a glimpse of him there.
And I spent so much time doing rewrites
I turned nervous, pale and drawn.
No wonder that when at last I saw him,
went up to him after a panel that he'd chaired,
he acted as though we'd never even met.

Men are like that, I thought.
The guy's an arrogant bastard.
He was right about one thing though:
The muse *is* a hard master.

PLEASE MASTER

- Allen Ginsberg

Please master can I touch your cheek
please master can I kneel at your feet
please master can I loosen your blue pants
please master can I gaze at your golden haired belly
please master can I gently take down your shorts
please master can I have your thighs bare to my eyes
please master can I take off my clothes below your chair
please master can I kiss your ankles and soul
please master can I touch lips to your hard muscle hairless
    thigh
please master can I lay my ear pressed to your stomach
please master can I wrap my arms around your white ass
please master can I lick your groin curled with blond soft fur
please master can I touch my tongue to your rosy asshole
please master may I pass my face to your balls,
please master, please look into my eyes,
please master order me down on the floor,
please master tell me to lick your thick shaft
please master put your rough hands on my bald hairy skull
please master press my mouth to your prick-heart
please master press my face into your belly, pull me slowly
    strong thumbed
till your dumb hardness fills my throat to the base
till I swallow & taste your delicate flesh-hot prick barrel
    veined Please
Master push my shoulders away and stare in my eyes, & make
    me bend over the table
please master grab my thighs and lift my ass to your waist
please master your hand's rough stroke on my neck your palm
    down my backside
please master push me up, my feet on chairs, till my hole
    feels the breath of your spit and your thumb stroke
please master make me say Please Master Fuck me now Please
Master grease my balls and hairmouth with sweet vaselines
please master stroke your shaft with white creams
please master touch your cock head to my wrinkled self-hole

please master push it in gently, your elbows enwrapped round
my breast
your arms passing down to my belly, my penis you touch w/
your fingers
please master shove it in me a little, a little, a little,
please master sink your droor thing down my behind
& please master make me wiggle my rear to eat up the prick
trunk
till my asshalfs cuddle your thighs, my back bent over,
till I'm alone sticking out, your sword stuck throbbing in me
please master pull out and slowly roll into the bottom
please master lunge it again, and withdraw to the tip
please please master fuck me again with your self, please
fuck me Please
Master drive down till it hurts me the softness the
Softness please master make love to my ass, give body to
center, & fuck me for good like a girl,
tenderly clasp me please master I take me to thee,
& drive in my belly your selfsame sweet heat-rood
you fingered in solitude Denver or Brooklyn or fucked in
a maiden in Paris carlots
please master drive me thy vehicle, body of love drops,
sweat fuck
body of tenderness, Give me your dog fuck faster
please master make me go moan on the table
Go moan O please master do fuck me like that
in your rhythm thrill-plunge & pull-back-bounce & push
down
till I loosen my asshole a dog on the table yelping with
terror delight to be loved
Please master call me a dog, an ass beast, a wet asshole,
& fuck me more violent, my eyes hid with your palms round
my skull
& plunge down in a brutal hard lash thru soft drip-flesh
& throb thru five seconds to spurt out your semen heat
over & over, bamming it in while I cry out your name I do
love you
please Master.

May 1968

C'MON JACK

- Allen Ginsberg

Turn me on your knees
Spank me & Fuck me
Hit my ass with your hand
Spank me and Fuck me
Hit my hole with your fingers
Hit my ass with your hand
Spank me and fuck me
Turn me on your knees
Ah Robertson it's you
Yes hit my ass with your hand
real hard, ass on your knees
sticking up hard harder slap
Spank me and Fuck me
Got a hard on Spank me
When you get a hard on Fuck me.

March 29, 1976

SWEET GWENDOLYN AND THE COUNTESS

- Edward Field

The Countess rode out
  on her black horse in spring
wearing her black leather riding costume.
She was scouting for disciples in the countryside
and flicked with her whip
  the rosebuds as she passed.

Sweet Gwendolyn in her white dress
was out gathering May flowers.
Under sunshade hat, her pale face
blushed to the stinging bees,

and her golden curls lay passive
  on bent shoulders
as she stooped to pluck a white lily.

The Countess passing by took one look,
galloped up,
  and reined her stallion sharply in,
high over the modest figure
of Sweet Gwendolyn with the downcast eyes.
She leaped down from her horse and knelt,
laying the whip in tribute
  before the golden girl.

That foolish one swooned forward to the ground
in a great white puff of dress fabric
and a scattering of flowers. At that,
The Countess rose in all her black pride
and put her dirty leather boot hard
  on Gwendolyn's bent neck
pushing down the golden head to the grass
and gave her a smart lash
  across her innocently upturned behind.

Gwendolyn looked up with begging eyes
and a small whimper of submission,
and The Countess pushed her over
  and threw the skirt over her head
exposing legs and bottom bare
and shoved the leather whiphandle
  between squeezed thighs of virtue
forcing them apart to reveal the pink
  pulsing maidenhood.

Foolish Gwendolyn for not wearing panties
but how could she have known what was in store?
Her skirt fell over her head like petals
  of a fully-opened flower
and her legs waved in the air
  like stamen and pistil
inviting the bee of The Countess' tongue
to slip in and sip nectar in the golden fuzz.

Poor Gwendolyn moaned with shame and pain
as she lay back crushing her May flowers,
  exposed and unresisting -
until The Countess, in full charge,
  pulled her to her feet,
tied the whip-end around her neck,
remounted the big black horse
and slowly trotted off
leading the sobbing girl a captive behind her
off to her dark castle.

THE MARRIAGE OF HEAVEN Y HIELO: A LOVE NARRATIVE OF SORTS

- Gerry Gomez Pearlberg

> *Think well and be a king,*
> *Think more and think again*
> Gertrude Stein
> from *Before the Flowers of Friendship Faded*
> *Friendship Faded*

Benson & Hedges swap candycorn hats,
leopard-spotted leotards,
leather caps, Orangina
tutus, and semiotic big black boots.

Benson & Hedges: two marshmallows on a stick
  impaled by fire.

Benson says: *Long live the King.*
King = top of the lesbian crop.

Benson's got a thing for King.
Hedges goes along for the ride.

King is an apothecary of desire, flooded
with rose-tinted cross-bone syrups
that magically transgress
to coughdrop green in bottles
hung from cage-like ceiling slings
of silver chain. King
paces her telescopic castle halls
of fanfare and fan tracery,
hourglasses, measuring cups,
and flasks of sleeping tongue.

Benson & Hedges, whose brains are blades,
glide toward the castle gate
wearing armors of intent for their
double-date with destiny.
Their lives a skating rink,
their silver blades saw stories into ice
flicking grit and ice cubes
in each other's eyes: those cocktail
party sound-effects of desire pouring in.

King is a cold fish, an effigy of herself on fire.
Burning always (or so it seems) on someone else's castle wall.

Desire is more than lipstick and a mouth.
It gnaws at Benson from the inside out.
False teeth, saber-tooth Swiss Army knives,
bicuspids, cupid's bows.
Benson has no date of birth, no ID card.
No beginning, middle, or end to what she wants,
that spiraling infinity of the reaching
for the out-of-reach.

King, an icon herself,
has a shelf of unwanted icons:
pin-headed dolls from ex's who hate her,
holograms from the scenes of the crime,
and a tarnished crown that whispers "Don't ask."

Sometimes King would like to rearrange her furniture:
replace the love seat with a single bed, toss out

the horsewhip and the other princely props,
pinprick the royal velvet cushions, deflate
the pedestal and throne. It's lonely being a top.

Sometimes Benson wishes an older, wiser Benson
would take matters into her own hands,
but that would be like putting a gun
to her head, blowing away the stellar
system of everything she knows
she cannot have, that parallel universe
of not-so-laughable lapses that always
seem to keep her
in the game.

Desire waves from the castle gate like a
    monogrammed hanky.
The initials keep changing but the script's always the same:
handwriting of a lonely girl trying to live up to being King.
It isn't easy being a man. It isn't easy being on top.

Tonight, the stars hovering by King's castle are alchemical,
an unfamiliar alphabet
                    souping down a river
                                        of new water,
                                                    a new water
one can skate across,
soft water transmuting all-too-readily to gold.
The night is a moat with a drawbridge that says:
Identify yourself to the dark.

King is a constellation shifting in the sky.
On this and every other night she'll sleep
and rise
with both boots on.
It isn't easy being the cream of the crop
and it's lonely, lonely, lonely
at the top.

TOP WOMAN

- Thaddeus Rutkowski

Usually, when it comes to sexual direction, I am top man. I take the dorsal position, stay in the saddle out of the chute, bounce to my feet if thrown. In this way I can relate easily to most women I meet. These women have intellects that squash my own.

Sometimes, I admit, a top woman needs to take me to the woodshed and hack me to size.

Verbal battery is satisfactory. My ax-happy top woman can back me into a corner and call me names like "kinky cowboy" and "little Willensky." Or she can forget to back me into a corner and forget to say anything. This treatment would be equally deserved.

But what I prefer is to be punched out physically. I need to feel my top woman's glove. I crave the impact of her padded fist on my unprotected noggin. I want to whimper, "Please, no thumbing, and no rabbit punching." I want to go down, sweaty and stunned, and find, to my delight, that my sparring partner is not through with me yet. She might poke me with her toe, walk slowly across my chest, and sit, finally, on my face.

Other times, I'd rather stay out of the ring and go to the mat. There, I can experience the full fury of my wrestling dominatrix. I can float through space as she topples me with the firefighter's takedown, taste vinyl as she drills me with the head-lever breakdown, feel my will snap as she punishes me with the double chicken wing, and see lights fade as she pins me with the twined-leg grapevine.

My top woman will quell any resistance I offer. If I squirm, she will use the old standby, the monster scissors. She will wrap her legs around my waist, inch her way up, and clamp my neck between her thighs.

I may pull lamely at her legs with my hands. I may gasp weakly for air. But the monster scissors will open for no man. She will flex, then squeeze, then twist, until my head is effectively unscrewed.

In this manner I will escape being crushed by my partner's intellect, but I will never be free of her tightening grip.

PERFECT VICTIM

- Thaddeus Rutkowski

If you want to tie me up, why don't you use the Venetian blind cord? I don't care if you cut it apart. I never pull the blinds anyway. Or use my shoelaces, or my bathrobe sash. I think I have some kite string around here somewhere.

Once I'm tied up, I don't care if you take advantage of me. My mother knows where I live. I don't care if you kill me - just as long as you show some interest.

I know what this is about. I've been to the Vault. I've seen gallows humor at Paddles. I used to see people waiting all night in that sling chair at Hellfire, hoping for some cruiser to poke them. I've slid down the pole to reach the mother lode at the Mineshaft. I'm a fetishist - I hope you don't mind.

Hang me like a pig. Belt me with a belt. Call me names. No, forget the names. Call me exactly what I am. That would be better. Tie me up and read a book. Forget about me until I scream. I don't care if you leave the building. Just call in and leave a message on the machine. I'll be able to hear it even though I won't be able to speak. Leave a funny message, like, "Don't go anywhere," or "I'm never coming back."

But if you do come back, take pictures of me writhing on my bed. Send them to my mother. Send them to my office. Demand money. I don't care if you take everything I have, just as long as you give me everything I want, okay?

SENTENCE D'AMOUR

- Jim Coughenour

She sat crazed in her corner, sipping cognac, her pupils like panicked insects, wondering why she'd left her plush stool by the bar to follow the fingers of his eyes when they directed her to this alcove, to this fragrant linen tablecloth laden with the most delicate midnight dishes, where he sat like an ancient sage muttering about the "teleological suspension of the ethical," meanwhile seducing her with what he wouldn't say, as if he were drawing from her womb some silken cord, extracting her essence so that he could savor, taste by forbidden taste, her most intimate reverie, insinuating himself into her reticence so that she climaxed repeatedly even before his fingers sought her beneath the candles and the dishes and the fragrant linen cloths -

- while he, on the other hand, had no idea what had brought this ravenfaced woman to his table at this late and dangerous hour as he tried to sum up what was left of his life in an epigram, some elegant aperçu, but found instead that he was transfixed by this creature who reminded him of a dominatrix he'd served one rainy summer long ago in Paris, an enchantress who had melted and molded him according to her whimsical cruelty, and who had left him at last suspended between passion and despair, a penis without a home, pregnant with a doomed desire that only she could deliver, lost, spiritless and so starved that he could only consume the shards of himself, until now, as the raspberry sorbet melted on his burning tongue, he dreamed of blood and barbs and tiny leather tortures and so surrendered to this woman he had conquered.

MAMA

- Jim Coughenour

"What on earth were you thinking of?" Mama asked when I came home from my first date with him. "What was going through your head? Didn't God give you a brain?"

"Mama, please," I said, "I'm old enough to know." I was still a little sore around the mouth, so it was hard to protest too vigorously.

"You'd think you would have figured it out by now," Mama said, implacable as ever. "There was that other one last summer - Rob or Bob or Slob - whatever he called himself. You couldn't go out for *weeks* after that one."

"That was different," I said, though I knew that it wasn't.

"No, it wasn't," Mama said. "You just did it again, that's all."

I wanted to sit down and weep like Christ Almighty, but didn't dare. It was still too sensitive down there too.

"Well, what about you and Daddy? I asked, gingerly feeling around my mouth with the tip of my tongue.

"I mean, how did you two ever manage..."

"Oh, him!" Mama said, throwing up her hands. "Don't even get me started."

THE FEEL OF TEETH

- Victor Borsa

not like snapping mongrel
nor north wind cruel
upon your face
is the feel of teeth
of your lover

there's something of flowers
when frost scars their bleeding
skins - predawn of October,
a gathering of roots

I call it hawk wing
in midnight winter   beak
upon my flesh in pause
of flight

music to break stillness
of a Sunday morning
(Russian as in
balalaika
wild
as in honey)

first then the lips and preliminary
drowning in arms
the drifting grass   burning
of hunger

yes and finally the pain
of teeth of your fine
barbarian love.

(Taste me gentle and be wild
and let me feel the color
of our flight)

FIRST LOVE

- Vidyapati
translated by Sam Hamill

The new moon stirs pangs of love.
Scratches mar her proud young breasts.
Often hidden, sometimes they lie revealed
like treasure in the hands of the poor.
Now she has known first love,
desires flood her mind,
she trembles with delight.
Safe from the eyes of gossipy friends,
she studies her reflection in a jewel,
knits her brow, and oh
so tenderly
touches the blossoming
love-bite on her lip.

- Steve Kowit
after Vidyapati

It was brutal. A country boy
without an iota of skill
in the art of love-making,
he scratched up my back,
manhandled my breasts,
bit on my throat,
& when he finally entered,
his boyish strength
was too much for me.
He was immense -
savage -
insatiable!
I pleaded & cried out,

but in vain.
I swear,
had the vow
not been sealed with a kiss
I would never meet him
again tonight
as I promised I would.
But it was,
& I cannot go back on my word -
it is out of the question.
I would run over thorns
with my bare feet
to be there on time -
for with me,
as you well know,
honor comes first!

- Steve Kowit
after Sonnoka

Daughter, when you frisk with the cat
take more care. See
that small discoloration
by your throat...
    & there,
those scratches on your breasts
& back?
Learn to play less passionately, dear.
- Mama, whatever are you driving at?
The roses that I gathered for the house
were full of thorns.

CLOSEUP

- Robert Peters

Your eyes are a basilisk's, for you sense what's coming. I require a simpler image, not one fraught with Bible business. When you bend over, whispering, you excite me, and I taste orange poppies, an epidermal mast. Do I know you? Your eyes are blue-gray, as blue smoke coils. Eyes. Don't be angry. You crave pain. Draw a noose around my throat. Bite my mouth. Bite my testes. Say you love me.

- Gavin Geoffrey Dillard

It at least will be a grand ego boost
when we're at a bar and everyone's
staring at me pretty young
me something you can tell your
crowd that that hot number over
there dressed to kill and
dancing so pornographically is
actually very in love with
you would die or spend the rest of
his life at your feet chained
to your wall for just those
occasional glimpses for
the smell of your body when
you walk by or the
looks when you say you really don't
care at all.

from TRUST/The Hand Book

- Bert Herrman

Polish the gemstones of my inner crown.
Twist lovingly through the inner halls,
  the deepest passages.
My thresholds give way to the mightiest of illusions
Caress, once again, the palatial essence of my being.

Excalibur thrusts deeply into the rock
Recapturing its primeval resting place.
Ours is the kingdom and ours, the glory.
My world is full of your glory.
The earth quakes
  ...the trumpets blast
    ...the kingdom comes.

Behold, we reside in a land ruled by kings and princes.
You are draped in my ermine robes, our bodies exalted.
There is peace and trust and love.
I feel and know the spirit of your nobility.
Once upon a time, yields to a new surreality.
Camelot is won and ours as never before.
Fairy tales and evil queens are banished forever.

- Gavin Geoffrey Dillard

With your
fist
inside me
at least
I know
I
have your
hand
to hold.

CONVERSATION OVER DINNER

- Jeff Crandall

"My fetish is fisting," he said.
I didn't blink. "Some think

that's S&M - It's not."
I nodded, trying not to look

too interested. My only
comment: "Esoteric."

"Reciprocal," he replied.
"I've reached inside

a hundred different men, but
back home I can't seem to find

a husband." "No small task," I said.
"Those southern states stick

to missionary positions."
He grinned. "So many people

don't understand - having a hand
enter your body, feeling

a heartbeat from the inside,
this is far more powerful union

than any mutual masturbation.
I'm not looking for perfect love.

Conversation, the color car he drives
or where he works don't mean shit.

But this - THIS is my highest priority.
Everyone else is missing it."

In two days he'd be gone,
back to the East Coast. I adjusted

my seat, set down my fork. Took
a drink of water and decided

to speak my mind. "Any time
a physical manifestation

is the highest qualification
of a relationship, you limit

the needs of the heart
and never will be content."

He scowled. "Do you know
what this means?" He thrust

a handful of tan
knuckles to my face.

"This fist," he said, "covered
with Crisco means -

Trust."

HANDMADE *(for DE)*

- Pat Califia

Give it up.

Arch
Your back,
Beat the mattress with your arms
Like wings,
Grab handfuls of
The sheet

And spread
Till you feel the pull
In the sockets of
Your thighs -

Spread for me.

Let it feel good -
The last finger,
The thumb tucked in,
My hand sliding in
The length of another knuckle

Until the idea that
This time it might really happen
Closes your cunt up
Tighter than a valve in the aorta
Sealing itself against
The heart's great thrust of blood.

I don't mind.
We can wait here,
You and I,
Until you decide
How much of me you want.

I move the tips of my fingers
Like a sea-flower
Combing the ebb tides for crumbs.
I slip more grease
Inside you,
And it melts off my fingers,
Dissolved by the heat
Of your lust.

You reach for me with your ass,
And I begin to fuck you again,
Pushing from the shoulder.
You distract yourself by
Making a noise
Your hips can keep time to.
You do not feel yourself slip down
Another crucial half-inch
Onto the biggest part of my hand.

You give,
Elastic in your need,
You give a little more,
You hover -

Contractions build
Too deep for you to feel them,
The tremors that herald
Orgasm.

For a split second,
You open
Like a balloon being blown up,
Like the tunnel that runs
Beneath the curling lip
Of an incoming wave.

We both yell
As I glide in.
The bolt of pain is
Followed by
Exquisite fullness.

You clamp around me,
Taking my measure,
Driving yourself crazy
Trying to push me out.

I push back.
I punish.
I coax.
I persuade.
I preach.
I lie.

And because you believe me
It is suddenly true

And you give
It all
To me
So hard
That if my fist wasn't in you
There would be come
All over
My face.

THE SLAVES OF PROMISE

- Zdzislaw Kurlowicz

If I were the slave
And you the master
I'd use my body to cushion your blows.
Let your arrogance rip at my soul
Allow your cruelty free passage to my heart.
And if the others plotted against you,
I would inform.
To your threats of life and death
I would obey

Leave nothing to chance
If you were concerned.
And when you die
I'll carpet the tomb with my flesh
To keep your passions warm.

PACKAGE

- Kirby Congdon

Undo me, cut me up,
strip me down, tear me
apart, rip me open, turn
me out, like a wish, an
expectation, a secret
exposed and, so ended,
destroyed.

For the death of the last
desire, the explosion in
the first surprise, for
eternities that lie in the
climax of instant joy,
come in. Open me!

"YES, I'M LIVING ON" #*XXIX*

- Emilio Cubeiro

I impress myself I do
I am inspired by me I can do
I am always given inspiration I shall do
as I am told
whatever you my master desire

I am yours
my heart beats for you
my lungs are yours especially since you smoke
  two packs a day that is why I stopped smoking
  so I can give you a lung when you lay dying
  and I say no to the cosmos and give you my lung
  and I am a martyr granted sainthood by all
  true visionaries of the masturbatory arts
my hair so dark and silky is for your fingers
my penis harder in intensity than in looks is for your majesty
my chest is for you to lie on
my nipples belong to you but don't start thinking
  of buying me gold earrings because I don't wear
  any jewels even if I shouldn't be telling you
  what to do but then again the slave is really
  the master here in a conscious sexual fantasy
  but not so in the subterranean realms of those
  in the political slave and master playground
  for here the sandbox contains gold
and my ass, my ass really rarely penetrated
  I give it to you   it is yours
  take me where you will
  it awaits your stab your pierce of
  vengeful oh so beautifully vindictive
  lustful passionate contempt-like
  thrusts containing an element of love
and my hands   they have been consecrated with
  musical ability   let me play on your
  body as one would on a harpsichord
  and my eyes that see through you to your core
  boring with drill-like precision to examine the essence
insult me   call me names   use outrageous words
show me you love me or hate me or
you love me and hate me but do something to me
use your imagination   go ahead   you can   relax
feel free and uninhibited   tell me what your wildest thought
  ever was   I won't tell anybody
  yes   yes and do you think of that a lot
I'm not into physical pain but you can beat me anyway
I'll do anything for you   I told you
if you want to kill me I won't try to stop you

but may I suggest strongly on being cremated
half of the ashes to be thrown to the wind
if not at least a mild breeze and the remaining
half to be smoked by a handful of friends in a
chillum mixed with hashish of superior qualité
and to spend a moment remembering some of the
good things they shared with me

S/M IS SUCH FUN

- Jamie Perry

to tie you up
    just to throw you down
        is nothing

only to hear your groans
and have my rock hard cock
pound against your inside
causing such pleasure,

slap you here,
    touch you there,
pinch that thing
    to cause such pain,
then to smooth it?
    by gentle caressing touch

chains and studs
leather-n-silk,
what fantasy we have
on the games we play -
no rules but one
to enjoy

a lustful bite
a sassy fuck

a hot load
dripping from your face

standing there helpless
    as a lamb
        to be slaughtered
by the hands of his master
    after the breeding is done

from CIRCUS POEMS

- Norbert Krapf

As the crowd roars
I step to the center
of the ring & shake
my shaggy hair.

I raise the whip
above my head,
you kneel on the stool
in your long-tailed suit
& raise your arms
behind you like wings.

When I crack
the whip & breathe
fire you flip
through the air
& burst headfirst
through the hoop
of my poem.

I whirl the whip
faster & faster,
you catch your
rhythm as the crowd

goes crazy & soar
higher & higher
into the ozone

but then I lower you
back to the ground,
remember my place,
sit on my haunches
& lick at my paws.

VENICE BEACH: MEMORIAL DAY

- Scott O'Hara

Lying on the beach with Sir, tightly handcuffed
to the stakes he's driven at my hands and feet
people strolling by, all unaware;
I can turn, rotisserate myself, but nothing more.
He relaxes, unconcerned, only attending me
to replace my beer each quarter-hour
- I suck them through a straw. "Please Sir" - I say,
on finishing my third - "I need to piss..."
He looks at me, and at the crowded beach.
"Turn on your back," he says, and I obey -
even bladder-bloated, hardon still won't go away,
tents my baggy running shorts - he smiles.
"So piss," he says.
The shorts are quickly soaked; the towel takes
a few more beers. Each time I ask - "Sir?" He nods,
and piss leaps up, bubbles through thin material,
puddles on my belly, as he watches.

Later, as I start to put the towel in the washer,
he corrects me. "Save it.
You can sleep with it tonight."

SAYING YES

- Scott O'Hara

I tried to tell him No, but then my lips said "Yes" instead
and not because I wanted any part of him:
he didn't have a single trait that I call "hot" -
his hair was stringy, brow pockmarked and haggard,
nose quite undistinguished, chin and hair alike
- receding - shoulders stooped, and body...
well, it wasn't exercised. A desk-job, obviously.
He had a look of perfect pathos in his eyes; and I,
who normally remain unmoved by sympathy,
discovered I'd said yes to him unwillingly.
Yes, I'll come home with you.

The journey in his car (a giant guzzler, just the type
I most abhor) was mostly silence and suspicion.
I wondered, am I crazy? What's my rationale
for being here? I found it shortly after we arrived
at his apartment: in his tawdry, tacky, prissy bedroom
(a drink and conversation was the last thing on my mind),
I took my clothes off while he went to pissssss...
and pondered whether loathing, lust, or pity'd driven me
to such extremity, but swallowed hard and told myself
to close my eyes and think of... something fun...
and while I listened to his stream, I noticed in the closet
(he'd left the door wide open after hanging up his coat)
a carefully-constructed noose depending from the ceiling.

Thirty minutes later, he climaxed quite emphatically
inside me, hissing violently, spasmodically,
a high-pitched, wailing, gurgling "Yessss!"
through throat encircled tightly by my hands.
His hands were bound securely to his feet.
I left him breathing shallowly, unconscious:
still tortured-looking, but with fantasies enough
(I think) to soothe a month of un-days
and still I dream about his "Yessss!"
I gave him my permission to desire;
and he gave me permission to despise...
but only one of us, I think, succeeded.

Mercedes

LOOKING FOR A LITTLE SPANK

- Thaddeus Rutkowski

I hit bottom on my birthday. Actually, I wanted to hit a bottom, but there were no buttocks to spank. I had my spanking apparati ready: the box-shaped attacher with straps for wrists and ankles, the low-spindled grasper with handles for trembling fingers, and the ceiling-anchored hoister with nooses for guilty feet.

I was feeling like an *hombre malo*. In fact, I was feeling *muy malo*. I was ready to cross the strike zone. I was prepared to go beyond no-hit sex and get into some real whacking. But I could not locate one live *derrière*.

So I called an old spanking-out partner. It had been a long time since we'd met for whippets and whipping. "Put on your knickers," I said, "and get ready to snort up and bend over."

"Okay," she said.

But when the big day - my birthday - arrived, she did not show. I waited a long while, then called her.

"Can I call you back?" she asked.

Needless to say, she never did.

So there I was, alone with my spanking stuff: the Ping-Pong paddle, the ruler, the yardstick, the willow switch, the birch twigs, the bamboo cane, the fly swatter, the wire hanger, the hairbrush, the wooden spoon, the crop, the quirt, the thong, the wet noodle, the nightstick, the strap, the back scratcher, and the plastic, hand-shaped slapper.

I spent the rest of the day thinking about how co-dependency works, how my enablers always eventually stop enabling me, how my compulsions supersede my feelings, and how, if I took the time, I could open a spanking museum. Or at least a paddling library.

I found some index cards and started cataloging.

SUMMER LOVE

- Robert L Rucker

Flex your muscles so I
can swing from your arm:
I want to feel like a
high-school girl
in summertime, in heat.
I want to fight with you
drunk behind bars
on Saturday nights,
then Sunday mornings
waking slow,
fucking 'til we cry,
and breakfast for lunch
at Denny's.
I need to know all about you:
the color of your blood,
the color of your pain,
the way you taste.
I'll make you feel stupid
with my words and you'll
slap me a little too hard
knowing it's what I want,
to be touched by you, hard.

me & ratboy run the gamut of literary lovers

- Michael Hathaway

sometimes we're jack & neal,
poking & challenging each others'
minds & histories,
entire belief systems
in motel rooms & cars
with no destinations

drunken thoughts & words
roll across the black manuscript
of strange city night skies

we move & run
as if our lives depend upon it

sometimes we are auden & kallman
and i hate him for being young.
i hate him for being in love
with the whole world.
i hate the whole world
for being in love with him.

sometimes i am
ginsberg & williams
& he is nameless tasty chicken,
i beg him to let me
help every inch
of his long brown body
into heaven

but he is most at ease
when we are Beavis & Butthead,
stuck in small Kansas towns
with no money,
punching each other,
biting each other,
exploring the taste of blood,
the art of pain,
creating fat purple bruises
on the canvas of our bodies.

i'm not a punching bag but...

- Michael Hathaway

he is stronger than me
and likes to hit

it is an art.
his eyes dilate,
his face gets a hard mean look,
he doubles his fist and swings wide,
brown biceps bulge

i like it,
the way it jars my whole being
that thud on my arm
or leg, or back, once in the eye
(you really do see stars)

the sheer male power behind the punch.
i never had that power,
it always mystifies, eludes me.

i like seeing it, feeling it,
understanding it

i take his touch, his skin
any way he offers it.

from NOTES FROM A MARRIAGE

- Gavin Geoffrey Dillard

It's no secret that he
loves me -

I beat it out of
him every nite.

He incites me to
violence,
when I respond his
body throbs with
excitation -

War is sweet.

I cringe in bed
plotting my escape

Helping him
bind my feet.

He says I'm only
interested in his butt -
I wanted to deny it
but my first thot is to
turn him over my
knee.

He seems to do everything he
can to get spanked -
I suppose if I had a
butt like his I'd
be the same way.

He tried to tell me he was
sorry

But I spanked
him anyway.

No more tears
we promised

And he bit my fist to
see if I could hold to it.

I don't cry anymore when he
hits me

It only
makes him stop.

- Michelangelo Buonarroti
translated by Sidney Alexander

Indomitable, savage
this woman would ravage
me, determined I should burn, die, disintegrate
for that which by weight
counts less than an ounce
and my blood quart by quart
she sucks from my veins: unfibres me, aborts
My body from my soul.
O the joy she takes in this toll!
Making up before her faithful mirror, she sees
herself equal to Paradise
then turning to me, sullies my every fold
So that simply by being old
My face makes hers more beautiful.
Whence have I decided
the more I am derided
for being ugly, yet that is my
great fortune, special feature
For increasing her beauty I conquer nature.

THE VAMPIRE

- Charles Baudelaire
translated by Jacques Leclercq

Thou, sharper than a dagger thrust
Sinking into my plaintive heart,
Thou, frenzied and arrayed in lust,
Strong as a demon host whose art

Possessed by humbled soul at last,
Made it thy bed and thy domain,

Strumpet, to whom I am bound fast
As is the convict to his chain,

The stubborn gambler to his dice,
The rabid drunkard to his bowl,
The carcass to its vermin lice -
O thrice-accurséd be thy soul!

I called on the swift sword to smite
One blow to free my life of this,
I begged perfidious aconite
For succor in my cowardice.

But sword and poison in my need
Heaped scorn upon my craven mood,
Saying: *Unworthy to be freed,*
From thine accursed servitude,

O fool, if through our efforts, Fate
Absolved thee from thy sorry plight,
Thy kisses would resuscitate
Thy vampire's corpse for thy delight.

ACHES-LES-BAINS

- Felice Picano

Smoking, smashed on my cot
locked back in my room
after trashing an hour
through showers and saunas
I heard a guy croon
through the next-door partition
"I love you as much as God."

The whistle of sheets.
A flash slap on skin.
Another. Another. Another.
A tumult of stumbles.
One splintered gasp.
A moan. A thud - and then:
"More, I mean. More than God."

SEVEN SEALS

- DH Lawrence

Since this is the last night I keep you home,
Come, I will consecrate you for the journey.

Rather I had you would not go. Nay come,
I will not again reproach you. Lie back
And let me love you a long time ere you go.
For you are sullen-hearted still, and lack
The will to love me. But even so
I will set a seal upon you from my lip,
Will set a guard of honour at each door,
Seal up each channel out of which might slip
Your love for me.

I kiss your mouth. Ah, love,
Could I but seal its ruddy, shining spring
Of passion, parch it up, destroy, remove
Its softly-stirring crimson welling-up
Of kisses! Oh, help me, God! Here at the source
I'd lie for ever drinking and drawing in
Your fountains, as heaven drinks from out their course
The floods.

I close your ears with kisses
And seal your nostrils; and round your neck you'll wear -
Nay, let me work - a delicate chain of kisses.
Like beads they go around, and not one misses
To touch its fellow on either side.

And there
Full mid-between the champaign of your breast
I place a great and burning seal of love
Like a dark rose, a mystery of rest
On the slow bubbling of your rhythmic heart.
Nay, I persist, and very faith shall keep
You integral to me. Each door, each mystic port
Of egress from you I will seal and steep
In perfect chrism.
Now it is done. The mort
Will sound in heaven before it is undone.
But let me finish what I have begun
And shirt you now invulnerable in the mail
Of iron kisses, kisses linked like steel.
Put greaves upon your thighs and knees, and frail
Webbing of steel on your feet. So you shall feel
Ensheathed invulnerable with me, with seven
Great seals upon your outgoings, and woven
Chain of my mystic will wrapped perfectly
Upon you, wrapped in indomitable me.

O DOES COBB'S CREEK

- Virginia Love Long

Knot the leather hood about my throat
With lashings pulled snug and tight.
Shut out any hint of day
And let darkness be my light,
Night ever the native habitat
And sole dress
For a prized falconess.

Clip my wings. Close.
Heap cold straw in the far corner
Of my cramped cage, dank and dark.
Feed me little: stale water, mildewed seed.
Keep me weak, a stranger to need.

Let nothing bespeak
Those wild sweet days
I soared far beyond the clouds for sport,
Raced the laughing winds for jest,
Mounting air, proud, high and free,
Spilling untethered song
To drown the eagle's call.

How we fare when felled and fallen,
Unfit for gaming or despair,
Is spelled by dull plumage
And drooping beak, listless eyes
Afixed, steady staring, unmoving,
Burning through the dungeon's thick air.

Chains,
Their clank and clink,
Dragging over dripping stone,
Tell all there is to know.

THE HOUSE BOY'S FIRST DAY

- Pat Califia

So many people say, "Please let me serve you, mistress"
When they really mean, "Why haven't you tied me up yet,
Whipped me, and fucked me yet?"
Tired of this, sometimes I won't bite,
But loneliness and a herniated disk encourage me to gamble
On the latest offer from a butch young farmboy
Who really wants to garden but will
Do housework if that's what it takes to get
Access to the topsoil of my overgrown back yard.

You arrive wearing shorts with your leather jacket,
And you've shined your beatup combat boots until
They look like patent leather.

Even your nose ring twinkles.
You dykes in your twenties with your bare knees and twenty-seven earrings
Seem to have enough energy to polish entire freeways.
It's endearing and a little scary
To someone like me who has been wearing pajamas
A lot more often than my leather.
Picking up the remote control hurts me, and
If I have to climb more than one set of stairs in a day,
I have to take a nap. Forget parallel parking.
I know there is gray hair under the bodacious burgundy
I've thrown on my hair.
I know this won't work; I have nothing for you.
But I've promised to give it a try,
And my sadism dictates that I give you a chance to fail.

So I leave you with a list, keys to the house,
Brand-new bottles of cleaning supplies.
When I return I expect to find a sullen house
Full of half-completed chores.

Instead, the rooms are full of peace, serenity, and Pine-Sol.
The vacuum cleaner is warm to the touch.
The corners of the kitchen floor wink like mirrors
Signaling rescue is on the way.
In the dish rack, plates wait to be used again,
Clean as an unopened deck of playing cards.
The cats are asleep, having accepted your service
As something natural and benevolent,
Like sunshine or the water in canned tuna.
As cats will, they leave the task of gratitude to me.

In my laundry basket,
A Japanese poem waits for me,
Formal in its simplicity,
Beauty made manifest by self-discipline
(Honor, like God, being in the details).

The T-shirt, socks and briefs
Are compartmentalized like the food in a TV dinner.
No sock has gone unmated.

The unwieldy Y-fronts have been turned right-side-out
And snapped into boot-camp shapes as rectangular as a shoebox.
The folded T-shirts are stacked up like coins.

And I suddenly feel rich
With the abundance of love
That has quietly waited
For me to come home and discover it
Like an unexpected inheritance.

No one could deserve such care.
I know myself incapable of this serene and graceful service.
Instead I offer you what chatelaines and overlords
Can spend upon their charges:
A list, my keys, the tools to do your work,
My name if it should ever be of use to you,
Hands to take your reins,
White gloves to run along your cracks and edges,
A roof to shield your fealty,
A vocation that deserves your loyalty.

With scrub brushes and dusters,
We craft a sort of romance
More potent than the love that's made
By most, who woo armed only with a kiss.

MINDBODY/BODYMIND

- Dawn McGuire

I know what she wants.
She wants her mind
You know
Respected.
We share this.
I want her.
I flirt with her mind.
We take up something, say
The Norman Conquest;
Plate Tectonics;
Pull up Pope Joan's robes;
Consider desire
In the Women Troubadours;
Build Catherine of Sienna's
Cathedral. I continue
Seduction in the sacristy.
My Irish tongue runs
Over the rim of her cortex,
Tips each gyrus, slips
Into each arousable sulcus
Like a bee's tongue in an orchid.
The wet does conduct electric
So well. I can hear the humming,
Hers, mine, in series.
I can see her eyes, salt
Lakes of language, silence, trace,
Begin to stir, change a little,
Just the smallest vexing
Of surfaces
And, near shore, the
Roiling round the rocks...
I know what she wants.
Our eyes strike and there,
There, yes, the quickening
Bulb sends up its first
Insistent shoot.

Our earth magnetic surfaces
Align: toe, toe, knee, knee,
The pelvic brims, two half
Rims become a fire bowl.
Fused at the waist, we each
Lean back, two principle
Leaves allowing the mental
Stem to rise. Then lips,
Hers, thick as stung,
Lean in to mine,
But there is time.
There is all this time.
Be still I sign, my finger
To her mouth.
I do this. I make her wait.
She bites. *Bitch* she whispers,
But I know
What gets to her.
It is her mind's
Engorged extravagance,
Its stem, sepal, lip
And, only lastly,
My combusting matter.

Kalika Mae's Wild Ride

Hardware
bikes, spikes and turnpikes

MYSELF WITH A MOTORCYCLE

- Mutsuo Takahashi
translated by Hiroaki Sato

Motorcycle, the vehicle for long-haired young gods.
My god sports a glans-shaped jeweled crown we call a helmet,
sticks his legs with long shins into azure jeans
puts on heavy boots adorned with many golden studs,
and dashes through the twilight of purple gods.
At the moment, midway on the stone steps behind a theatre, for example,
my god is in the midst of a blood-reeking conspiratorial discussion with other long-haired gods.
Their youthful conspiracy is too dazzling, too fragrant
for me, passing the foot of the stone steps, to clearly discern.
Below the stairs, only the god's seat made of steel gleams like a living thing.
I touch the motorcycle, particularly that part of its seat which was just glued to the ass of my god,
still retaining the ass's warmth.
My god eats Kentucky fried chicken, drinks Coca-Cola,
and from the dawn-colored slit of his beautiful ass he ejects shit.

DAREDEVIL

- Kirby Congdon

Hard helmets and high boots
tumescent in the sun,
got-up in rubber skin
and leather hide,
black, strapped, laced,
buckled with grommets,
chrome and brassy-eyed,
their dress itself is an act of sex,
as the body, used,
tumbles to its end
like jointed dolls we outgrew
and threw aside.
So the exalted race
to their base death
in self-abuse begins,
as the body's transient existence
sings its violent end,
to replace that dull, dull death
that waits upon the rest of us
behind a desk,
behind another desk,
behind the coffin lid
closing like an office door.

MOTORCYCLIST

- Kirby Congdon

The intoxicating stench of gas
mixes with the body's sweat
and smell of musk.
Their leather torsos,

riding iron bulls,
intimate and crouched,
intense in the lover's act,
copulate with their hot machines.
Blood and oil are one.
They eat and digest
death.

MOTORCYCLISTS

- Kirby Congdon

burn tire tracks
through my guts;
roar, exhausting,
under rearing buttocks;
cut corners
across my taut chest;
like roving lovers,
leave me, strapped,
silent and stranded.
Their intricate engines
are merciless,
blasting through
the insides of my torn-out heart,
ripping ragged holes
out of the night,
shaking space
with black sound
across the asphalt of heaven,
their staccatos scattering
sparks, hearts, stars.

THE MOTORCYCLE SOCIAL CLUB

- Kirby Congdon

After the run, we all meet at the Club - those of us who haven't broken down, dropped their bikes, or gotten hurt, injured or killed. We play pool and drink, and move in even strides about the room, showing off the thick backs of our curving thighs, gleaming where the black leather stretches tight. We spend the evening sending messages - flowers, emergency telegrams and time-bombs - with our eyes. When we pair off, we are casual and conceal the excitement we feel at our public but silent commitment to destruction. The veteran members disappear one by one to recover in hometowns, or to wait in hospitals or graves. But the membership grows, though the initiations become more stringent. The local people laugh nervously at our public image, or they ask, Where will it all end? But the game, underneath, is serious and there is no end. In the land of plenty, death grows, fertilized and lush. And we get drunk on the habit-forming perfumes of its secret and majestic, its black and addictive blooms, and each flower broken off sheds a glittering shower of hard new seeds. There's the fascination. To join the Club is difficult; to be a member is final and permanent. Meanwhile, as we wait for our own last night, we drink and play pool.

HARLEY-DAVIDSON

- Harold Norse

I climb on the Harley-Davidson
behind him. "Hold me," he says,
"around the waist!" my arms
petrified as we hurtle through Brooklyn.
he glances over his shoulder.

to show appreciation I smile, thighs
numb with tension. the feel
of his lean belly under the leather
is soothing. Nick's slant
blue Russian eyes sheathed
in the Jaeger like that scene
of Slavs and Teutons on the ice
in *Alexander Nevsky*, he turns
into a knight, I his vassal.
we ride the lancing air,
one with the machine
alive and leaping, sailing
a concrete sea. words
had not brought us together, words
made us "comrades". we never spoke
intimately. teenage marxists.
slum intellectuals.
                    we shoot
by dazzling shores, roar
at the rocks - then back,
I pry loose. Nick grins,
removes the Jaeger. lank
blond hair over high
cheekbones. "Were you
scared?" still trembling I frown.
"Nah. Let's do it again next Sunday."

RIDING

- Robert L Rucker

Vibration from grooves
in the freeway
make my cock stiff
where it shoves against your ass
as I ride behind,
my face next to yours,

arms snaking around your belly,
hands between your legs
rubbing the place
where you always dress left,
feeling you come
through tightened denim
while the wind caresses us
faster and harder
as we speed up past families
in strictly practical sedans
and I pull my hand
to my mouth
and lick you off.

BELLEROPHON IN LEATHER

- Paul Mariah

Blood and wind grew wings, bled
that is how I was born.
You were sent out to kill

the beast. I went with you,
you in leather, cycle,
a reconciling of hides.

I, an agent of travel,
upgrading and tanning
a way of blood-life.

You want to tame me,
to speed, to tilt and ride
the steed bareback, bearable.

Even Poland seems conquerable
or possible in cold war:
To ride the wind in exile

and taking impossible grades
and making them after all
possible, Polish possible.

You gun me and we speed
off into the night together,
Bellerophon in leather

and I, the wingéd horse,
Pegasus, the wild steed,
the impossible chase

after the beast. After
wards you lie on small
of my swayback, fagged

and I charge for the mare
of my night's dream. Tomorrow
we must continue the rites.

RIDDEN *(for Joan Colby)*

- Paul Mariah

I too have been ridden
and have felt like the back
of a cycle seat,
curled and warped with wear.

The spine swerves &
bends to the current
of the warp & where it's been
pressed and pressured.

These old Levi's are
so holy that my knees
are always smiling
at other pedestrians.

The sideloop for the belt
continues to sag under
the ghosts of old keys,
leatherbelt & other riders.

Leathern & seared.
I continue to churn
to work the knots out
& to undo the network

That others tied while
riding me: wardens, lovers,
brothers, fathers,
poverty, churches and other

Spectacular ghosts.
I have watched
riding and being ridden
simultaneously. Love.

- Gavin Geoffrey Dillard

There was no bike, no offending noise
no caustic smells or carnivorous show of leather

My hands held tight to two steaming armpits,
trickled down to his legs

Another sharp turn would send us
flying

- Gavin Geoffrey Dillard

Flying to Santa Barbara
on the back of his bike,
willing to die at every
turn;
this man is a stranger
and I am excited
by all dark secrets
yet to learn.

Flying to Santa Barbara
on the back of this man,
holding every inch of
flesh that I can;
his name is Dave
and I am unafraid
of decisions my soul has
already made.

SHE DROVE HER PELVIS

- Cheryl Townsend

like a Porsche 928
wide open into his
thick shift overdrive
burning rubber and the
odometer checks the
distance from here
to there finishing
first as exhaust
drips down her thighs

CHANGING THE OIL

- Eloise Klein Healy

I get her up on the curb, two wheels off the street
and dive under with my tools - my favorite blue-handled
wrench and a drop-forged hammer with a no-slip grip.

Her, her, her - always the female car. And now I'm under,
lying on the news of the day before yesterday, slowly turning
the warm nut. She's above me like a womb or heaven
about to rain. I'm slowly turning my way into her
black blood, slipping on the wet bolt, diving into
the underworld we women crawl into with our new pride
fresh from the parts store. Turning the beautiful
implements over in my hands, tenderly
the oil spurts free - and I have done it.

JONAS' FIAT

- Trebor

Jonas used to pick me up
and take me to school
in his little yellow Fiat

He was my Spanish teacher
Jonas and I started fucking halfway through the second week
but we never spent the night together
Jonas lived with his family
and I lived with somebody else's

Jonas would take me for long rides
through the mountains
up to San Miguel de Allende and Guanajuato
Once he fucked me on the hood of the car

I fucked him on the roof
and we screwed endlessly inside

When I got robbed in Mexico City 3 months later
I called Jonas and told him
all my money, my plane ticket, passport, everything
Jonas said I could drive his car home if I promised to come back for good

Jonas and his Fiat, both so sweet

But I'd forgotten about Jonas by the time I got back to San Francisco
At night out in the Sonora Desert, I'd pull off to sleep
First I thought about Jonas and jacked off inside
Subsequent nights I moved to the front hood
By the end of the week, as I approached the border
I was opening the hood and dumping my semen into the crankcase
I liked to pull over and piss on the engine when it was hot

When I finally got Jonas' Fiat into my garage at home
it was all I could do not to peel the paint right off its body
I opened all its doors, trunk, hood, windows
I unclamped a fat rubber hose from the radiator
packed it with solvent and fucked Jonas' Fiat
while I revved the carburetor to 4000 rpms with my hand

I wanted to make Jonas' Fiat blow a rod
suck a valve
I wished then I had a metal cock
what a poor lover I was for Jonas' Fiat
All I could fuck were his hoses
and no matter how much rubber I wrapped around his exhaust pipe
he was just too big and hard for me

But Jonas' Fiat didn't seem to mind
He was some kind of bottom
Long as I gave him gas and oil
he made more noise than any lover I'd ever had

I looked ridiculous at the self-serve station
pumping the hose into Jonas' Fiat with a big hard-on
pushing out of my pants

I started leaving the oil cap off while I fucked Jonas' Fiat
I liked to watch him pump, uncontained
Hot black gushers of 20-weight-50 slopped out of the
head of the engine
scalded my skin
and ran down my legs

And Jonas' Fiat never ran out of cum
I kept a case of it at my feet
and I'd just refill him when he ran low

I still haven't figured out a way to kiss Jonas' Fiat
or get him to stay warm when we sleep
He's awful quiet sometimes
and I sense we both feel kinda bad about Jonas

I fear we won't last either
I've already got my eye on a smogcheck device down at the
Shell Station
- I like its air of authority
It could teach me a thing or two

But while Jonas' Fiat has got a few thousand miles left
I'll keep sucking dry his brake fluid and loosening all his
bearings
One day I'll take him out and get him so hot with speed
he'll cum fire
and
hot molten tears and black tragic streaked mascara skidmarks
will scar the long highway
on the day I kiss him goodbye

timmy, age 16, decides to be fighter pilot

- Carl Miller Daniels

goes to air show
stands by himself
watches all

blue angels
turning those jets
into paintbrushes
painting
red-white-n-blue
blossoms
rainbows
sunbursts

timmy goes home
sleeps
has major
wet-dream
bathed in
sweat
cums in
patriot colors
cums
till he's near
awake
his
screaming
mach-1
thruster
firing
hot
plumes into
jet-streaked
sky

BIKER BROAD

- Fred Voss

Ruth lifted her head,
as she rocked on her hands and knees,
her pussy an inch above Dave's face.
She looked out over Dave's toes
as Dave began to tongue her.
She looked across her bed at Dave's leather jacket and his
boots on the floor against the wall.
She could see Dave riding his bike,
drunk and on pills,
crazy with his fear of going back to prison.
She saw Dave racing down the streets,
and her nipples swelled.
She shivered and groaned with pleasure
as she saw
Dave's hand slamming his bike through its gears,
as Dave took the street corners faster and faster.
She lifted her neck and widened her eyes
as she saw Dave go down.
Her body jerked and twitched
with enthusiasm
as she watched Dave slide and twist under his bike
as his bike pulled him 40 feet across the asphalt,
skinning and crushing him
and fracturing his skull.
She dropped her shoulders and head
and climaxed
crouched down on the street next to Dave's body,
peering into his fixed open eyes
to make sure that he was dead.

JAGANNATH

- Kirby Congdon

...and when, after years of developing it, he had molded every contour of his body to perfection, marveling in the cold mirror the taut curves of the pectorals, the lean, hard undulations of his abdomen, and the restrained power of his swollen thighs, with hypnotic fascination - almost greed - in his eyes, he pushed his middle finger under his testicles, into his rectum and pressed forward. So, he ejaculated before the mirror, and as often as possible. His eyes gobbled up all the different and perfected sections of his straining body until, throwing his head back, and rising on his toes, his pelvis shoved forward, the semen jerked out like his very soul, arching in space, thick in its glorious waste, uniting itself with the empty air like far-flung and briefly luminous constellations which fell in their destruction with soft splats against the mirror and onto the floor until he doubled over in exhaustion and then leaned, breathing heavily, against the wall and watched his body slowly relax its magnificent tensions.

He exercised and manipulated his beauty every day, sharing it only in the sidelong glance of strangers who watched his athletic movements or caught a glimpse of his body which revealed itself as a living explication of the human form - to be handled and coddled and toyed with, roughed about and teased and mistreated until that body broke in its purest function and lay, still beautiful, like a great imaginary landscape, with a thigh or a breastplate glistening with his own body's juice where, far-flung, it had landed and was just beginning to leak out from its own heavy substance, to define a muscle's shape like a painful tear. Obsessed with himself, he was happy to enjoy the workings of his interior body, to have those strange unknown motors move, run, churn and race, pumping up a wellful of compressed sludge until this volcano of lava vomited up his very loins under the studied, shameless gaze of his one admirer in the mirror.

But now he found a silent place in a desert area, on a hilltop close to heaven which looked down on him with its great indifferent eyes, pretending not to care or to watch, as he removed his clothes. Lying down, he inserted the gun barrel into his rectum and aggravated himself in an almost ugly and mean fashion, his fist on his erect cock, stroking and twisting it cruelly over and over again to the breaking point, releasing his hand just quickly enough to forestall an ejaculation, as the head of the penis alternately shone with its anticipatory lubricant.

Finally, as the afternoon wore on, he knew it was time. He rested until all was quiet and relaxed so that he could appreciate the full sweep of his excitement. He began slowly and forced himself not to rush his progress, and then he attacked his cock roughly, occasionally rolling over, the gravel scrubbing his driving-rod knuckles raw and the gun barrel jabbing his rectum compulsively. His throat clutched at the air in gasps as he felt his loins convulse at the center of his being. The throbs sped through his fingers where the semen rushed through his flaming cock in hard pellets. As the first glob seemed to push his thighs apart with its force, his cock broke out of his blinded hand and as the second burst fell on his body like fireworks, he pulled the trigger of the gun. Its one expensive bullet lunged its way deep into his stomach without time, and blasted a white hole that seemed larger than his own torso for the length of his prostrate body. His penis continued to break forth in ruptured joy until at last it subsided, and he was left for the rest of the afternoon bathed in his own sweat, under his own semen, and on top of his own blood, under the impassive sky which looked down on him as indifferently as before.

His pain lifted him out of himself, his brain a mass of shapeless fire, a molten, boiling stone of hideous sensitivity and feeling that swarmed over him and advanced and retreated like the sun moving in and out of focus, or like galaxies of time itself exploding and shrinking in the slow motions of astronomical speeds. In time, before the sun itself had set, he died.

When his admirer came from out of his mirror and found the corpse, he saw the position of the gun and understood. He looked close and saw where the semen had dried in shallow, almost invisible scabs on his still body. The visitor knelt down on the ground beside the body, withdrew his cock, waited dispassionately for it to grow full and large, and then covered the suicide once more with medallions of come. Then he removed his own clothes and lay down naked with the corpse for a while, chest to chest. Having regained his strength, he put his clothes back on and headed down the hill toward the town and the people.

It was a beautiful day, filled with love. It was holy and the people in it seemed, all of them, to be saints. And the dying and the dead - martyrs whom he alone had blessed and whose transfiguration he alone had witnessed, and whose meaninglessness he alone knew - had more meaning than existence itself - an existence which was the fulfillment of life into the very extremes of its far-flung boundaries, which are those far-off yet so close frontiers of death.

HORSE-OPERA

- Kirby Congdon

His very victims
also overcome,
drunk with death,
prostrate,
and past ecstasy,
the cowboy-hero, cool,
blows smoke
from his hot gun's barrel
that banged his leather-vested
partner/villain
down to dust,
and tucks the rod away

like a still-stiff cock
that's just shot off
its stinging load
into the second-man's entrails
and marries,
in love's hate,
and war's own peace,
his mirror's mate;
re-enacts a myth,
a play of words,
a game of wish
and all of it
hides love's hard kiss.

MANDRAKE OF THE RIFLE RANGE

- *Paul Weinman*

is quick a
split second
from spotting that
bullseye to barrel
aimed set
finger to trigger
pause
squeezing it
explosion
ripping through
scoring for the
kill of that red
eye of meat

LINES ADDRESSED TO A YOUNG LADY

- Lord Byron

As the author was discharging his pistols in a garden, two ladies passing near the spot were alarmed by the sound of a bullet hissing near them; to one of whom the following stanzas were addressed the next morning.

Doubtless, sweet girl! the hissing lead,
  Wafting destruction o'er thy charms,
And hurtling o'er thy lovely head,
  Has fill'd that breast with fond alarms.

Surely some envious demon's force,
  Vex'd to behold such beauty here,
Impell'd the bullet's viewless course,
  Diverted from its first career.

Yes! in that nearly fatal hour
  The ball obey'd some hell-born guide;
But Heaven, with interposing power,
  In pity turn'd the death aside.

Yet, as perchance one trembling tear
  Upon that thrilling bosom fell;
Which I, th' unconscious cause of fear,
  Extracted from its glistening cell:

Say, what dire penance can atone
  For such an outrage done to thee?
Arraign'd before thy beauty's throne,
  What punishment wilt thou decree?

Might I perform the judge's part,
  The sentence I should scarce deplore;
It only would restore a heart
  Which but belong'd to thee before.

The least atonement I can make
  Is to become no longer free;
Henceforth I breathe but for thy sake,
  Thou shalt be all in all to me.

But thou, perhaps, may'st now reject
  Such expiation of my guilt:
Come then, some other mode elect;
  Let it be death, or what thou wilt.

Choose then, relentless! and I swear
  Nought shall thy dread decree prevent;
Yet hold - one little word forbear!
  Let it be aught but banishment.

EVA BRAUN'S DREAM

- Lawrence Durrell

First come the Infantry in scented bodices,
Deployed, and after them the Birdwomen,
(The Ladies Air Arm) clad in shirts of male,
And riding gravid chargers shod with spurs.
In shrill capitulation like some endless wife.

After them in rumbling families
Symbolic engines only found in Jung,
Bombs polished on the lathe like eggs,
Grey mammary tanks, forceps and hooks with eyes,
Unbuttoned panzers, huge uncircumcised artillery,
Grave in procession rustle past the stand.

'One age, one land, one leader and one sex.'

IN THE HANDS OF THE ENEMY

- Vytautas Pliura

Their skin was ivory
The jungle was emerald
They kept me in a bamboo cage
I was given, quite mysteriously, a
  mahogany chair to sit in
A strange privilege

Because I was known to be gay
  they let me grow orchids in my cell
Orchids don't lust after much light
I also fed the monkeys and the peacocks
  and was let out to make rice paper at the
  blind woman's hut

Often
when a South Vietnamese prisoner was to be
  executed
that prisoner could request to humiliate a
  prisoner from the USA by making him give
  the condemned person
  oral sex

Mark and Willard both had jet black hair
  and did not impress the Montagnards
One mountain man traveled 250 kilometers to
  cut off some of my blonde ringlets to
  weave into dolls for his children

I, blue-eyed Central Illinois farm boy a
  little speck of purple-mountain-majesty among the
  hobbled rubber trees and the elf-like golden
  shimmering teak trees
  was led into a clearing

The prisoner to be shot was tied to a post, I could
  hear the women washing their clothes in the Red River
  singing lullabyes

Hands tied behind my back
I was lowered to my knees

One boy shot his semen down my throat as he lurched with bullets

Loins quivering
It took him ten minutes to die
It took them that long to free his fingers
from my hair

SCOTT

- Vytautas Pliura

I spoke to a very young boy in a bar
He said, "Wanna go to your place?"

We got in my Chevy, cherry red.
He looked like a movie star. Thick black hair. Like Matt Dillon.

"How old are you?" I said.
"Where do you live?" he said.
"Not far."
"My mother died today."
"I'm sorry."
"Look, the moon looks like a cheap earring. L.A. is cool, man."

The only thing I had in the house to drink was Tang.
When he took off his preppie cream-colored coat I noticed he had a tattoo of a dragon with one fang.

"Where's the bedroom?"
"Would you like some Tang?"
"Cool, man."

He turned on my radio to a station playing Bach.

He took off his pants.

He had a beautiful cock.
"Wanna fuck on the floor?" he said.
"I was hoping for more."
"Like what, man?"
"I guess I wanted to talk a little."

He took off his football jersey.

I noticed fresh razor cuts up and down both arms.

Still bleeding.

His chest was mutilated with cuts.
He had used a knife to cut a large heart on his chest.

"What happened to your arms?"

"My mother's death, you know,
I broke up with my boyfriend the other day, too.
A lot of things.
A zebra wouldn't eat outta my hand at the zoo,
  he was cool with everyone but me. I haven't had Tang for
  years, man.
They drank this in outer space."

We made love on the rug. Okay we fucked on the floor.

I discovered he'd mutilated his penis.

After his orgasm he trembled like a deer I once ran over on
  a Wisconsin highway, the beautiful tan buck lay there
  twitching and dying in a ditch with tiny antlers coming
  out of his head.

I gave him my jar of Tang.

It wasn't until after he left that I realized he'd cut
himself up to resemble the striped zebra that refused to
eat from his hand.

I realized that the scars he wore openly on the outside
I wore on the inside.

NEEDLE

- Kelvin Beliele

his strong muscles bulging,
my handsome nurse wears blinding white,
calloused hands with silky black hair -
his eyes nail me to this pillow

the syringe hard and erect,
spurting like an eternal cock
the sharp needle, brittle and certain
pierces my blue-veined arm

needle man fucks my muscle, deep and hard
I flinch, surging toward his heavy voice -
liquid fills me, calming my blood,
soothing this curséd fever - I breathe again

the needle withdraws,
a small spot of blood remains,
I lick the needle, tasting my salty blood -
my dick is full, throbbing

my nurse snaps the needle off - BIOHAZARD
he is sweaty, his breath shallow
a thick syrupy stain on his pants -
and drops the syringe into the hole

I sink into this lumpy, hostile mattress -
he smiles and our lips finally touch
the edge of my pain softens
allowing me to sleep - for now

KNIFE 'N' EASY

- Thaddeus Rutkowski

I have no patience for partners who refuse to seek higher levels of behavioral perversity and believe that, in so refusing, they represent the American female majority. I have no time for date mates who rely on their childhood piety as protection against the patently kinky. That is why I am looking for a *compadre* who wants me to put on a ski mask, break into her house, roust her from bed, take out a knife, slice off her pajamas, and rub the deadly point up and down her goose-bumped body.

When I creep from the bushes in my burglar outfit, reach for my pig-sticker and release the blade, I expect my girlfriend to be happy. When I cut through the elastic of her stays and garters after taping her to a chair and ransacking the place, I expect her to travel to ecstasy. When I trace complex patterns on her skin with my weapon after muffling her mouth with a sock and a stocking, I expect her demeanor to be relatively cheery. When I say, "Don't move a muscle, don't go for the phone, don't scream for help, and, above all, don't do anything involving stupidity," I expect her to follow my instructions to a T.

I know I belong to a demographic minority. I realize I've missed out on parochial theory, burned my option to seek comfort in family, and openly disregarded dating philosophy. But I see no reason to abandon my search for psycho-tragicomedy. I am ready to put on my Spandex cat suit, strap on my machete, pull the wool over my eyes, and play.

THE HITCHHIKER

- Lynne Savitt

lucite blue eyes
fox tattoo on his hip
sun spitting on him
turned his hair Velveeta yellow
his body bran-muffin brown

Always taking the curves
slow
I stop
to pick up
the hitchhiker

grinning erection in his faded jeans
gearshifting fingers
sweating the electric
love of other women

My nipples pen points
write on his chest
(I know there's a knife in his boot)

Back to an idle
in my empty car
I sometimes run
my fingers over the slit in the upholstery

Tell me if
you see the hitchhiker

lucite blue eyes
fox tattoo on his hip
indelible ink scrawled
across his chest

Boy with Jockstrap

CONVERSATION WITH MY RAPIST

- Barbara Hauk

When he sneaks around the corner
and enters through the open door,
I will look up and smile.

"Oh, you're here to read the meter," I'll say.

He doesn't answer but shows his knife.
His fly is open, his cock hard.

"If that's the way you want to be," I say,
"I have no way to defend myself.

"But, listen, don't you know it's not necessary?
I'm in the mood for a good fuck,
a quick and violent thing between a man and a woman."

He pauses, knife at my throat.
"Bitch," he growls at me.

"No, really," I say, a water-rolling duck,
"Your violence,
your wild sexy eyes,
your tense muscles,
I know just how lonely you feel,
I've felt that way myself.

"Come now - I like your eyes, they turn me on.
Put down the knife and let's go upstairs
where we can be comfortable."

I glow at him and he snarls but puts down the knife.

I put my arm around him, kiss his cheek softly.
"See," I say in sympathy, "Love is just a baby."

When we get upstairs, he doesn't rip off my pants,
he cries.

THREE FOR SCOTT TAYLOR

- Gavin Geoffrey Dillard

1.

He traveled as a
carny for a
freak show,

Then on his own
shoving razor blades in the
pee hole of his
killer cock;

Much too timid now to
try to use the
thing,

He kisses me in
bed and shows me his
scars.

2.

The hole in his dick is so
enlarged that an
average penis (mine)
can slide right in;

This is a magic I had
never dreamed.

3.

When he talks of suicide I
tremble and hide the razor
blades;

When he talks of love I
shiver and
sharpen the knives.

- Gavin Geoffrey Dillard

Would that he were Prometheus (well he
may be) shining god of fire,

bound on craggy Caucasus in
adamantine chain -

and I the scarlet eagle, sent down by wrathful
Zeus, to tear each immortal sinew -

bone to socket, socket to
bone -

this handsome deity who can never
die - his flesh forever

in my teeth.

AN ARRANGEMENT OF SKIN

- Walter Griffin

My Grandmother was a
taxidermist. She skinned
dead animals, slit their
bellies and stuffed them
with straw. I slept in the

room with them at seven;
their glass eyes looked
down on me every night after
the chain light was pulled. I
covered my face at first but

later grew used to their stare.
Sometimes, just before daylight,
I would wake and see them all
watching me: the alligators,
snakes, the mounted bass and

buck's head; the baby octopus
floating inside the mayonnaise jar.
Now, after all these years when
I am out on the road by the
fields, every scarecrow waves

in my headlights; and when I
stop at a motel by the Interstate,
I always dream of a stuffed and
mounted head hanging from the
ceiling, while the stranger from

the lounge sleeping next to me
does not know my eyes do not
close during the night, does
not feel the prickly straw
against her naked back.

from WATCHER IN THE SKY

- Harold Norse

Sebastian Rainbow had no choice. He spreadeagled
In the iconic position. Times were getting hard
For crucifixion addicts. The guy nearly tore him open
With his belaying pin. In the straw hut at the edge
Of town. But to Sebastian, who was used
To far greater pain and humiliation
It served merely as another trial to be patiently endured
On his way to the Watcher in the Sky.
On the bamboo wall hung a single picture

Whose eyes penetrated Rainbow's. No matter which way he
turned
The eyes followed. He lay with a straw-filled pillow
Under his midriff, looking up at the eyes and thorns,
admiringly.
Blood gushed from an open heart that seemed to palpitate
and throb
With every bang of the dong. Mesmerized by tongues
Of flame in the man's eyes, black pupils like nails hammered
into his brain,
The man's immensity filled the skies. Blue clouds hovered
Around long silky hair. White space spread
Like ocean waves. Infinite foam of space. He felt
Seized with immeasurable awe. It was Easter.

from THE BLACK MASS

- Aleister Crowley

I

Lord! on love's alter lies the sacrament.
O willing victim, eager to be slain,
Lusting to feel the knife, the life-veil rent,
Assumption energized by death! O fain
To feel the murderous ardour of the priest
Clutch at his throat, theurgic frenzy fly
About the initiates of the Paschal feast
And know it centered in the dim dead I
Loosed by the pang - even thus you know it is,
Even thus, when I invoke your harsh caress,
Put up my mouth to your immortal kiss,
Confess you for my lady and murderess -
In mine own life-blood I exult to float
Even as your white fangs fasten in my throat.

II

You stand away - to let your long lash curl
About this aching body, fiery rings
Of torture, o my hot enamoured girl
Whose passion rides me like a steed and stings.
Like to a wounded snake infuriated
With pain, you drive your reeking kisses home
Into my flesh, their poisonous frenzy mated
With this delirious anguish, bitter foam
Of storm on some innavigable sea.
Whip, whip me till I burn! Whip on! Whip on!
Is it not madness that you wake in me?
Is not this curse the devil's orison?
Ah, devil! devil! when you grip me and glare
Into mine eyes, and answer all the prayer!

III

A virgin with the lusts of Messaline,
A goat-soul in the body of a saint,
You writhe on me with cruel and epicene
Phrenzy and agony of acute restraint.
You ache - you burn - you dizzy me with blows -
You call me coward and eunuch, who say No.
Volcanic child! upon your masking snows
I will not raise my rod, that forth may flow
Torrents of blazing lava, that shall hiss
And roar, and ruin all the glad green world.
I like the attack of your seducing kiss,
The lashes of your love about me curled,
Better than slack delight and murmuring sigh -
Flowers by the road to sad satiety.

IV

Spit in my face! I love you. Clench your fists
And beat me! Still, I love you. Let your eyes
Like fiery opals or mad amethysts
Curse me! I love you. Let your anger rise
And with your teeth tear bleeding bits of flesh
Out of my body - kill me if you can!

I love you. I will have you fair and fresh,
A maenad maiden maddening for a man.
Ay! you shall weary in the erotic craving!
I'll have you panting - aching to the marrow -
Exhausted, but a maiden (Lesbia raving:
"Catullus brings a song and not a sparrow")
Famished with love, fed full with love, your soul
Still on the threshold of the unenvied goal.

V

The goal of love is gotten not of these
White-blooded fools that haste and marry and tire.
They grasp and break their bubble ecstasies;
We know desire the secret of desire.
We have the wisdom of the saints of old
Who know that what divinely is begun
Glows from dawn's grey to noon's deliberate gold
Darkens to crimson - and day's race is run.
For us the glamour of the dawn suborning,
We escape the enervating heat of noon:
We hear Astarte for Adonis mourning,
And close our lover's calendar at June.
Ah, Lola! but we suffer. Hell's own worm
Aches less than this, and hath an earlier term.

VI

You grind your tiny shoes into my face;
You roll upon the furs before the fire,
Smiting and cursing in the devil's race
Whose goal and prize is Unassuaged Desire.
You rub your naked body against mine:
You madden me by blows and bites and kisses;
You make me drunken with your stormy wine;
We swoon, we roll into unguessed abysses
Of torture and of bliss; we wake and yearn,
Doing violence on ourselves - anon we are slain,
Slain and reborn again to ache and burn:
Aeon on aeon thunders through our brain.
- At last you see, my maiden? Kiss me! Kiss!
There is no end - happy or not - to this!

VII

There is a respite - we must part anon.
  Short are the hours of sweetness: it is well.
  Could such a bout of murder carry on
  We should drink poison and awake in hell;
Or being but mortal, or nearly mortal, yield
  Exhausted spirit to the clamant flesh;
  The book of common love should be unsealed,
  And we be caught within the common mesh
That catches common folk. O God! bite hard!
  Smite down rebellious flesh with hideous pain!
  Bite hard! Smite hard! By bruises scarred and marred
  Love this exultant face! Again! Again!
O Lola! Lola! Lola! Kiss me, Kiss!
  Nay - nay! Kiss not! I cannot bear the bliss.

VIII

You are a devil gloating on the pain
  You suffer and I suffer; you laugh shrill
  Over the pangs of those pale fools, the twain
  Whom we deceive, whom we shall surely kill
Whispering a word of this. Ah! joy it is
  That false to faith is all the honied pressing;
  A traitor triumphs in each stolen kiss,
  Caligula and Cressida caressing.
You love yourself for stealing me away
  From the proud lovely wife; you love me more
  That in my arms a prostitute you lay,
  And to your troth-plight lover played the whore
When mouth to mouth we clung, and breath for breath
  Exchanged the royal accolade of death.

IX

I love you for your cruelty to them;
  I love you for your cruelty to me;
  I see their blood glittering a diadem
  Upon your dazzling brows; my blood I see
Sucked deep into your body, curling round
  Like fire in every artery and vein

Massed in your heart, colossal and profound.
I am mad for you to brand me with the stain
Of your own vice. Our souls, a murdering crew
Of itching Mullahs, wallow, dervish-drunk.
Love surges at the pang! Our poisonous dew
Of sweat and kisses blinds us. A mad monk
Kissing fanatically the cross that had
Devoured his vitals is not half as mad!

X

Ay! rub yourself, you big lascivious cat,
On the electric soft, the wanton fur!
Call upon Hera! You've a furious gnat
Worth any gadfly ever sent from her!
Call upon Aphrodite! she will send
No sparrows from her prudish Paphian home!
Call upon Artemis! She will not bend
To lift you from your seas of bitter foam!
Nay! wrap yourself and rub yourself in silk!
Drink of my blood, engorge my fruitless sperm!
For you were suckled on the poisonous milk
That betrays virgins to the deathless worm.
Are we not glad thereof? Kiss, Lola, kiss,
Comrade of mine in the uttermost abyss!

VERY PERSONAL AD

- Rane Arroyo

I want you if you are
a vampire. Blood
gusher here. Your man-on-

the-moon-teeth in my neck,
ok. Day job just
not important. Please don't

answer ad more than once
unless you're a vampire at last.
Brad Pitt not welcomed to

my erection. Morning beard
at midnight is good. Boy with
his own cape even better.

I'll shave you if you offer
fangs. Be discreet after you
leave me, after you wake up

with my blood in your bed.
Death is bisexual, straight men,
so take off my black clothes.

VAMPIRE SADIST OF SODOM

- Thaddeus Rutkowski

Like a true, nobly born, epileptic-orgasming sadist, I am not content to see my partner sweat or hear her squeal. Like a genuine, title-holding, grand mal-seizure ejaculator, I am not happy feeling the narrow warmth of her rectum ensleeving my penis. No, to get the full, decadent-aristocratic wad-shooting effect, I must see blood.

To start, I use the puncture method, with sewing needles and rubbing alcohol. When I see a trickle oozing from my partner's skin, I slide into God-given scrotal conniptions.

Needless to say, needles aren't all that's needed. What is required is a blowgun, through which I can shoot darts at my partner's buttocks. At the sight of a cluster of darts in her gluteal cushion, and the resulting red rivulets, my entitled bonal tip jumps.

But when someone has taken my blowgun away, the authorities are on my trail, and my cold-blooded mother-in-law is demanding imprisonment without trial, I resort to the kingly cane. After a few skin-breaking slices, my entire five-foot frame goes royally ape.

18th song

- ron androla

sputtering, back-firing, i bounce twice
turning into my driveway
i am dracula half-mist, half-cape with a key to the door
my casket home
neck of susan
turning to ask for a screwdriver
i did not order
i gazed upon with growl hunger
o to bite that, fully drinking

curtained from daylight, prone on my dry dirt
i evaporate
to susan's bedroom
her blood
sweet as midnight menstruation

MOON

- Allyson Shaw

When I reached her lips she said, blushing, It's my period.

He said my pussy looked like an alien. I know
I have every B-movie inside me, all the gore inverted. *Just my luck!*

I was as erect as a bare-footed friar,
and she was looking at my prick good-naturedly.
I have an upside-down doll, a red riding-
hood with a wolf under her skirt, *What big teeth she has -*

she plays with it prettily. My jaw stretches, then the bone
snaps and the skin is taffy.

At least I could amuse myself with her hanging
gardens. With or without the moon
I'll do it,

I opened her jacket and her breasts slipped into my waiting
hands - I count my thumbs,

Like the girl, they were freckled; I sit on my haunches,

I saw nothing
to reproach them for. I don't know, is there
blood in the corner of my mouth?

[Note: Italicized text is from Memoirs of a Young Rakehell *by Guillame Apollinaire, Paris 1959.]*

sang brulé à la mode

- Ruan Bone

'I'm strictly vegetarian
I only drink menstrual blood periodically
no one gets killed after all.
Let me take out your tampon with my teeth.'

'Will that be extra?'

'Yes only I'll pay you ducky
in monthly instalments
with my - do you accept Visa?'
'What do I taste like?'

'Anchovy fresh-flattened skunk and lemons
a cross between the fish market in Athens
and the cosmetics counter at JC Penney
alfalfa rubbed between finger and thumb
sweet tassled corn with a shade of boiled parsnip.'

'Parsnips stink like sweaty armpits.'

'I was going to have it for my afters
use it as a swizzle stick
infuse it for my tea
couple it with Cool Whip
Sang Brulé - the latest yuppie vampire's dessert
I can hardly wait for the clots on the second day...'

'Menopausal blood, hardly a romantic theme
filled with its quota
iron, oxygen and protein
edgy metallic as raw wine
sangue fresca petillant as vinho verde.'

'Your blood makes my blood boil
my hair twists into rrringlets
my toenails start to curl.'

'I know you only want me for my iron!'

'Throaty - coats your nostrils - musky
keep those witching day blues away-ay!'

'Strange bird, odd appetite!'
the raven flew away...

RITES

- Terry Wolverton

She used to like to take me to the graveyard, half-daring me to be afraid, but of course, I would never resist her, my dark-eyed Valkyrie, two years older than me. She was seventeen and I thought she owned the whole world, owned it and cast it aside, finding it beneath her standards.

Her name was Leah, and she lived on her own, no mother or father, apparently for years. Her body thin and angular, sharply jutting bones, planes you could cut yourself on. Maybe that's why she wasn't afraid of anything.

She used to pick me up at school, waiting on the street astride her black motorcycle just before sixth period. I had a class sixth period - History - but I wouldn't keep her waiting; I'd pass through those doors, leaving history behind, and settle myself on the seat in back of her, not daring to look left or right, not wanting to read the faces of my peers.

She didn't have any peers, didn't care what anyone thought. She used to like to take me to the graveyard; we'd sail past those iron gates like two dark birds mating in flight, plunge deep along the path beside the silent grave-stones.

After the first time, she always made me pick the site. I'd walk among the monuments while she leaned against the bike, watching. She never said anything, no matter what I chose, but I was always nervous, wanting to please her, wanting to make the right choice.

Springer, Myron 1917 - 1974.

Alicia Corland Dyson, Beloved Mother, b. 1932 - d. 1968.

Miller, Bradley 1971 - 1976.

Once I found a spot I'd sit down on the grassy rise of earth, nestling into a cushion of fresh flowers or a rustle of dried leaves. She'd strut over then and stand above me. I'd stare up at the sharp white corners of her collarbone, visible in the open triangle of her shirt. "Take your clothes off," she'd tell me, neither gently nor meanly, and she'd watch, carefully but without hunger, as I discarded my sweater, my plaid skirt, my loafers and knee socks. "Everything," she'd instruct me further, until I reluctantly yielded my bra and panties.

Then she'd have me stretch myself prone on top of the grave. I'd lie in the grass, feeling the wind over me, the earth beneath, and deeper still, the spirit in its house below the ground. I wondered what it thought, if it could think at all. I never saw what we did as desecration or sacrilege; she was the object of my worship then, and if she asked, it was mine to do.

Sometimes she would stretch out full beside me, and run her hands over every part of me until I gasped and wailed. Sometimes she would work me with her teeth, sharp, voracious. Sometimes she would not touch me at all, only talk to me about what she would do if she were to touch me, while I moaned and begged for her. One time she turned me over on my stomach and lay her whole body atop mine, thumping at my ass with the stiff denim of her crotch. "Come on, baby, fuck the corpse," her breath hissed in my ear, and I felt the taut embrace of bone.

At night, at home, alone in the white bathtub, far from the murmurs of my parents and the television downstairs in the living room, I used to love to search my body for the signs she left, the dark bruises on my hip, scratches on my thigh, teeth marks just above my breast. Neck-deep in steaming water, I'd remember the mound of the grave beneath me, her dark mystery spread above, the cloying scent of lilies overpowering me still.

LONELY UNDERTAKER THROWS DINNER PARTY FOR THREE CORPSES

- Susan Terris

A chignon for Mme. Eissler,
braided coronet for Mme. Halliday,
but his *pièce-de-résistance* was
corkscrew curls on Bibi Lemieux,
arranged to camouflage
bullet holes in her jaw. The party
was for Bibi who -
judging by fishnets, ragged nails,
brown-smudged bustier - hadn't
been someone's best-beloved.

Mmes. Halliday and Eissler
wore subtle make-up, but
Bibi warmed to Very Berry Red,
to Allspice, to beauty marks
above her lip and Brandied Peach
nails. When candelabra were
lit and Merlot pooled in crystal,
the undertaker draped Bibi
with lace, lay her on
his ottoman beside the others.

Lonely Undertaker, headlines
shrieked after policemen found
him. Puzzled by
their failure to comprehend
friendship, the undertaker lifted
his goblet, continued to murmer
reassuring words. "*Chérie*,
do not lose heart. God bless you.
Mon chou-chou - comme tu es
belle. Yes, yes - you are special..."

ANNABEL LEE

- Edgar Allen Poe

It was many and many a year ago,
    In a kingdom by the sea,
That a maiden there lived whom you may know
    By the name of Annabel Lee; -
And this maiden she lived with no other thought
    Than to love and be loved by me.

She was a child and *I* was a child,
    In this kingdom by the sea,
But we loved with a love that was more than love -
    I and my Annabel Lee -
With a love that the wingéd seraphs of Heaven
    Coveted her and me.

And this was the reason that, long ago,
    In this kingdom by the sea,
A wind blew out of a cloud by night
    Chilling my Annabel Lee;
So that her highborn kinsmen came
    And bore her away from me,
To shut her up in a sepulchre
    In this kingdom by the sea.

The angels, not half so happy in Heaven,
    Went envying her and me: -
Yes! that was the reason (as all men know,
    In this kingdom by the sea)
That the wind came out of a cloud, chilling
    And killing my Annabel Lee.

But our love it was stronger by far than the love
    Of those who were older than we -
    Of many far wiser than we -
And neither the angels in Heaven above
    Nor the demons down under the sea,

Can ever dissever my soul from the soul
  Of the beautiful Annabel Lee: -

For the moon never beams without bringing me dreams
  Of the beautiful Annabel Lee;
And the stars never rise but I see the bright eyes
  Of the beautiful Annabel Lee;
And so, all the night-tide, I lie down by the side
Of my darling, my darling, my life and my bride,
  In her sepulchre there by the sea -
  In her tomb by the side of the sea.

NECROPHILIA

- Aleister Crowley

Void of the ecstasies of Art
 It were in life to have lain by thee,
 And felt thy kisses rain on me,
And the hot beating of thy heart,

When thy warm sweat should leave me cold,
 And my worn soul find out no bliss
 In the obscenities I kiss,
And the things shameful that I hold.

My nostrils sniff the luxury
 Of flesh decaying, bowels torn
 Of festive worms, like Venus, born
Of entrails foaming like the sea.

Yea, thou art dead. Thy buttocks now
 Are swan-soft, and thou sweatest not;
 And hast a strange desire begot
In me, to lick thy bloody brow;

To gnaw thy hollow cheeks, and pull
  Thy lustful tongue from out its sheath;
  To wallow in the bowels of death,
And rip thy belly, and fill full

My hands with all putridities;
  To chew thy dainty testicles;
  To revel with the worms in Hell's
Delight in such obscenities;

To pour within thine heart the seed
  Mingled with poisonous discharge
  From a swollen gland, inflamed and large
With gonorrhoea's delicious breed;

To probe thy belly, and to drink
  The godless fluids, and the pool
  Of rank putrescence from the stool
Thy hanged corpse gave, whose luscious stink

Excites these songs sublime. The rod
  Gains new desire; dive, howl, cling, suck,
  Rave, shriek, and chew; excite the fuck,
Hold me, I come! I'm dead! My God!

ANDROGYNOUS KISS

- Tess Gallagher

It is not the sex washed out
but intensified past its difference -
the archangel Saint Michael painted
by Gentile de Fabriano with his wings
crossed to shelter his too omnipotent sex.
Or Joan of Arc in armor stroked
in a scald of black against red velvet
by Rubens, her burnished hair
flowing, the iron gloves laid by,
her hands bare, praying.

Where is that point of intersection
between holy and unholy? they asked of her
who was never unaccompanied
because she believed in her voices, even
when they changed her story: Margaret
of Antioch in holy simplicity tending sheep
as the Roman prefect sullenly rides by;
Saint Catherine of Alexandria, patron saint
of prisoners, tortured on the wheel, tended
then by angels.

Still the Maid's accounts were restrained,
unadorned by supernatural
ornament. Always to accept the miracle
but to refuse adoration. Kiss of
sacrament, kiss of private fervor,
friendless kiss of the virgin pledged
to God alone. Rarest kiss of innermost blood
and the arrow six inches deep between her neck
and shoulder. Under her, the duke's black horse,
deemed holy as her sword
which, as she said, "gave good blows
and good slashes."

AUTOPYROTECHNICS

- Kirby Congdon

As I sat cross-legged before the universe,
reeking of gasoline, soaked in the gorgeous fashion
of the times, my public cock, demanding and merciless,
reached proudly to my navel.

I hardly had a chance to see the match ignite
before heaven and earth were enflowered in my own
body's extravagant flame.

WILL'S SUICIDE, MAY 18th, 1976:

- Gavin Geoffrey Dillard

I could have raped him then
in that instant jumped,
would've fought to detain him
between trembling legs pumped,
then released him with seed
into calloused cold air,
toward the street
a vanishing flower of hair.

SHALLOW GRAVE

- MJ Arcangelini

Make mine a shallow grave,
and place my body there naked,
clothed in neither coffin
nor robe, but directly into the
earth where worms may have
their way as I would never permit
a man to have when I lived. And
in time, when these servants
of the soil are done,
dig up the bones.
Make from my skull a bowl,
fill it with wine and pass it
among my friends. Then carve
from the long shafts of femur,
fibula, humerous - flutes, that
I may sing again. And from other
bones make combs and handles
for brushes. Take fingers and
toes, carve beads and string them.
Then give all these things to
handsome young men that they
may hold me to their lips,
draw me through their hair,
and carry me resting against
the firm flesh of their chests -
never knowing what they hold,
never questioning why.

Pat and Sally

Family and Pets
dads, dugs and dogs

THOMAS

- Vytautas Pliura

I believe the hardest thing I ever did
was coping with the fact, growing up,
that I was in love with my brother

He was five years younger
and his shoulder blades changed from balsa wood airplane
wings into a ship's mast in the eighth grade year
Under each of his arms was the beginning of a robin's nest

He slept in his underpants, sheetless, the moon watching us
like a restless nun, in a bed a body's length away from me
His skin was ivory
His curly chestnut-colored hair slept on his forehead
He looked like the boy on the Grecian urn in my
textbook at school
He was my brother
I wanted to take him in my arms and make passionate
love to him

In the summer we baled hay together
We herded cattle together
We swam in the pond together
seeing who could hold their breath the longest
I drove him in town to the Piggly Wiggly so he could
buy his race car magazines
I drove him to the new Dairy Queen on the new highway
so he could buy a pineapple malt
We laughed at dirty jokes
He would take off his T-shirt as we sped down the back
roads
Central Illinois farms would whiz by us like a green-
colored Oz
His hard chest looked like butterscotch

Sweat glistened on his body like diamonds
I wanted to lick them off

I hated myself
I felt like a pervert
I felt like an assassin
I felt like a man moments away from the gallows
His eyes were as green as the pond on a bright, cloudless June afternoon

I watched his buttocks move in his jeans
I watched his square jaw eat the oatmeal I'd fix him in the morning
He was as beautiful as our walnut grove
He was as beautiful as Huckleberry Finn
He was as beautiful as a warm spring rain
He was as spunky as the wind that kept up our homemade kites
He was my brother

How do you tell your fourteen year old brother you want to kiss him on the mouth until the world ends and the angels rest in our maple trees

He looked up to me as a hero
I was president of the senior class
I was starring in the senior play
I had the 4th fastest two-mile in McLean county

I wanted to put my face on his chest and travel to a world as yet undiscovered by explorers
Perhaps his chest was the surface of the moon
There was a mystery in his taut little man-boy chest, butterscotch flavored, that would rival all the mysteries of Egypt
I had a dream that he, in a former life, had been sacrificed to a Pharaoh
I wanted to eat his soul

I wanted to...........

It was these feelings that pushed me toward suicide.

Nobody in their right mind falls in love with their younger brother.

I felt filthy
Rodent-like
I may as well have eaten the mud pies Thomas and I made after a violent spring shower, the rich Illinois loam soil as black as a moonless midnight

I rocked him in my arms for hours that first day my parents brought him home from the hospital

I was almost five

My brother
My brother
My brother
Rocking Rocking   Rocking   Until the end of the world

I felt I had given birth to him
He was as big as a football
He cried when I stopped rocking

Angels in the maple trees

He was a mystery
What was he going to become

If it had just been sexual desire I may have been able to cope and tuck it away in an appropriate coffin

But I was feverishly in love with him
I was obsessed with him like early man was obsessed with the sun

My body ached for him in the night
Our bodies as close to each other
as two soldiers who had killed each other in a trench
Toy soldiers papered our bedroom walls
The moon looked in through the shutters, blinking like a senile, old, ruby-eyed, judging nun

One night
I got up from my bed
and I stood over him
His face was crushed into his pillow
as vulnerable as a girl

I had to know what his buttocks felt like
I lay my hand on his thigh, through his underpants
like a museum guard reaching out for a statue
It lasted all of thirty seconds
He was made of elephant tusk.

I returned to my bed

The next afternoon my father called me into his room
"Last night did you touch your brother?"
It was the end of the world

Thomas had not been asleep
I was turned in
Like Nazi children turn in their parents
I tasted vomit in my mouth
My father smoked cigarette after cigarette
Shaking like a cocker spaniel that had been kicked, he
choked on his Old Golds
The end of the world was now
The angels watched from low branches of the maple trees
their wings beating as though they were underwater
"Yes, I did."
The angels looked at me sternly, also smoking
Old Gold cigarettes
nervously

My father suggested a psychiatrist
I was the golden boy turned into a slimy eel

My father was more jittery than angry
His hands missed his mouth several times in an attempt to
smoke his cigarette
He was wearing a beautiful three-piece suit
I never saw him in anything but a dark, three-piece suit

I think he slept in his three-piece suit
He was a surgeon
He could slice into people's brains
but he could not deal with his son

The angels languished in the maple trees, wearing three-piece suits, blowing smoke rings, double smoke rings that transformed themselves into Thomas' buttocks

A darkness overtook me
I walked around in a daze
Soon my mother would know
The angels were whispering among themselves
This was the end of the world
I was one of Columbus' sailors and my ship fell off the edge of the world
I felt I was falling through darkness so dark it was God
The angels watched uncaringly as I hurled down into Satan's jaws
Numb   A sinner falling through the hands of an angry God
Dead   A corpse on the shore of the Sea of Tranquility
Without hope
Exiled from Eden, I had touched the forbidden marble statue, flecked with topaz and gold
Mindreaders
They knew I wanted to drink the saliva of an angel

The night before I was to go to see the psychiatrist
I took a bottle of sleeping pills from my father's bathroom
I went to bed feeling dizzy and sick and happy, contented
I saw my brother stretched out on his bed like a mummy
He had pulled the covers up over himself tightly
That whole week he hadn't said two words to me
The apocalypse had arrived

All I thought was
"At least I don't have to spend another night lying next to him, lusting like a rabid dog.

This will be my last."

I wasn't the least bit afraid of dying.
I was relieved.
I was at peace.
I had eaten the entire bottle of pills as if they were M&M's.
I laid my head on my pillow, serene, thankful.
A delicious feeling crept over me like someone pouring bubble bath over me. Thomas' face floated by like a crystal ball.

I began to lift away like a child's balloon escaping from the child.
I was thankful that it was all over.

Then the pills began to pull at me like dragon's claws.
I remembered Thomas in his Casper the Friendly Ghost Halloween costume when he was ten.
He held out his trick-or-treat bag to me. We were swimming in the pond naked during an electrical storm. We were riding in the pickup, he threw his malt out the window. I was kissing him on the mouth in the barn. I was rocking him as a baby.

My baby brother.
My baby brother.

I woke up in the hospital with a tube down my nose that hurt like hell.
My stomach was being pumped.

Thomas had awakened my parents because I was vomiting in my sleep.

My father was very angry that I should "try such a stunt."
I told him that I was even angrier.
I told him I was angry to be alive.
I spit in his face.
He, the man dressed in the three-piece suit.
He, the god-like doctor.
He, sperm-maker of Thomas and me.
I watched the spit roll down his cheek.

Then I gagged on the hose in my nose.
The nurses soon turned into angels in three-piece suits smoking Old Gold cigarettes. The smell of maple leaves was everywhere.

Thomas came to visit me.

He stood there like the boy on the Grecian urn.
I was as cold as the stone urn he was made of. I did not speak to him.
I rang the nurse to remove him. "I love you," he said. He began to cry.
He tried to hug me.
I heaved him away. The intravenous needle broke in my arm.
The urn broke.
Shattered on the floor.
An orderly who looked like Rumpelstiltskin breezed in and swept up the fragile pieces. Outside the clouds rolled by like elephant kings.

I was taken away to a mental institution where I drew watercolors and occasionally saw a doctor who looked like President Garfield after he was shot.
There were three women who each thought they were Joan of Arc and continually fought with each other like alley cats, calling the others impostors.

I think Frances was the real Joan of Arc.
She did the most convincing recreation of being burned alive.

Occasionally we took a bus trip to go bowling.
Nothing more hilarious than a bunch of mental patients bowling.
Frances wore her rented bowling shoes home on purpose because they were more comfortable than her institution shoes.

I had shock treatments.

I did not recognize Thomas when I got home. I did not know my sisters or my mother or my father.

Now, these many years later, Thomas is a doctor, handsome as ever.
We are friends.
He hugs me a lot when I visit.
He has full-fledged robin's nests under his arms.

- Gavin Geoffrey Dillard

I remember my brother making a deal with me, that if I would let him do it to me, he would let me do it to him.

Well, I did. But he didn't.

That was thirty years ago. Now he's married, with kids, and I'm embarrassed to ask...

- Gavin Geoffrey Dillard

Frank's father used to take him out in the
barn and fuck him between
the cows
the cows grew up with complexes and
Frank went on to become a
child psychologist

And me,
I never got so much as a hand
shake from my dad.

THREE RHYMES FOR MY FATHER

- Gavin Geoffrey Dillard

1. Is sex with Dad always bad
or is it sometimes good?
When I think of all the sex I've had, it
wasn't half of what I could've.

2. When Mamma took me off the tit
I took rubber nips undaunted,
for after all, a tit's a tit -
'twas the breasts of Dad I wanted.

3. I sat upon his hairy thighs
and rode upon the pony -
little boys little boys don't fall down
who hold on Daddy's bonie.

NUDE FATHER IN A LAKE

- Robert Peters

I've never stopped, even in my sleep,
seeing him in the lake
facing me with his hands all wax
over his sex.   His throat
and his wrists are burned.
He is so white.
He splashes me with water.

I yank my baggy swim trunks off,
dive, and reach cold mud.
I hold a submerged branch.
His nudity no longer shimmers...
a dance... a fish... green cartilage
between his eyes... a hinged mouth.

I surface and watch dad
retrieve his clothes from a bush.
He keeps on walking, without asking
me, entices me to follow, from the rear.

pretend you're

- Carl Miller Daniels

pretend you're wyatt
8 yrs old
waiting to get
a beatin
waiting for dad to come
in and take off his
belt and beat ya
pretend that's the only
time dad really notices wyatt
at all, the only time
dad seems wholly 100%
emotionally involved
at all with 8-yr-old son wyatt
and wyatt sits there
waiting to get his beatin
wyatt's little dick is
a little hard and he is
feeling a little sick to
his stomach as if
there's somethin dead
inside it
and dad comes on
in and strips off
the big leather belt and
flails away at wyatt's
butt and the backs
of wyatt's legs

wyatt's little dick
doesn't stay hard
for the whole beatin
but it sure
tingles a while
afterward
his heart beatin crazy
fast and his stomach
feeling like there's
something dead
inside

ECONOMY LESSON

- Donna Hilbert

My father lay on his back,
me balanced on his feet
until I was miserable with dread.
Then he would thrust me into the air,
catching me with his hands
before I hit his chest.

Everything we did together had its cost.
He'd pay a nickle if I kissed his feet.
A raspberry kiss under my arm -
was worth a dime,
an Indian burn - a nickel,
Dutchman's rub - four *Little Abies*.

I kept my booty in a blue ceramic pig.
And, I never earned the quarter
for kissing his hairy armpit.

LOT'S REFRESHMENT

- GG *Belli*
translated by Harold Norse, Rome, 1955

So, already at Sodom and Gomorrah
Everyone was roasted and baked like mullet,
And from so many families in that horror
The only one that escaped was that of Lot.

Without ever taking a breath or pulling the reins
The Patriarch kept running the whole day:
But then, as it usually is, to his daughters there came
With dusk a fantasy to want to lay.

But because on that far border they were sunk,
Not even one cock with a spark of life,
They said: "Daddy is sexy!" and they got him drunk.

Then having thrown two glances at his dumdumdangle
Those randy sisters happily all night
Divided between themselves the bang-bang-bang-o.

[Translator's note: Dumdumdangle: *in the original,* dumpennente, *a portmanteau word Belli created from* dum pendebat *from the* Stabat Mater.*]*

DADDY

- *Michael Lassell*

Oh Daddy,
I'm far away and miss you
so much. The bogeyman is on the
prowl again, draped in last year's
judgment. Things go bump
in the cold sweaty night,
growl in the swelling neck and

sunken groin where men have danced
on points of pins
and Sabu rode his elephant
all the morning long in rain.

Kiss me quiet in the
moonless room. Tell me about
Heaven and how good boys turn
to angels when they die;
how you'll be there to meet me -
like that dream of disembarking
in the Land of Dead and
Grandpa's Airedale Mickey
lumbered up to lick my hand -
how you played hooky from school and
snuck off to Broadway to
steal a piece of Fanny Brice;
and how God loved his only son
so much He killed him.

Remember the time we went to
Radio City and saw
Ben Hur from the first and only
row? You ate popcorn and were
Charlton Heston with
your arm around my chair,
your shoulder straining on the
reins. I was happy as Haya
Harareet to ride your chariot
anywhere.

I dreamed I was crucified once
but felt nothing, was shot
as many times as St. Sebastian
but did not complain, was
hoisted by a hook around my
breastbone - eyes skyward like
a saint or martyr - but
it did not hurt. That's how
pain is in dreams: all concave
terror, but pain in life is

terror and agony too. No wonder
passion can have two meanings.

And God whispered:
This is my beloved son in whom I am well pleased.
And Jesus was so moved
he gladly gave his life
for a stranger.

Oh Daddy,
all I ever wanted was to
crawl into your arms, as firm
as hairless Samson's buttock cheeks.
Naked and enslaved, he grunts the
prison treadmill round, trapezius muscles
rising to the task. You bought me that
beefcake Bible for my confirmation
and it more or less confirmed
what you feared.
I was grateful for Samson's he-man flesh, for
Jesus' long untangled hair
and angels gentle as
bathing or Hedy Lamarr.

Oh Daddy,
wherever you are, I still want to
suck your chest hair, sink
into your skin like the
painless dream lashings of
a leather scourge, spread
tattoos across your stung trunk
like oil from Hedy's cruet
rubbed into the sore and
musk Semitic meat of Victor Mature
as John the Baptist - no!
that's not right (that was Rita
Hayworth dropping veils) -
as *Samson*, rather, pulling down
the temple by its columns,
loincloth stiff on glistening limbs
anointed by angry desire.

Secrets spill in the dark aisles
of theaters and churches
like blood from test tubes spreading
contagion. All I wanted was to
touch your cock that time
in the shower once when
I was small. Shame feels like
déjà vu these days, but still
I love a shower room full of
nude men dripping water through
marble swirls of hair.

Oh Daddy,
it was you all the time in those
backroom bars and bathhouse crannies
at four a.m.,
all those men who
filled me with the
Holy Spirit. I was
speaking in tongues. And when the
profane angel death comes
flapping down with winks and
wings akimbo, I will
recognize his sultry and
engendering breath, will
look into his bedroom eyes,
and see you there:
the dusky idol of my
'50s matinee,
strong and silent,
sullen as Gregory Peck's
lower lip lusting after
Bathsheba in a Technicolor dream.

DADDY'S LITTLE MAN

- Kelvin Beliele

My father lives in that part of town -
junkies by the plasma joint
hookers and skull-eyed thugs
smoky bars and porno shops -
an old wino with wet brain now
shuffling about his flop house room

Remembering all the times -
I quiver now just like then
in the cornfield, bathtub, bed

his overalls unbuttoned
pocket watch loud in my ear
whisky breath and dirty hands
his young hardness - pretty man! - in me
scared and excited I strove to please

Daddy loves his boy - don't it feel good?
sons should love their fathers
if you ever tell....

I still want him close and warm
all wrapped up in Daddy's love -
drunken sexy men to care for
just like Daddy

but now I offer only pity and lust -
I gave all my love to Daddy

CONFESSIONS OF AN IDIOT OLD MAN

- François Coppèe

Bless me, Father...
Young, at our county fairs,
I left the repetitious wheels of chance,
To seek the neighing darkness beyond the tents
Where the cart horses from their steaming loins
Thrust out those blood-choked, glistening tubes
Whose memory terrifies me still;...
And my mother,
Whose nightdress had a bitter smell,
Frayed at the hem and yellowed as a rotting fruit,
Would get to bed with such strange sounds...
...This daughter of the soil!...her full thigh,
Enormous loins...where damp linen caught in cracks
And gave me fevers that I never told...

More crude, but calmer, was the shame I felt
When my little sister, coming home from class,
Her muddy boots worn down by sharp ice,
Went out to piss, and watched the delicate urine spurt
Over the rosy lower fold of flesh!...
Father, forgive me!
...I dreamt of my father:
Card games late at night, exciting army-words;
A neighbor visiting - myself sent off to bed, watching...
A Father's a frightening thing! Imagining things...
Up on his knee: in his lap: my finger
Trembling to touch the front of his pants...Oh, God!
To feel the enormous stump, dark and hard,
My father had!
While his hard hand stroked me...

I cannot talk about the chamber pot, the things
That I caught sight of in the attic,
Almanacs and their red covers, and the rag basket,
The Bible, the toilets, and our maid,
The Holy Virgin and the crucifix...

Oh, no one ever
Was so much tormented, so thunderstruck by sin!

And to obtain a pardon...
Since these terrors of the flesh have slain my soul,
I confess to God and you my childhood crimes...

And now...Father, let me address the Lord!
                                        Why?
Why this stubborn puberty, this curse of
An insistent gland, too often listened to? Why,
Why this slow darkness creeping from my loins?
These swarming terrors overwhelming all my joy
Like some great black avalanche?
I was always paralyzed before it!
                                    ...to know what?

Contrition?
        Father, put back on
That purple stole.
              Oh, childhood!

                                    ...Let's jack each other
                                                  off!

DOMESTICITY

- Catullus
translated by Geoffrey Cook

What is Gellius doing?
    with his mother & his sister!
    massaging them naked all night long?
What is he doing to his uncle!
    not allowing him to perform his marriage duties?
Do you know how much karma Gellius is taking on?
So much that not even far-off Tethys
nor Oceanus, the father of the sea spirits
        could wash it away
for there isn't a worse crime
- not even if he could blow himself.

- Charles Olson

one night Ma
lay with Pa
and I was around

That changed Ma

one night Ma
lay with Pa
and I happened to

her eyes her teeth her tongue
out her nails clawing him
her hair all over
her look

That changed me

MY MOTHER MEMORY POEM

- Peter Orlovsky

My mothers very funney some times,
    when I was 17teen she told me
        she sucked my gigger when I was 3 months old
& sucked my dildo in frunt of my farther
& he got jelous she said & he told her to quit haveing fun.

I always loved that storey & tell it fast when ever I can
to sweet friendley girls.

JERKED OFF

- Peter Orlovsky

I rubbed my two comes all over my cat
& now she has something to do
under the belley, on the paw,
behind the ear
near the tail

- Gavin Geoffrey Dillard

I always stop to
stroke a fur or
kiss a fuzzy
face

Love is where you
make it

Often
sitting on walls

COITUS FELINUS

- Gavin Geoffrey Dillard

There are a multitude of ways to have sex with a cat.

Whenever I bathe, Samadhi, whose mother was pedigree Siamese, runs into the bathroom to play this game: I get my hands wet and stroke her madly against the bath rug until she's slick as a sea otter. She mews passionately, ecstatic tribbling sounds; when I stop she begins tonguing the water off herself until, dry, she sits up and asks for more - we do it again, ad infinitum, and rarely a day goes by that we don't indulge.

Mr Baggins is my alpha male. It is his prerogative to eat first and his duty to guard the catdoor. Exercise is rare and usually restricted to pursuit of the occasional marauder in the yard. Sex for Mr Baggins is the typical American variety. When the oil hits the skillet he is there and ready. The first morsel of pancake is always his, blown cool, avec butter but sans syrup. After six or seven pieces he is in my lap, a veritable harbor seal, clawing and pushing his heft into my thighs, drooling like an invalid. The cakes were good for him; good for me...

Marlene is into heavy confinement. Any box or bag will send her straight into the ethers. The smaller and titer the better, and even at thirteen years and after hip surgery she can hop in and out of an upright brown grocery sack without knocking it over. Her rustling will tell you: she needs no human now, no intruding hands, she is in her own world and she is happy.

Buddha resents the hell out of not being alpha male and only comes in when it's raining and such boundaries dissolve. He feathers my quilts with leaves and mud and we both work out the knots around the collar. If I get too rough with the comb he bites me and we wrestle until some equilibrium is achieved. He nibbles on my toes and I nibble his, the dank and fertile terrains of wet fur. We nap with tails twitching.

Sponge Muffin is my favorite and she knows it. When I nabbed her, among thousands of screaming urchins at the LA City Pound, the dyke guards all smiled knowingly. We were wondering who would get her, one of them spoke. A baby raccoon in plush calico, she has always caused heads to turn. No one can make love like Sponge. But she doesn't come easy. In fact she'll work you from one end of the fence to the other, always two steps away from your hands, a plaintive cry that warns of her wanton pent-up desires. But once in bed she is insatiable - especially after a wee cocktail of brewer's yeast - her mouth a river of exudate, claws and haunches in continual motion. I mount her like a panther and she coos beneath my belly, submissive but not resigned. In an instant she is off into the nite and I am left with but teethmarks and blood...

Kalika Mae and Miss Mousey join me then - sisters of a less exotic countenance - kneading the covers from both sides, until, wet with spilt passion, they bathe away the stars and settle in for a long and dreamless nite, we all purring.

- Gavin Geoffrey Dillard

My Buddha cat's so big
he can spoon me like a lover -
what dreams have I then,
this great furry beast,
his tongue in my ear...

WET DREAM

- Edward Field

Often in dreams I make love
with a dog or a horse.

In the middle of a kiss
animal mouth turns to lips

and everything works in harmony
to a perfect orgasm.

THE FAMILY DOG

- Edward Field

As the children grew up
they each passed through a phase
where they jerked off the old family dog
who tolerated them all happily,
wagging his tail.

A DOG FOR THE KINSEY STUDY

- Paul Mariah

"When I was seven
there was a neighborboy
who used to suck
off his dog;
then he started on boys,
me included."

TOUCHING YOU

- DS Lawson

I rest my head on your chest
And diddle with your privates.
You groan and roll onto your stomach.
I rub your back slowly.
"Nice dog," I say. "Nice dog."

GUY AND RITA DROPPED BY

- Fred Voss

Guy carried a derringer
that fired hollow bullets and fit inside his closed fist.
His girlfriend Rita had a 12-inch rubber dildo.
She was throwing it back and forth across my backyard,
training my dog Herman to fetch it.
Guy strutted about my house
laughing at me and insulting me,
as he drank beer after beer
and stomped the empty cans into my carpet.

Rita walked back inside my house
and opened up her jeans
and yanked out a pubic hair
and handed it to me
as I was backing away,
thinking about Guy's derringer.
Rita backed me against the wall
and unzipped my fly and pulled my cock out.

Guy fell back into my sofa.
Rita backed away from me
and climbed on top of Guy and opened Guy's pants.
Guy invited me to watch.

Herman came running in from my backyard
with Rita's dildo in his mouth.
Herman was breathing hard,
his eyes asking me to play fetch.

WITH DOG AND DAME - *An October Idyll*

- Aleister Crowley

The ways are golden with the leaves
  That Autumn blows about the air,
  The trees sing anthems of despair,
And my fair mistress binds the sheaves
Of yellow hair more loose, and weaves
  More subtly bars of song, that bear
  Bright children of love debonair,
And laughter lightly comes, and reaves
The garland from our sorrow's brow,
  Life rises up, is girt with song,
    Joy fills the cup, that flashes clear.
The year may fade in whispers now,
  Shadow and silence now may throng
    The seasons - we are happy here.

Autumn is on us as we lie
  In creamy clouds of latticed light
That hint at darkness, but descry
  A rosy flicker through the night,
My mistress, my great Dane, and I.

We linger in the dusk - her head
  Lolls on the pillow, and my eyes
Catch rapture, as upon the bed
  He licks her lazy lips, and tries
To tempt her tongue. My fires are fed.

Her heavy dropping breasts entice
  My teeth to jewel them with blood,
Her hand prepares the sacrifice
  She would desire of me, the flood
That wells from shrines of Paradise.

Her other hand is mischievous
  To bid the monster Dane grow mad,
His red-haw gaze grows mutinous,

Her eyes have lost the calm they had,
My body grows all amorous.

My tongue within her mouth excites
Her dirtiest lust, her vilest dream;
His greedy mouth her bosom bites;
He cannot hold, his eyeballs gleam;
He burns to consummate the rites.

I yield him place: his ravening teeth
Cling hard to her - he buries him
Insane and furious in the sheath
She opens for him - wide and dim
My mouth is amorous beneath.

Her lips devour me, and I rave
With pleasure to discern the love
They twain exert, my lips who lave
With double dew distilled above;
To dog and woman I'm a slave,

Nor move, though now essays the Dane
To cool his weapon in my mouth;
Her lust bestrides me, and is fain
To quench in his sweet sweat her drouth
Her finger probes my bowel again.

All three enjoy once more, and I
Am ready ever to renew
These bestial orgie-nights, whereby
Loose woman's love is spiced, as dew
On tender spray of spring doth lie.

Like the cold moon to earth and sun
My mistress lingers in eclipse,
We wake her passion, either one
Licking each pouting pair of lips
Till new sweet streams of nectar run.

'Tis Autumn, and the dying breeze
Murmers 'embrace'; the moon replies

'Embrace'; the soughing of the trees
  Calls us to linger loverwise,
And drain our passion to the lees.

'Tis Autumn. The belated dove
  Calls through the beeches, that bestir
Themselves to kiss the skies above,
  As I will kiss with him and her.
Leave us, sweet Autumn, to our love.

HUMANBOYCOME VS. ANIMALBOYCOME

- Antler

"Who wants the come of human boys that eat junkfood?
When you can have boycougarcome, boyottercome,
    boycoyotecome, boyhorsecome, boydolphincome,
When you can become a connoisseur of boychipmunkcome,
When you can jack off an adolescent elephant,
When you can persuade a boybluewhale
    to perform fellatio on his boybluewhale bestfriend
        in front of you in the moonlight.
Who wants the come of boys of the human kind
    who spend more time inside than out,
        who never strode a mountain or forest
    or slept out under the stars,
        when you can have boydeercome.
Ha, centuries of boymountaingoatcome
    ejaculated from pinnacle and precipice
        while Christianity, Judaism,
    Hinduism, Buddhism, Islam,
Have been oblivious of
    its beauty, reality, color, trajectory,
        taste, potency, cosmicity
    in girlmountaingoat velvet pussy!
Boymountaingoat semen for me!"

EVERYTHING IS DIFFERENT NOW

- Antler

Everything is different now,
Now that I know that octopus penises detach
    and wander alone through the Ocean
        seeking a mate,
So that right now, and throughout
    all human history,
        and millions of years before
    humans were even at
        the tree-shrew level,
Octopus penises wandered alone
    without eyes or ears or noses
        through vast vastnesses
            of Ocean
        searching for a lady-love.

GIANT PACIFIC OCTOPUS

- Edward Field

I live with a giant pacific octopus:
he settles himself down beside me on the couch in the
    evening.
With two arms he holds a book
that he reads with his single eye:
he wears a pair of glasses over it for reading.

Two more arms go walking over to the sideboard across the
room where the crackers and cheese spread he loves are,
and they send back endless canapés, like a conveyor belt.

While his mouth is drooling and chomping,
another arm comes over and gropes me lightly:
it is like a breeze on my balls, that sweet tentacle.

Other arms start slipping around my body under my clothes.
They wiggle right in, one around my waist,
and all over, and down the crack of my ass.

I am drawn into his midst where his hot mouth waits for
kisses and I kiss him and make him into a boy
as all giant pacific octopuses are really
when you take them into your arms.

All their arms fluttering around you
become everywhere sensations of pleasure.
So, his sweet eye looks at me and his little mouth kisses me
and I swear he has the body of a greek god,
my giant pacific octopus boychik.

So this was what was in store
when I first saw him in the aquarium
huddled miserably on the rock
ignoring the feast of live crabs
they put in his windowed swimming pool.

You take home a creature like that, who needs love,
who is a mess when you meet
but who can open up like a flower with petal arms waving
    around - a beauty -
and it is a total pleasure to have him around,
even collapsible as he is like a big toy,
for as long as he will stay, one night or a lifetime,
for as long as god will let you have him.

PORNO STUDIES

- Paul Weinman

We watched a sleepy classroom video
were languid witnesses of sucking
that silent, slow feeding process
of starfish easing onto so slow clam.
Wrapping those leathery arms
around bivalve hardness; that seam
with fleshly lips pressed tight.
But then, the hundreds of cups
tiny, pulsing suctions that pull, pull
then pop open that seam, moistness
seeping from the good flesh within.
And out comes that echinoid stomach.
Oozes down into that bivalve split
to digest, eat the sweetness within
as I start to breathe too hard.

BUTCH

- Jameson Currier

Dressage in Westchester
is supposed to be so elegant,
controlled.
Some people think, well,
it's so prissy, too.
But I was still surprised to find Otis
so pumped up with muscles,
more macho than his trainer.
Anne offered me a lesson and
I had to climb three steps just to
mount him.
Is it the same with girls and horses

as with boys and boys? I quizzed her,
wishing, of course, that Otis
could talk and date.
She laughed and led us into a canter
into the center of a rink of manicured dust.
Riding like a piston,
my jeans squeezed his chest,
hands clutched at his coarse black hair,
while sweat crept up through
the back of my T-shirt.
Up in the air that day
I felt ten years younger,
sexier,
and more handsome.
What a tonic
to feel gracefully so butch.

horse.

- Jules Mann

you can't sleep.

ride a horse
when you can't sleep.

little finger
slides the rein

squeeze
with thumb.

squeeze
with thigh.

think
of leg against

shoulder and press.
roll knees forward.

grip. bone
against wither.

ass against back.
inner thigh

wither. hips
roll.

knees a long
muscle.

pelvis and
bones.

grip. fingers
and leather.

move elbows in.
coax with shin.

knees to shoulder
calves and hair.

at the edge
of the meadow.

begin
to canter.

A DOE AT EVENING

- DH Lawrence

As I went through the marshes
a doe sprang out of the corn
and flashed up the hill-side
leaving her fawn.

On the sky-line
she moved round to watch,
she pricked a fine black blotch
on the sky.

I looked at her
and felt her watching;
I became a strange being.
Still, I had my right to be there with her.

Her nimble shadow trotting
along the sky-line, she
put back her fine, level-balanced head.
And I knew her.

Ah yes, being male, is not my head hard-balanced, antlered?
Are not my haunches light?
Has she not fled on the same wind with me?
Does not my fear cover her fear?

OVATION

- Deena Metzger

Yesterday the blood lined slit of the antelope
opened. He followed her logically
as the wolf follows his tongue to his balls
licking shit and mud from the winter fur,
in an orgy of pricks and nipples,
brazen as a baboon with emblazened ass.
If the grass parts, why not walk through it?
While our hands have the reluctant habit of fists,
we come to the trail with back pack, jerry cans of water,
too safe and therefore ill prepared,
neither on the road nor lost.
The passing birds are the gusts of wind
and the lizard knows more than we do about the sun.

In the Sinai dunes the winds blew
the shape of a bed under my buttocks
then the menstrual dawn announced the rut
in trumpets of tiger lilies across the sky.
At dusk, the red sea is red
and when the sea parts it is to be entered.
So my hair is silver! The gray wolf
licks his ass and dreams of the delicate
ellipses of blood. It's the season everywhere.
Get down on your hands and knees.

MOON IN TAURUS

- Deena Metzger

Across the barbed wire, the bull takes my hand. It is lost in his mouth, deeper, softer, warmer than I dare think. This is what it must be to sink into a large woman, to submit to her ample thighs. I am aware of boundaries, his teeth, used to grass, will not close on me, he wants the salt, wants me to sweat for him.

I have had to come east to learn this animal, a real not mythic beast, attended by dozens of heifers, who seeks me out under the horned, full moon. My hands, stained with mulberries, come clean on that great tongue slapping between my fingers, his tail flits across his back, his silken tassel quivers.

I have dreamed this animal but not his gentleness, not that I would herd with him, not that I would wish him to nudge my flanks, his skin slouched over bones, a tent of a beast, not that he would drive me forward

head down
hungry
through the
night fields.

AFTERNOON PILLOW

- Deena Metzger

Afternoon pillow between my legs, feathers grind another
dream from the back of the wild goose, the swan coming
down, that insistent visitation in clouds and thunder.

Who wouldn't fall on her knees, deaf to ordinary day, the footsteps of dust, the egg woman entering, who would listen for the car when she is lost in wings and chariots, the beak rising, talons clamped on her nipples, trying to learn the bird calls?

Once, the gift of two black swans, emerging from the water, twisting, one about the neck of the other, pink billed and trumpeting, then drowning again; and two rhinoceri, heaving, one great stone wheel rubbing for a millennium against the other, also the lion, opening the burning air of the great savannah with his tawny rod.

But here the woman locks the door against all blind witnesses to the churning air, the down feathers, the white squawks. She hunkers down in stealthy prayer, praising the single hand of god, the secret kingdom of the lonely afternoon.

- *Catullus*
translated by James Michie

Sparrow, my Lesbia's darling pet,
Her playmate whom she loves to let
Perch in her bosom and then tease
With tantalising fingertips,
Provoking angry little nips
(For my bright beauty seems to get
A kind of pleasure from these games,
Even relief, this being her way,
I think, of damping down the flames
Of passion), I wish I could play
Silly games with you, too, to ease
My worries and my miseries.

TRYST

- Kelvin Beliele

shimmering green feathers
tiny and fragile he descends
humming in my face
his beak shyly touches my lips
sticky syrup of soda pop
he hovers above my torso
his wings graze my nipples
as no human lips can

he lingers near my cock
his beak dipping to sip of a drop
of thick clear man nectar
then he is gone until next time
spirit brother sweet winged lover

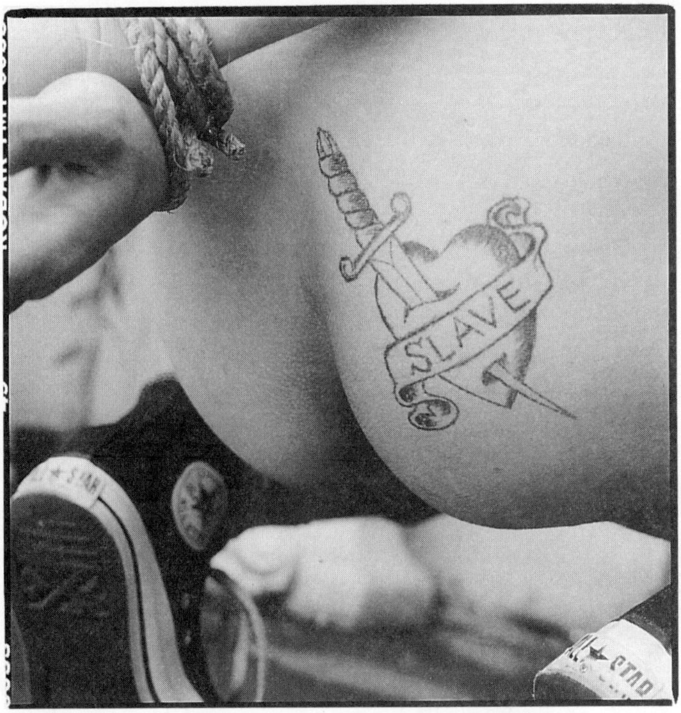

All-Star

Biographies

YOSANO AKIKO (Japanese: 1878-1942).

ANAKREON (Greek: c. 560 BC).

RON ANDROLA has been active in the underground press since the 70's, has been featured in *Chiron Review* and *Atom Mind*, in addition to some 40 book credits, his work appears widely in such magazines as *Poetry Motel*, *Impetus*, *Bogg*, etc. He's been married for 17 years.

ANTLER, from Milwaukee, author of *FACTORY* (City Lights), *LAST WORDS* (Ballantine) and *EVER-EXPANDING WILDERNESS*, has poems in over 80 anthologies including *GAY AND LESBIAN POETRY IN OUR TIME*, *EROS IN BOYSTOWN*, *THE BADBOY BOOK OF EROTIC POETRY*, *RECLAIMING THE HEARTLAND: Lesbian and Gay Voices from the Midwest* and *AMERICAN POETS SAY GOODBYE TO THE 20th CENTURY*.

MJ ARCANGELINI, born in 1952 in Pennsylvania, at age 11 awoke with pencil piercing his side and a poem in the bed - hasn't stopped writing since. Academically dismissed from Cleveland State in 1972, he rode the road until 1979, settling in Northern California where he writes, photogs and practices law without a license.

RANE ARROYO is author of *THE SINGING SHARK* (Bilingual Press) and other books of poems. His plays include *Prayers for a Go Go Boy*, *Buddha and the Señorita* and *Wet Dream With Cameo by Fidel Castro*. He is a Scorpio in and out of bed.

PIERRE CHARLES BAUDELAIRE (French: 1821-1867).

IF THE SHOE FITS, a collection of KELVIN BELIELE's short erotica has been published by Masquerade Books. His story "Strawberries and Cream" is included in *DOING IT FOR DADDY* (Alyson). Beliele and his lover Dennis Weber are the subject of a profile in *LESBIAN AND GAY MARRIAGE* (Temple University Press).

GG BELLI (Italian: 1791-1863).

ANNA BERGMAN is enrolled in the MA program at San Francisco State University. She has performed her work throughout the Bay Area and writes for *Cuir Underground*.

PAUL BLOOM lives in Oakland. He is the godfather of Hannah and Carly Maria, and the uncle of Mira.

LAUREL ANN BOGEN teaches poetry and performance for the UCLA Extension Writer's Program. She is author of nine collections of poetry and short fiction, the most recent, *THE LAST GIRL IN THE LAND OF THE BUTTERFLIES*, was published in 1996 by Red Wind Books.

RUAN BONE is originally from England where she edited *Lunch*, a literary gay magazine; she was the first person to interview Quentin Crisp and

David Hockney on their homosexuality. She's been writing poetry for seven years, is published in *Sierra Heritage, Kumquat Meringue, Sirens, Backspace* and *The Squaw Review.*

VICTOR BORSA was born in Saskatchewan, Canada in 1931. Began writing at age 16, published in various journals in Canada and US. His two books are *UNTANGLE THE WIND* (1967) and *A SEARCH FOR THE WILD* (Fiddlehead Poetry Books, New Brunswick, 1971).

GLORIA G BRAME has appeared in *Boulevard, Plum Review, Sparrow, Bad Henry Review, ELF, Cosmopolitan, Working Woman...* is co-author of *DIFFERENT LOVING: The World of Sexual Dominance and Submission* and founder of the first SM support and education group online on *Compuserve.* World Wide Web site *http://gloria-brame.com.*

JAMES BROUGHTON, poet/film-maker, has received two Guggenheims, two NEAs, plus lifetime achievement awards from National Poetry Association and American Film Institute. Most recent books are (his memoir) *COMING UNBUTTONED* (1993), *MAKING LIGHT OF IT* (1992), *THE ANDROGYNE JOURNAL* (1991) and *SPECIAL DELIVERIES* (1990). He lives in Port Townsend, Washington.

MICHELANGELO BUONARROTI (Italian: 1475-1564).

LORD BYRON (English: 1788-1824).

PAT CALIFIA is a widely published leatherdyke author who believes it is vital to celebrate our sexuality. Her most recently published work includes *PUBLIC SEX*, a collection of essays about sex radicalism, and *THE SECOND COMING*, a leatherdyke reader edited with Robin Sweeney. Her first collection of poetry, *DIESEL FUEL*, is in press with Masquerade Books.

MIKE CASTRO was Administrator for Community Arts of San Diego (1979-1982) where he helped co-ordinate California Poets-in-the-Schools programs for the San Diego area. He is copyeditor for *Caffeine Magazine* and staff member of Beyond Baroque Literary Arts Center.

GAIUS VALERIUS CATULLUS (Roman: 84? BC-54? BC).

CONSTANTINE CAVAFY (Greek: 1863-1933).

KIRBY CONGDON was born in 1924. His books include *IRON ARK, JUGGERNAUT, A KEY WEST REBUS, DREAM WORK* and *BLACK SUN.* He lives in Key West, Florida, with long-time spouse Ralph Simmons.

FRANÇOIS COPPÈE (French: contemporary of Rimbaud).

JIM CORY, a journalist, lives in downtown Philadelphia with his partner Dan Gardner and three cats. He is a 1994 Yaddo fellow. Chapbooks include *CROSSING THE STREET IN THE RAIN* (1982), *TENNESSEE WILLIAMS IS DEAD* (1987), *MACHO POET* (1987), *THOSE ROSES YOU SENT* (1992), *WIFE* (1993) and *THE REDHEADS* (1996).

JIM COUGHENOUR, born in Indiana, educated at Taylor, Andover-Newton and University of Chicago. Temporary office worker in San Francisco, creator of *Daimonix Raw Art Cards* and occasional author of minimal fictions, including *INSTANT NOIR: Savage Tales for Short Attentions*. His latest cultural productions may be viewed at http://www.daimonix.com.

JEFF CRANDALL (unknown).

ALEISTER CROWLEY (English: 1875-1947).

EMILIO CUBEIRO was born in New York City in 1947. He is a playwright, actor and performance artist.

JAMESON CURRIER is the author of *DANCING ON THE MOON: Short Stories about AIDS*, published by Viking Penguin, and the documentary film, *Living Proof: HIV and the Pursuit of Happiness*.

By his own description, CARL MILLER DANIELS is "a skinny, cold-hearted, mean-spirited 44-year-old ex-school teacher." His poetry has appeared in *Bouillabaisse*, *Chiron Review*, *Holy Titclamps*, *pLopLop*, *Slipstream*, *Rant* and *Wormwood Review*. Daniels resides in Prell, Virginia.

DAN DIAMOND (American: 1949-1996).

EMILY DICKINSON (American: 1830-1886).

GAVIN DILLARD is the author of seven or so volumes of poetry, one lengthy memoir, *IN THE FLESH*, co-editor (with Ian Young) of *RETURN OF THE MALE MUSE*, song-writer, artist, photographer and faded porn star. His new project is "the great San Francisco musical", *Bags*. He raises cats and orchids on Maui. His dharma name is *Sankara*.

DENISE DUHAMEL has recently appeared in *American Poetry Review*, *Ontario Review*, *Ploughshares*, *Partisan Review* and in the anthology *MONDO BARBIE*. She is the author of four full-length books: *KINKY* (Orchises Press, 1997), *GIRL SOLDIER* (Garden Street Press, 1996) *THE WOMAN WITH TWO VAGINAS* (Salmon Run, 1995) and *SMILE!* (Warm Springs Press, 1993).

LAWRENCE DURRELL (English: 1912-1990).

LORI FAULKNER. Previously published works can be found in *COMMON LIVES, LESBIAN LIVES*; *WE TALKED ABOUT BEING A WOMAN*; and *MY LOVER IS A WOMAN: Contemporary Lesbian Love Poems*. She lives on the shores of Puget Sound with Mike and Jasper Lily.

EDWARD FIELD's collected poems, *COUNTING MYSELF LUCKY*, was published by Black Sparrow Press. He is editor of the Alfred Chester Society Newsletter. He lives in Manhattan.

TESS GALLAGHER, poet, short-story writer, essayist. Books of poetry include *PORTABLE KISSES EXPANDED* (Capra, 1994), *INSTRUCTIONS TO THE DOUBLE* (Carnagie-Mellon, 1994), *MOON CROSSING BRIDGE* (Graywolf, 1992). A collection of short stories is forthcoming from Scribner, and essays are collected in *A CONCERT OF TENSES* (University of Michigan Press, 1986).

JOHN GILGUN is the author of *EVERYTHING THAT HAS BEEN SHALL BE AGAIN: The Reincarnation Fables of John Gilgun* (Bieler, 1981), *MUSIC I NEVER DREAMED OF* (Amethyst, 1989), *FROM THE INSIDE OUT* (Three-Phase, 1991), *THE DOOLEY POEMS* (Robin Price, 1991) and *YOUR BUDDY MISSES YOU* (Three-Phase, 1995).

ALLEN GINSBERG won widespread fame for his book *HOWL* (City Lights Press). His *COLLECTED POEMS* was just published by HarperCollins, along with a new volume, *COSMOPOLITAN GREETINGS*. He lives in Manhattan.

JOHN GIORNO, Buddhist, Warhol's first star, the originator of *Spoken Word* and *Performance Poetry*, as Giorno Poetry Systems has produced 40 LPs and CDs, numerous poetry videos, films, silk-screens and performances, started the *AIDS Treatment Project* in 1984. His most-recent book is *YOU GOT TO BURN TO SHINE*.

LISA GLATT's first book, *MONSTERS AND OTHER LOVERS*, was published by Pearl Editions in 1996. She has been awarded several residencies, including Yaddo, The MacDowell Colony, and Fundacion Valparaiso in Mojacar, Spain. She teaches at Cal State University, Long Beach, and in the UCLA Extension Writer's Program.

LYNN GOLDFARB, a "nice girl" from Connecticut, loves women, the guitar, poetry and dance. Educated at Stanford and Wesleyan universities, she recently published her first poem in Lesléa Newman's *MY LOVER IS A WOMAN*.

GARY GOUDE was born in a trailer across the street from Santa Anita racetrack, where he, his mom and sister, lived in poverty after dad ran off with a prostitute met at the track. Since his wife left him, five years ago, he has had sex with various fruits, vegetables and household appliances. His poems have appeared in many a mag & zine.

WALTER GRIFFIN's poems have appeared in *Poetry, The Paris Review, The Kenyan Review, Sewanee Review, the Southern Review, The New England Review, Harper's, The Atlantic* and *Evergreen Review*. His recent collection, *WESTERN FLYERS*, was the 1991 winner of the University of West Florida's "Panhandler Series."

MICHAEL HATHAWAY works as a supported living assistant for an organization that serves people with mental disabilities. He edits and publishes *Chiron Review*, a literary magazine he founded in 1982 with his mother, Jane. He lives in St John, Kansas, with his parents, brother, and 15 cats.

BARBARA HAUK is the author of one book of poetry, *CONFETTI* (Event Horizon Press, 1993) and co-editor of *Pearl* magazine. She lives in Huntington Beach, CA.

ELOISE KLEIN HEALY teaches at Antioch University, Los Angeles. She has published four books of poetry. The most recent, *ARTEMIS IN ECHO*

PARK (Firebrand Books) is also available in CD/audiotape.

ROBERT HERRICK (English: 1591-1674).

BERT HERRMAN is editor of *TRUST/The Handballing Newsletter*, author of *BEING;BEING HAPPY;BEING GAY* and author/publisher of *TRUST/The Hand Book*. He is publisher of Alamo Square Press, offering books and periodicals to serve the gay/lesbian community. He resides in the mountains of New Mexico.

DONNA HILBERT's short fiction collection *WOMEN WHO MAKE MONEY AND THE MEN WHO LOVE THEM* was published in England in July, 1994, winning the *Staple* First Edition competition. Her books of poetry include *DEEP RED*, *MANSIONS* and *FEATHERS AND DUST*, Event Horizon Press. She lives in Cerritos, CA.

TOM HOUSE is a poet and songwriter in Nashville. Recent work has appeared on an "insurgent country" CD by Bloodsport Records out of Chicago, and three poems just in *HOME WORKS*, an anthology of Tennessee writers (Bicentennial Project). He has had more than 600 poems in print and is cofounder/MC of The Working Stiff Jamboree.

JR KANGAS, a librarian and a musician, has had pieces in *New Letters*, *Poet & Critic*, *South Carolina Review*, *New York Quarterly*, *Bay Windows*, *Chiron Review*, *Evergreen Chronicles*, *RFD*, *Washout Review* and *Windless Orchard*. He hails from Flint, MI.

Born in Seoul, Korea, and raised in New Jersey, AMY KASHIWABARA is a recent graduate of UC Berkeley where she won the Academy of American Poets 1994 Competition. She has two book-length collections, *BUG* and *POCKET METEORS*, both by Cyborg Productions. She currently lives in Corte Madera, CA.

ELIZABETH KINCAID-EHLERS was born in 1933. Beginning at age fourteen, she worked. She also went to school constantly, married, tended four children, was divorced, changed careers. These days she makes her living as a psychotherapist. Whenever she can get away, she goes to her cabin on an island in the St Lawrence River.

RON KOERTGE's *NEW & SELECTED POEMS* is due from the University of Arkansas Press late in 1996. He is also the author of a series of award-winning novels for young adults. He will go anywhere in any weather to bet on a horse race.

STEVE KOWIT is the author of several volumes of poetry, the publisher of Gorilla Press, and is the translator of a collection of Pablo Neruda's political verse. He lives in San Diego and is on the faculty of The University of California at San Diego, San Diego City College, and San Diego State University. He founded the Animal Rights Coalition of California.

NORBERT KRAPF's nine poetry collections include *CIRCUS SONGS*, a collaboration with his late friend Alfred Van Loen, *SOMEWHERE IN SOUTHERN INDIANA*, and *BLUE-EYED GRASS: POEMS OF GERMANY*. He directs the CW Post Poetry Center of Long Island University.

ZDZISLAW KURLOWICZ (Canadian: unknown).

MIKHAIL KUZMIN (Russian: 1875-1936).

JACQUELINE LAPIDUS, born 1941 in New York City, spent more than 20 years abroad in Greece and France where she became active in international feminist groups. Her poems have appeared in numerous magazines; her books are *READY TO SURVIVE, STARTING OVER, ULTIMATE CONSPIRACY* and *YANTRAS OF WOMANLOVE* (with Tee Corinne).

MATTHEW S LaPIERRE lives in Portland, Maine. His work has appeared in *Chiron Review, Cokefish, Atom Mind, Midwest Quarterly, Parnassus* and others. He's worked a bunch of dumb jobs and now works in a bank, which isn't as bad as it sounds.

MICHAEL LASSELL is the author of many poems, some of which appear in books and magazines. His books include *POEMS FOR LOST AND UN-LOST BOYS, DECADE DANCE, THE HARD WAY, THE NAME OF LOVE,* and *EROS IN BOYSTOWN.*

DAVID LAURENTS is the editor of *WANDERLUST: Homoerotic Tales of Travel, SOUTHERN COMFORT, BADBOY BOOK OF EROTIC POETRY* and *HARD AT WORK* (all published by Badboy). His stories and poems have appeared in *Drummer, Torso, Mandate, First Hand, Steam, Gay Scotland, FLASHPOINT* (Richard Kasak Books) and other anthologies and magazines.

DH LAWRENCE (English: 1885-1930).

DS LAWSON teaches writing, literature and film studies at Lander University in South Carolina. His work has appeared in *Five Fingers Review, Bay Windows, RFD, Pivot, Widener Review, Backspace, The James White Review, Evergreen Chronicles, Wormwood Review,* and the anthology, *EX-LOVER, WEIRD SHIT.*

ALI LIEBEGOTT is a diner waitress in NYC. Her four chapbooks are: *THE DAZE OF MY LIFE, NO PINK BOWS, I NEVER PROMISED YOU AN OPIUM DEN* and *LIVE FROM THE ROTTEN APPLE.* Her work has appeared in: *Sinister Wisdom #55, The Haight Ashbury Literary Journal, BEYOND DEFINITION, TEN CALIFORNIA POETS...*

LYN LIFSHIN has published many books including *BLACK APPLES, KISS THE SKIN OFF, NOT MADE OF GLASS, MARILYN MONROE, BLUE TATTOO* and *COLD COMFORT* (Black Sparrow, 1997). She has edited four anthologies of women's writing, *ARIADNE'S THREAD, LIPS UNSEALED,* two editions of *Tangled Vines,* and is the subject of a documentary film, *Not Made of Glass.*

JEFFREY LILLY just completed his MA in Russian literature from San Francisco State, is a board member of The National Poetry Association, and co-editor of the AIDS anthology/literary-quilt, *ART MUGS THE REAPER.* He has produced a poetry music cassette entitled *Promised Land Poems.*

GERALD LOCKLIN has published over a thousand poems in periodicals such as *The Wormwood Review* and over seventy volumes of poetry, fiction and essays, most recently, *CHARLES BUKOWSKI: A Sure Bet*, essays, memoirs and poems from Water Row Books.

VIRGINIA LOVE LONG is an award-winning poet with 11 collections, including three collaborations with Rochelle Lynn Holt. Twice a Pulitzer nominee, she was recipient of the 1988 Oscar Arnold Young Award for the best volume by a NC poet for *SQUAW WINTER* (Kindred Spirit). In 1995, Chiron released her Wiccan exorcism, *SWEEPINGS*.

JULES MANN gets her inspiration by walking her handsome hunk of a golden retriever around the gay ghetto of Castro Street. Her poetry has been published in *Carbuncle*, *Jejune*, *Blind Date*, *Backspace*, *The Evergreen Chronicles*, *modern words* and *Exquisite Corpse*. She's a freelance wine consultant, desktop publisher, grantwriter and book designer.

PAUL MARIAH (American: 1937-1996).

CATFISH McDARIS is a New Mexican rapscallion desperado recently published in *Atom Mind*, *Chiron Review*, *Slipstream* and *Sivullinen* from Finland, and is contributing editor to *Latino Stuff Review* from Little Havana/Miami.

WHITMAN McGOWAN's most recent publication is *CONTENTS MAY HAVE SHIFTED* (Viridiana Publishing, San Francisco, 1994), a book of humorous poetry illustrated with cartoons by underground artist Momo. McGowan was nominated for a 1995 Pushcart Prize.

DAWN McGUIRE is a neurologist-poet with one published book, *SLEEPING IN AFRICA*, and is a member of the Squaw Valley Community of Writers. Her second manuscript, *NERVE*, is making the rounds.

LOUIS McKEE's poems have appeared in numerous journals. Wampeter Press published his book, *SCHUYLKILL COUNTY*, in 1982. *THE TRUE SPEED OF THINGS*, *SAFE WATER*, *NO MATTER* and *ORANGES* (chapbooks) have appeared since then. For years he edited *The Painted Bride Quarterly*. He was recently featured on NPR's *Morning Edition*.

DEENA METZGER's publishings include *WRITING FOR YOUR LIFE: A Guide and Companion to the Inner Worlds* (HarperSF), *WHAT DINAH THOUGHT* (Viking), *LOOKING FOR THE FACES OF GOD* and *A SABBATH AMONG THE RUINS* (Parallax Press), *THE WOMAN WHO SLEPT WITH MEN TO TAKE THE WAR OUT OF THEM* and the diary/novel *TREE* (Wingbow Press).

MICHAEL GREGG MICHAUD was born in a potato field in Readfield, Maine, and currently lives in the killing fields of Los Angeles, just seven miles from Keanu Reeves. His work has been widely anthologized in English speaking nations, and he once stole, and continues to wear, a pair of Matt Dillon's sneakers.

EDNA ST VINCENT MILLAY (American: 1892-1950).

EDMUND MILLER, Chairman of the English Department at a large university in New York, is the author of several books of poetry, including the legendary *FUCKING ANIMALS*. He is the author of scholarly books about 17th-century British literature, and is currently at work on a sonnet sequence about the go-go boys of New York.

THÉRÈSE MURDZA lives and writes in Rehoboth Beach, Delaware, where she works as a bookseller. Her poetry has been published in *Evergreen Chronicles*, *Cumberland Poetry Review*, *The Pearl* and *MY LOVER IS A WOMAN* (Ballantine Books, 1996).

HAROLD NORSE was born in New York City in 1916. His books include: *THE UNDERSEA MOUNTAIN*, *THE ROMAN SONNETS OF GG BELLI*, *THE DANCING BEASTS*, *KARMA CIRCUIT*, *HOTEL NIRVANA*, *SELECTED POEMS 1953-1973*, *CARNIVOROUS SAINT: Gay Poems 1941-1976* (Gay Sunshine Press, 1977) and his memoirs, *BASTARD ANGEL*. He lives in San Francisco.

TAVYA NYONG'O was born in Illinois and grew up in Michigan, Connecticut and Kenya. He graduated from Wesleyan University in 1995, and is currently studying in the United Kingdom. He has written for the gay press, and has had poems published in *modern words*, *Colorlife!* and *Friend's Journal*.

SCOTT O'HARA is rentable at your local video store in about twenty-six different skinflicks; he also founded and edited, for three years, the journal *Steam* ("the Literate Queer's Guide to Sex and Controversy"). His first books are *DO-IT-YOURSELF PISTON POLISHING (for Non-Mechanics)* and *AUTOPORNOGRAPHY*. He is available, but not marriageable.

CHARLES OLSON (American: 1910-1970).

PETER ORLOVSKY, born in 1933, was portrayed by Kerouac as hospital nurse/saint Simon Darlovsky among *DESOLATION ANGELS*. Books include *DEAR ALLEN: Ship will land Jan 23, 58* (Intrepid, 1971), *LEPERS CRY* (Phoenix, 1972), *CLEAN ASSHOLE POEMS & SMILING VEGETABLE SONGS* (City Lights, 1978) and (with Ginsberg) *STRAIGHT HEARTS' DELIGHT* (Gay Sunshine, 1989).

ORLANDO PARIS was the pseudonym for PAUL O WELLES, the author of numerous volumes from Greenleaf Classics, including *THE SHORT HAPPY SEX LIFE OF STUD SORRELL AND 69 OTHER FLIGHTS OF FANCY*, from which his poem was drawn.

GERRY GOMEZ PEARLBERG's writings have appeared in *Plazm*, *WOMEN ON WOMEN 3*, *The James White Review*, *modern words*, *Chelsea*, *Apalachee Quarterly*, *Global City Review*, and *Pucker Up*. She's edited *THE KEY TO EVERYTHING: Classic Lesbian Love Poems* and *THE ZENITH OF DESIRE: Contemporary Lesbian Poems About Sex*.

JAMIE PERRY (American: 1961-1993).

ROBERT PETERS, indefatigable poet, critic, playwright, actor, lives in Southern CA with his life-mate, poet and fiction-writer Paul Trachtenberg. Some books are: *LOVE POEMS FOR ROBERT MITCHUM*, *WHAT JOHN DILLINGER MEANT TO ME*, *LUDWIG*

OF BAVARIA, THE BLOOD COUNTESS, SNAPSHOTS FOR A SERIAL KILLER and *POEMS SELECTED AND NEW: 1967-1992*.

FELICE PICANO, author of fifteen books, which range from the best-selling thriller *THE LURE* to *THE NEW JOY OF GAY SEX* (written with Charles Silverstein) and his most recent, *LIKE PEOPLE IN HISTORY*. He lives in Los Angeles.

VYTAUTAS PLIURA grew up in a farm town in Southern Illinois and is first generation Lithuanian. He has a degree from UCLA in Motion Picture Production and worked as a screenwriter until discovering poetry. He has been published in *James White Review, Bay Windows, Evergreen Chronicles, Chiron Review* and *GENTS, BAD BOYS & BARBARIANS*.

EDGAR ALLAN POE (American: 1809-1849).

RHONDA C POYNTER has been published in 400 mags and journals and presently writes more for zines than slicks. She has had two beat chapbooks released in '96 and has a "rigid" book of poetry coming out in '97 in the UK. She has a little boy named Gannon Blue.

STAN RICE was for many years associated with San Francisco State University, as Professor of English and Creative Writing, Assistant Director of the Poetry Center, and Chairman of the Creative Writing Department. Books include *FEAR ITSELF, SINGING YET, BODY OF WORK, WHITEBOY* and *SOME LAMB*. He lives in New Orleans where he writes and paints.

ARTHUR RIMBAUD (French: 1854-1891).

ROBERT L RUCKER is a queer hermit who lives, writes poetry and fiction, and fishes for the big bass on a small island in a small river in Oregon. He is the author of two volumes of poetry, *LEX-I-CON* and *LIFE FLIGHT* by Trout Creek Press, 1996.

THADDEUS RUTKOWSKI's chapbook *SEX-FIEND MONOLOGUES* was published by Venom Press, 1994, New York. Previous chaps include *SUPER NATURE* (Power Trio Press), *DESPERATE MEASURES* (Pinched Nerves Press), *BEAUTIFUL YOUTH* (Talent House Press) and *NEAR WILDERNESS* (ABC No Rio Gallery). He was a featured reader in the New York Poets Live festival at the Literatur Werkstatt in Berlin.

LYNNE SAVITT's work speaks for itself. Her titles include *LUST IN 28 FLAVORS, EROS UNBOUND, NO APOLOGIES, PLUMP PASSIONS, DREAMS AS ERECT AS NIPPLES ON ICE, SLEEPING RETROSPECT OF DESIRE*. Her next books will be *THE BURIAL OF LONGING BENEATH THE BLUE NEON MOON*. Sex is her metaphor.

ALLYSON SHAW has been published in various literary reviews and has work forthcoming in *THE SANTA MONICA REVIEW, ERRANT BODIES*. Her work has been shown in video format on the PBS series, "*The Works*", which featured LA artists and writers. She currently teaches writing at Irvine Valley College.

SELENA ANNE SHEPHARD/ANDY PLUMB is a transgenderal poet

who lives, writes and makes videos in Marin, California.

SIMON SHEPPARD's work has been published in magazines as diverse as *The James White Review* and *Drummer*. Primarily a writer of cutting-edge porn, his smut can be found in books including *THE BADBOY BOOK OF EROTIC POETRY, BEST GAY EROTICA 1996, HAPPILY EVER AFTER: Erotic Fairy Tales for Men, RITUAL SEX* and *SWITCH HITTERS*.

LINDA SMUKLER is the author of two books of poetry: *NORMAL SEX* (Firebrand Books, 1994) and *HOME IN THREE DAYS. DON'T WASH.*, a multi-media project with accompanying CD-ROM (Hard Press, 1996). Her work has appeared in numerous journals and anthologies, and she is co-editor (with Susan Fox Rogers) of the forthcoming *PORTRAITS OF LOVE* (St Martin's Press, 1997).

BELINDA SUBRAMAN holds an MA from CA State U, has appeared in such journals as *Puerto del Sol, Social Justice* and *Yellow Silk*, edited and published *Gypsy* magazine from 1984 to 1994, is a martial artist, Middle-Eastern dancer and nursing student. Her papers are collected by the Center for Southwest Research at NMSU.

MUTSUO TAKAHASHI, friend of Yukio Mishima, is Japan's foremost gay poet. Books include *POEMS OF A PENISIST, A BUNCH OF KEYS* and *SLEEPING SINNING FALLING*, all three translated into English by Hiroaki Sato.

SUSAN TERRIS' recent works include *AUTHOR! AUTHOR!* and *NELL'S QUILT* (Farrar, Straus & Giroux) and *KILLING IN THE COMFORT ZONE* (Pudding House Press) and many journal publications including *Antioch Review, Calyx, Iowa Woman, Kansas Quarterly, Negative Capability, Poet & Critic, Poetry Northwest, Spoon River Poetry Review, Southern California Anthology* and *The Southern Poetry Review*.

CHERYL A TOWNSEND is the editor of *Impetus* magazine and publisher at Implosion Press. She founded The Impecunious Poetry Project and recently has opened a bookstore in Kent, OH, called "cat's Impetuous Books & stuff". Her own poetry has been read in *Paramour, Atom Mind, Erotic By Nature* and hundreds of periodicals and anthologies internationally.

TREBOR is the author of five chapbooks and has recently been published in *Eidos, Black Sheets* and *THE BADBOY BOOK OF EROTIC POETRY*. He is a regular at Wordfuck events in San Francisco and Los Angeles, and co-editor of *BEYOND DEFINITION: New Writing from Gay and Lesbian San Francisco* (Manic D Press).

PAUL VERLAINE (French: 1844-1896).

VIDYAPATI (Indian: 15th Century).

Published extensively internationally, FRED VOSS won the 1988 Wormwood Award, and in 1995 did a whistlestop reading tour of England to relaunch his first full length collection of poems, *GOODSTONE*, published in England by Bloodaxe Books and in the US by Event Horizon Press.

ELISSA WALD is a writer, dancer, and long-distance runner. Her first book, *MEETING THE MASTER*, a collection of erotic fiction, was released by Prowess Press in 1995. She lives in New York City and is working on a novel.

CHARLES WEBB's work has appeared or is forthcoming in *American Poetry Review, Iowa Review, Michigan Quarterly Review, Agni, Paris Review* and *THE BEST AMERICAN POETRY, 1995*. He edited *STAND UP POETRY: The Anthology* from The University Press, CSULB, and *GRAND PASSION: The Poetry of Los Angeles*.

PAUL WEINMAN is the Education Supervisor for the New York State Museum; won the 300th game '95 as modified-fast softball pitcher, archived by Suny-Buffalo.

KATHLEENE WEST has published seven books of poetry and fiction. Two books of poetry are in print: *WATER WITCHING* (Copper Canyon Press) and *THE FARMER'S DAUGHTER* (Sandhills Press). She is an Associate Professor at New Mexico State University and the Poetry Editor of *Puerto del Sol*.

WALT WHITMAN (American: 1819-1892).

DIANE WILLIAMS is a 38-year-old economy-sized black lesbian who is beginning to realize her potential as a writer and a woman. Her work has appeared in *B City, Chicago Outlines, Reclaiming the Heartland, The Country of Herself, West Side Stories, Puck, Chiron Review, Blacklines*... She teaches creative writing at the College of Lake County in Grayslake, IL.

San Francisco poet AD WINANS' poetry has appeared in over three hundred literary magazines and anthos worldwide. His collections include *NORTH BEACH POEMS, IN MEMORIAM* and *THIS LAND IS NOT MY LAND*. His book, *CHARLES BUKOWSKI/THE SECOND COMING YEARS*, was published in 1996 by Beat Scene Press.

TERRY WOLVERTON is the author of the poetry collection, *BLACK SLIP*. Her novel, *BAILEY'S BEADS*, will be published by Faber and Faber in 1996. She teaches creative writing and has edited several literary compilations, among them *INDIVISIBLE, HIS* and *HERS*. Terry lives in Los Angeles with her lover, artist Susan Silton.

IAN YOUNG is the author of *YEAR OF THE QUIET SUN, SOME GREEN MOTHS, COMMON-OR-GARDEN GODS* and *SEX MAGICK*, and has edited several anthologies of gay literature including *THE MALE MUSE*. His most recent titles are *THE STONEWALL EXPERIMENT: A Gay Psychohistory* and *THE AIDS CULT* (with John Lauritsen). He lives in Toronto with Wulf.

PERMISSIONS

Grateful acknowledgement is made for permission to reprint the following poems. All poems not acknowledged are printed courtesy the respective poets, when known, all copyrights remain with the authors. My sincere apologies to those poets unfound - if you exist, please send word:

"What can I put in..." by Yosano Akiko is from *RIVER OF STARS: Selected Poems of Yosano Akiko*, translated from the Japanese by Sam Hamill and Keiko Matsui Gibson to be published by Shambhala Publications, Spring 1997.

"Artemon once traveled in shadow" by Anakreon was first published in *THE INFINITE MOMENT* by Sam Hamill, copyright ©1991, 1992 by Sam Hamill. Reprinted by permission of New Directions Publishing Corp.

"18th song" is from *erie blues* (translucent tendency press) and is copyright ©1996 by ron androla. "as simple" is copyright ©1996 by ron androla.

"Everything is Different Now" was first printed in *Paramour* and is copyright ©1995 by Antler. "The Ultimate Pomposity", "Skullcups Vs. Boymouthcups", "Origami Vs. Origasmi" and "Humanboycome Vs. Animalboycome" are all copyright ©1996 by Antler.

Excerpts from "Ben's Whips", "Shallow Grave" and "Bicycle Seat Envy" are copyrighted ©1996 by MJ Arcangelini.

"Very Personal AD" is copyright ©1996 by Rane Arroyo.

"Tryst" was first published in *RFD #60* and is copyright ©1989 by Kelvin Beliele. "Daddy's Little Man" and "Needle" are copyright ©1996 by Kelvin Beliele.

"Convalescence" and "Pantoum: This time will end" are both copyright ©1996 by Anna E Bergman.

"Love Poem #9" is copyright ©1996 by Paul Bloom.

"Love of Shoe" is from *THE PROJECTS* (Illuminati) and is copyright ©1987 by Laurel Ann Bogen. "Pirates" is from *THE BURNING: New and Selected Poems 1970-1990* (Red Wind Books) and is copyright ©1991 by Laurel Ann Bogen.

"Sang brulé à la mode", "Current Attraction" and "Love Satisfied" are from *LOUD NIPPLES* (Chi Chi Press, 1994) by Ruan Bone and are copyright ©1994 by Ruan Bone.

"The Feel of Teeth" and "Transvestia" by Victor Borsa are from *A SEARCH FOR THE WILD* (Fiddlehead Books, 1971) and are copyright ©1971 by Victor Borsa.

"The Rape" was previously published in *Sparrow*, and is copyright ©1995 by Gloria G Brame. "The Bath" and "Bruises" are both copyright ©1996 by Gloria G Brame.

"The Odors of God" was first published in *GRAFFITI FOR THE JOHNS OF HEAVEN* by James Broughton (Syzygy Press, 1982) and is copyright ©1982 by James Broughton.

The poems of Michelangelo Buonarroti, translated by Sidney Alexander, are from *THE COMPLETE POETRY OF MICHELANGELO*, Ohio Press, and are copyright ©1991 by Sidney Alexander.

"Handmade" was first published in *THE ZENITH OF DESIRE* (Crown, 1996) and is copyright ©1995 by Pat Califia. "Street Theatre" and "The House Boy's First Day" are both copyright ©1996 by Pat Califia.

"Piranesi's Last Supper" is copyright ©1996 by Mike Castro.

"Jagganath" is from *BLACK SUN* (Pilot Press, 1973), "Horse Opera" and "Motorcyclist" are from *JUGGERNAUT* (Interim Books, 1966), and are copyright ©1966 by Kirby Congdon. "Daredevil", "Motorcyclists", "Motorcycle Social Club", "Autopyrotechnics" are copyright ©1970 by Kirby Congdon. "Package" is copyright ©1995 by Kirby Congdon.

"Feet" is from *FEET* and is copyright ©1995 by Jim Cory.

"Sentence D'Amour" and "Mama" are copyright ©1993 Jim Coughenour

"Conversation Over Dinner" appeared in *Northwest Gay and Lesbian Reader* and is copyright ©1992 by Jeff Crandall.

"Yes, I'm Living on" was first published in *ANGELS OF THE LYRE* (Gay Sunshine Press) and is copyright ©1975 by Emelio Cubeiro.

"Peter" is copyright ©1995 and "Butch" is copyright 1996 by Jameson Currier.

"timmy" will first appear in *Chiron Review*, 1996, and is copyright ©1996 by Carl Miller Daniels. "pretend you're" is copyright ©1996 by Carl Miller Daniels.
"Constructive Instructions" is copyright ©1996 by Dan Diamond.
"My Heart upon a little Plate..." is from *THE COMPLETE POEMS OF EMILY DICKINSON*, Back Bay Books, and is copyright ©1960 by Mary L Hampson.
"from NOTES FROM A MARRIAGE" and "He peed on my" are from *NOTES FROM A MARRIAGE* by Gavin Dillard (Sea Horse, 1983) and are copyright ©1983 by GAVCO.
"Will's Suicide" is from *PAGAN LOVE SONGS* (Bhakti Books, 1987) and is copyright © 1987 by GAVCO. "501" was first published in *Frontiers* and is copyright ©1991 by GAVCO.
"His bad breath...", "Three for Scott Taylor", "I remember my brother...", "Yellow Snow", "He could work in any..." and "A sucker for a hairy ass..." are all from *YELLOW SNOW* by Gavin Dillard (Bhakti Books, 1993) and are copyright ©1993 by GAVCO. "Flying to Santa Barbara...", "My Buddha cat's...", "It's Been a Long Time Since I've Lived with a Straight Boy", "I bathe, he showers...", "Three Rhymes for my Father", "Coitus Felinus", "With your fist...", "Courting Rodney", "Alexander Peeing", "Drinking Trebor's Pee", "Would it be rude to..." and "Would that he were Prometheus..." are all copyright ©1996 by GAVCO.
"Kinky" first appeared in *MONDO BARBIE* and is copyright ©1993 by Denise Duhamel.
"First of the Motorcycle Poems" and "Second of the Motorcycle Poems" are reprinted from *MY LOVER IS A WOMAN* (Ballantine Books, 1996, Edited by Lesléa Newman) and are copyright ©1988 and 1996 by Lori Faulkner.
"Sweet Gwendolyn and the Countess" and "Giant Pacific Octopus" are copyright ©1992 by Edward Field. Reprinted from *COUNTING MYSELF LUCKY: Selected Poems 1963-1992* with the permission of Black Sparrow Press. "Street Instructions", "Wet Dream", "The Family Dog" and "Satyagraha" are copyright ©1996 by Edward Field.
"Androgynous Kiss" is copyright ©1992 by Tess Gallagher. Reprinted from *PORTABLE KISSES* by Tess Gallagher, Capra Press, 1992, by permission of the author.
"Beau Blows Himself" is copyright 1996 by John Gilgun.
"The Night-Apple", "Please Master", "C'mon Jack" are from *COLLECTED POEMS 1947-1980*, Harper & Row, and are copyright © 1984 by Allen Ginsberg.
"I sat on his face..." is from *CANCER IN MY LEFT BALL* and is copyright ©1973 by John Giorno, "I'm giving it to you..." copyright ©1979 by John Giorno, "Hi Risque" is copyright ©1990 by John Giorno. "I'm giving it to you..." and "Hi Risque" first appeared in *YOU GOT TO BURN TO SHINE* (Serpent's Tail Press, 1994).
"Hungry" was first published in *A NEW GEOGRAPHY OF POETS*, copyright ©1992 by Edward Field, Gerald Locklin and Charles Stetler, and is in *MONSTERS AND OTHER LOVERS* (Pearl Editions) and is copyright ©1996 by Lisa Glatt.
"Poem with an Attitude" was published in *MY LOVER IS A WOMAN*, edited by Lesléa Newman (Ballantine, 1996) and is copyright ©1994 by Lynn Goldfarb.
"You're My Rock" is from *A CRUSHED, ROTTING DOG* by Gary Goude (Fine Human Wreckage Press, 1995) and is copyright ©1995 by Gary Goude.
"The Arrangement of Skin" has been published in the *North Dakota Quarterly* and is copyright ©1996 by Walter Griffin.
"me & ratboy run the gamut..." is copyright ©1996 by Michael Hathaway. "i'm not a punching bag but..." is from *RATBOY, ETC.* (Kings Estate Press, 1994) and is copyright ©1994 by Michael Hathaway.
"Baldness Abolishes Comfort and Creates Anxiety" first published in *Nausea*, copyright ©1975 by Barbara Hauk; "Conversation With My Rapist" published in *Format*, copyright ©1978 by Barbara Hauk.
"Changing the Oil" is from *ARTEMIS IN ECHO PARK* by Eloise Klein Healy, Firebrand Books, and is copyright ©1991 by Eloise Klein Healy.
"Polish the gemstones..." is from *TRUST/The Hand Book*, by Bert Herrman, 1991, Alamo Square Press, and is copyright ©1991 by Bert Herrman.
"Economy Lesson" is from *DEEP RED*, Event Horizon Press, and is copyright ©1993 by Donna Hilbert.
"The Safe-sex Cell.", "Laurie's Transexual Fantasy." and "The Professional Psycho-Drama." are all copyright ©1996 by Tom House.

"Breath of Eden" was first published in *Windless Orchard* and is copyright ©1995 by JR Kangas.
"Grapes" and "A Fine Wine" are from *BUG* (Cyborg Productions) and are copyright ©1993 by Amy Kashiwabara.
"Kinky Rubs Plums" is copyright ©1996 by Elizabeth Kincaid-Ehlers.
"Dildo" is copyright ©1996 by Ron Koertge.
"It was brutal. A country boy..." and "Daughter, when you frisk..." are both from *PASSIONATE JOURNEY* (City Miner, 1984) and are copyright ©1984 by Steve Kowit.
"from Circus Songs" was originally published in *CIRCUS SONGS*, Floating Island Publications, copyright ©1984 by Norbert Krapf. "Strawberry Harvest" is copyright ©1996 by Norbert Krapf.
"The Slaves Promise" is from *THE MALE MUSE* and is copyright ©1973 by Zdzislaw Kurlowicz.
"You look divine in drag..." copyright ©1985 by Jacqueline Lapidus, first published in *MY LOVER IS A WOMAN* (ed. Lesléa Newman).
"Black Bra" is copyright ©1996 by Matt LaPierre.
"I want my dick sucked" was first published in *Drummer* and is copyright ©1996 Michael Lassell. "Dancer(s) with Dick(s) at the 1 Saloon" first published in *EROS IN BOYSTOWN* (Crown, 1996 - ed. by Michael Lassell) and is copyright ©1996 by Michael Lassell. "Daddy" first published in *DECADE DANCE* (Alyson, 1990) by Michael Lassell and is copyright ©1990 by Michael Lassell. "Personal foibles #2" is copyright ©1996 by Michael Lassell.
"Arse Poetica" and "The Autofellator" are copyright ©1996 by David Laurents.
"Abrasions on the Body" and "Touching You" are copyright ©1996 by DS Lawson.
"On Being Fucked By a Talk-Show Panelist" is copyright ©1996 by Ali Liebegott.
"Whips at the Ritz" and "Mad Girl is Sick of Pouring..." are copyright ©1996 by Lyn Lifshin.
"Marilyn" is copyright ©1996 by Jeffrey Lilly.
"clothes make the woman" was first published in *Sierra Madre Review* and is copyright ©1985 by Gerald Locklin.
"O Does Cobb's Creek" is copyright ©1996 by Virginia Love Long.
"Fixing the Bracelet" and "late" are from *LOUD NIPPLES* by Jules Mann (Chi Chi Press, 1994) and are copyright ©1994 Chi Chi Press. "horse", "private OBsession" and "when I take it into my mouth" are copyright ©1996 by Jules Mann.
"High Ho Silver" and "pierced pandemonium" are copyright ©1996 by Catfish McDaris.
"A Couple More Poetic Feet" and "Anonymous Sex Dream" are copyright ©1996 by Whitman McGowan.
"Mindbody/Bodymind" is copyright ©1996 by Dawn McGuire.
"What Money Can Buy" was first published in *pinchpenny* and is copyright ©1985 by Louis McKee.
"Sunday, August 1st, 1977" is excerpted from *TREE* by Deena Metzger (Wingbow Press, 1983) and is copyright ©1978 by Deena Metzger. "Moon in Taurus" is from *A SABBATH AMONG THE RUINS* (Parallax Press, 1992) and is copyright ©1992 by Deena Metzger. "Raspberries", "Afternoon Pillow", "Ovation" are copyright ©1996 by Deena Metzger.
"July 15, 1974", "July 30, 1974", "August 8, 1974", "The Night Keanu Reeves Kicked Me In the Face" and "The Night Joe Dallesandro Puked On Me" are all copyright ©1996 by Michael Gregg Michaud.
Both "Most Valuable Rookie" and "Oh, To Keep Beauty Back From Vanishing Away" are from *FUCKING ANIMALS* by Edmund Miller, Florida Literary Association and STARBooks, and are copyright ©1994 by Edmund Miller.
"eating szechuan eggplant" was previously published in *MY LOVER IS A WOMAN*, edited by Lesléa Newman (Ballantine, 1996) and is copyright ©1993 Thérèse Murdza. "I'd venture to say that, yes" is copyright ©1996 by Thérèse Murdza.
"Popess Joan" and "Lot's Refreshment" by GG Belli, translated by Harold Norse, are from *THE ROMAN SONNETS OF GG BELLI* and are copyright ©1960 by Harold Norse. "Auto Fellatio", "Survivor", "Harley-Davidson", and "Sonnet to the Asshole" (by Verlaine/Rimbaud, translated by Norse) are from *CARNIVOROUS SAINT* (Gay Sunshine) and are copyright ©1977 by Harold Norse. "Eric Heiden's Thighs" and "from Watcher in the Sky" are from

THE LOVE POEMS (Crossing Press) and are copyright ©1986 by Harold Norse. "Big Thick Dick" and "A Nice Young Man" are copyright ©1996 by Harold Norse.
"Drag" was first published in *modern words* and is copyright ©1994 by Tavya Nyong'o.
"Straps" is copyright ©1996 by 1996.
"Venice Beach: Memorial Day" was first printed in *THE BADBOY BOOK OF EROTIC POETRY* and is copyright ©1995 by Scott O'Hara. "Saying Yes" is copyright ©1996 by Scott O'Hara.
"My Mother Memory Poem" and "Jerked Off" are both from *CLEAN ASSHOLE POEMS AND SMILING VEGETABLE SONGS* by Peter Orlovsky (City Lights Books, 1978) and are copyright ©1978 by Peter Orlovsky.
"My Hero" is from *THE SHORT HAPPY SEX LIFE OF STUD SORRELL AND 69 OTHER FLIGHTS OF FANCY* (Greenleaf Classics) and is copyright ©1996 by Orlando Paris.
"My College Sex Group" is from *ORIGINAL LOVE: Poems by Molly Peacock*. Copyright ©1995 by Molly Peacock. Reprinted by permission of WW Norton & Company, Inc.
"Viewings I" was first published in *THE ARC OF LOVE* (edited by Clare M Coss, Scribner) and is copyright ©1996 by Gerry Gomez Pearlberg. "Shave" and "Happy Birthday Baby" first appeared in *modern words*, and are copyright ©1996 by Gerry Gomez Pearlberg. "The Marriage of Heaven y Hielo" is copyright ©1996 by Gerry Gomez Pearlberg.
"Nude Father in a Lake" is from *WHAT DILLINGER MEANT TO ME* by Robert Peters (Sea Horse Press, 1983) and is copyright ©1983 by Robert Peters. "Essence of Mitchum", "Mitchum's Navel", "Testicles" and "The Mitchum Tomato" are from *LOVE POEMS FOR ROBERT MITCHUM* by Robert Peters (Chiron Review Press, 1992) and are copyright ©1992 by Robert Peters. "Closeup" is from *SNAPSHOTS FOR A SERIAL KILLER* by Robert Peters (GLB Publishers, 1992) and is copyright ©1992 by Robert Peters.
"The Deformity Lover" was first published in *Gay Sunshine* (1977) and "Aches-les-Bains" was first published in *Mouth of the Dragon* (1975). Both are from *THE DEFORMITY LOVER and Other Poems* by Felice Picano (Sea Horse Press, 1978) and are copyright ©1978 by Felice Picano.
"In the Hands of the Enemy" was first published in *GENTS, BADBOYS & BARBARIANS* (editor Rudy Kikel, Alyson Press, 1993) and is copyright ©1993 by Vytautas Pliura. "Scott" is from *SKATING ON THE DARK SIDE OF THE MOON* (Alpha Beat Press, 1995) by Vytautas Pliura and is copyright ©1995 by Vytautas Pliura. "Thomas" was first published in *Chiron Review* and is copyright 1995 by Vytautas Pliura. "Eat Your Sperm" is copyright ©1996 by Vytautas Pliura.
"the prophecy" is copyright ©1996 by Rhonda C Poynter.
"The Catalog Goddesses" is from *FEAR ITSELF* (Knopf, 1995) by Stan Rice and is copyright ©1995 by Stan Rice. "Lust" is copyright ©1996 by Stan Rice.
"Prayer" was published in 1993 by *RFD* and is copyright ©1993 by Robert L Rucker. "Summer Love" was published in 1996 by *Modern Words* and is copyright ©1996 by Robert L Rucker. "Riding" and "Christ in Chains" are copyright ©1996 by Robert L Rucker.
"Hair Care" was first printed in *Vital Pulse* and is copyright ©1992 by Thaddeus Rutkowski.
"TV Guide" first appeared in *Pinched Nerves* and is copyright ©1992 by Thaddeus Rutkowski.
"Top Woman" first appeared in *Pink Pages* and is copyright ©1993 by Thaddeus Rutkowski.
"Perfect Victim" and "Vampire sadist of Sodom" are from *SEX-FIEND MONOLOGUES* (Venom Press, 1994) and are copyrighted ©1994 by Thaddeus Rutkowski. "Looking for a Little Spank" has been published in *Paramour* and is copyright ©1996 by Thaddeus Rutkowski. "Sock Man", "Knife 'n' Easy" and "Blade Runner" are copyrighted ©1996 by Thaddeus Rutkowski.
"Mechanics of Love" and "The Hitchhiker" appeared first in *Second Coming* and then *LUST IN 28 FLAVORS* by Lynne Savitt (Second Coming Press) and are copyright ©1979 by Lynne Savitt. "For a Confused Friend with Two Lovers..." is from *SLEEPING RETROSPECT OF DESIRE* by Lynne Savitt (Konocti Books) and are copyright ©1993 by Lynne Savitt.
"Moon" is copyright ©1996 by Allyson Shaw.
"Pretty Persuasion" was first published in *modern words* and is copyright ©1995 by Selena Anne Shephard/Andy Plumb. "Latex Dreams", "Yellow Fever" and "The Real World" are all copyright ©1996 by Selena Anne Shephard/Andy Plumb.

Simon Sheppard's "A Shropshire Lad" was previously published by *THE BADBOY BOOK OF EROTIC POETRY* ©1995 by David Laurents. "Wing", "An Architecture of Pain" and "Poetic Discipline" are all copyright ©1996 by Simon Sheppard.

"Telephone II" was anthologized in *THE ARC OF LOVE* and is copyright ©1996 by Linda Smukler. "Trash" was originally published in *Girlfriends* and is copyright ©1995 by Linda Smukler. Both appear in *HOME IN THREE DAYS. DON'T WASH.* (Hard Press, 1996) by Linda Smukler.

"A Pentecostal Neighbor" and "She Said" were first published in *Vergin' Mary & Madonna* (Vergin' Press) and are copyright ©1986 by Belinda Subraman. "She'll Show You Hers..." was published by *Whoreson Dog* and is copyright ©1993 by Belinda Subraman.

"Ode" was first published in 1971 and is copyright ©1971 by Mutsuo Takahashi. "Myself with a Motorcycle" was first published in *SELF-PORTRAITS 50* in 1975 and is copyright ©1975 by Mutsuo Takahashi. Both translations are from *A BUNCH OF KEYS* (Crossing Press) and are copyrighted ©1984 by Hiroaki Sato.

"Lonely Undertaker Throws Dinner Party for Three Corpses" was previously published in *Poets On* and is copyright ©1996 by Susan Terris; "Cotton Candy" was published in *Pearl* and is copyright ©1996 by Susan Terris.

"Ditty" is from *PARALLELS AND REBUTTALS* (xib Press) and is copyright ©1992 by Cheryl Townsend. "She Drove Her Pelvis" was first published in *Journal of Sister Moon* and is copyright ©1992 by Cheryl Townsend. "He Liked to Fuck Me" was first published in *MACHO SEX* (Hyacinth House, 1993) and is copyright ©1993 by Cheryl Townsend. "With One Red Stiletto" is from *RED STILLETOES* (Mulberry Press, 1993) and is copyright ©1993 by Cheryl Townsend. "Breakfast Between My Thighs" is from *WANT TO SING* (X-It Press, 1994) and is copyright ©1994 by Cheryl Townsend. "Masturbation" was first in *Plain Brown Wrapper* and is copyright ©1994 by Cheryl Townsend. "The Cobble Stone Street", "New Tricks", "Her Hot Piss" and "His Face Was" are all copyright ©1996 by Cheryl A Townsend.

"Mouse" and "Jonas' Fiat" are both copyright ©1996 by Trebor.

"First Love" by Vidyapati is from *THE EROTIC SPIRIT: An Anthology of Poems of Sensuality, Love and Longing*, edited by Sam Hamill, copyright ©1996 by Sam Hamill. Reprinted by arrangement with Shambhala Publications, Inc, 300 Massachusetts Ave, Boston, MA 02115.

"Biker Broad" was published in *GOODSTONE AIRCRAFT COMPANY* (PO Press) by Fred Voss and is copyright ©1988 by Fred Voss. "Guy and Rita Dropped By" appeared in *GENRE 11: EROTICISM* (CSULB Press) and is copyright ©1989 by Fred Voss.

"Meeting the Master", "Masochist's Love Song", "The Joy of Woman's Desiring", "Heat", and "Prometheus and Hercules" are from *MEETING THE MASTER* (Prowess Press, 1995) and are copyright ©1995 by Elissa Wald.

"976-CHAT" is copyright ©1996 by Charles Webb.

"Mandrake of the Rifle Range" is from *Mandrake Makes Madonna in Marmelade* and is copyright ©1996 by Paul Weinman. "Porno Studies" is copyright ©1996 by Paul Weinman.

"Borrowed Time" was first published in *Santa Clara Review*, Fall, 1992, and is copyright ©1992 by Kathleene West.

"The Big Bang Theory" is copyright ©1996 by Diane Williams.

"S and M Games" and "S and M Games Two" first appeared in *Abuse* magazine and are copyright ©1995 by AD Winans. "Lily was an Expert", "Love Comes in Different Flavors", "S and M Games" are all copyright ©1996 by AD Winans.

"Black Slip" was first published in *The Jacaranda Review* and is used by permission of the author. Copyright ©Terry Wolverton, 1988. "Ties" was first published in a slightly different form in *Outweek* and is used by permission of the author. Copyright ©Terry Wolverton, 1991. "Rites" was first published in *Zyzzyva* and is used by permission of the author. Copyright ©Terry Wolverton, 1992.

"Standing and Kneeling Figures", "Absence Makes the Heart Grow Stronger", "Jeff" and "Honeysuckle" all appeared in Ian Young's *SEX MAGICK* (Stubblejumper Press, Toronto) and are copyright ©1986 by Ian Young. "The Skull" is from *YEAR OF THE QUIET SUN* (House of Anansi, Toronto) and is copyright ©1969 by Ian Young.

Books available from Daedalus Publishing Company

Ties That Bind
The SM/Leather/Fetish Erotic Style
Issues, Commentaries and Advice

The writings of a well-known psychotherapist and one of the most respected and knowledgeable people on the subject of the SM/leather/fetish erotic style has been compiled in this book. Price: $14.95

Learning the Ropes
A Basic Guide to Safe and Fun S/M Lovemaking

This book, by S/M expert Race Bannon, guides the reader through the basics of safe and fun S/M. Price: $12.95

The Master's Manual
A Handbook of Erotic Dominance

In this book author Jack Rinella examines various aspects of erotic dominance including SM, safety, sex, erotic power, techniques, and more. Price: $14.95

Beneath The Skins
The New Spirit And Politics Of The Kink Community

This book examines the many issues facing the modern leather/SM/fetish community. Price: $12.95

Leathersex
A Guide for the Curious Outsider and the Serious Player

The reader will find much wisdom between these covers about this often misunderstood form of erotic expression. Price: $14.95

My Private Life
Real Experiences of a Dominant Woman

Within these pages the author, Mistress Nan, allows the reader a brief glimpse into the true private life of an erotically dominant woman. Price: $14.95

Leather And Latex Care
How To Keep Your Leather And Latex Looking Great

This concise book by Kelly J. Thibault gives the reader all they need to know to keep their leather and latex items in top shape. Price: $10.95

Leathersex Q&A
Questions About Leathersex and the Leather Lifestyles Answered

Author Joseph Bean answers a wide variety of questions about leathersex sexuality. Price: $16.95

Between The Cracks
The Daedalus Anthology of Kinky Verse

Editor Gavin Dillard has compiled this impressive selection of erotic poetry that celebrates the edgier side of sexuality. Price: $18.95